THE MARINE ELECTRICAL AND ELECTRONICS BIBLE

THE MARINE ELECTRICAL AND ELECTRONICS BIBLE

Second Edition

JOHN C. PAYNE

SHERIDAN HOUSE

For my sons David and Andrew,
For you the adventures are yet to begin

This edition first published 1998 by
Sheridan House Inc.
145 Palisade Street
Dobbs Ferry, NY 10522
http://www.sheridanhouse.com

Library of Congress Cataloging-in-Publication Data

Payne, John C.
    The marine electrical and electronics bible / John C. Payne. -
2nd ed.
        p.   cm.
    Includes bibliographical references and index.
    ISBN 1-57409-060-7 (alk. paper)
    1. Boats and boating-Electronic equipment-Handbooks,
manuals, etc. 2. Boats and boating-Electric equipment-
Handbooks, manuals, etc. I. Title.
VM325.P39 1998
623.8'5-dc21   98-27298
                                                          CIP

Illustrations by Paul Checkley

Printed in the United States of America

ISBN 1-57409-060-7

FOREWORD

Think of your electrical system as parts of the body—arteries, veins and capillaries (wires) providing blood (electricity) to all areas of the body (boat). If you wish to keep your boat healthy and safe you must have an electrical system based on sound principles.

As a competitor during the 1990/91 BOC challenge solo around the world yacht race, I had on many occasions to witness potentially life threatening dramas being played out on fellow competitors' yachts. Deep in the Southern Ocean, amongst icebergs and raging gales, simple electrical problems snowballed into potential disasters. It is just as easy to experience your own life threatening drama out in the bay or on some quiet backwater if your electrical system is not up to standard.

I have known John Payne for many years, his professional reputation a by-product of an exhaustive professional career so it was understandable that all three Australian BOC competitors (myself included) sought his advice and involvement for on-board charging and electrical systems, which went on to function efficiently under the most demanding conditions.

Whilst the BOC is only for a select few, the experience gained is of benefit to all cruising or professional mariners.

This publication is of real value to every boating person. If you are a builder, it lays the foundations; if you are employing a professional marine electrician, it will give you an insight into why he does certain things and if you have bought your boat and plan to set sail, it will become a bible for maintenance and repair when no one else can get to you!
To stop blood flow to any part of your body would have disastrous consequences!
This comprehensive publication can be the key to your healthy boat.

DON MCINTYRE
McIntyre Marine Services
"Buttercup"
2nd Class II, BOC Challenge

CONTENTS

SECTION TWO   ELECTRONICS SYSTEMS

INTRODUCTION

The modern cruising yacht now carries an array of electronic equipment that rivals many merchant vessels. Unfortunately, the electrical system that supports this equipment is often poorly planned, installed, and maintained.

This manual is written to meet the real and practical requirements of cruising yacht systems. Electrical theory is explained to allow proper consideration, selection, installation, operation, maintenance, and troubleshooting. I have deliberately attempted to correct the dangerous illusion that vessel and automotive systems are alike except for the voltage levels. Electrical problems are an inevitable part of cruising, and an acceptable level of reliability is possible.

Marine electronics system technology is advancing at a spectacular rate. The greatest impact in the coming two years is the introduction of the Global Maritime Distress and Safety System (GMDSS). In this second edition, the marine communications chapters have been rewritten to reflect this large change, and the ramifications are profound for all boaters. Ultimately it will result in a much safer and more efficient distress and safety system afloat. Pocket satellite telephones are imminent, Internet and e-mail afloat worldwide are a reality and easy to set up, and a handheld GPS costs less than a hundred dollars.

An inherent danger with automation is the surrendering of seamanship skills. Far too many people sail away without the knowledge or ability to survive a loss of electronics aids or to maintain the equipment to support them. These high technology systems are only aids to navigation, and there is no substitute for seamanship, a well-found vessel, properly corrected charts, and the ability to find out where you are using traditional methods.

This book encapsulates 23 years of professional experience on merchant vessels, offshore oil exploration vessels, dive support and salvage vessels, and cruising and power vessels. I have attempted to answer many of the frequently asked questions and requests, and addressed criticisms, both constructive and destructive. I cannot overstress the importance of adopting a keep-it-simple approach to electrical and electronics systems. Successful and trouble-free cruising depends on simplicity.

Contact the author, John Payne, at jolly-jack@cheerful.com or
http:www.cruising-yacht.net.

ELECTRICAL SYSTEMS

Batteries

1.0   Batteries. The heart of any vessel power system is the battery. It has a primary role as a power storage device, and a secondary one as a "buffer", absorbing power surges and disturbances arising during charging and discharging. The battery remains the most misunderstood of all electrical equipment. In the majority of installations, it is improperly selected and rated, with a resulting decrease in vessel seaworthiness. For a system to function correctly, the power system must be able to provide power reliably and without disturbance. The following chapters explain all the factors essential to the installation of a reliable power system. The following battery types are examined:

a.   **Lead Acid Batteries.** The lead acid battery is used in the majority of marine installations and therefore will be covered extensively.

b.   **Nickel Cadmium Batteries.** These batteries are usually found on larger cruising vessels and are a viable alternative to lead acid batteries.

c.   **Low Maintenance Batteries.** The viability of these batteries for cruising is considered.

d   **Gel Cell Batteries.** Gel cell batteries are a relatively new battery type and their suitability for cruising applications will be analyzed.

1.1 **Battery Safety.** The lead acid battery, which is used on the majority of cruising vessels, is potentially hazardous; use the following safe handling procedures:

a. **Gas.** Battery cells contain an explosive mixture of hydrogen and oxygen gas at all times. A risk of explosion is always possible if naked flames, sparks or cigarettes are introduced into the immediate vicinity:

  (1) Always use insulated tools.

  (2) Cover the terminals with an insulating material to prevent accidental short circuit. Watchbands, bracelets, and neck chains can accidentally cause a short circuit.

b. **Acid.** Sulfuric acid is highly corrosive and must be handled with extreme caution. If there is ever a need to refill a battery with new acid on yachts, observe the following precautions:

  (1) Wear eye protection during any cell filling.

  (2) Wear protective clothing at all times.

  (3) Avoid splashes or spills as acid can cause severe skin and clothing burns.

  (4) If acid splashes into the eyes, irrigate with water for at least 5 minutes. Seek immediate medical advice. Do not apply any medications unless directed to do so by a physician.

  (5) If electrolyte is accidentally swallowed, drink large quantities of milk or water, followed by milk of magnesia. Seek immediate medical attention.

c. **Manual Handling.** Observe the following when handling batteries:

  (1) Always lift the battery with carriers if fitted.

  (2) If no carriers are fitted, lift using opposite corners to prevent case distortion and electrolyte spills.

d. **Electrolyte Spills.** Electrolyte spills should be avoided, but take the following measures if a spill occurs:

  (1) Spillage of electrolyte into salt water generates chlorine gas. Ventilate the area properly.

  (2) Neutralize any spills immediately using a solution of baking soda.

1.2   **Lead Acid Batteries.** The fundamental theory of the battery is that a voltage develops between two electrodes of dissimilar metal when they are immersed in an electrolyte. In the typical lead acid cell, the generated voltage is 2.1 volts. The typical 12-volt battery consists of 6 cells which are internally connected in series to make up the battery. The primary parameters of a lead acid battery consist of the following:

      a.   **Cell Components.** The principal cell components are:

            (1)   Lead Dioxide (PbO_2) — the positive plate active material.

            (2)   Sponge Lead (Pb) — the negative plate material.

            (3)   Sulfuric Acid (H_2SO_4) — the electrolyte.

      b.   **Discharge Cycle.** The battery discharges when an external load is connected across the positive and negative terminals. A chemical reaction takes place between the two plate materials and the electrolyte. During the discharge reaction, the plates interact with the electrolyte to form lead sulfate and water. This reaction dilutes the electrolyte, reducing its density. As both plates become similar in composition, the cell loses its ability to generate a voltage.

      c.   **Charge Cycle.** Charging simply reverses this reaction. The water decomposes to release hydrogen and oxygen. The two plate materials are reconstituted to the original material. When the plates are fully restored, and the electrolyte is returned to the nominal density, the battery is completely recharged.

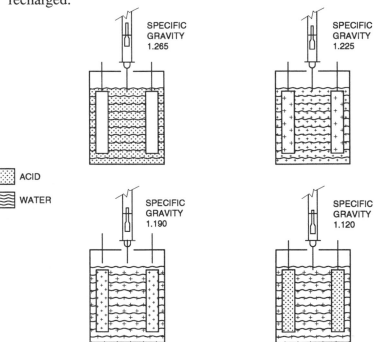

Figure 1-1 Lead Acid Chemical Reaction

3

1.3   **Battery Electrolyte.** The cell electrolyte is a dilute solution of sulfuric acid and pure water. Specific Gravity (SG) is a measurement defining electrolyte acid concentration. A fully-charged cell has an SG typically in the range 1.240 to 1.280, corrected for temperature. This is an approximate volume ratio of acid to water of 1:3. Pure sulfuric acid has an SG of 1.835 and water a nominal 1.0. The following factors apply to battery electrolytes:

     a.   **Temperature Effects.** For accuracy, all hydrometer readings should be corrected for temperature. Ideally, actual cell temperatures should be used, but in practice ambient battery temperatures are sufficient. Hydrometer floats have the reference temperature printed on them and this should be used for calculations. As a guide, the following should be used for calculation purposes in conjunction with Table 1-1:

         (1)   For every 1.5° C the cell temperature is *above* the reference value, *add* 1 point (0.001) to the hydrometer reading.

         (2)   For every 1.5° C the cell temperature is *below* the reference value, *subtract* 1 point (0.001) from the hydrometer reading.

         (3)   Celsius x $^9/_5$ + 32 = Fahrenheit — F-32 x $^5/_9$= C

     b.   **Nominal Electrolyte Densities.** Recommended densities are normally obtainable from battery manufacturers. In tropical areas, it is common to have battery suppliers put in a milder electrolyte density, which does not deteriorate the separators and grids as quickly as electrolytes for temperate climates.

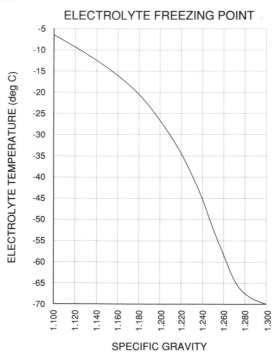

Figure 1-2 Electrolyte Temperature Effects

1.4   Battery Water. When topping up the cell electrolyte, always use distilled or deionized water. Rainwater is acceptable, but under no circumstances use tap water. Tap water generally has an excessive mineral content or other impurities which may pollute and damage the cells. Impurities introduced into the cell remain, and concentrations will accumulate at each top up, thereby reducing service life. Water purity levels are defined in various national standards.

Table 1-1 Electrolyte Correction at 20°C

Temperature	Correction Value
-5° C	deduct 0.020
0° C	deduct 0.016
+5° C	deduct 0.012
+10° C	deduct 0.008
+15° C	deduct 0.004
+25° C	add 0.004
+30° C	add 0.008
+35° C	add 0.012
+40° C	add 0.016

1.5   Battery Additives. There are a number of additives on the market, namely Batrolyte and VX-6. The claims made by manufacturers appear to offer significant performance enhancement. The compounds are specifically designed to prevent sulfation or dissolve it off the plate surfaces. If you read the fine print on one brand, it is not recommended for anything other than new or near-new batteries. If the additive is to dissolve sulfates on battery plates, it will be only on the surface, as plate sulfation occurs through the entire plate, so only a partial improvement is achieved. Recently a friend of mine returned after an extended Pacific cruise and called over a charging problem. I had installed a TWC Regulator three years previously and he had managed the entire period as a liveaboard without a problem, until he put in an additive. My advice is to leave such stuff alone; your battery electrolyte should remain untouched. Just make sure the battery is properly charged and topped off and you won't need to resort to such desperate measures.

1.6   Battery Ratings. Manufacturers often quote a bewildering set of ratings figures to indicate battery performance levels. When selecting a battery, it is essential to understand the ratings and how they apply to your own requirements. The various ratings are defined as follows:

    a.   Amp-hour Rating. Amp-hour rating (Ah) refers to the available current over a nominal time period until a specified final voltage is reached. Rates are normally specified at a 10- or 20-hour rate. This rating generally applies only to deep-cycle batteries. For example, a battery is rated at 84 Ah at 10 hour rate with a final voltage of 1.7 volts per cell. This means the battery is capable of delivering 8.4 amps for 10 hours, when a cell voltage of 1.7 volts is attained. (Battery Volts = 10.2 V DC).

b. **Reserve Capacity Rating.** This rating specifies the number of minutes a battery can supply a nominal current at a nominal temperature without the voltage dropping below a certain level. This rating, normally used only in automotive applications, indicates the power available when an alternator fails and the power available to operate ignition and auxiliaries. Typically, the rating is specified for a 30-minute period at 25° C with a final voltage of 10.2 volts.

c. **Cold Cranking Amps (CCA).** This rating defines the current available at -18° C for a period of 30 seconds, while being able to maintain a cell voltage exceeding 1.2 volts per cell. This rating is only applicable for engine starting. The higher the rating, the more power available, especially in cold weather conditions.

d. **Marine Cranking Amps (MCA).** This newer rating defines the current available at 0° C for a period of 30 seconds, while being able to maintain a cell voltage exceeding 1.2 volts per cell. Again, this rating is only applicable for engine starting. If you are in cold climate area (UK/Europe and USA) then CCA is more relevant.

e. **Plate Numbers.** Data sheets state the number of positive and negative plates within a cell. The more plates, the greater the plate material surface area. Greater plate surface area increases the current during high current rate discharges and subsequently improves cranking capacity and cold-weather performance.

f. **Casing Type.** Battery casings are either a rubber compound or plastic. Where possible, always select the rubber types as they are more resilient to knocks and vibration.

g. **Marine Battery.** This often misused sales term applies to certain constructional features. Plates may be thicker than normal or there may be more of them. Internal plate supports are also used for vibration absorption. Cases may be manufactured with a resilient rubber compound and have carry handles fitted. Filling caps may be of an anti-spill design. These days, batteries are of a similar design, with very little except the label to distinguish marine batteries from the automotive types. Buyer beware; in many cases you are paying a premium for a label.

1.7   Battery Selection. The foundation of a reliable and efficient power system is a correctly specified and rated battery. A battery is required to supply two different types of loads:

a. **Service Loads.** These loads draw current over extensive time periods. Equipment included in this category are lights, instruments, radios, radar, and autopilots.

b. **Starting Loads.** These loads require large current levels for a relatively short time. Loads in this category include engine starter motors, engine preheating, anchor windlass, electric winches, and inverters.

1.8   **Service Loads.** Service loads require a battery that can withstand cycles of long, continuous discharge, and repeated recharging. This deep cycling requires the use of the suitably named deep-cycle battery. The deep-cycle battery has the following characteristics:

a.   **Construction.** The battery is typified by the use of thick, high-density, flat-pasted plates, or a combination of flat and tubular plates. The plate materials may contain small proportions of antimony to help stiffen them. Porous, insulating separators are used between the plates. A glass matting is also used to assist in retaining active material on the plates. Plate material can break away as plates expand and contract during charge and recharge cycles. As this material accumulates at the cell base, a cell short circuit may occur, although this is less common in modern batteries. As plate material is lost, the plates will have reduced capacity or insufficient active material to sustain the chemical reaction and the cell will fail.

b.   **Cycling.** The number of available cycles varies between individual battery makes and models. Typically, it is within the range of 800-1500 cycles of discharge to 50% of nominal capacity and complete recharging. Battery life is a function of the number of cycles and the depth of cycling. Batteries discharged to only 70% of capacity will last appreciably longer than those discharged to 40% of capacity. In practice, you should plan your system so that discharge is limited to 50% of battery capacity. In cruising yachts where batteries are properly recharged and cycle capabilities are maximized, battery life is around 5 years.

c.   **Plate Sulfation.** Sulfation is the single greatest cause of battery failure. It occurs in the following way:

(1)   During discharge, the chemical reaction causes both plates to convert to lead sulfate. If recharging is not carried out promptly (within a couple of hours), the lead sulfate starts to harden and crystallize. This is characterized by white crystals on the typically brown plates and is almost non-reversible. If a battery is only 80% charged, this does not mean that only 20% is sulfating; the *entire* plate material has not fully converted and subsequently sulfates.

(2)   The immediate effect of sulfation is a partial and permanent loss of capacity as the active plate materials are reduced. Electrolyte density also partially decreases as the chemical reaction during charging cannot be fully reversed. Sulfated material causes higher resistances within the cell and inhibits charging. As the level of sulfated material increases, the cell's ability to retain a charge is reduced and the battery fails. The deep-cycle battery has unfairly gained a bad reputation, but the battery is not the cause; improper and inadequate charging is. As long as some charging is taking place, even from a small solar panel, a chemical reaction is taking place and sulfation will not occur.

d. **Efficiency.** Battery efficiency is affected by temperature. At 0° C, efficiency falls by 60%. Batteries in warm, tropical climates are more efficient, but may have reduced life spans. (Batteries commissioned in tropical areas often have lower acid densities to extend battery life.) Batteries in cold climates have increased operating lives, but are less efficient.

e. **Self Discharge.** During charging, a small quantity of antimony or other impurities dissolve out of the positive plates and deposit on the negative ones. Impure topping-up water can introduce other impurities which also deposit on the plates. A localized chemical reaction then takes place, slowly discharging the cell. Self-discharge rates are affected by temperature, with the following results:

(1) At 0° C, discharge rates are minimal.

(2) At 30° C, self-discharge rates are high and specific gravity can decrease by as much as 0.002 per day, typically up to 4% per month.

(3) Regular and complete recharging, or the use of a small solar panel, will prevent permanent damage as it can equal or exceed the self-discharge rate.

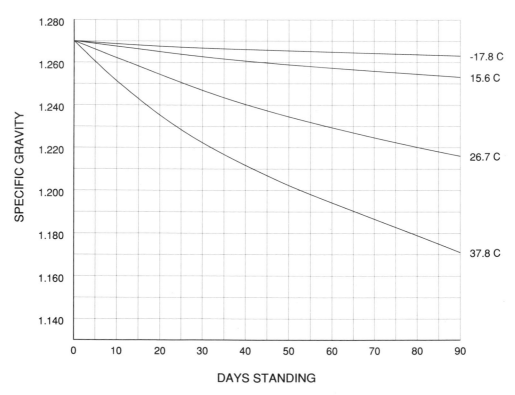

Figure 1-3 Self-Discharge Rates

f. **Charging.** The recommended charging rate for a deep-cycle battery is often given as 15% of capacity. In vessel operations, it is not possible to apply these criteria accurately. Essentially, the correct charge voltage (corrected for temperature) should be used. Deep-cycle battery charging characteristics are as follows:

(1) During charging, a phenomenon called "counter voltage" occurs. Primarily, this is caused by the inability of the electrolyte to percolate at a sufficiently high rate into the plate material pores and subsequently convert both plate material and electrolyte. As the battery resists charging, plate surface voltage rises artificially high and "fools" the regulator into prematurely reducing charging.

(2) To properly charge a deep-cycle battery, a charge voltage of around 14.5 volts is required, corrected for temperature. Contrary to some amazing assertions in some marine electrical books, a charge level of approximately 80% does not represent a fully-charged battery, and is not acceptable if you want a reliable electrical power system and reasonable battery life. If you do not fully recharge the battery, it will rapidly deteriorate and sustain permanent damage.

g. **Equalization Charge.** An equalization charge consists of applying a higher voltage level at a current rate of 5% of battery capacity. This is done to "reactivate" the plates. There is a mistaken belief that this will also completely reverse the effects of sulfation. There may be an improvement following the process, but it will not reverse long–term permanent damage. Equalization at regular intervals can increase battery longevity by ensuring complete chemical conversion of plates, but care must be taken.

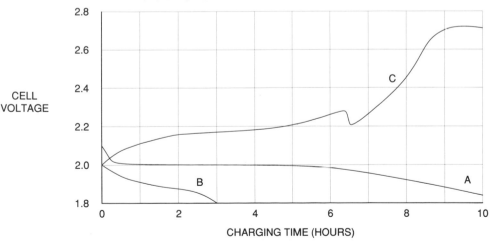

Figure 1-4 Lead Acid Battery Characteristics

1.9   Starting Loads. The starting battery must be capable of delivering sufficient current for the auxiliary engine starter motor to turn and start the engine. This starting load is affected by engine compression, oil viscosity, and engine-driven loads. Some loads, such as an inverter or an anchor windlass under full load, require similarly large amounts of current. Starting batteries have the following characteristics:

  a.   **Construction.** The starting battery is characterized by thin, closely spaced porous plates which give maximum exposure of active plate material to the electrolyte and offer minimal internal resistance. This enables maximum chemical reaction rates, and maximum current availability. Physical construction is much the same as deep-cycle batteries.

  b.   **Cycling.** Starting batteries cannot withstand cycling, and if deep cycled or "flattened," they have an extremely short service life. Ideally, they should be maintained within 95% of full charge.

  c.   **Sulfation.** In practice, sulfation is not normally a problem, as batteries are generally fully charged if used for starting applications only. If improperly used for deep-cycle applications and under-charged, they will sulfate.

  d.   **Self Discharge.** Starting batteries have low self-discharge rates and this is generally not a problem in normal engine installations.

  e.   **Efficiency.** Cold temperatures dramatically affect battery performance. Engine lubricating oil viscosities are also affected by low temperatures, and further increase the starting loads on the battery. The reduction in battery capacity in low temperatures combined with the increased starting current requirements amplifies the importance of having fully charged starting batteries. Table 1-2 illustrates the typical cranking power lost by the battery when the temperature falls from 27° C to -18° C and the increased percentage of power required to turn over and start an engine, using a typical 10W-30 multi-viscosity lubricating oil.

Table 1-2 Battery Power Table

Temperature	Battery Level	Power Required
+ 27° C	100 %	100 %
0° C	65 %	155 %
- 18° C	40 %	210 %

f. **Charging.** Recharging starting batteries is identical to deep-cycle batteries. Additional factors to consider are as follows:

(1) Discharged current must be restored quickly to avoid damage. Similarly, temperature compensation must be made.

(2) Normally after a high current discharge of relatively short duration, there is no appreciable decrease in electrolyte density. If the battery is quickly recharged, the counter-voltage phenomenon does not have time to build up and affect charging.

g. **Battery Ratings.** Starting batteries are normally specified on the basis of engine manufacturers' recommendations, although I have found these to be vague. The following is given as a guide only. Table 1-3 shows recommended battery ratings and plate numbers for various diesel engines, as well as the current typically used by their starter motors.

(1) **Starting Capability.** Calculate a good safety margin that allows for multi-start capability. Some classification societies specify a minimum of 6 consecutive starts, and this is a good practical guide to abide by.

(2) **Temperature Allowance.** Additional allowances should be made for the decreased efficiency in cold climates as a greater capacity and greater load current is required.

h. **Additional Starting Battery Loadings.** The starting battery should also be used to supply short-duration, high-current loads. Check with your engine supplier for the recommended battery rating, and then add a margin for safety. Also factor in the following:

(1) **Windlass.** Normally, the recommended engine battery rating will suffice.

(2) **Electric Winches.** To cope with the very heavy current loadings that electric winches demand, I would recommend simply doubling the battery bank by connecting two identical batteries in parallel.

(3) **Generator.** In some cases, the engine battery can be used for starting. Be careful when starting the engine while the generator is running. Small 10- to 15-amp alternators regularly suffer damage from the engine starting motor's high current load.

Table 1-3 Battery Ratings Table

Engine Rating	Current Load	Battery CCA	Plate No.
10 hp 7.5 kW	59 Amps	375 CCA	9
15 hp 11 kW	67 Amps	420 CCA	11
20 hp 15 kW	67 Amps	420 CCA	11
30 hp 22 kW	75 Amps	450 CCA	13
40 hp 30 kW	85 Amps	500 CCA	13
50 hp 37 kW	115 Amps	500 CCA	13

1.10   Battery Rating Selection. This chapter covers the important task of selecting suitable batteries for use in service roles. Most problems arise from improper battery selection. Battery bank capacities are either too small, with resultant power shortages, or they are so large that the charging system cannot properly recharge them, resulting in premature battery failure due to sulfation. Initially, it is essential to list all equipment on board along with power consumption ratings. Ratings can usually be found on equipment nameplates or in equipment manuals. I recommend that these ratings, usually expressed in watts, be converted to current in amps. To do this, simply divide the wattage by your system voltage. Calculate the current consumption for 12, 24 and 36 hours, day and night, at sea and in port. Table 1-4 illustrates typical power consumption for most equipment aboard boats. There is space for you to insert and calculate the data for your own vessel. Base your calculations as follows:

a.   **Load Calculation Table.** To calculate the total system loading, multiply the total current values by the number of hours to get the amp-hour rating. If an electrical device uses 1 amp over 12 hours, then it consumes 12 amp-hours.

b.   **Capacity Calculation.** Select the column that matches the frequency of your charging periods. The most typical scenario operates the engine every 12 hours to pull down refrigerator temperatures with an engine-driven eutectic refrigeration compressor. A 24-hour rating may give a greater safety margin. If your port usage figure is larger, then select that as the worst-case scenario.

eg.   Total consumption is 120 Ah over 12 hours = 10 amps/hour

c.   **Capacity Derating.** As we wish to keep our discharge capacity to 50% of nominal battery capacity, we can assume that a battery capacity of 240 amp-hours is the basic minimum level. In an ideal world this would be a minimum requirement, but certain frightening realities must now be introduced into the equation. The figures below typify a common system, with alternator charging and standard regulator. Maximum charge deficiency is based on the premise that yacht batteries are rarely above 70% charge and cannot be fully recharged with normal regulators, and that there is reduced capacity due to sulfation, which is typically a minimum of 10% of capacity. The key to maintaining optimum power levels and avoiding this common and frightening set of numbers is to install an efficient charging system, covered extensively in Chapter 2.0.

Nominal Capacity		240 Ah
Maximum Cycling Level (50%)	Deduct	120 Ah
Maximum Charge Deficiency (30%)	Deduct	72 Ah
Lost Capacity (10%)	Deduct	24 Ah
Available Battery Capacity		**24 Ah**

d. **Amp-hour Capacity.** It is important to discuss a few more relevant points regarding amp-hour capacity, as it has significant ramifications on the selection of capacity and discharge characteristics.

    (1) **Fast Discharge.** The faster a battery is discharged over the nominal rating (either 10- or 20-hour rate), the less real amp-hour capacity there is. For example, if we discharge our 240 amp-hour battery bank, which has nominal battery discharge rates for each battery of 12 amps per hour at a rate of 16 amps, we will actually have approximately 10-15% less capacity.

    (2) **Slow Discharge.** The slower the discharge over the nominal rate, the greater the real amp-hour capacity. If we discharge our 240 amp-hour battery bank at 6 amps per hour, we will actually have approximately 10-15% more capacity. The disadvantage here is that slowly discharged batteries are harder to charge if deep cycled below 50%.

e. **Battery Load Matching.** Ideally, the principal aim is to match the discharge characteristics of the battery bank to that of our calculated load of 10 amps per hour over 12 hours. Assume that we have a modified charging system so that we can recharge batteries to virtually 100% of nominal capacity. The factors affecting matching are as follows:

    (1) **Discharge Requirement.** The nominal required battery capacity of 240 Ah has been calculated as that required to supply 10 amps per hour over 12 hours to 50% of battery capacity. In most cases, the discharge requirements are worse for the night period, and this is the 12-hour period that should be used in calculations. What is required is a battery bank with similar discharge rates as the current consumption rate.

    (2) **Battery Requirements.** As the consumption rate is based on a 12-hour period, a battery bank similarly rated at the 10-hour rate is required. In practice, you will not match the precise required capacity, therefore you should go up to the next battery size. This is important also because the battery will discharge longer and faster over 12 hours, so a safety margin is required. If you choose a battery that has 240 amp-hours at the 20-hour rate, you will, in effect, be installing a battery that in the calculated service actually has 10-15% less capacity than is stated on the label, or approximately 215 Ah, less than you need. This is not the fault of the supplier, but simply a failure to correctly calculate and specify the right battery to meet system requirements.

f. **Battery Capacity Formulas.** There are a range of formulas frequently used to determine battery capacity. These are as follows:

(1) **Four-Day Consumption Formula.** One of the more unrealistic formulas states that you should be able to supply all electrical needs over four, complete, 24-hour periods without recharging batteries. Given that an average 10 amps per hour is a typical consumption rate, the four-day formula tells us we'll use 960 amp-hours. If we only discharge to 50%, that translates into an incredible 2000 amp-hour battery capacity. In addition, the recharging period, which requires an additional 20%, must replace about 1200 amp-hours. Even with a fast-charge device, a 100-amp alternator, the finite charge acceptance rate of the battery will force you to spend at least 12 hours charging.

(2) **75/400 System.** This was included in a recent magazine article as one of three formulas for various sized vessels, and was for a 40- to 45-foot yacht. This was the nearest I have seen to a rational set of numbers, based on a 75-amp consumption over 24 hours. Though perhaps too conservative, the formula is based on a 130- or 150-amp alternator with fast-charge device to recharge half of a 400 amp-hour battery bank.

(3) **Personal Formula (240/460 System).** My own personal formula is based on the worst-case consumption of 240 amp-hours over 24 hours. This entails the installation of two banks of 230-hour batteries, each bank made up of two 6-volt batteries. The batteries each supply a split switchboard, with electronics off one bank and with pumps and other circuits off the other, limiting any interference. Charging is from an 80-amp alternator with a cycle regulator (TWC, Ample Power, Adverc) through a diode isolator. It's simple and able to cope with all load conditions. Charging is relatively fast, and at a rate similar to the battery's ability to accept it. In reality, there are no easy formulas. Each vessel has different requirements, and systems must be tailored to suit.

1.11 **Sailing Load Calculations.** It is essential to list all equipment on board along with power consumption ratings. Ratings can usually be found on equipment nameplates or in equipment manuals. To convert power (in watts) to current (in amps), simply divide the power by your system voltage. Unlike normal consumption tables, these tables are broken down into different load consumption scenarios.

    a. **Sailing Modes.** Add up all the current figures relevant to your vessel and multiply by hours to get an average amp-hour consumption rate for each sailing mode. Space is reserved to add in specific values.

    b. **Cumulative Load.** Add both day and night figures together to get the average current drain on your batteries over the selected period.

Table 1-4 (a) DC Load Calculation Table

Equipment	Typical	Actual	12 Hours	24 Hours	Other
DAY SAIL					
Radar-Standby	1.5 A				
Autopilot	4.5 A				
SSB-Receive	1.0 A				
VHF-Receive	0.5 A				
CB-Receive	0.4 A				
Weatherfax	1.0 A				
GPS/LORAN	1.0 A				
Stereo	1.0 A				
Gas Detector	0.3 A				
Inverter-Stby	0.4 A				
S/Board Lights	0.3 A				
Electric Refrig.	4.0 A				
Sub Total					
NIGHT SAIL					
Radar - On	3.5 A				
Tricolor Light	1.0 A				
Compass Light	0.2 A				
Chart Light	0.5 A				
Instrument Lts.	0.5 A				
GPS Light	0.5 A				
Bunk Lights	1.0 A				
Red Night Lt.	0.5 A				
Sub-Total					
SAIL TOTAL					

1.12   Additional Load Calculations. There are other basic loads that have to be factored in to load calculations. Add up all the current figures relevant to your vessel and multiply by expected run times to get an average amp-hour consumption rate.

a. **Intermittent Loads.** It is often hard to quantify actual current demands with intermittent loads. My suggestion is simply to use a baseline of 6 minutes per hour, which is .1 of an hour.

b. **Anchorage/Port Loads.** Port or anchorage loads vary greatly and you will have to carefully assess your own load characteristics.

c. **Motoring Loads.** Certain loads are also added when motoring, and these are in addition to any combination of listed values. Loads must be subtracted from charge current values. Loads include navigation lights, refrigeration clutch, desalinator clutch, and ventilation fans.

Table 1-4 (b) DC Load Calculation Table

Equipment	Typical	Actual	12 Hours	24 Hours	Other
Other Loads					
Bilge Pump	3.5 A				
Shower Pump	3.5 A				
Water Pump	4.0 A				
Salt Wtr. Pump	2.5 A				
Toilet	18.0 A				
Macerator	15.0 A				
SSB -Transmit	15.0 A				
VHF -Transmit	4.0 A				
Deck Spot Lt.	3.0 A				
Extraction Fan	1.5 A				
Inverter	40.0 A				
Cabin Lights	2.0 A				
Port Loads					
Anchor Light	3.5 A				
Spreader Light	1.0 A				
Cockpit Light	0.2 A				
Cabin Lights	0.5 A				
Bunk Lights	0.5 A				
Cabin Fan	0.5 A				
Bunk Lights	1.0 A				
LOAD TOTAL					

1.13 **Battery Installation**. Batteries must be installed correctly. There are a number of important criteria to consider.

    a. **Cell Size.** Battery banks may be installed either in cell multiples of 1.2 volts, 6 volts, or 12 volts. Each configuration has advantages, both physically and operationally:

        (1) **1.2 Volt.** Though the battery plates are generally more robust and thicker, which means an increased service life, this is an expensive option and generally impractical because the batteries take up so much space.

        (2) **6 Volt.** This is the ideal arrangement. The cells are more manageable to install and remove. Large capacity batteries are simply connected in series. Electrically, they are better than 12-volt batteries, generally having thicker and more durable plates. Contrary to some opinions, a series arrangement does not necessarily reduce the available power range, nor does it require an equalization network, and these are rarely found. The one proviso is that batteries in series must be of the same make, model and age. If one battery requires replacement, then the other should also be replaced at the same time.

        (3) **12 Volt.** This is the most common marine battery. Physically, batteries up to around 105 Ah are easily managed. If the battery space is available to connect three batteries in parallel, it is relatively easy to replace one unit. Additionally, if you have a multiple bank and lose one from cell failure, you still have two. It is not uncommon to see traction or truck batteries of very large dimensions installed on a boat, but this is totally impractical from any service standpoint.

        (4) **24 Volt.** This is simply any of the above battery or cell sizes connected in series to get 24 volts.

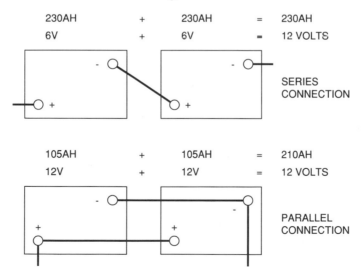

Figure 1-5 Cell and Battery Arrangements

b.   **Battery Housing.** The batteries should be installed in a lined box protected from temperature extremes. The preferred temperature range is 10°C to 27°C. The box should be made of plastic, fiberglass, or lead-lined plywood to prevent any acid spills contacting the wood or water. The box should be located as low as possible in the vessel for weight reasons, but high enough to avoid bilge water or flooding.

c.   **Battery Ventilation.** The area should be well ventilated and vented to the atmosphere. An extraction fan is rarely required, though I have started to use the solar-powered vent fans with integral battery for round-the-clock positive ventilation with great success. The larger the battery bank, the more ventilation required.

d.   **Battery Lighting.** Sufficient natural light should be available for testing or servicing. If this is not possible, a vapor-proof light can be installed.

e.   **Battery Access.** Allow sufficient clearance to install and remove batteries. Make sure there is sufficient vertical clearance to allow hydrometer testing.

f.   **Battery Electrical Equipment.** Do not install electrical equipment adjacent to batteries if at all possible. Sparks may be accidentally generated and cause hydrogen gas to ignite, particularly after charging.

g.   **Battery Orientation.** The ideal configuration is to arrange the batteries athwartships. This offers marginally better protection against acid spilling under excess heel. Yet even in a fore-and-aft layout, I have not come across any adverse problems. On a friend's steel cruising yacht, I have seen a gimballed tray to prevent electrolyte spills when heeling, although I think this is an impractical and unnecessary innovation.

h.   **Battery Security.** Physically secure batteries with either straps or a removable restraining rod across the top. Batteries must not be able to move around. Insert rubber spacers around the batteries to stop any minor movements and vibrations.

i.   **Battery Location.** Ideally, batteries should not be located within machinery spaces where they might be exposed to high ambient temperatures:

    (1)   **Monohulls.** Battery boxes or compartments should be mounted clear of areas liable to flood. After a bad knockdown, and with water over the sole, many boats have compounded their problems by having the batteries contaminated with salt water.

    (2)   **Multihulls.** Trimaran battery locations are the same as monohulls. Catamaran batteries should either be located centrally in the mast area, or be divided into two banks with one bank in each hull. This effectively gives two separate house banks, plus two engine-start batteries.

1.14   Battery Commissioning. After installation, the following commissioning procedures should be carried out:

    a.   **Battery Electrolyte Level.** Check the electrolyte level in each cell.

        (1)   Cells with separator guard — fill to top of guard.

        (2)   Cells without guard — fill to 2mm above plates.

    b.   **Battery Electrolyte Filling.** If the level is low, and evidence suggests a loss of acid in transit, refill with an electrolyte of similar density. Specific Gravity is normally in the range 1.240 to 1.280 at 15° C. If no evidence of spillage is apparent, top up electrolyte levels with deionized or distilled water to the correct levels.

    c.   **Battery Terminals.** Battery terminals are a simple piece of equipment, yet they cause an inordinate amount of problems:

        (1)   **Terminals.** Install heavy-duty, marine-grade brass terminals. Do not use the cheaper plated brass terminals; they are not robust and fail quickly. Don't use the snap-on, quick-release terminals or those with integral security switch. These tend to fail prematurely at the worst possible time because they introduce resistance into the circuit, causing voltage drops, and often form a hot spot under high-current conditions.

        (2)   **Clean Terminals.** Ensure that terminal posts are clean, that they do not have any raised sections, and that they are not deformed, or a poor connection will result.

        (3)   **Replace Connections.** Replace the standard wing-nuts on terminals with stainless steel nuts and washers. Wing-nuts are very difficult to tighten properly without deformation and breakage. I have encountered many installations where the wings and the casting are broken.

        (4)   **Coat Terminals.** Coat the terminals with petroleum jelly.

    d.   **Battery Cleaning.** Cleaning involves the following tasks:

        (1)   **Clean Surfaces.** Clean the battery surfaces with a clean, damp cloth. Moisture and other surface contaminations can cause surface leakage between the positive and negative terminals.

        (2)   **Grease and Oil Removal.** Grease and oil can be removed with a mild detergent and cloth.

    e.   **Battery Charging.** After taking delivery of a new battery, perform the following:

        (1)   **Initial Charge.** Give a freshening charge immediately.

        (2)   **Routine Charging.** Give a charge every week if the vessel is incomplete or not in service.

1.15   **Battery Routine Testing.** The following tests can be made on a daily and weekly basis to monitor the condition of the battery. Battery status can be measured by checking the electrolyte density and the voltage as follows:

a.   **Stabilized Voltage Test.** Voltage readings should be taken with an accurate voltmeter. Switchboards should incorporate a high-quality meter, not a typical engine gauge charge indicator. The difference between fully charged and discharged is less than 1 volt, so accuracy is essential. A digital voltmeter is ideal. Battery voltage readings should only be taken a minimum of 30 minutes after charging or discharging. Turn off all loads before measuring. Typical values at 15°C are shown in Table 1-5. Manufacturers have slightly varying densities; check with your supplier.

Table 1-5 Typical Open Circuit Voltages and Densities

Charge Level	SG Temperate	SG Tropical	Voltage
100%	1250	1240	12.75
90%	1235	1225	12.65
80%	1220	1210	12.55
70%	1205	1195	12.45
60%	1190	1180	12.35
50%	1175	1165	12.25
40%	1160	1150	12.10
30%	1145	1135	11.95
20%	1130	1120	11.85
10%	1115	1105	11.75
0	1100	1090	11.65

b.   **Battery Electrolyte Specific Gravity.** A hydrometer should be used to check acid density every week. The hydrometer is essentially a large syringe with a calibrated float. The calibration scale is corrected to a nominal temperature value, normally marked on the float. The following points should be observed when testing with a hydrometer:

(1)   Never test immediately after charging or discharging. Wait at least half an hour until the cells stabilize; this is because it takes some time for the pockets of varying electrolyte densities to equalize.

(2)   Never test immediately after topping up the electrolyte. Wait until after a charging period, as it similarly takes some time for the water to mix evenly.

(3)   Ensure the float is clean and not cracked and the rubber bulb has not perished.

(4)   Keep the hydrometer completely vertical and take care that the float does not contact the side of the barrel, which may give a false reading.

(5)   Draw enough electrolyte into the barrel to raise the float, but not so much that the top of the float touches the bulb.

(6)   Observe the level on the scale. Disregard the curvature caused by surface tension, then adjust your reading for temperature to obtain the actual value.

(7)   Wash out the hydrometer with clean water when finished.

c.   **Battery Load Test.** The load test is carried out only if the batteries are suspect. The load tester consists of two probes connected by a resistance and a meter. The tester is connected across the battery terminals effectively putting a heavy load across it. The load is typically 275 amps at 8 volts. Take your suspect battery to your nearest automotive electrician or battery service center for a test.

1.16   **Battery Maintenance.** Battery maintenance is simple and not the tedious chore that it is often made out to be. The following tasks should be carried out:

a.   **Battery Terminal Cleaning.** (Bi-monthly). Remove battery terminals and ensure that terminal posts are clean and free of deposits. Refit and tighten terminals and coat with petroleum jelly, not grease.

b.   **Battery Electrolyte Checks.** (Monthly). Check levels along with density. Record each cell density so that a profile can be built up. Record the battery voltage as well. Top up cells as required with distilled or deionized water.

c.   **Battery Cleaning.** (Monthly). Wipe battery casing top clean with a damp rag. Moisture and salt can allow tracking across the top to ground or negative, slowly discharging the battery. A common cause of flat batteries, and the mysterious but untraceable system "leak."

Table 1-6 Lead Acid Battery Troubleshooting

Symptom	Probable Fault
Will not accept charge	Plates sulfated
	Maximum battery life reached
Low cell electrolyte SG	Cell sulfated
Low battery SG value	Low charge level (regulator failure)
	Plates sulfated (undercharging problem)
Will not support load	Low charge level (undercharging problem)
	Plates sulfated
Cell failure	Improperly commissioned
	Electrolyte contaminated (impure water)
	Overcharging problem (regulator failure)
	Undercharging problem (regulator failure)
	Excess vibration and plate damage
	Cell internal short circuit
Battery warm	Plates sulfated
	Excessive charge current (regulator failure)
	Cells damaged.

1.17 **Low Maintenance Batteries.** Sealed low maintenance batteries are not suited to cruising vessel applications. Frequently, they are installed without considering their performance characteristics or their various advantages and disadvantages.

    a. **Low Maintenance Principles.** Basic chemical reactions are similar to the conventional lead acid cell. The differences are as follows:

        (1) **Lead Acid Batteries.** In a normal lead acid battery, water loss occurs when water is electrically broken down into oxygen and hydrogen close to the end of charging. In any battery during charging, oxygen will develop at the positive plate at approximately 75% of full charge level. Hydrogen is generated at the negative plate at approximately 90% of full charge. These are the bubbles seen in the cells during charging. In normal batteries, the gases disperse to atmosphere, resulting in electrolyte loss that requires periodic water replacement.

        (2) **Low Maintenance Batteries.** The low maintenance recombinational battery has different characteristics. The plates and separators are held under pressure. During charging, oxygen is only able to move through the separator pores from positive to negative, reacting with the lead plate. The negative plate charge is then effectively maintained below 90%, inhibiting hydrogen generation.

    b. **Low Maintenance Battery Safety.** Batteries are totally sealed, but incorporate a safety valve. Each cell is also sealed, with a one-way vent. When charging commences, oxygen generation exceeds the recombination rate and the vents release excess pressure within the battery. Excessive charge rates can create internal pressure build-up. If the pressure exceeds the safety vent's discharge rate, an explosion can occur.

    c. **Charging.** Low maintenance batteries must only be charged at recommended charging rates and charge starting currents. The result of any overcharging may be explosion.

    d. **Advantages.** The following are advantages of low maintenance batteries:

        (1) **Low Water Loss.** Low water loss is the principal advantage; however performing a routine monthly inspection and occasional topping up of a lead acid battery is not so labor intensive or inconvenient. I am amazed that this factor is the main one put forward as the criterion for these batteries. If you are continually topping up, then you have a charging problem or a high ambient temperature.

        (2) **Inversion, Heel and Self Discharge.** The batteries are safe at inversion or excessive heel angles without acid spilling, and have a low self-discharge rate.

e. **Disadvantages.** There are two major disadvantages that make low mainte-nance batteries unsuitable for cruising applications:

(1) **Over-Voltage Charging.** Low maintenance batteries are incapable of withstanding any over-voltage during charging. If they are sub-jected to high charging voltages (above 13.8 V), water will vent out and they have been known to explode. This means no fast charging devices should be installed to charge them.

(2) **Cycle Availability.** Cycle availability is restricted, and an approxi-mate lifespan of 500 cycles to 50% of nominal capacity is typical. Any discharge to 40% of capacity or less makes recharging extreme-ly difficult if not impossible, and requires special charging tech-niques.

1.18 **Gel Cell Batteries.** These battery types are known as Dryfit or Prevailer batteries. Their principal characteristics are as follows:

a. **Electrolyte.** Unlike normal lead acid cells they have as an electrolyte a thixotropic gel which is locked into each group of plates. Thixotropic gels have a reduced viscosity under stress. Sonnenschein are the major manufac-turers of these batteries; they have advanced the chemical technology by the use of phosphoric acid to retard sulfation hardening.

b. **Construction.** The batteries have plates that are reinforced with calcium, rather than antimony, thus reducing self-discharge rates. The plates are rela-tively thin, which facilitates gel diffusion into them, and does make charge acceptance easier, as diffusion problems are reduced.

c. **Charging.** A number of important factors affect the charging of gel cells:

(1) **Over-Voltage Intolerance.** Gel cells are unfortunately intolerant to over-voltage charge conditions and will be seriously damaged in any over-charge situation. The normal optimum voltage tolerance for these battery types is 13.8 volts, 14.2 volts being the absolute maxi-mum.

(2) **Charge Acceptance.** A gel cell has a much higher charge accep-tance rate, and therefore a more rapid charge rate is possible. Gel cells cannot tolerate having any equalizing charge applied and this over-charge condition will seriously damage them.

(3) **Fast Charging.** Although accepting a higher charge rate than a lead acid deep-cycle battery, and consequentially charging to a higher value, there is at a certain point the problem of attaining full charge, and therefore capacity usage of the battery bank. As no fast charge devices can be used, a longer engine run time is required for com-plete recharging.

d. **Selection Criteria.** While the technology is very good, these batteries are not suited to serious offshore cruising yacht applications for the following reasons:

(1) **Cycle Life.** A quality deep-cycle lead acid battery can have a life exceeding 2500 cycles of charge and discharge to 50%. A gel cell has a life of approximately 800-1000 cycles. Gel cell batteries do have a much greater cycling capability than normal starting batteries, but not of good deep-cycle batteries.

(2) **Cost.** It is difficult to justify a battery that initially costs up to 50% more, is more susceptible to problems encountered on the average yacht, lasts less than half the time of a conventional battery, and all that based on not spending five minutes a month checking electrolyte densities and levels.

(3) **Charging.** While these batteries will accept some 30-40% greater current than an equivalent lead acid battery, they are restricted in the voltage levels allowed, so you cannot use any fast-charging system.

e. **Suitable Applications.** Gel cells are ideally suited to the following:

(1) **Short Charge Periods.** If you are a weekend, harbor or river cruiser, doing little motoring out of marinas or moorings, then the gel cell will not suffer adversely through incomplete charging.

(2) **Unattended Vessels.** If you leave the vessel unattended for extended periods, then the gel cell is a viable proposition, as it has low self-discharge rates, and is less prone to the problems of deep-cycle batteries. If a small solar panel is left on with a suitable regulator, they will recoup the annual costs of replacing deep-cycle batteries by lasting a few seasons.

1.19   Nickel Cadmium Batteries. Nickel Cadmium batteries are not used extensively on vessels, but they should be considered. The principal factors are cost (typically 500% greater), excessive weight, and large physical bank size. Normally these batteries will only be found in larger cruising vessels for those reasons. They have completely different operating characteristics from the lead acid cell.

     a.   **Cell Components.** The components of the cell are as follows:

          (1)   Nickel Hydroxide ($2Ni(OH)2$) — the positive plate.

          (2)   Cadmium Hydroxide ($Cd(OH)2$) — the negative plate.

          (3)   Potassium Hydroxide (KOH) — the electrolyte.

     b.   **Discharge Cycle.** Cells are usually classified by their rate of discharge characteristics, such as low, medium, high, or ultra high. Classification UHP is for starting applications and VP for general services. There is also a category for deep-cycle applications. Discharge ratings are given at the 5-hour rate and typically they will deliver current some 30% longer than lead acid equivalents. The amp-hour capacity rating remains fairly stable over a range of discharge currents values. An over-discharge condition can occur when the cell has been driven into a region where voltage has become negative. A complete polarity reversal takes place. No long-term effects occur on occasional cell reversal at medium discharge rates.

Curve A - Discharge current reduces cell voltage from 1.3 volts to 1.0 volt over 10 hours.

Curve B - Discharge over three hours.

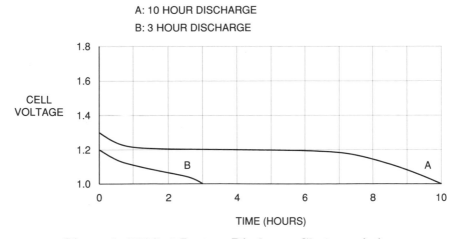

Figure 1-6 NiCad Battery Discharge Characteristics

c.   **Charge Cycle.** During charging, the negative material loses oxygen and converts to metallic cadmium. The positive material gradually increases in the state of oxidation. While charging continues, the process will proceed until complete conversion occurs. Approaching full charge gas will evolve and this results from electrolysis of the electrolyte water component. NiCad cells can be charged rapidly with a relatively low water consumption. The disadvantages are that cell imbalances may occur and this can cause thermal runaway. The NiCad cell will generally absorb maximum alternator current for about 85% of the cell charge period, so the alternator must be capable of withstanding this load and have adequate ventilation:

(1)   **Regulator Voltage Settings**. Typical alternator voltage regulator settings for a nominal 12-volt battery bank of 10 cells over a 2-4 hour period should be in the range of 15 to 15.5 volts maximum. A NiCad battery accepts high charge currents and will not be damaged by them. At 1.6 volts per cell a NiCad can absorb up to 400% of capacity from a charging source. In most cases it will accept whatever the alternator can supply. The problem with normal alternator regulators is that they fix the output at only 14 volts which is far too low for proper charging. Absolute maximum charging rates require a 1.6 to 1.8 volts per cell which is 16-18 volts on a typical 10 cell battery bank.

(2)   **NiCad Charging Controllers**. The typical 14-volt output of an alternator is a float charge voltage level only for a NiCad battery. An alternator controller is essential for correct charging, and the Solent Chargemaster ideally suits this application, enabling setting of the required level. I have set up this type of regulator with a CAV alternator successfully. Constant voltage charging is the only practical method of charging on vessels. Regulator setting should be typically around 15.5 volts for a 2-4 hour charge period, higher voltages will increase current.

Charging cell voltage 1.5 times the 10 hour discharge current.

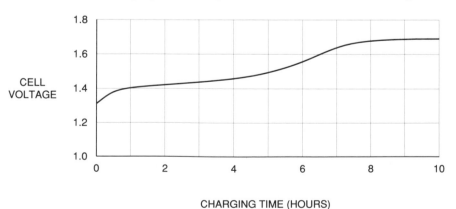

CHARGING TIME (HOURS)

Figure 1-7 NiCad Battery Charge Characteristics

1.20 **NiCad Electrolyte.** The obvious difference is the use of an alkaline electrolyte instead of an acid. Unlike lead acid cells, plates undergo changes in their oxidation state, altering very little physically. As the active materials do not dissolve in the electrolyte, plate life is very long. The electrolyte is a potassium hydroxide solution with a specific gravity of 1.3. The electrolyte transports ions between the positive and negative plates and the alkaline solution is chemically more stable than lead acid cell electrolytes. Unlike lead acid cells, the density does not significantly alter during charge and discharge and hydrometer readings cannot be used to determine the state of charge. Electrolyte loss is relatively low in operation. There are two basic factors to consider with NiCad cells:

    a. **Electrolyte Topping Up.** Water additions should be made immediately after charging, and never after discharging.

    b. **Mixed Battery Installations.** Lead acid and NiCad batteries should never be located in the same compartment as the acid fumes will contaminate the NiCad cells, causing permanent damage.

1.21 **NiCad Battery Characteristics.** The NiCad battery has the following characteristics:

    a. **Open Circuit Voltage.** The typical open circuit voltage of a vented cell is 1.28 volts. This depends on temperature and time interval from the last charge period. Unlike a lead acid cell, the voltage does not indicate the state of charge.

    b. **Nominal Voltage.** Nominal voltage is typically 1.2 volts. This voltage is maintained during discharge until approximately 80% of the 2-hour rated capacity has been discharged. This is also affected by temperature and rate of discharge.

    c. **Closed Circuit Voltage.** This voltage is measured immediately after load connection. Typically it is around 1.25-1.28 volts per cell.

    d. **Working Voltage.** This voltage is that observed on the level section of the discharge curve of a NiCad cell, voltage plotted against time. Typically, the voltage averages 1.22 volts per cell.

    e. **Capacity.** Capacity is specified in amp-hours. Normally it is quoted at the 5-hour rate.

    f. **Nominal Rating.** The nominal rating is the amp-hour delivery rate over 5 hours to a nominal voltage of 1.0 volt per cell.

    g. **NiCad Internal Resistance.** Internal resistance values are typically very low, due to the large plate surface areas used. That is why the cells can deliver and accept high current values.

Battery Charging Systems

2.0   **Battery Charging Systems.** An efficient battery charging system is essential for optimum battery and electrical system performance. I receive literally hundreds of letters and phone calls from cruising yacht owners who are totally confused by conflicting information and simply want a reliable system. The principal charging systems on cruising vessels consist of the following:

a.   **Alternators.** The alternator is the principal charging source on the majority of cruising yachts. In many cases, it is the only source utilized, even at the dock, due to the alternator's higher available charging currents.

b.   **Alternative Energy Systems.** The following methods of alternative energy charging are available as options to augment engine charging sources:

- Solar Panels

- Wind Generators

- Prop Shaft Alternators

- Water-Powered Charging Systems

c.   **Battery Chargers.** When a vessel is in port, and particularly in liveaboard situations where the main power source is via a shore-powered charger, the battery charger has an important role in the power system.

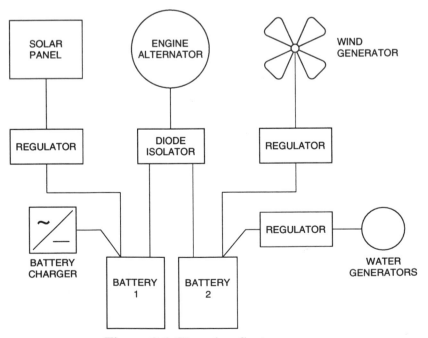

Figure 2-1 Charging Systems

28

2.1   Charging Cycles. There are four recognized parts of any charging cycle; understanding these parts is crucial to understanding charging problems.

    a.   **Bulk Charge.** The bulk-charge phase is the initial charging period before the gassing point is reached. This is typically in the range 14.4 to 14.6 volts, corrected for temperature, though with a traditional alternator and regulator, output is fixed at 14 volts. The bulk charge rate can be anywhere between 25% and 40% of rated amp-hour capacity at the 20-hour rate as long as temperature rises are limited.

    b.   **Absorption Charge.** After attaining the gassing voltage, the charge level should be maintained at 14.4 volts until the charge current falls to 5% of battery capacity. This level normally should equate to 85% of capacity. In a typical 300 amp-hour bank, this will be 15 amps.

    c.   **Float Charge.** The battery charge rate should be reduced to a float voltage of approximately 13.2 to 13.8 volts to maintain the battery at full charge.

    d.   **Equalization Charge.** A periodic charge rated at 5% of the installed battery capacity should be applied for a period of 3-4 hours until a voltage of 16 volts is reached. A suitable and safer way of equalizing is applying the unregulated output from the wind generator or solar panel once a month for a day.

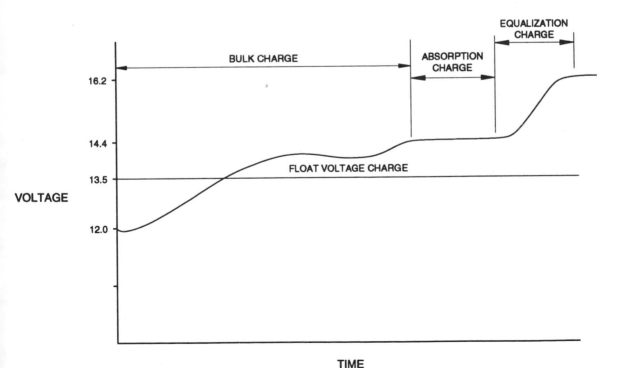

Figure 2-2 Charging Cycles

29

2.2   Charging Efficiency. Before any charging systems can be considered, a number of factors must be summarized and taken into account.

a.   **Battery Capacity.** Nominal capacities of batteries are specified by manufacturers, and the total capacity of the bank must be taken into consideration.

b.   **Battery Age and Condition.** Older batteries have reduced capacities due to normal in-service aging, and plate sulfation. Sulfation increases internal resistance and therefore inhibits the charging process.

c.   **Electrolyte.** The electrolyte is temperature dependent, and the temperature is a factor in setting maximum charging voltages.

d.   **State of Charge.** The state of charge when charging begins can be checked using the open circuit voltage test and electrolyte density. The level of charge will affect the charging rate. Also critical to the state of charge is the temperature. It has a dramatic effect on charge voltages as indicated in the curve below.

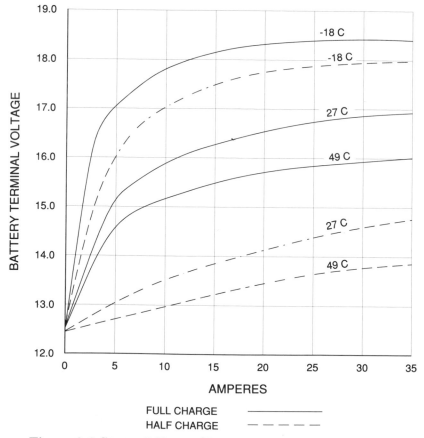

Figure 2-3 State of Charge/Temperature Characteristics

e. **Charging Voltage.** Charging voltage is defined as the battery voltage plus the cell voltage drops as follows:

   (1) **Cell Volt Drops.** Cell volt drops are due to internal resistance, plate sulfation, electrolyte impurities, and gas bubble formation that occur on the plates during charging. These resistances oppose charging and must be exceeded to effectively recharge the battery. Resistance to charging increases as a battery reaches a fully-charged state and decreases with discharge.

   (2) **Charge Regulation.** A battery is self regulating in terms of the current it can accept under charge. Over-current charging at excessive voltages (which many so-called fast-charging devices do) simply generates heat and damages the plates, which is why fast-charging devices are not recommended (see Cycle Regulators).

2.3 **Alternator Charging.** A robust and reliable piece of equipment, the alternator is the principal charging source on most marine installations. Automotive alternators, or derivatives, are used in the majority of marine installations. Most alternators, however, are incorrectly rated for the installed battery capacity and therefore are unable to properly restore the discharged current.

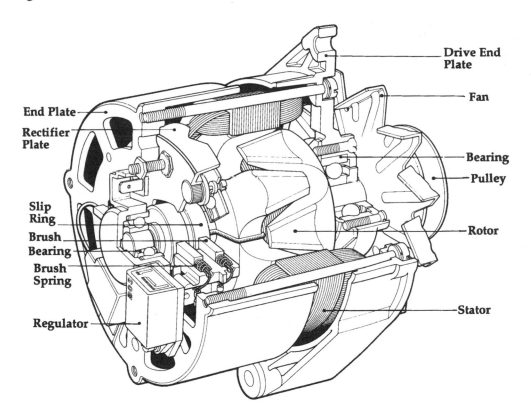

Figure 2-4 Bosch Alternator

2.4   **Alternator Components.** The alternator consists of several principal physical components.

  a.   **Stator.** The stator is the fixed winding. It consists of three windings that are interconnected in a "star" or a "delta" arrangement. These windings supply three phases of alternating current (AC) to the diode bridge (rectifier).

  b.   **Rotor.** The rotor is the rotating part of the alternator. It consists of the slip rings, and the rotor winding, which are interconnected.

  c.   **Rectifier.** The rectifier or diode bridge consists of a network of six diodes. This rectifies the three generated AC phase voltages into the DC output used for charging. Two diodes are used on each winding to provide full wave rectification. The three DC voltages are connected in parallel to the main output terminal.

  d.   **Exciter Diodes**. The exciter (D+) consists of three low power diodes which independently rectify each AC phase and provide a single DC output for the warning light or auxiliary control functions.

  e.   **Brushgear.** The brushgear consists of the brush holders, brushes and springs. The brushes are normally made of graphite, or on some high performance alternators, copper graphite. The brushes are spring-loaded to maintain correct slip ring contact pressure and are solder connected to the terminals.

  f.   **Regulator.** The regulator, if integral to the alternator, is often combined with the brushgear or mounted adjacent to it. The field control output of the alternator is connected to one of the brush holders, which then supplies the rotor winding though the slip ring. Regulator sensing is normally connected to the D+ output circuit.

2.5 **Field Circuits.** The field circuit is used to vary the output of the alternator. It can be simply defined as the alternator "controller" because all alternator output is controlled by the field current level. There are a number of variations in the connection of fields besides the normal regulator; these are as follows:

a. **Advanced Field Switching.** This method is comparatively rare in modern integral regulator alternators. The field is taken through the battery selector switch auxiliary contacts, so that the field circuit is broken, de-energizing the alternator immediately before the main output contacts break. This will prevent any accidental circuit interruption and subsequent diode destruction through generated surges.

b. **Oil Pressure Switch Control.** This method has two configurations. The first senses battery voltage through an oil pressure switch on the engine. The alternator does not commence generating until after engine oil pressure has built up. The second method takes the field directly through an oil pressure switch.

c. **Field Isolation Switch.** This circuit is common in small engines or where small output auxiliary engines drive more than one piece of equipment. This enables the alternator to be switched off to reduce engine loadings so that other equipment such as refrigerators or desalinators can operate. To avoid circuit disturbances and possible damage to alternator from surges and spikes, it is advisable to operate the switch before starting the engine, or stop the engine and operate.

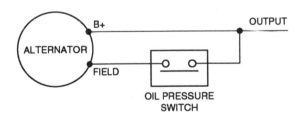

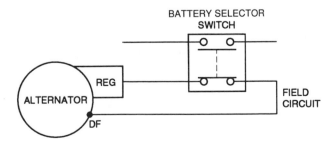

Figure 2-5 Field Circuits

2.6   **Alternator Selection.** Boat owners have a number of important factors to consider when selecting alternator output ratings. Along with regulators, the alternator is probably the most common item to fail onboard, therefore careful selection is required. The factors are summarized as follows:

a.   **Engine Run Times.** The engines in a majority of cruising vessels are run excessively in an attempt to recharge batteries. The maximum run time goal is one hour in the morning and one hour in the evening, which coincides with refrigeration pull down times.

b.   **Engine Loading.** Diesel engines should not be run with light loads because unloaded engines suffer from cylinder glazing. A high output alternator can provide loads of up to 1.5 horsepower at rated output.

c.   **Engine Speeds.** Ideally, the engine should be able to charge at maximum rates at relatively low speeds. The preferred speed is generally a few hundred revs/min above idle speed. Alternator speed is dependent on the drive-pulley ratio and the alternator cut-in speed.

d.   **Battery Capacity.** Nominal charging rates are specified by manufacturers, and they generally specify starting and finishing rates. A battery requires the replacement of 120% of the discharged current to restore it to full charge. This value is required to overcome internal resistances within the battery during charging.

e.   **Charging Current.** As a battery is effectively self limiting in terms of charge acceptance levels, we cannot simply push in the discharged value and hope that it will recharge. The battery during charging is reversing the chemical reaction of discharge, and this can only occur at a finite rate. If possible, therefore, the alternator must recharge the battery at the optimum charge rate specified. Charging by necessity tapers off as full charge is reached, which is why start and finishing rates are specified. These ratings are largely impractical in marine installations. Alternator output current is the sum of electrical loads on the system during the charging period, plus the actual battery charging current.

f.   **Charge Voltage.** The majority of alternators have a fixed output of 14 volts, with some makes having the option of regulator adjustment up to around 14.8 volts for isolation diode voltage drop compensation. Charge voltage is probably the single most important factor in charging, as all other factors are related to it.

g.   **Alternator Output Current Selection.** From the power analysis table, we have calculated the boat's maximum current consumption. Added to this is a 20% margin for battery losses, giving a final charging value. One popular opinion is that alternator ratings should be approximately 30% of battery capacity. In practice, this is at best optimistic and difficult to achieve.

I always specify and install an 80-amp (eg, Bosch) alternator, which is about the highest rating possible without going into high-priced or exotic alternators. I avoid wherever possible installing a battery bank in excess of 300 amp-hours and usually fit a bank of two 6-volt cells rated at 230 amp-hours. With a suitable regulator system, I have never found this to be inadequate for charging and load requirements. You can go and fit large output units, but economic considerations weigh against that solution.

h.   **Marine Alternators.** Marine alternators are essentially enclosed and ignition protected with a UL listing to prevent accidental ignition of hazardous vapors. Windings are also protected to a higher standard by epoxy impregnation. Marine units have a corrosion-resistant paint finish and are designed for higher ambient operating temperatures. Their output characteristics are generally similar to automotive types.

i.   **Marinized Alternators.** An alternator can be marinized to a reasonable degree. If you wish to marinize and improve your alternator, perform the following:

   (1)   **Bearings.** Bearings should be totally enclosed. Replace if they are not.

   (2)   **Windings.** Windings should be sprayed or encapsulated with a high-grade insulating spray.

   (3)   **Diode Plate.** The back of the diode plate can also be sprayed with an insulating coating to prevent the ingress of moist, salt-laden air and dust which can short out diodes and connections.

j.   **High-Output Alternators.** It is, regrettably, a fact of life that many so-called marine electrical people push high output alternators (typically 130 amps or more) as the first step toward solving battery charging problems. These alternators are expensive, and in many cases mask the more common problems of poor circuit design, poor installation, and inedequate regulation. Be warned! This is the typical automotive electrician's answer, but not a marine one; a high output alternator will not necessarily solve your charging problems. In most cases, an 80-amp alternator is all that's required. A considerably cheaper and more reliable solution may be to replace the regulator. If you choose to upgrade your alternator, install a quality unit such as Silver Bullet, Lestek, Balmar, Niehoff or Powerline. Beware of rewound standard alternators; they are notoriously unreliable.

k.   **Outboard Motor Alternators.** On many multihull vessels up to 40 feet which use outboard motors, charging problems are commonplace. Outboards have a flywheel driven alternator, and they are generally have a low output, typically in the range 10-15 amps.

l.   **Surge Protection.** Some alternators are provided with separate surge protection units. Unfortunately, very few alternators are fitted with any surge protection and few options are available:

(1)   **Lucas Systems.** Lucas/CAV alternators have these units available. Some series of Lucas alternators also incorporate a surge protection avalanche diode within the alternator (ACR and A115/133 range); this protects the main output transistor in the regulator.

(2)   **Zap Stop (Cruising Equipment Co.)** This device is a high-voltage spike suppressor that shunts excess voltages to ground. The device is connected across the main alternator output and ground. It is essential equipment on any modern yacht.

(3)   **Additional Protection.** Simple surge protection can be installed by fitting a Metal Oxide Varister (MOV) across B+ and negative or ground. Another good method is to solder a capacitor rated at 0.047F/250 V across each of the AC windings.

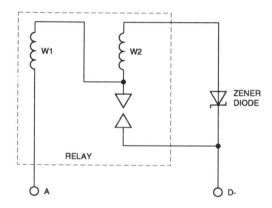

(a) LUCAS SURGE PROTECTION UNIT

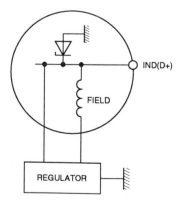

(b) LUCAS AVALANCHE DIODE REGULATOR PROTECTION

Figure 2-6 Surge Protection

36

2.7 **Alternator Installation.** Optimum service life and reliability can only be achieved by correctly installing the alternator. The following factors must be considered during installation:

    a. **Alignment.** It is essential that the alternator-drive pulley and the engine-drive pulley be correctly aligned. Pulley misalignment can impose twisting and friction on drive belts and additional side loading on bearings. Both can cause premature failure.

    b. **Drive Pulleys.** Drive pulleys between the alternator and the engine must be of the same cross section. Differences will cause belt overheating and premature failure. Ideally, the split, automotive-type pulleys on some alternators should be replaced by solid pulleys of the correct ratio.

    c. **Drive Belt Tension.** Belts must be correctly tensioned. Maximum deflection should not exceed 10 mm. When a new belt is fitted, the deflection should be re-adjusted after 1 hour of operation and again after 10 hours. Belts will stretch in during this period.

        (1) **Under Tensioning**. This causes belt overheating and stretching, as well as slipping and subsequent undercharging. The excess heat generated also heats up pulleys and the high heat level conducts along the rotor shaft to the bearing, melting bearing grease and increasing the risk of premature bearing failure.

        (2) **Over Tensioning**. This causes excessive bearing side loads, which leads to premature bearing failure. Signs of this condition will be characterized by sooty deposits around the belt area and wear on the edges of the belt.

    d. **Drive Belts.** Belts must be of the correct cross section to match the pulleys. Notched or castellated belts are ideal in the engine area as they dissipate heat easily. If multiple belts are used, always renew all belts at the same time to avoid varying tensions between them. For any alternator over 80 amps, a dual-belt system should be used because a single belt will not be able to cope with the mechanical loads applied at higher outputs.

    e. **Ventilation.** An alternator, similar to electrical cable, cannot achieve its rated output in high temperatures. Ideally, a cooling supply fan should be fitted to run when the engine is operating and its airstream should directed to the alternator. Many alternator failures occur when boost charging systems are installed because such systems run at near maximum output for a period in high ambient temperatures. Always ensure when fitting an additional alternator that the alternator's fan is rotating in the correct direction.

f. **Mountings.** Mountings are a constant source of problems. Make sure you take the following steps:

(1) **Tensioning.** When tensioning the alternator, always adjust both the adjustment bolt and the pivot bolt. Failure to tighten the pivot bolt is common and causes alternator twisting and vibration. Vibration fatigues the bracket or mounting and may cause it to fracture. Additionally, this can cause undercharging and radio interference.

(2) **Adjustment Arm.** Ensure that the slide adjustment arm is robust. Most marine engines have a vibration level that will fatigue the slide and break it. In my experience, Volvo engines are notorious for this problem. I always recommend taking off the Volvo's old arm and having another one custom made.

g. **Warning Light.** The light circuit is not simply for indicating failure—the lamp excites the alternator. In many cases, an alternator will not operate if the lamp has failed because the remnant voltage or residual magnetism has dissipated. Ideally, a lamp should be in the range of 2-5 watts. Undersized lamps are often characterized by the need to "rev" the engine to get the alternator to "kick" in. This is often highly visible with alternator driven tachometers. Many newer engine panels have a printed circuit board type of alarm panel. I recommend, where possible, installing a separate light.

h. **Interference Suppression.** Alternator diode bridges create radio frequency interference (RFI) which can be heard on communications or electronics equipment. Always install an interference suppression capacitor. As a standard, install a 1.0 microfarad suppressor. In some cases, a suppressor is required in the main output cable.

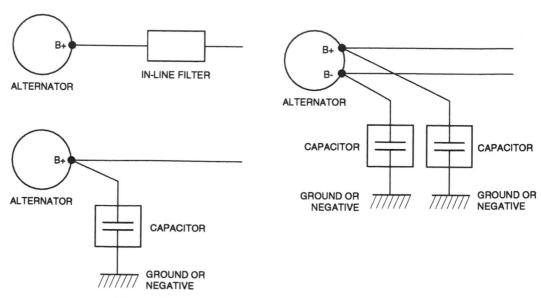

Figure 2-7 Alternator Interference Suppression

2.8   Alternator Drive Pulley Selection. Ideally, maximum alternator output is required at a minimum possible engine speed. This is typically a few hundred revs/min above idle speed. Manufacturers install alternators and pulleys assuming that the engine is only run to propel the vessel, when in fact engines spend more time functioning as battery chargers, at low engine revolutions. Alternators have three speed levels that must be considered and the aim is to get full output at lower speeds.

      a.   **Cut-in Speed.** This is the speed at which a voltage will be generated.

      b.   **Full Output Operating Speed.** This is the speed where full rated output can be achieved.

      c.   **Maximum Output Speed.** This is the maximum speed allowed for the alternator, otherwise destruction will occur.

      d.   **Pulley Selection.** An alternator is rated with a peak output at 2300 revs/min. At a typical engine speed of 900 revs/min and a minimum required alternator speed of 2300, a pulley ratio of approximately 2.5:1 is required. The alternator's maximum output speed is 10000 rev/min. Maximum engine speed is 2300, so 2300 multiplied by 2.5 = 4000 revs/min. This falls well within safe operating limits and is acceptable. A pulley with that ratio would suit the service required.

      e.   **Selection Table.** Table 2-1 gives varying pulley ratios with an alternator pulley diameter of 2.5 inches.

Table 2-1 Drive Pulley Selection Table

Engine Pulley Dia.	Pulley Ratio	Engine RPM	Alternator RPM
5 inch	2:1	2000	4000
6 inch	2.4:1	1660	4000
7 inch	2.8:1	1430	4000
8 inch	3.2:1	1250	4000

f. **Alternator Characteristics.** The graph below illustrates the relationship between output current, efficiency, torque, and horsepower against rotor revolutions. The optimum speed can be selected from these characteristics. The performance curves and characteristics illustrated are for a Lestek high output alternator, and for a 9135 series 135-amp alternator.

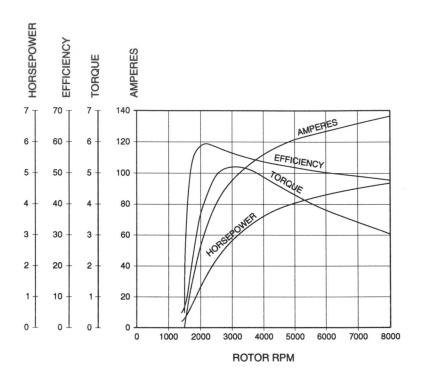

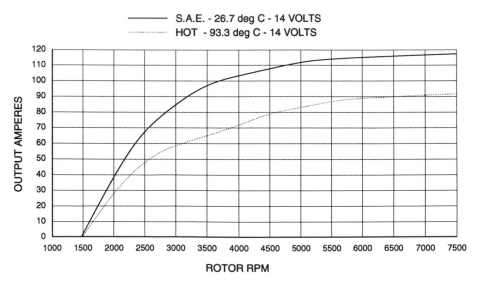

Figure 2-8 Alternator Output Characteristics

2.9   **Alternator Maintenance.** Many alternator failures can be avoided by performing basic maintenance tasks. The following tasks should be carried out.

    a.   **Drive Belts.** Check monthly as follows:

        (1)   Check and adjust tension. Deflection: 10mm maximum.

        (2)   Examine for cuts, uneven wear or fatigue cracks.

        (3)   Ensure belts are clean, with no oil or grease.

    b.   **Connections.** Check monthly as follows:

        (1)   Clean and tighten all alternator terminals.

        (2)   Check cable and connectors for fatigue.

    c.   **Vibration.** Check monthly as follows:

        (1)   Check alternator for vibration when running.

        (2)   Examine mounts for fatigue cracks.

    d.   **Bearings.** Check every 1500 operating hours as follows:

        (1)   Remove alternator and turn rotor. Listen for any bearing noises.

        (2)   Renew every 3000 hours or at major overhaul.

    e.   **Brushes.** Check every 1500 operating hours as follows:

        (1)   Check brushes for excess or uneven wear.

        (2)   Check slip rings for scoring.

    f.   **Cleaning.** Clean yearly as follows:

        (1)   Wash slip rings, diode plate, and brushgear with electrical solvent. Do not use any abrasives on slip rings; they must be cleaned only to preserve a film that is essential for brush contact.

        (2)   Wash out windings and dry.

    g.   **Pre-cruise.** Take alternator to a quality marine or automotive electrical workshop. Request the following tests:

        (1)   Test alternator output for maximum current.

        (2)   Check diodes.

        (3)   Clean windings, slip rings and brushgear.

        (4)   Renew bearings.

        (5)   Renew brushes.

2.10   **Alternator Faults and Failures.** Failures in alternators are primarily due to the following causes, many of which can be prevented with routine maintenance.

a.   **Diode Bridge Failures.** Diode failures are generally caused by:

(1)   **Reverse Polarity Connections.** Reversing the positive and negative leads destroys the diodes. This is a common occurrence.

(2)   **Short Circuiting Positive and Negative.** A short circuit will cause excess current to be drawn through the diodes and the subsequent failure of one or more diodes. The most common cause is reversing the battery connections.

(3)   **Surge.** A high voltage surge is generated by the inductive effect of the field and stator windings. This occurs if the charge circuit is interrupted, most commonly when an electrical battery selector switch is accidentally opened.

(4)   **Spikes.** Short-duration, transient voltages several times greater than the nominal voltage can be caused by high inductive loads when starting up, say, a pump. Most spikes, however, are caused by lightning strikes. Countermeasures are covered in the lightning protection chapter.

b.   **Winding Failures.** Stator winding failures are usually due to the following causes:

(1)   **Overheating.** Normally due to insufficient ventilation at sustained high outputs, causing insulation failure and intercoil short circuits.

(2)   **Short Circuit.** Due to mechanical winding damage, overheating, or ingress of moisture.

(3)   **Rotor Winding.** Short circuit or a ground fault due to overheating or over-voltage if the voltage regulator fails.

c.   **Brushgear.** Brushgear failures are not that common in a properly maintained alternator, but they are generally due to:

(1)   **Brushes.** Brushes worn and sparking, and characterized by fluctuating outputs and radio interference.

(2)   **Slip Rings.** Scoring and sparking due to build-ups of dust, also causing radio interference.

d.   **Bearing Failure.** The first bearing to fail is normally the front pulley bearing. Rotating it by hand will usually indicate grating or noise.

2.11   Alternator Troubleshooting. Alternator troubleshooting should be carried out in conjunction with the charging system troubleshooting described in Table 3-1.

a.   **Check Output.** This initially depends on the lamp and the regulator. Using a voltmeter, check that the output across the main B+ terminal and negative rises to approximately 14 volts. No output indicates total failure of the alternator or regulator. Partial output indicates diode failure or a regulator fault.

b.   **Check Components.** After confirming the function of the regulator, test the components. I recommend first removing the alternator, and taking it to any good automotive electrician with a test bench. If you don't carry spares, then you can do little. To get home with partial diode failure, you can disconnect the regulator and apply a full field voltage to get maximum output.

2.12   Alternator Terminal Designations. Alternators have a variety of different terminal markings, which are listed in Table 2-2.

Table 2-2 Alternator Terminal Markings

Make	Output	Negative	Field	Auxiliary	Tachometer
Bosch	B +	D -	DF	D+/61	W
Ingram	B +	B -	F	IND/AL	W
Lucas	BAT	E	F	L	
Paris-Rhone	+	-	DF	61	W
Sev Marchal	B +	D-	DF	61	
Motorola	+	-	F	AUX	AC
CAV	D +	D -	F	IND	
AC Delco	BAT	GND	F		
Niehoff	BAT+	BAT -	F	D+	X
Valeo	B +	D -		D+	W
Mitsubishi	B +	E	F	L	
Nippon Denso	B +	B	F	L	
Prestolite	POS+	GND		IND LT	AC TAP
Silver Bullet	+	-	F		R

2.13   Alternator Test Specifications. The following specifications are typical for a range of Bosch alternators. Those for other makes are similar.

Table 2-3 Alternator Test Specifications

Model	Output	Speed	Stator Ohms	Rotor Ohms
14V 35A	10 A	1300 rpm	0.24	4.0
	23 A	2000 rpm		
	35 A	6000 rpm		
14V 55A	16 A	1200 rpm	0.14	4.0
	36 A	2000 rpm		
	55 A	6000 rpm		

2.14 **Alternator Remagnetization.** After dismantling or stripping down an alternator, it is not uncommon to find it simply won't work at all. Before you hurriedly dismantle it again to find your mistake, perform the following checks:

a. **Field Disconnect.** Disconnect the regulator field connection (assuming you have installed a separate regulator or controller).

b. **Manual Field Activation.** With the engine running at idle speed and all electrical and electronics equipment off, temporarily touch the field connection to the following:

 (1) **Positive Control.** (Bosch, Paris-Rhone, Motorola, new Sev-Marchal) If the field control is on the positive side, touch the lead to main alternator output terminal B+; or if a diode is fitted, then to the diode battery output terminal.

 (2) **Negative Control.** (Lucas, CAV, Hitachi) If the field control is on the negative side, touch the lead to the negative terminal or to the case.

c. **Output.** If the alternator is operational, it will immediately generate full output, you will hear the engine load up, and voltage will rise up to 16 volts. Only do this for a second or two. Reconnect the regulator back to normal. In many cases, this will restore magnetism to the alternator and it will operate normally. If there is little or no output after this test, it generally indicates a fault in the alternator. Normally this is caused by a faulty diode bridge or the brushes not seating on slip rings.

d. **Warning Light.** Ensure the light is operating and on when the ignition switch is turned on. If not, the following may be faulty:

 (1) Lamp fault, or seating badly if a replaceable lamp.

 (2) Lamp connection fault.

 (3) Wire off D+ terminal, or a loose connection.

 (4) Faulty alternator excitation diodes.

2.15 **Emergency Repairs and Getting Home.** The following gives basic survival methods where an alternator or regulator has failed and you have neglected to carry spares. In some cases it may not work, but anything is worth trying in such cases.

    a. **Regulator Failure.** This may be simply no output or full, uncontrolled high voltage output:

        (1) **No Output.** To overcome this, apply full field voltage as described in Chapter 2.14. For sustained motor sailing in this condition, place a spare navigation lamp or bunk light in the field circuit to limit field current value.

        (2) **High Voltage Output.** Run the engine for limited periods only, until the voltage rises across the battery. Disconnect all electronics to avoid damage. The internal regulator should also be disconnected and a lamp placed in the circuit if motoring for extended periods.

    b. **Alternator Diode Failure.** This is indicated by low charge voltage. In many cases, only a few diodes may have failed. If you do not carry a spare diode plate, the following actions are required to get some charging capability:

        (1) Identify any short-circuited diodes using a multimeter.

        (2) Disconnect and remove the short-circuited diodes.

        (3) Reduce battery capacity to one battery to prevent overloading the reduced diode bridge.

    c. **Warning Light Failure.** In many cases, an alternator will not operate without a warning light. Place any small lamp in series with the lead off the auxiliary output (D+), and touch it to the battery's positive terminal. Excitation is usually immediate. Remove straight away.

Alternator Charging Systems

3.0   Alternator Regulators. The regulator is the key to all alternator charging systems. The function of the regulator is to control the output of the alternator and to prevent the output from rising above a nominal set level, typically 14 volts. Higher voltages would damage the battery, alternator, and equipment.

   a.   Principles. An alternator produces electricity by the rotation of a coil through a magnetic field. Its output is controlled by varying the level of the field current. This is achieved by applying the field current through one brush and slip ring to the rotor winding, and completing the circuit back through the other slip ring and brush. Essentially, the regulator is a closed loop controller, constantly monitoring the alternator output voltage and varying the field current in response to output variations.

   b.   Regulator Operating Range. A regulator does not control the charging process significantly until the battery's charge level reaches approximately 50%. When the voltage of the battery rises to this threshold, the regulator starts limiting the voltage level. The charge current levels off as the voltage level rises; this is called the regulation zone.

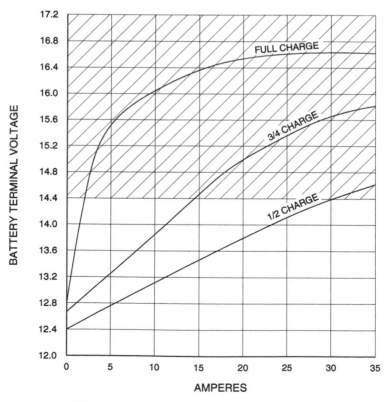

Figure 3-1 Regulator Operating Range

46

c.   **Standard Regulators.** The traditional automotive alternator is fitted with a regulator designed for automotive service. This requires the replacement of a relatively small amount of discharged power within a short time. The alternator then supplies the vehicle's electrical power as the engine runs. This arrangement is totally inadequate for marine applications. To recharge a battery properly on a boat, the charging system must overcome the battery's counter voltage, which increases as charging levels increase. The typical scenario is one of a high charge at initial start-up and then a rapidly decreasing current reading on the ammeter. As a result, few yacht batteries are ever charged much above 70% of capacity. One of the many undesirable effects of standard regulators is that when a load is operating on the electrical system, charging current also decreases. As an example, I tested an alternator with a total output of 30 amps at 14 volts aboard a vessel with an electrical load of 24 amps. I found that only 6 amps was flowing into the battery with a terminal voltage of only 13.2 volts. The more load you apply on the system during charging, the less goes to charging the battery. It is better to have as much load switched off as possible.

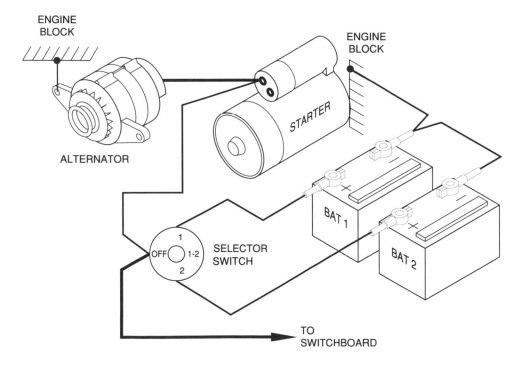

Figure 3-2 Standard Engine Charging Configuration

3.1   **Alternator Regulator Sensing.** With any type of charging system, there is a voltage drop between the alternator output terminal and the battery. With a nominal alternator output of 14 volts, it is not uncommon to have a totally inadequate 13 volts reach the battery. This voltage drop increases as current increases. Regulator sensing consists of the following configurations:

   a.   **Machine Sensed.** The machine-sensed unit simply monitors voltage at the output terminal and adjusts alternator output voltage to the nominal value, which is typically 14 volts.

      (1)   **Charge Circuit Voltage Drops.** The machine-sensed regulator makes no compensation for charging circuit voltage drops. Voltage drops include inadequately rated terminals, cables, and negative path back through the engine block.

      (2)   **Diode Isolators.** If a diode-isolator, charge-distribution system is installed, this also contributes a further drop, typically 0.75 volt.

   b.   **Battery Sensed.** The battery-sensed unit monitors the voltage at the battery terminals and adjusts the alternator output voltage to the nominal voltage. Always install battery sensing if possible.

      (1)   **Charge Circuit Voltage Drops.** The battery-sensed regulator compensates for voltage drops across diodes and charge circuit cables. By sensing the battery terminal voltage, the regulator varies the output from the alternator until the correct voltage is monitored at the battery. Some alternator manufacturers such as Bosch, Lucas, Prestolite, and Sev-Marchal are introducing modifications so that regulators can be compensated with a separate sense connection that goes directly to the battery.

      (2)   **Caution.** In some cases, the voltage drop between alternator terminals and battery may be considerable, and figures of 1.5 to 2 volts and above are not uncommon. With a multimeter, check the output and battery voltage to find out the drop, ideally at the full output current. An excessive voltage drop is a fire risk. Excessive current flow, along with high, ambient engine space temperatures, can literally melt and ignite the cable insulation, or typically first burn off the terminals. Check output terminal to see if it is hot.

   c.   **Temperature Compensation.** Very few alternator manufacturers incorporate temperature compensation, even though electrolyte is affected by temperature. In hot climates, charge voltage should be marginally decreased; in cold climates, it should be increased. Regulators with compensation usually have it sensed at the regulator, as the sensing element is part of the regulator circuit. In most vessels, however, batteries are not located near the engine, so the regulators reduce charging output when they sense high engine compartment temperatures. Compensation should be based on the ambient temperature of the batteries.

3.2   Alternator Regulator Types. It is extremely important to distinguish between a regulator and a controller. There are a number of new alternator-control devices which do not fit into the definition of a regulator.

   a.   Regulator Function. A regulator is a fully automatic device which ensures a stable output from the alternator. The primary function of a regulator is to prevent overcharging the battery and damaging the alternator. This crucial function is frequently forgotten—with disastrous results—when selecting a controller.

   b.   Alternator Control Devices. There are now five main categories of alternator control devices:

   (1)   Standard Regulators. These are factory fitted to alternators.

   (2)   Cycle Regulators. These devices use a cyclic regulator control principle that is microprocessor controlled.

   (3)   Stepped Cycle Regulators. These use a timed cycle of voltage steps.

   (4)   Regulator Controllers. These devices either parallel connect or override existing standard regulators.

   (5)   Manual Controllers. These devices have no regulator function and control alternator output manually by operator control.

3.3   Standard Regulators. Standard alternator regulators are simple and inexpensive voltage regulators with associated circuitry. They are normally an integral part of the alternator, are incorporated with the brushgear as a removable module, or are located externally on the engine or an adjacent bulkhead. The best arrangement is to have a separate regulator mounted on an adjacent bulkhead to minimize engine heat and vibration damage.

3.4   Regulator Polarity. Regulators and field windings have two possible field polarities. It is important to know the difference when installing different regulators or testing regulator function. The two types are as follows:

   a.   Positive Polarity. The positive regulator controls a positive excitation voltage. Inside the alternator, one end of the field is connected to the negative polarity. Alternators with this configuration include Bosch, Motorola, Ingram, Sev-Marchal (older models), Silver Bullet, Lestek, Balmar:

   (1)   Polarity Test. To test, use a multimeter on the ohms x 1 range and connect across the field connection to an unpainted part of the alternator case or negative output terminal.

   (2)   Meter Reading. The reading should be in the range of 3 to 8 ohms.

b. **Negative Polarity.** The negative regulator controls a negative excitation voltage. Inside the alternator, one end of the field is connected to the positive polarity. Alternators with this configuration include Hitachi, Lucas A127, ACR 17-25, and AC5, CAV, Paris-Rhone, new model Sev-Marchal, and Valeo, AC Delco, Mitsubishi:

(1) **Polarity Test.** To test, use a multimeter on the Ohms x 1 range and connect across the field connection to the alternator's positive terminal.

(2) **Meter Reading.** The reading should be in the range of 3 to 8 Ohms.

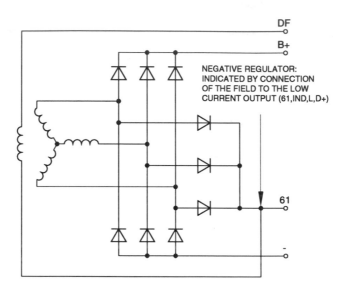

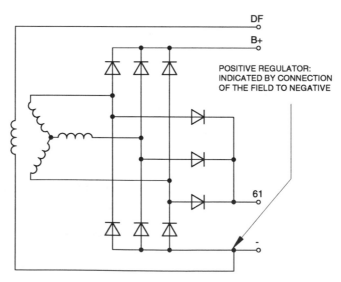

Figure 3-3 Alternator Regulator Field Polarity

3.5   Regulator Removal. If a regulator must be removed or checked, certain procedures should be used to avoid damage. The following diagrams illustrate various alternators and disassembly procedures. Mounting a separate regulator on the engine bulkhead makes replacement simple and inexpensive, and makes testing easier.

   a.   **Bosch (K1/N1 Series).** Dismantle as follows:

   (1)   Unscrew the two screws retaining the regulator.

   (2)   Carefully lift the regulator up and out. Be careful not to damage the brushes.

   (3)   Disconnect the (D+) lead from the back of the regulator.

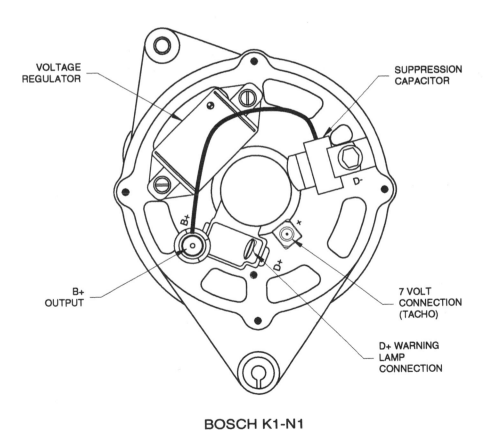

BOSCH K1-N1

Figure 3-4 Bosch Series K1/N1 Alternator

51

b. **Lucas.** This is the standard type fitted to Perkins engines. There are a large number of Lucas alternators around and all are different. This procedure covers both removal and conversion to an external regulator:

(1) Unscrew and remove the two screws securing the integral regulator and brushgear to the alternator housing.

(2) Carefully lever open the two halves of the regulator, which are held together with an adhesive.

(3) Cut and disconnect the three joining links from the brushes.

(4) Solder a new wire to the spring-loaded connector immediately below the inner brush-holder. You must use a special solder to do this because normal solders will not work. (RS Stock Number 555-099) Run it out through the cover for connection to the new regulator. This is the field control connection.

(5) Place the two regulator halves together and refit into the alternator.

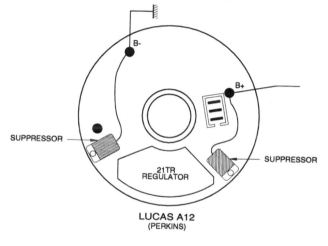

LUCAS A12
(PERKINS)

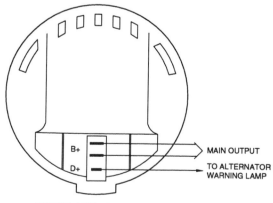

LUCAS ACR 16,17,18,25

Figure 3-5 Lucas Alternator

c. **Paris-Rhone/Valeo.** Usually a standard type fitted to Volvo engines, Paris-Rhone and Valeo are now all the same as Valeo alternators, though there are some differences in the design. Use the following procedure to disconnect and install a new, external regulator system, or to replace the existing one:

(1) Unscrew and remove the 4 screws securing the regulator to the casing.

(2) There are 4 cables leading from the regulator (5 on the new Valeo). If you are replacing the regulator with an external type, cut the cables off at the regulator. The regulator and housing act as a spark arrestor cover for the brushgear.

(3) Remove the negative cable to the regulator entirely.

(4) Take the cable running internally under the plastic cover to terminal 61 and solder it to one of the brush-holder connections. This cable was initially connected to the regulator until cut off.

(5) Solder a wire to the remaining brush-holder and run it out through the cover for connection to the new regulator. This is the field control connection.

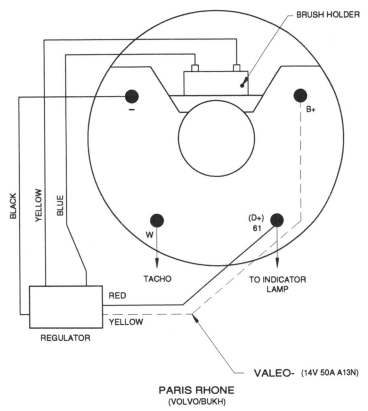

Figure 3-6 Paris-Rhone/Valeo Alternator

d. **Hitachi.** This is the standard alternator fitted to Yanmar engines (Models LR 135-74 35A, LR 155-20 55A and LR 135-105 35A). Use the following procedure:

(1) Remove the rear casing from the alternator. The screws are generally torqued extremely tight, so use the correct screwdriver size.

(2) Carefully cut off the connections to the existing regulator. There are 5 in total.

(3) Solder a 1.5 mm bridging wire between the R and F terminals, as illustrated.

(4) Replace the rear casing.

(5) Connect the external field connection to the socket at the rear of the alternator. A cable and plug are normally fitted and can be removed.

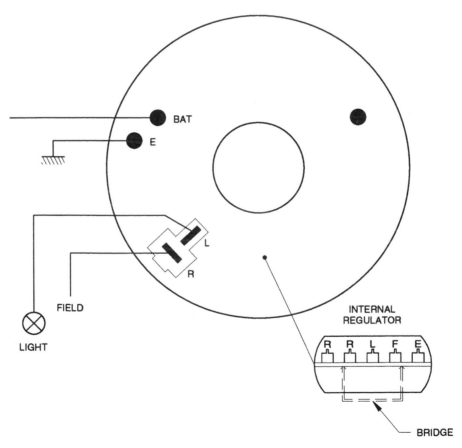

HITACHI (YANMAR)
LR 135-74 35A
LR 155-20 55A
LR 135-105 35A

Figure 3-7 Hitachi Alternator

e. **Motorola.** Model 9AR is usually fitted to Nanni and Universal engines. Remove as follows:

(1) Unscrew and remove the two retaining screws holding in the existing regulator.

(2) Either cut or remove the two cables connecting the regulator to the alternator.

(3) Fit a new wire to the vacated lower terminal and run it out through the cover for connection to the new regulator. This is the field control connection.

(4) Refit the old regulator and housing, which acts as a spark arrestor cover for the brushgear.

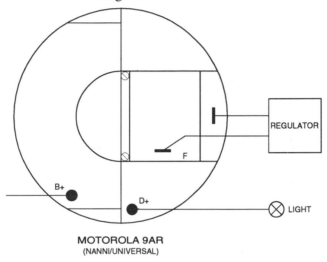

MOTOROLA 9AR
(NANNI/UNIVERSAL)

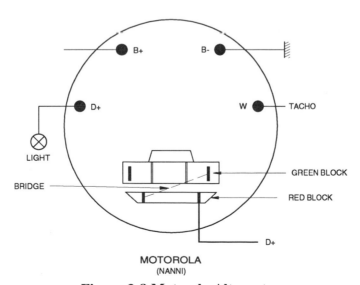

MOTOROLA
(NANNI)

Figure 3-8 Motorola Alternator

f. **Prestolite.** Model 8EM2017KA, 51 Amp. is the standard alternator now often fitted to Universal and Westerbeke engines. Remove and modify as follows:

(1) Disconnect cables and make a note of installation points.

(2) Unscrew and remove terminal nuts and washers.

(3) Remove the two hex head bolts in the center of the rear casing and remove the black plastic cover.

(4) Remove the nut securing the bridging link from the brush terminal to the indicator light terminal.

(5) Carefully unscrew the two hex head bolts securing the brushgear and regulator. Slide up brushgear/regulator and remove.

(6) Turn over the regulator, and using a screwdriver, pry off the metal plate to which the regulator is attached. Remove the regulator completely and clip off connection tags.

(7) Attach a crimp ring connector to a piece of cable and fasten to the right-hand brush terminal. This is for field control from external regulator.

(8) Carefully replace the brushgear and refit and tighten the bridging link.

(9) Refit black plastic cover and terminal nuts. Lead out the field wire though the casing. Be careful that no wire becomes trapped under casing.

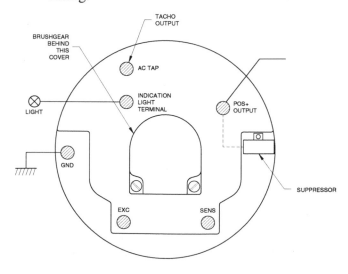

PRESTOLITE 8EM 2017kA 51 AMP
(UNIVERSAL/WESTERBEKE)

Figure 3-9 Prestolite Alternator

3.6 **Cycle Regulators.** In my experience, cycle regulators are the most efficient for fast charging. The TWC Regulator from Megalans in Sweden pioneered the "smart" or "intelligent" cycle regulator concept back in 1985. I have installed many hundreds successfully in yachts ranging from BOC entrants to cruising and racing boats of all sizes. A recent U.K. magazine survey of ocean-cruising yachts showed more than 40% of vessels now have such intelligent regulators.

3.7 **TWC Regulators.** The TWC (now called Hella Power) regulator consists of a patented microchip with a charging program. Like the machine-sensed regulator, it monitors alternator output voltage. Being battery sensed, it also monitors the battery voltage and compensates for the difference between them. The regulator also receives input from a temperature sensor adjacent to the batteries and uses this value when calculating charging voltage. The charging program consists of eight phases. The alternating high and low charging voltage phases effectively exercise the battery. The result is similar to that obtained from periodic equalization charges, which stops the charge being held close to plates and enables complete electrolyte plate percolation, and therefore complete charging. After each low voltage phase, a high current surge of short duration is applied which causes a stirring action within the electrolyte, limiting sulfation, and breaking up smaller and unhardened sulfate deposits.

    a.   **TWC Cycle Phases.** The main cycle phases are as follows:

- **Phase A.** Charging proceeds at a low level (13.8 to 14.0 volts).

- **Phase B.** Charging ceases; battery voltage is measured.

- **Phase C.** Charging resumes at a high level (14.6 volts) for 12-minute period if voltage is below a preset level.

- **Phase D.** Charging decreases to 13.8 volts for a 2-minute period, before the next measurement phase.

- **Phase E.** Charging ceases and battery voltage is measured again (on models 1985-89). If required, the cycle continues for another 12 minutes on high charge. If measured voltage exceeds preset level, the regulator goes into a compensating charge mode.

- **Phase F.** Charging continues for an extended period, at reduced alternator output. Time metering ceases and charging period extends until normal conditions resume.

- **Phase G.** Rest period; charging is automatically interrupted after eight 12-minute cycles, or if preset level is exceeded. A compensating charge period then begins.

- **Phase H.** After a heavy discharge, one hour of low, compensating charging takes place before resuming Phase A. Gassing is eliminated.

- **Phase I.** After the one-hour rest period, battery status is measured. If required, a new cycle period starts.

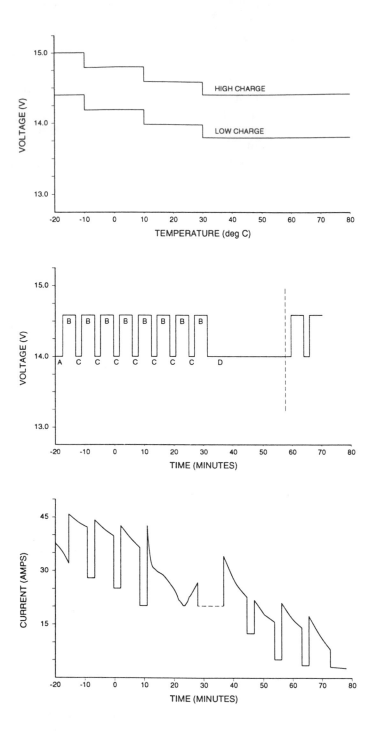

Figure 3-10 TWC Charging Program Cycle Phases

b. **TWC Troubleshooting.** With nearly 60,000 units in service, some troubleshooting advice is appropriate. The newest Hella Power unit (1994) does not have any alarm-indicator function.

(1) **Warning Light Slow Flash.** This can be due to low engine speed, too many electrical accessories in operation, a faulty alternator, a detached sensor, or an over-voltage condition due to a faulty regulator or ground leakage. The alarm is usually cleared by increasing engine speed so that the alternator is at full output, or by switching off some equipment to reduce the load. An engine running at low speed is often thought to be charging the battery. In fact, the opposite is often the case if a number of accessories are operating. It should be also noted that heavily discharged batteries will activate the slow flash function for up to 20 minutes or more as voltage rises across the battery.

(2) **Warning Light Fast Flash.** If charging circuit losses increase to abnormally high levels due to oxidation or corrosion of terminals and connections, the warning lamp flashes fast (3 flashes per second). Excessive voltage drops represent a fire hazard because cables may overheat and melt or ignite the insulation.

c. **TWC/Adverc Regulator Color Codes.** The following are the color codes for TWC regulators:

(1) **Green.** Connects to the field connection of the alternator.

(2) **Brown.** Connects to the auxiliary D+ output terminal.

(3) **Yellow.** Connects to alternator warning light, taken off the D+ terminal of the alternator at installation. Splice them together.

(4) **Black.** Connects to the alternator negative or case.

(5) **Blue.** This is a sense wire that connects to the alternator main output B+, but note that where a diode isolator is used, it must be connected to the house battery side of the diode isolator. This may entail lengthening the blue wire.

(6) **Red Sense Wire.** Connects to the house battery or battery-selector switch common terminal.

d. **Operational Checks.** Units usually fail when either full on or off. If you suspect that your TWC or Adverc is faulty, first check the following:

(1) Check that output voltages during charging are correct and that cycling does occur. This generally proves that the processor is working.

(2) If voltage or charge current appears low, an alternator diode may be faulty. Connect a spare regulator and check. If the fault still persists, then take ashore for a full bench test to verify.

3.8   **Smart Regulator (Ample Power Co. Seattle).** The Ample Power Smart regulator uses a cycle-type program that is microprocessor controlled. It has no operator adjustable functions with respect to the charging cycle, and operates based on 12 programmed charging cycles. Battery temperature compensation is incorporated. The Smart regulator is for use with P-type alternators only. Features include the following:

a.   **Alarm Indication.** This function uses a coded flash system.

b.   **Runaway Voltage Detection.** This circuit detects over-voltage conditions that occur when regulator output circuits short circuit and run away. These are indicated via the alarm lamp circuit.

c.   **Current Limiting.** This is a user adjustable function that requires connecting an externally operated switch. The switch will reduce output to a relatively low level to avoid overheating the alternator or to remove a load from a smaller engine.

d.   **Equalization.** This is a user-adjustable feature that requires connection of an externally operated switch. The function enables an equalization current to be applied until the battery reaches 16.2 volts.

e.   **Protection.** The regulator has some very commendable features. The field output driver protects the regulator from damage in the event of a field circuit failure. Additionally, all inputs are protected from transient surge and spike voltages, although normal precautions should still be installed. The lamp circuit is also over-rated to provide alarm buzzer load capability.

f.   **Voltage Limiting.** This voltage lock function enables charge voltage to be held at 13.8 volts.

3.9   **Adverc Cycle Regulator (U.K.).** This regulator was developed to overcome certain deficiencies in the TWC regulator. It utilizes similar principles to the TWC regulator, but has a number of different features. A cycle program is also the basis of the charging system. The regulator is designed for parallel connection to the existing regulator, giving some redundancy should failure occur.

a.   **Cycle Period.** The cycle periods on the Adverc system consist of four 20-minute intervals followed by a one-hour rest period. Voltage levels within the charging cycle are at the normal charge rate of 14.0 volts, with a high level of 14.5 volts.

b.   **Temperature Compensation.** Temperature compensation also takes place, but where the TWC has a stepped characteristic, the Adverc has a linear one.

c.   **Warning System.** The Adverc system has a warning light system, with indication given for low- and high-voltage conditions or the loss of sensing leads.

d.   **Engineering Standards.** Adverc regulators are designed with value engineering principles, and components are over-rated by 400%. This of course is important for cruising yachts where robust construction is a key consideration.

3.10   Stepped (Multiple) Cycle Regulators. Stepped cycle regulators are not really "intelligent" or "smart" cycle regulators. They are essentially timed charging systems that incorporate a microprocessor-based timing circuit to supervise the charging process. Unlike "smart" regulators, stepped cycle regulators often permit a level of operator control or have settings that can be altered. I would caution any user not to experiment with settings, as I have seen many problems on vessels due to incorrect or dangerously high voltage settings.

3.11   Ideal Regulator (Cruising Equipment, Seattle). This new regulator is unique in that current is a factor in the charging process, not just voltage. I have not seen this in any other regulator types I have come across. The Ideal regulator is used in conjunction with a digital circuit monitor.

    a.   **Charge Program.** The Ideal regulator has the following program:

        (1)   **Delay Period.** A 20-second delay after voltage is applied from ignition allows engine speed to rise to normal running speed.

        (2)   **Ramping Up Period.** This feature allows a controlled increase of alternator output over a 10-second period until the default current limiting value is reached. This reduces shock loadings, allows belts to warm up, and reduces powerline surges that occur when full outputs are applied.

        (3)   **Charge Cycle.** The charge cycle allows full alternator output until the battery voltage reaches 14.3 volts.

        (4)   **Acceptance Cycle.** Charging continues at 14.3 volts until charge current decreases to a default value of 2% of capacity. Once the 2% level is reached, the acceptance hold cycle begins.

        (5)   **Acceptance Hold Cycle.** Charging is held at 14.3 volts and charging current is monitored and continues for a minimum of 10 minutes or a maximum of 20 minutes.

        (6)   **Float Ramp Cycle.** This is a transition phase between charged and float cycles. Voltage is reduced to the float setting of 13.3 volts during this cycle.

        (7)   **Float Cycle.** Voltage is held constant at 13.3 volts.

        (8)   **Condition Cycle.** This is a manually activated function. Current is held at 4% of battery capacity, until a maximum of 16 volts is attained. Once voltage reaches 16 volts, it is maintained until charge current falls to charged current percent setting. The cycle then automatically terminates. On termination, it reverts to the float ramp cycle to bring the voltage down.

b. **Regulator Characteristics.** The characteristics illustrated below show the previously described program steps. The relationship between voltage and current is graphically illustrated. Also note the conditioning cycle. The steadily rising voltage shows why such conditions should be carefully monitored.

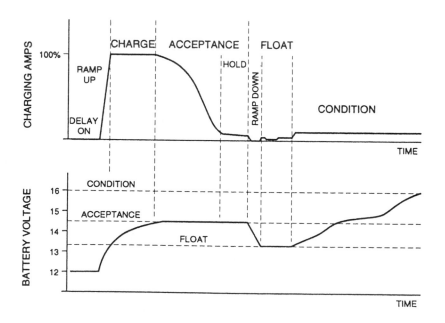

Figure 3-11 Quad Cycle and Ideal Regulator Characteristics

3.12   Three-Step Deep Cycle Regulator. (Ample Power, Seattle)   The Three-Step device uses a step-type program that is fully automatic and operates based on the charging cycles of absorption and float The unit consists of a timer circuit rather than an intelligent program chip, and has simple battery and ignition inputs.

    a.   **Charge Program.** The regulator has the following features:

        (1)   **Step 1.** The alternator is controlled to give full output until the absorption setpoint is reached. The time required to reach this level depends on the initial battery level and output speed of the alternator.

        (2)   **Step 2.** The absorption setpoint (14.5 volts) is maintained for a period of 45 minutes.

        (3)   **Step 3.** The charge level reduces to the float voltage setpoint (13.8 volts).

    b.   **Adjustment Options.** Users are able to manually alter absorption and float voltage settings. This is useful in applications such as NiCad cells that require different charging voltage levels.

    c.   **Installation Notes.** The following notes are given by the manufacturer:

        (1)   Due to the full alternator output requirement in Step 1, many alternators may not be able to cope and may suffer failure. This is generally due to windings overheating and diode failure.

        (2)   The regulator is suitable for P-type alternators only (i.e. Bosch, Prestolite, Motorola, Valeo/Paris-Rhone, etc.).

3.13   Next Step Regulator. (Ample Power, Seattle)   The Next Step device is an improved version of the Three-Step unit. The unit is microprocessor-controlled and also incorporates temperature compensation. Due to its requirement for full alternator output (Step 1), many alternators may not be able to cope, and may fail. This is generally due to windings overheating and diode failure.

    a.   **Charge Program.** The regulator has the following features:

        (1)   **Step 1.** The alternator is controlled to give full output until the absorption setpoint is reached. The time required to reach this level depends on the initial battery level and the output speed of the alternator.

        (2)   **Step 2.** The absorption setpoint (14.5 volts) is maintained for a period of 45 minutes.

        (3)   **Step 3.** The charge level reduces to the float-voltage setpoint (13.8 volts).

    b.   **Adjustment Options.** Users are able to manually alter both absorption voltage and time, as well as float voltage settings.

3.14   BEP Electronic Regulator. (BEP Marine, NZ). The unit also incorporates temperature compensation. Due to the full alternator output requirement in step 1, many alternators may not be able to cope if undersized for battery capacity, and may suffer damage or failure.

The regulator has the following charge steps:

(1)   **Step 1.** The alternator is controlled to give full output until a voltage of 14.6 volts is reached. The time required to reach this level depends on the initial battery charge level and output speed of the alternator.

(2)   **Step 2.** The 14.6-volt setpoint is maintained for a period equal to that required to reach the setpoint.

(3)   **Step 3.** The charge level reduces to the float voltage setpoint of 14 volts, which is maintained until engine shutdown.

3.15   Alternator Manual Control Devices. Manual devices are those which require total operator control of the alternator output. Some handbooks give information on how to make your own controllers. From personal experience, I can say that once these home-grown controllers and circuits are installed, the charging system, batteries, and alternator will be burned out not too far into the future. There is no such thing as a cheap solution, and if you really care about your power system, don't risk it. There is no sense in having electronics worth thousands only to balk at paying relatively small sums to improve charging. Use the following control methods at your own risk. While there are many who boast how reliable and cheap these devices are, I make a very nice living off the majority who subsequently have problems. The savings initially achieved with these methods are more than negated by one mishap which often shortens battery life through overcharging and plate damage.

a.   **Field Switches.** A typical manual method is to connect the switch directly to the field connection. It simply puts on a full field voltage resulting in maximum alternator output. The results can be quite spectacular and very damaging to both battery and alternator. Once, while his boat was crossing a dangerous bar, a friend casually flicked a switch, which was followed by sparks and smoke curling out of the engine compartment. After investigating, I found this same set-up, which nearly led to a disaster.

b.   **Field Rheostats.** The most common type of control is the rheostat. A rheostat is simply a variable resistance rated for the field current. The term rheostat is still in common usage and low-value variable resistances are generally termed potentiometers. Rheostats are totally reliant on operator control, with no safety cutouts or regulation. As a general alternator charging control, it is not recommended, because both alternator and battery are easily and commonly damaged.

3.16   Alternator Controllers. Controllers are devices that require the yacht owner to manually select or partially override the existing regulator to deliver a fast charge. It is important to remember the basic phases of charging a battery (bulk, absorption, float, and equalization) and that at no stage should battery voltage exceed gassing level. In most cases, controllers do not adhere to these basic charging principles.

a. **Operating Principles.** Controllers are either direct regulator replacement units or are connected in parallel to the existing regulator. Some units have an ammeter to monitor output and require continual adjustment of field current to maintain the required charge current level, but they do not monitor or take into account the high and damaging system voltages that are imposed while maintaining the initial high charging currents.

b. **Precautions.** All controllers will have some beneficial aspects, and can improve the charging process to varying degrees. There are, however, serious risks that must be considered to avoid damage.

    (1)   **Power System Disturbances.** If you apply excessive voltages or full alternator outputs, spikes and surges can arise that will damage regulators and electronics equipment.

    (2)   **Battery Damage.** Forcing current into batteries above their natural ability to accept a charge will damage plates, heat the battery up, and generate potentially explosive gases. The failure of automatic cut-outs, or forgetting to adjust the regulator may cause all of the problems mentioned.

c. **Performance and Efficiency.** There are some important factors to consider before purchasing controllers.

    (1)   **Efficiency.** At best, these types of units offer a 10-15% improvement, which brings charge levels up to approximately 85% of nominal capacity.

    (2)   **Performance.** It is interesting to note that virtually none of the controller manufacturers can offer any verifiable proof or independent testing to support claims that they in fact improve charging. So far, only TWC has had verifiable and independent testing carried out.

d. **Controller Types.** Some of the more common controllers on the market are as follows:

    (1)   **AutoMAC (USA).** This regulator is connected in parallel to the existing regulator. A potentiometer is used in conjunction with an ammeter to adjust alternator current. When a predetermined voltage is reached, the unit automatically cuts off and the existing regulator takes over. Failure of automatic cut-offs is relatively frequent, as is subsequent overcharging.

    (2)   **Kestrel 90 Controller (U.K.).** This device is connected in parallel to the existing regulator. When the engine starts, the controller activates and applies a boost charge level until a programmed time limit cuts the controller off and the normal regulator takes over.

    (3)   **Altimo Controller (Aust).** This controller uses a stepped voltage increase. Its reliability is questionable. The upper voltage levels are too high and may cause electronics damage.

3.17   Regulator Troubleshooting. There is a simple test to check whether your regulator or controller is working properly. This is not difficult with external regulators, but if an internal regulator is fitted, the alternator will need to be opened and a wire attached to a brush-holder. Switch off all electrical and electronic equipment at the switchboard circuit breaker before starting this test. *If in doubt, don't try it.*

> a.   **Alternator Test.** Check that the alternator gives full output. If the alternator operates after testing, then the regulator is suspect.

> b.   **Rotor Testing.** If a regulator has failed, particularly in an overcharge condition, checked the rotor for damage before replacing the regulator. The test is as follows and is illustrated below:

>> (1)   **Test Insulation Resistance.** Place one multimeter probe on a slip ring, and the other on the rotor core. Resistance should be infinite or over-range.

>> (2)   **Test Winding Resistance.** Place the multimeter probes on each slip ring. Resistance should be around 4 ohms. If it is very high, an open circuit may exist; if very low, a coil short circuit may exist.

> c.   **Auxiliary Diode Test.** On some occasions, the auxiliary diodes may fail. Put your multimeter on the 20-volt range and connect across 61/D+ and negative. If there is any reading, the diode may be faulty. Turn on the ignition key without starting. The reading should be around 1-2 volts. If less, the wiring may be faulty; if higher, the diode may be faulty, there is excessive rotor resistance or there are bad connections.

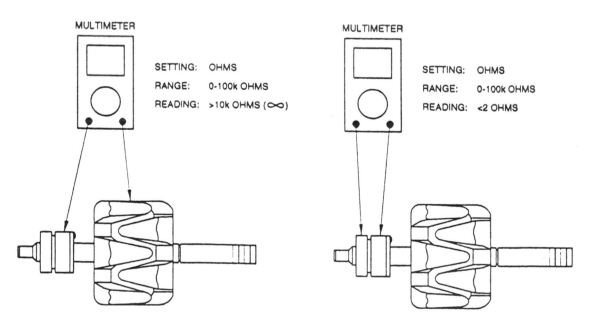

Figure 3-12 Rotor Testing

3.18   Charging System Configurations. The three principal systems are the battery selector switch, the relay, and the diode isolator.

    a.   Battery Selector Switch. The charging system on most engines uses the same cabling as the engine starter circuit. Basically, it consists of a switch with 3 positions and off. The center position parallels both battery banks. It is not uncommon to see both batteries left accidentally parallelled under load so that both are flattened. Parallelling a heavily discharged battery and a fully charged one during charging can also cause some instability in the charging as they both equalize.

        (1)   Switch Operation During Charging. If a battery selector switch is operated under load during charging and accidentally switched to the off position, the resultant surge will normally destroy the alternator diodes, and charging will cease. With poor quality switches even switching between batteries causes a noticeable disturbance as the circuit is temporarily interrupted. Switches should be turned off only after the engine has stopped.

        (2)   Surges. If both batteries are parallelled during an engine start, sensitive electronics can be damaged by the surge.

        (3)   Circuit Resistance. In most cases, the cables must run from the batteries to the switch location and back to the starter motor, causing voltage drops. Switches are notoriously unreliable and can introduce voltage drops into the circuit or cause alternator or switch to fail.

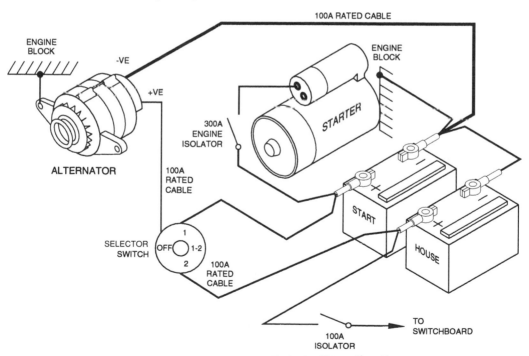

Figure 3-13 Battery Selector Switch Charging System

b. **Relay/Solenoid Configuration.** This system improves on the switch system by separating the charging system from starting circuits. The relay connects both batteries during charging, and separates them when off, preventing discharge between the batteries. The relay operating coil is interlocked with the ignition and energizes when the key is turned on. When modifying the system, it is necessary to separate the charging cable from the alternator-to-starter-motor main terminal where it is usually connected. Lead a cable directly from the alternator output terminal to the relay, as illustrated. A relay or solenoid can fail if incorrectly rated for the task. Relay ratings should at least match the maximum rated output of the alternator, and it is prudent to over-rate the relay. Relays are marketed in various forms, the most common being automotive solenoid types. Some are manufactured specifically for this task.

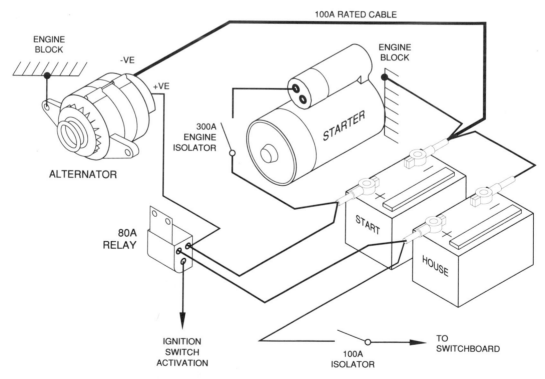

Figure 3-14 Relay Charging System Configuration

c.　**Diode System.** The diode system is the simplest configuration and the most reliable. A diode has an inherent voltage drop of typically 0.7-0.8 volts. This is unacceptable in a charging circuit. If the alternator is machine-sensed and does not have any provision for increasing the output in compensation, the diode should not be used. Essentially, a diode isolator consists of two diodes with their inputs connected. They allow voltage to pass one way only, so that each battery has an output. This prevents any backfeeding between the batteries. Professionally built diode isolators should be used, such as the American-manufactured Surepower isolator. They are mounted on heat sinks specifically designed for the maximum current carrying capacity and maximum heat dissipation. Homemade units are notoriously unreliable and have given diode isolation systems an unfair reputation. Diode isolators must be rated for at least the maximum rating of the alternator, and if mounted in the engine compartment, must be over-rated to compensate for engine heat. Not all diodes are heat sink mounted. Lucas manufactures a cylindrical, oil-filled unit. Mount diodes in the coolest area possible. Heat sink units should have the cooling fins in the vertical position to ensure maximum convection and cooling. Do not install switches in the cables between the diode and the batteries. A diode is an isolator, so a mechanical switch is redundant.

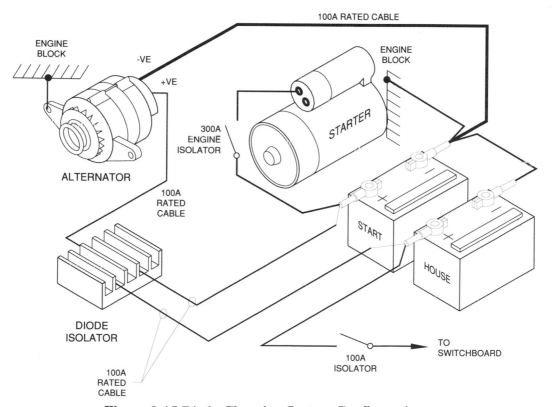

Figure 3-15 Diode Charging System Configuration

69

d. **Automatic Charge Distributors.** These are characterized by the following systems:

(1) **EDR Electronically Controlled Relays (LEAB, Sweden).** These devices allow charging of two or more batteries from one alternator or battery charger. One battery, normally the house battery, is selected as the priority unit. During charging, once the priority battery has reached the preset voltage level, the EDR automatically selects and connects the next battery. If the charge level of the priority bank drops during charging, the EDR will revert back to ensure that it remains fully charged.

(2) **CDB Charging Distributor (LEAB, Sweden).** This device functions as charge distributor, battery isolator, and regulator. The regulator function is not strictly true in that it has no control over field voltage. The device and connections are illustrated below.

(3) **Isolator Eliminator (Ample Power).** This is a multi-step regulator that controls the charge to the secondary battery bank, typically used for engine starting. It is temperature compensated like an alternator control system.

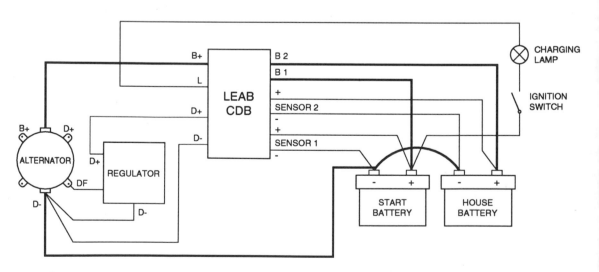

Figure 3-16 Automatic Charge Distributors

3.19   Multiple Alternator Charging System Configurations. Many vessels have a second alternator installed. Generally, charging problems can be solved without extra alternators, but the multiple alternator system does have advantages, mainly that of charging source redundancy. There are a number of different system configurations for multiple alternator installations, which are as follows:

> **a.   Discrete Systems.** These systems often use the original engine alternator to charge only the engine start battery. The additional alternator, usually a higher-rated type of 80 amps or more, charges only the house batteries. If there is more than one bank, this may be split either through a diode isolator or a switch. Given that start batteries require very little charging, an under-utilized start battery alternator can be used to charge a third battery bank.

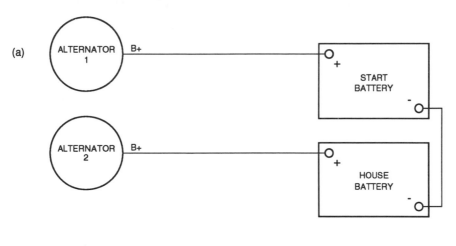

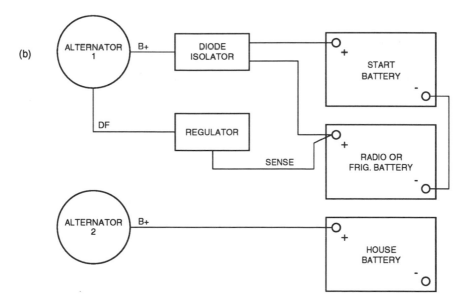

Figure 3-17 Two-Alternator Discrete Charging Systems

71

b.   **Cross Feed Systems.** In these systems, each alternator usually charges a primary battery bank and cross feeds to the other battery bank via a diode isolator. Ideally, a fast-charge device should still be used. Although it looks complicated, it is in fact a simple arrangement. The advantages of such a layout are as follows:

(1)   **Alternator Redundancy.** The arrangement allows charging of both battery banks even if one alternator should fail.

(2)   **Load Balancing.** It is easier to balance loads between battery banks to achieve similar discharge levels over the same time period. This allows both batteries to be charged at a similar rate, which overall is faster, assuming the alternators and regulators are the same.

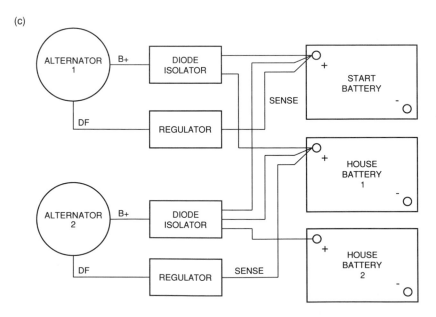

Figure 3-18 Two-Alternator Cross Feed Charging Systems

3.20   Diode Isolator Testing. On rare occasions, a diode isolator may fail because of an external event such as a surge or spike. The following tests can be carried out to verify its operation:

      a.   **Engine Operating.** Output terminal voltages should be identical. The input terminal should read approximately 0.75 volt higher if a non-battery-sensed regulator is being used. The diode system should not be used in these installations.

      b.   **Engine Off.** Output terminal voltages should read the same as the service and starting batteries. The input terminal from the alternator should be zero.

      c.   **Ohmmeter Test.** Make sure all power is off before testing.

          (1)   Disconnect battery input and output cables.

          (2)   Set meter scale to x1.

          (3)   Connect red positive probe to input terminal.

          (4)   Connect black negative probe to output terminals 1 or 2.

          (5)   If the diode is good, the meter will indicate minimal resistance.

          (6)   Reverse the probes, and repeat the test. The reading should indicate high resistance, or over range.

3.21   Charging System Recommendations. I recommend the following modifications to every vessel charging system:

      a.   **Install a Separate Negative Cable.** I strongly recommend that a separate negative conductor of at least 10 mm^2 (see Tables 6-1 and 6-2 for equivalents) be installed from the alternator case or negative terminal directly to the battery's negative terminal. This by-passes the engine block, offers a good, low-resistance path, and reduces stray currents through the block, which can cause bearings to pit.

      b.   **Replace Positive Cable.** Most installed positive cables are too small, especially if a fast-charge device is installed. The cable size should be doubled. Ideally, install a minimum of 10 mm^2. When using fast-charge devices or when recharging heavily discharged batteries, one problem is that the heat of the engine compartment lowers the maximum current capacity of the cable. In most cases, a significant voltage drop develops across the cable under full output conditions.

      c.   **Connectors.** Do not use the yellow insulated crimp ring connectors to terminate at the alternator, as they are not rated for the full alternator output current. Use higher-rated crimp connectors. Also, do not solder in place of crimping. If a connection is loose and develops a high resistance, the heat at the joint along with engine space temperatures will soon melt the connection. Additionally, a large amount of vibration is transmitted through to the connections, and fatigue of soldered lugs is a common cause of failure.

d. **Install Suppressors.** Many alternators do not have these fitted, so install them, especially if you have noticed radio noise or interference on electronics equipment. Start with a 1.0 microfarad suppressor, or experiment with a couple of simple and inexpensive automotive types.

e. **Separate Charging System.** If you can, separate the charging system from the starting circuit. Previous illustrations show how various methods can be done. In the long term, this will considerably reduce problems and increase reliability.

Table 3-1 Charging-System Troubleshooting

Symptom	Probable Fault	Corrective Action
Reduced Charging	Drive belt loose	Adjust to 10 mm
	Oil on belt	Clean belt
	Loose alternator connection	Repair connection
	Partial diode failure	Repair alternator
	Suppressor breaking down	Replace suppressor
	Regulator fault	Replace regulator
	Diode isolator fault	Replace diode
	Negative connection fault	Repair connection
	Solder connection fault	Resolder connection
	Under-rated cables	Uprate cables
	In-line ammeter fault	Repair connections
	In-line ammeter fault	Replace ammeter
	Ammeter shunt fault	Repair connections
Over Charging	Regulator fault	Replace regulator
	Sense wire off	Replace wire
No Charging	Drive belt loose	Retension belt
	Drive belt broken	Replace belt
	Warning lamp failure	Replace lamp
	Auxiliary diode failure	Repair alternator
	Regulator fault	Replace regulator
	Diode bridge failure	Repair alternator
	Jammed brushes	Clean brushgear
	Stator winding failure	Repair alternator
	Rotor winding failure	Repair alternator
	Output connection off	Repair connection
	Negative connection off	Repair connection
Fluctuating Ammeter	Alternator brushes sticking	Repair alternator
	Regulator fault	Replace regulator
	Loose cable connections	Repair connections
	Ammeter fault/overcurrent	Replace ammeter
High Initial Start	Batteries sulfated	Replace batteries
Current, Low Charge	Battery cell failure	Replace batteries
Current	Battery charge very low	Recharge for extended time

3.22   Power Charging Systems. Instead of or in addition to the main propulsion energy charging systems, vessels can have a dedicated engine powering an alternator, with possible extra power take-offs for compressors, pumps, or desalinator/high-pressure water pump. These engines can be either diesel or gasoline driven. A traditional method has been the use of lay shafts, but they are often complicated and cause difficulties. Systems are as follows:

a.   **Diesel Alternator Systems.** Typical units are as follows:

   (1)   **Balmar.** Balmar (U.S.) has a unit driven by an air-cooled, 4-horse-power Yanmar diesel. Weighing only 65 lbs, it is fitted with 100-amp or greater alternator.

   (2)   **Ample Power Genie.** This unit uses a raw water cooled Kubota diesel fitted with a 120-amp alternator and Smart regulator system.

b.   **Water Cooled Diesel.** SeaFresh(U.K.) manufactures a multipurpose desalination system that integrates charging and a reverse-osmosis, high-pressure pump into a single unit. The system also integrates the hot-water heater and refrigeration compressor to utilize engine power economically.

c.   **Gasoline.** MASE of Italy makes a gasoline-powered portable unit that has an output of 50 amps DC at 14.2 volts. Weight is only 28 kg, including an integral fuel tank:

   (1)   **Multihulls.** This is the perfect solution for multihulls where only an outboard is used for main propulsion. It is a considerably cheaper and more efficient charging source than several solar panels.

   (2)   **Trailerable Yachts.** Many small cruising yachts 26-feet or less have only outboards with limited charging ability. Gasoline-powered portable chargers provide a good DC power supply in these situations. In many cases, the outboard is a cheaper option to a small diesel, so the charging units can be easily installed in the vacant engine space.

d.   **Custom Units.** Units can be made to suit individual requirements, as some leading singlehanded sailors have found:

   (1)   An air-cooled Yanmar engine was used on Australian Kay Cottee's *Blackmores First Lady.* (This was Kay Cottee's record-breaking effort as the first woman to solo around the world non-stop.) I installed a belt-driven 80-Amp Bosch alternator with TWC regulator to improve the charging characteristic. This eliminated the need to use the more fuel-hungry main engine for charging. As a back-up, the small diesel also had charging output from a flywheel generator.

   (2)   To reduce main engine run times, I have also used a 10-horsepower Kubota diesel to run an AC alternator, refrigeration compressor, air compressor, and DC charging alternator.

Alternative Energy Systems

4.0   Alternative Energy Charging Systems. More misconceptions exist about the capabilities of alternative energy systems on cruising yachts than virtually any other equipment. In most cases, expectations are wildy optimistic, and the realities are at best disappointing. Some absolute truths must be recognized before embarking on projects that entail large expenditures, and often a lot of engineering. They must be faced in spite of the philosophical and environmental arguments. The important factors are outlined below for consideration in that decision-making process.

a.   **Secondary Power Sources.** Alternative energy sources at the prevailing technology levels can only be considered as auxiliary charging sources. They should be integrated into the power system as a secondary power source where no further charging capacity can be derived from the engine alternator. In most cases, alternative generation sources significantly reduce dependence on engine-based systems. A battery on a poorly maintained vessel can lose as much as 14% of its charge per month, so an alternative energy charging system would be ideal in this situation.

b.   **Primary Power Sources.** Many people, for a variety of reasons, choose to rely solely on renewable power sources to supply electrical power. Yet I have observed in a large number of cases a complete lack of understanding of basic electrical design.

(1)   **Design Considerations.** Alternative energy systems require considerably more stringent design criteria, a sailing philosophy that excludes a large number of electrical and electronics equipment, and a very disciplined lifestyle while cruising. If you want all the comforts and technologies of home, you are going to require a very large number of solar panels, wind generators, and probably water-powered ones as well. Regrettably, the natural forces that control alternative sources are far from predictable, which is why many have had to adjust their cruising behavior to one dominated by the search for ways to conserve battery power, and recharge batteries.

(2)   **Output Data.** You must realize that the quoted output data is almost always in absolutely ideal laboratory conditions. In practice, you will require a large safety factor to get a reasonable result.

(3)   **The Downward Spiral**. In practice, battery charge levels tend to slowly spiral downward. The real trick in getting the most out of alternative energy systems is to fully charge the battery to 100% with a good, fast-charge engine system before the batteries sink low enough to be damaged. That allows the alternative systems to keep up.

4.1 **Solar Systems.** Solar energy is not a new concept. It dates back to 1839 when the French scientist Becquerel discovered the photovoltaic phenomenon. Solar systems are the most commonly used alternative energy sources on boats and offer a renewable and nearly maintenance-free energy source. In many cases, attempts to make panels the primary charging system are unrealistic. At best, solar panels should be considered an auxiliary charging source, although new advances over the next decade may well change that.

    a. **Theory.** Solar cells consist of two layers of silicon, one positive, and one negative. When photons enter the cell, some are absorbed by the silicon atoms. This frees electrons in the negative layer, which then flow through the external circuit (the battery) and back to the positive layer. This is the photovoltaic principle. When manufactured, the cells are electronically matched and connected in series to form complete solar panels with typical peak power outputs of 16 volts.

    b. **Cell Types.** There a number of solar-cell types based on the cell material or structure used.

        (1) **Mono-crystalline.** Pure, defect-free silicon slices from a single, grown crystal are used for these structures. The cell's atomic structure is rigid and ordered and cannot easily be bent. The cells are approximately 15-20% efficient. The thin, pure silicon wafers are etched with a caustic solution to create a textured surface. This textured surface consists of millions of four-sided pyramids which act as efficient light traps, reducing reflection losses. Panels are made by interconnecting and encapsulating 34-36 wafers onto a glass back.

        (2) **Multi-crystalline.** These arrays use wafers of silicon cut from a cast block. The multi-crystalline cell has better low-light-angle output levels and is now the most commonly used.

        (3) **Amorphous Silicon.** Unlike crystalline cells, these thin film panels have a loosely arranged atomic structure. They are also much less efficient; their power output is nearly a quarter of crystalline cells the same size. Amorphous cells are normally used in watches and calculators. They do have the advantage that they can be applied to flexible plastic surfaces, which is how flexible panels are made. In addition, the cells are capable of generating under low light conditions. I have heard of one enterprising yachtsman who always tries to park his stern panel under the marina floodlights so he can get some trickle charging at night. Crystalline cells won't do this.

c.   **Construction.** Cell arrays are normally laminated under Ethylene Vinyl Acetate (EVA). Anti-reflection coatings using titanium dioxide are used, and some are characterized by a blue coloring. This also increases the gathering of light at the blue end of the light spectrum. Panels are constructed to be moisture and ultraviolet resistant. Glass surfaces are tempered and sometimes textured to reduce reflection, increase surface area, and improve light gathering at low lighting angles. Solar arrays often utilize front and rear connections to improve faulty cell redundancy.

d.   **Ratings.** Efficiency is at an optimum when a solar panel is angled directly towards the sun. The most efficient panels are rigid units while the flexible units have significantly lower outputs.

e.   **Output Specifications.** These are normally quoted to a standard, typically $1000W/m^2$ at 25° C cell temperature and spectrum of 1.5 air mass. The level of irradiance is measured in watts per square meter. The irradiance value is multiplied by time duration to give watt-hours per square meter per day.

f.   **Efficiency.** Location and seasonal factors affect the amount of energy available. Cells are approximately 15% efficient and start producing a voltage as low as 5% of full sunlight value:

(1)   **Solar Angles.** Solar angles are important to panel efficiency. With the sun at 90° overhead, panels give 100% output. When angled at 75°, the output falls to approximately 95%. At 50°, output falls to 75%. A light angle of 30° reduces output by 50%.

(2)   **Average Seasonal Hours.** Table 4-1 shows typical seasonal hours and yearly averages based on a solar array tilted towards the sun at an angle equal to latitude of the location +15°.

Table 4-1 Peak Solar Level Table

Location	Winter Hours	Summer Hours	Average
California	4.0	5.0	4.5
Florida	3.6	6.2	4.9
Central Pacific	4.5	6.0	5.3
Caribbean	5.5	5.5	5.5
Azores	2.2	6.0	4.1
Northern Europe	1.5	4.0	2.7
Southern England	0.6	5.0	2.8
South France	2.5	7.5	5.0
Greece	2.4	7.4	4.9
SE Asia	4.0	5.5	4.7
Cape Town	4.0	5.0	4.5
Red Sea	6.0	6.5	6.3
Indian Ocean	5.0	5.5	5.3
Eastern Australia	4.5	5.5	5.0

g. **Panel Regulation.** In any panel larger than a small 12-15 watt unit, a regulator is required to restrict the voltage to a safe level. It is not uncommon to have solar panel output rise to 15-16 volts and boil batteries dry over an extended, unsupervised period. There are solar control devices in use which must not be confused. One simply limits voltage to safe levels and the other device, called a linear current booster, increases power for certain conditions:

(1) **Regulators.** The regulator serves to limit panel output to a safe level and prevent damage to a battery. Some units simply limit voltage to 13.8 volts, the maximum float level, and dissipate heat through a heat sink. More sophisticated regulators get more from the panel. These units incorporate an automatic boost level of 14.2 volts and a float setting of 13.8 volts. The regulator float charges the battery until a lower limit of approximately 12.5 volts is reached before switching to boost. The units normally eliminate the need for an additional blocking diode. Check the manufacturer's data sheet first. Some regulators also have temperature compensation and must be installed adjacent to the batteries.

(2) **Linear Current Booster.** These electronic devices boost current from the solar module. They are designed to prevent permanent magnet motors from stalling, but effectively they are constant current devices. Such units are used primarily in applications where panels directly supply a load. They are not useful on boats where the panel is used to charge a battery.

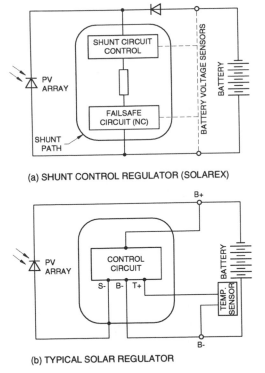

(a) SHUNT CONTROL REGULATOR (SOLAREX)

(b) TYPICAL SOLAR REGULATOR

Figure 4-1 Typical Solar Regulator Systems

h.   **Diodes.** Most panels have diodes installed. There is a rather flawed argument that the use of a a diode reduces charging voltage. This is true, as a diode reduces voltage by approximately 0.75 volt. But if you are installing a couple of 3-amp panels, which is typical, you will need a regulator to reduce the voltage to avoid overcharging and damaging your batteries. If the regulator is a good unit, the control will float between 14.5 and 13.8 volts, so the small voltage drop will not be a problem. If the regulator has the appropriate reverse-current protection diode, then the panel-installed diode can be removed to increase the input voltage to the regulator, which gives a marginally higher output. If you do not regulate the solar supply, then failing to install or removing the diode will result in a flat battery overnight. There are two functional uses of diodes:

(1)   **By-pass Diodes.** By-pass diodes, normally installed at the factory in solar module junction boxes, reduce power losses that might occur if a module within the array is partially shaded. For 12-volt systems, these offer sufficient circuit protection without the use of a blocking diode. A 24-volt array requires two 12-volt panels in series. An array for larger current outputs requires the parallel connection of these series arrangements. If one module of a parallel array is shaded, reverse current flow may occur.

(2)   **Blocking Diodes.** Blocking diodes are often connected in series with the solar panel output to prevent the battery from discharging back to the array at night, but not all manufacturers install them as standard. If the panels do not have a diode, then a diode rated to 1.5 times the maximum output (5 amps) should be installed at the regulator input. Most solar regulators will have the diode incorporated. Generally, all panels with a by-pass diode installed in the connection box do not require any further diode.

JUNCTION BOX LAYOUT

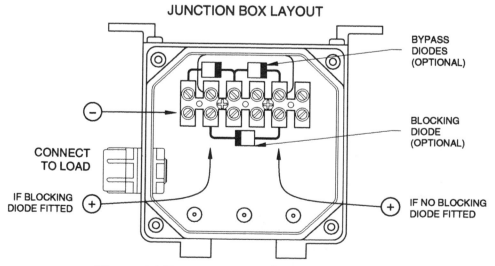

Figure 4-2 Typical BP Solar-Diode Junction Box

i. **Charging System Interaction.** There is often an interaction between solar panels and alternator charging regulators during engine charging. If the solar panels are not regulated, it is quite common to see a voltage of up to 16 volts or more across the battery. When an alternator's regulator senses this high voltage level, it simply registers it as a fully charged battery, and as a result the alternator does not charge the battery, or does so at a minimal rate. When installing panels and regulators, consider the following features:

    (1) **Isolation Switch.** Install an isolation switch on the incoming line to the panel so that it can be switched out of circuit.

    (2) **Regulator By-pass Switch.** Always install a switch that can by-pass the regulator and apply full-panel output to the battery. This will make periodic equalization easier and charging a dead battery more efficient.

    (3) **Engine Interlock.** This circuit automatically disconnects the solar panel via a relay so that the solar panel does not impress a higher voltage and "confuse" the alternator's regulator.

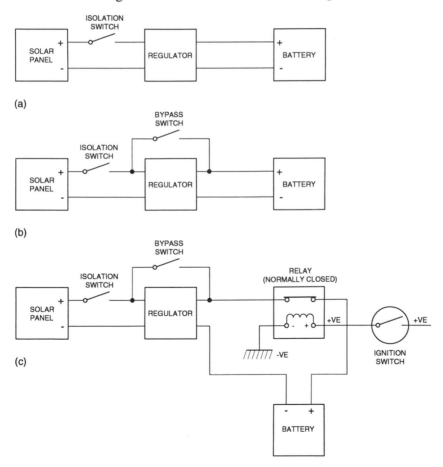

Figure 4-3 Typical Solar Interlock Systems

j.   **Site Selection.** Solar-panel siting is largely dependent on the physical space available for installation. The following options are the most common and most efficient. In all cases, it is essential to ensure that panels are not shadowed by sails, spars, or any other equipment. Ideally, panels should be angled towards the sun if at all possible, but on a cruising yacht this is not always practical. Generally, flat-mounted panels offer the best compromise, which is why the stern arch configuration is becoming so popular:

(1)   **Coach House.** Panels can be mounted on coach-house tops, but one panel will often be shaded and the other illuminated, depending on the tack .

(2)   **Stern Mounting.** This arrangement is really only suitable for a single panel, and is usually designed to allow the panel angle to be adjusted. The panel support brackets are welded to the stern pulpit rail.

(3)   **Stern Arches.** This is becoming the most popular method as it allows the easy installation of at least two clear and unobstructed 3-amp panels.

(4)   **Stern Pulpit (Pushpit) Rails.** This arrangement uses two panels mounted on swing-up brackets on each side of the vessel, normally close to and on the pulpit rails. Depending on tack, or direction of sun, the panels can be put into service, and folded down if not used.

(5)   **Multihulls.** The greater deck area of a multihull and its nearly flat sailing attitude make site selection much easier, and offer increased efficiency. In most cases, a large coach house can be utilized, and on trimarans, arrays can be mounted on the outer hulls well clear of shadows.

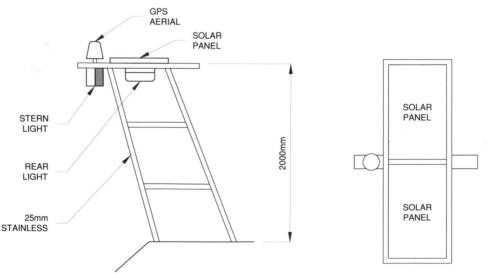

Figure 4-4 Stern Arch Arrangement

k. **Installation.** Solar panels are manufactured in either rigid or flexible form. Cabling should be properly rated to avoid voltage drop. To cope with two 65-watt panels, 2.5 mm^2 (15-amp) cable is the minimum size. Use only tinned copper marine cable. Most panels have weatherproof connection boxes and connections can be simply twisted and terminated in terminals. Do not use connectors or solder the wire ends. Manufacturers also specify grounding the array's or the module's metallic frames. I have heard concerns about corrosion aboard vessels with automatic bilge pumps and a solar panel charging the battery. If the pump cable develops a fault, once the battery is flat, serious electrolytic corrosion may corrode through-hull (skin) fittings and hull as a voltage is being applied directly to them. Although theoretically possible, I have never heard of this occurring and it would be extremely rare. If it is a concern, operate the bilge pump off the non-charging battery:

   (1) **Panel Safety.** Cover solar panels to prevent voltage from being generated during installation or removal so that accidental short circuiting of terminals or cables cannot occur.

   (2) **Mounting.** Each panel should be securely mounted and able to withstand mechanical loads. Ideally, they should be oriented to provide unrestricted sunlight from 9 to 3 PM solar time.

   (3) **Stand-offs.** Allow sufficient ventilation under the panel. Excessive heat levels will reduce output and damage cells. Most panels in frames have sufficient clearance incorporated into them.

l. **Maintenance.** Maintenance requirements for solar panels are minimal:

   (1) **Cleaning.** Panels should be cleaned periodically to remove salt deposits, dirt, and seagull droppings. Use water and a soft cloth or sponge. Mild, nonabrasive cleaners may be used; do not use scouring powders or similar materials.

   (2) **Connections.** Make sure the terminal box connections are secure and dry. Fill the box with silicon compound (sealer).

m. **Troubleshooting.** Faults are normally the result of catastrophic mechanical damage. A single cell failure will not seriously reduce performance as multiple cell interconnections provide some redundancy. Reliability is very high and manufacturers give 10-year warranties to support this. Faults can be virtually eliminated by proper mounting and regular maintenance. As with all electrical systems, the most common faults are cable connections. The following checks should be carried out if charging is not occurring:

   (1) Check regulator output for rated voltage, typically 13.2 V DC.

   (2) Check regulator input; voltage will typically be 14+ volts. Disconnected from battery, it can be up to 17-18 volts.

   (3) Check panel junction boxes for moisture or corroded connections.

4.2 **Wind Charging Systems.** Wind generators are the second most used alternative energy source. As with all charging systems, there are important factors to consider when deciding whether to install a unit as part of a balanced power system. The following chapter outlines the various factors to consider.

a. **Cruising Patterns.** Wind generators are more effective in some areas than others. In the Caribbean, they are very effective. In the Mediterranean, solar power is considered more efficient. If you sail downwind following the trades, wind generators are not effective as the apparent wind speed is reduced, along with charging capability. In his survey of the Europa 92 Round-the-World Rally, Jimmy Cornell said that all performed badly for this reason. If your cruising takes you primarily to sheltered anchorages, they may not be an economical or practical proposition. It is at anchorages, however, that wind generators can be the most useful and give 24-hour charging.

b. **Generator Types.** Essentially, a wind generator is either a DC generator or an alternator driven by a propeller. In the U.S., the trend is toward large, two- or three-bladed DC generator units which give relatively good outputs at low wind speeds. The Fourwinds II and Windbugger appear to be the most popular models. The U.K./European trend is for smaller diameter, multi-bladed AC alternator units designed to operate at and withstand greater wind speeds. These units incorporate a heavy hub that acts as a flywheel to maintain blade inertia.

c. **Generator Operation.** Many units have a permanent magnet rotor, with up to 12 poles. A 3-phase alternating current is generated and rectified to DC, similar to engine-driven alternators. The Rutland 910 unit circuit is illustrated below.

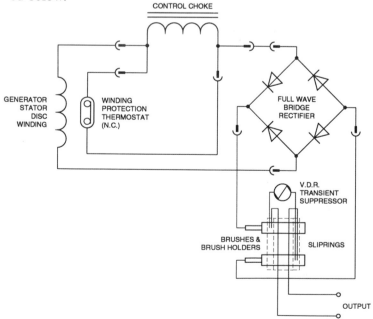

Figure 4-5 Rutland Wind Generator Circuit

d. **Ratings.** The average wind generator produces anything from 1 to 10 amps maximum. Ratings curves are always a function of wind speed and are quoted at rated output voltages.

e. **Charging Regulation.** There are a number of features incorporated into wind generators to protect batteries and generators. These are as follows:

Table 4-2 Wind-Generator Output Table

Make and Model	Output Current	Wind Speed
Aerogen 3	1 Amp	10 knots
	2	13
	3	18
	6	25
	10	35
Rutland 910	2 Amps	15
	3	18
	5	27
	6	35
	8	45
Ampair 100	1 Amp	10
	3	15
	5.5	25
Fourwind III	4 Amps	10
	7	15
	12	25
Windbugger	4 Amps	10
	8	15
	13	25

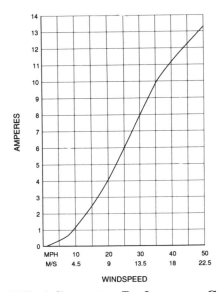

Figure 4-6 Wind Generator Performance Curve

85

(1)   **Regulators.** A regulator is required to limit normal charging voltages to a safe level (14.5 volts) and to limit output at high wind speeds. Normally, a shunt regulator is preferred over a normal solar panel regulator as it is more suited to constant loads. Shunt regulators divert excess current to a resistor which functions as a heater and dissipates heat through a heat sink. If series regulators are used, a power zener diode should be installed to provide some load when the battery is fully charged. Twelve-volt systems should use an 18-volt zener diode. The zener must be rated for at least half the generator's rated output.

(2)   **Regulator Interaction.** Like solar panel installations, interaction may occur with alternator charging systems. The charging should be either switched out of circuit or diverted to a battery other than the sensed one (e.g., the start battery).

(3)   **Chokes.** Some units incorporate a choke to limit the charge produced at high wind speeds.

(4)   **Winding Thermostats.** A number of generators incorporate a winding embedded thermostat which opens in overload conditions when the winding overheats.

(5)   **Transient Suppressors.** These suppressors are installed to minimize the effects of intermittent spikes being impressed on the charging system. These could damage the rectifier and onboard electronics. The suppressor is usually a Voltage Dependent Resistor (VDR).

f.   **Installation.** Selection depends largely on available mounting locations. Arrangements vary. Some are mounted on the front of the mast. Others are hoistable.

(1)   **Stern Posts.** The ideal mounting arrangement is on a stern post, which keeps the blades clear of crew and feeds it air coming off the mainsail. One of the major complaints is that under load wind generators create vibration. It is essential that the post section be as thick as possible and well supported. Usually this extra support is on the stern pulpit (pushpit); some install stainless steel wire stays.

(2)   **Mountings.** Mountings can be cushioned with rubber blocks or similar material to reduce the transmission of vibrations. Rutland chargers have a tie-bar modification that strengthens the blades and prevents excessive blade deformation under load and the increased vibration that occurs. Newer models have improved blade design and strength that prevents blade breakage.

g.   **Troubleshooting.** Always secure the turbine blades when installing, servicing, or troubleshooting a wind generator. The following performance tests should be carried out:

(1)   If no ammeter is installed on the main switchboard, install an ammeter in line and check the charging current level. If there is no output, then check the system according to the manufacturer's instructions.

(2)   If there is no output and the generator has brushes, check that they are not stuck and are free to move. Instead of brushes and commutators, many generators have a set of slip rings installed with brushes to transfer power from the rotating generator down through the post to the battery circuit. They can jam, and on rare occasions cause loss of power.

(3)   Some generators have a winding embedded thermostat. Check with an ohmmeter that it is not permanently open circuited. If it is open circuited, the generator will not charge. The thermostat opens in high wind charging conditions. If the thermostat has not closed after these conditions and the generator case is cold, the thermostat is defective. Regrettably, it cannot be repaired unless a new winding is installed. To get the generator back into service, connect a bridge across the thermostat terminals. Remember that there will be no protection in high wind and heavy charging conditions, so the winding may burn out.

(4)   Excess vibration may be caused by bearing wear. If the unit is a few years old, renew the bearings. Vibration can also be caused by damage to one or more blades, and these should be carefully examined for damage that may cause imbalances.

(5)   Check the rectifier to be sure that it is not open or short circuited.

(6)   If the generator output is correct, check for a malfunctioning regulator. The voltage input should be in the range 14-18 volts, and the output approximately 13-14 volts.

(7)   Ensure that all electrical connections are secure and in good condition.

4.3 **Prop Shaft Charging Systems.** Prop shaft generator systems are either traditional alternators with prop shaft gearing to achieve rated output, or alternators wound to generate outputs at low speed. These systems can be used as an extra energy source while under power (not an economic proposition), or to take advantage of a free-wheeling propeller under sail. The following points must be considered:

a.   **Cruising Patterns.** The viability of these units depends on your cruising pattern. Consider that only about one quarter to one third of your time is spent passage making, so the shaft alternator is used for a limited period.

b.   **Drag.** Under any load, the alternator will brake the shaft by slowing shaft rotation, causing drag and a reduction in vessel speed. On a lightweight vessel, this can be as high as half a knot. On steel or other heavy displacement vessels, the inertia of the vessel will generally minimize the drag effect. For such cruising yachts, prop systems are a useful proposition. With an increasing number of yachts opting for two- and three-bladed folding props, shaft alternators may rarely be used.

c.   **Output.** The maximum output will generally be in the region of 5-10 amps. The Lucas unit has a maximum output of 12 amps, with an approximate output of 1 amp per knot. Cut-in speed is 600 rev/min and requires a shaft-pulley ratio of 5:1. One major fear has been gearbox damage due to improper lubrication while freewheeling, but many major gearbox manufacturers have dispelled this fear.

4.4 **Water Charging Systems.** Water-based charging systems come in two configurations:

a.   **Towed Turbine Generator.** The towed turbine water generator is essentially a slow speed alternator with the drive shaft mechanically connected to a braided rope and turbine assembly. When streamed off the stern, the turbine turns and rotates the alternator. Typical output is approximately 6 amps. The trail rope is typically around 30 meters long:

(1)   **Drag.** Typical drag speed reduction is around half a knot. The trailing generator, like the old-fashioned trailing log, is reliable, and hungry ocean denizens rarely eat the turbine.

(2)   **Turbine Skipping.** One problem is that the turbine tends to skip out of the water at speeds over 6 knots. There are a variety of methods to reduce skipping, which include adding sinker weights to the turbine, increasing the towline length, and increasing the towline diameter. The Ampair units have two turbine types, one for speeds up to 7 knots, and another coarse pitch turbine for higher speeds.

b. **Submerged Generator.** These units comprise a forward facing, three-bladed propeller that drives a permanent magnet alternator. The propeller is mounted at the end of a tubular arm at a depth of approximately one meter. As a water-driven power source, they are a good option, being easy to lift and service. Maximum output is approximately 8 amps.

    (1)   **Drag.** The drag on a submerged generator is approximately double that of a towed generator.

    (2)   **Physical Characteristics.** As the electrical alternator is underwater, the generator housing has double seals, as do the cable glands. The alternator body is filled with hydraulic fluid to equalize external pressures when fully immersed. A reservoir is fitted to allow for oil expansion and contraction.

    (3)   **Mounting Locations.** Generators can be mounted directly on the transom or on the taffrails.

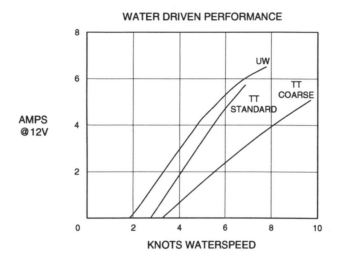

UW = UNDERWATER GENERATOR
TT STANDARD = TOWED TURBINE - STANDARD PITCH
TT COARSE = TOWED TURBINE - COARSE PITCH

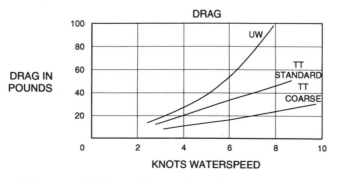

Figure 4-7 Ampair Water Generation System Characteristics

Battery Chargers

5.0   Battery Chargers. Battery chargers are generally used as the primary charging source in large vessels with AC generators in continual service. Many vessels have had batteries ruined by poor quality chargers due to a marginal overcharge voltage level. In reality, battery chargers are not a principal charging source on a cruising yacht, and a relatively small output automatic charger of approximately 10-15 amps will meet the normal requirements while in port. The basic principles of most battery chargers are as follows:

> **a.   Transformation.** The AC voltage, either 220/230 or 110 volts AC, is applied to a transformer. The transformer steps down the voltage to a low level, typically around 15/30 volts depending on the output level.

> **b.   Rectification.** The low level AC voltage is then rectified by a full-wave bridge rectifier similar to that in an alternator. The rectifier outputs a voltage of around 13.8/27.6 volts, which is the normal float voltage level.

> **c.   Regulation.** Many basic chargers do not have any output regulation. Chargers that do have regulation are normally those using control systems to control output voltage levels. These sensing circuits automatically limit charge voltages to nominal levels and reduce to float values when the pre-determined full-charge condition is reached.

> **d.   Protection.** Battery chargers have a range of protective devices that range from a simple AC input fuse to the many features that are described as follows:

>> **(1)   Thermal Overload.** This device is normally mounted on the transformer, or rectifier. When a predetermined high temperature is reached, the device opens and prevents further charging until the components cool down.

>> **(2)   Input Protection.** This is either a circuit breaker or fuse that protects the AC input against overload and short circuit on the primary side of the transformer.

>> **(3)   Reverse Polarity Fuse.** A fuse is incorporated to protect circuits against accidental polarity reversal of output leads.

>> **(4)   Current Limiting.** Limiting circuits are used to prevent excessive current outputs, or to maintain current levels at a specific level.

>> **(5)   Short Circuit Protection.** This is usually a fuse that protects output circuits against high current short circuit damage.

> **e.   Interference Suppression.** Most chargers have an output-voltage ripple superimposed on the DC. This is overcome by the use of chokes and capacitors across the output. This ripple can affect electronics and cause data corruption on navigation equipment.

5.1   **Battery Charger Types.** There are a number of charger types and techniques in use as follows:

    a.   **Constant Potential Chargers.** Chargers operate at a fixed voltage. The charge current decreases as the battery voltage reaches the preset charging voltage. Unsupervised charging can damage batteries if electrolytes evaporate and gas forms. Additionally, such chargers are susceptible to input voltage variations. If left unattended, the voltage setting must be below 13.5 volts or batteries will be ruined through overcharging.

    b.   **Ferro-Resonant Chargers.** These chargers use a ferro-resonant transformer which has two secondary windings. One of the windings is connected to a capacitor, and they resonate at a specific frequency. Variations in the input voltage cause an imbalance, and the transformer corrects this to maintain a stable output. These chargers have a tapered charge characteristic. As the battery terminal voltage rises, the charge current decreases. Control of these chargers is usually through a sensing circuit that switches the charger off when the nominal voltage level is reached, typically around 15% to 20% of the charger's nominal rating.

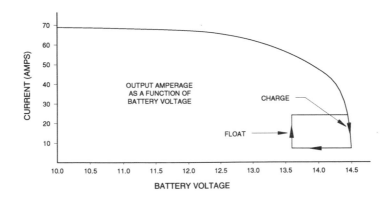

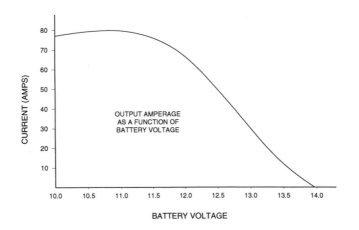

Figure 5-1 Newmar Battery Charger Characteristics

c.   **Switch Mode Chargers.** Compact switch mode chargers are becoming increasingly popular due to their compact size and low weights. These charger types convert the input line frequency from 50 to 150,000 hertz, which reduces the size of transformers and chokes used in conventional chargers. An advantage of these chargers is that line input and output are effectively isolated, eliminating the effects of surges and spikes. These chargers are my favorites, and the units from LEAB of Sweden are technically very advanced. The chargers are battery-sensed, temperature-compensated, have integral digital voltmeters and ammeters, and are compact. The illustration below shows the principle of operation and the various waveform conversions from the AC input to a stable DC output.

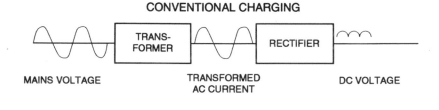

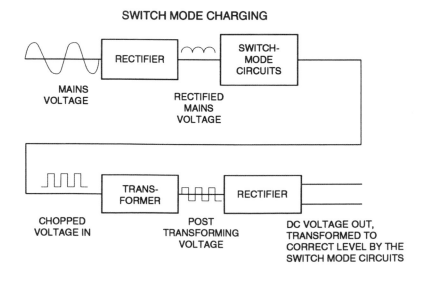

Figure 5-2 LEAB Switch Mode Charger System

d. **Automatic Chargers.** This term covers a wide range of electronically controlled charging systems. These include chargers that have SCR or Triac control, a combination of current and voltage settings with appropriate sensing systems and control systems, as well as overvoltage and overcurrent protection. The ideal charger characteristic is one that can deliver the boost charge required and then automatically drop to float charge levels so that overcharging does not occur.

5.2 **Battery Charger Installation.** Chargers should be mounted in a dry and well ventilated area. The following precautions should be undertaken when using chargers:

a. Always switch off battery charger during engine starting if connected to the starting battery.

b. The AC connection should be an industrial grade outlet in engine areas or normal outlet in dry areas.

c. The metal case of any charger must be properly grounded to the AC ground.

d. To prevent cables from moving, clips or permanent fasteners should be used on cables if the charger is permanently installed .

e. Switch off the charger before connecting or disconnecting cables from battery.

f. Do not operate a large inverter off a battery with a charger still operating. The large load will overload the charger and may damage circuitry.

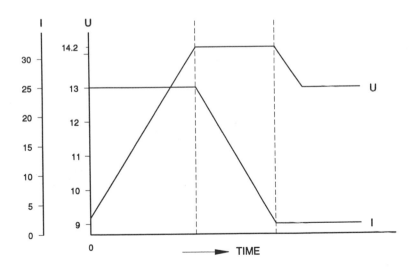

I = CHARGING CURRENT (AMPS)
U = CHARGING VOLTAGE (VOLTS)
13V = MAINTENANCE /FLOAT VOLTAGE

Figure 5-3 Automatic Charger System Characteristic

DC Systems Installation

6.0   **DC Systems.** It is estimated that up to 80% of electrical system failures can be directly attributed to incorrectly selected or installed cables, or improper connections and terminations. The majority of failures can be eliminated by using simple accepted practices. Unfortunately, the common attitude is to treat vessel low voltage systems like automotive installations, and the high failure rates on cruising vessels reflect this attitude. Exposure of DC systems to water is capable of causing a potentially fatal fire, shock, and possibly catastrophic damage.

6.1   **Electrical Standards.** The question of installation standards is an important one. The systems should be installed to comply with one of the principal standards in use. In reality most standards are consistent, and a decision must be made in accordance with requirements. The following are what I would consider the most recognizable standards, and for the purposes of this chapter, all references will quote the International Standards Organization (ISO) Standard and the United States National Fire Protection Association (NFPA) Standard as required.

   a.   **International Standard ISO 10133.** *Small Craft – Electrical systems – Extra-low-voltage d.c. installations,* 1994. This standard is the preferred one. The standard is prepared and ratified by a large group of nations including the U.S., France, and the U.K. Standards are also made in conjunction with the International Electrotechnical Commission (IEC).

   b.   **NFPA 302,** *Fire Protection Standard for Pleasure and Commercial Motor Craft,* 1994 Edition. This standard is approved by the American National Standards Institute and is applicable to cruising yacht installations. The technical committee includes representatives from ABYC, USCG, Underwriters Laboratories (UL), and others such as the National Association of Marine Surveyors.

   c.   **Lloyd's Register of Shipping.** *Rules and Regulations for the Classification of Yachts and Small Craft.* Normally used when a vessel is to be built to class, it serves as a very high benchmark for those who choose to use it.

   d.   **American Boat and Yacht Council (ABYC).** *Standards and Recommended Practices for Small Craft.* These are voluntary standards and recommendations that are widely used by many builders.

6.2   **Planning the Wiring System.** A cruising boat has a great number of systems that have to be considered and installed. Nowhere are there more serious mistakes and bad installations than with electrical wiring. More often than not, the equipment is specified and purchased before the boat is even launched and the actual impact on the system is considered. Planning the electrical installation requires a carefully considered systems approach. It should never be undertaken on the "run wires to it when you fit it" basis. More importantly, your new and very expensive vessel is not the place to be experimenting with basic electrical theories. An electrical system should be simple, and with that comes reliability. You will always meet someone who did something that worked; in the large majority of cases, however, accepted electrical practice has not been followed, and subsequently these vessels will have inherent built-in problems, overcome only with total rewires or major systems alterations. Do it once, and do it right!

a.   **Planning.** Plans should be made right at the beginning, not when you are ready to put in wires. Making an electrical plan involves more than simply jotting down which equipment is being used and current ratings. The calculations have to be precise and logical.

b.   **List Equipment and Power Requirements.** Make separate lists for equipment operated all the time at sea, in port, at night, and intermittently. Your load requirements then become functional blocks that enable you to look properly at load usage, and realistic loads over typical periods.

c.   **Wiring Plan.** Make a plan drawing of your vessel and locate every item of equipment on it. This will enable you to plan ahead for cable access and control equipment.

d.   **Battery Requirements.** The battery requirements to support the load over the calculated period will be based on those carefully calculated power requirements.

e.   **Charging System Requirements.** In turn, the charging system's rating and capabilities will depend on the battery requirements, the major question being, "will it satisfactorily recharge the expended power in the time required?" More often than not, the realities are very different from expectations.

f.   **Power Usage.** You must bear in mind that when you go cruising the electrical usage pattern is often very different from what you experienced at your home anchorage.

g.   **Equipment Procurement.** Make a list of all the requirements. Find the source for each item. It is worth shopping around for basics. It might be better to go directly to the importers or suppliers than to "specialist" marine electrical equipment suppliers. If you do visit one of those "marine electrics emporiums," do not be fazed by the masses of equipment and gadgets on display. In actual fact, you don't need most of it. The common goal of a simple and reliable electrical system must not be forgotten.

6.3   **Wiring Considerations.** There are a number of important considerations, which are as follows:

    a.   **Hull Material.** The hull construction has important implications for the electrical and electronics installation on any vessel. For steel or alloy boats, special considerations must be given to wiring systems and grounding, in particular the effects of corrosion. This question is important right at the outset, because if you can purchase an engine which has a fully isolated electrical system for a steel or alloy vessel, you can plan before starting construction, as it must be often specially ordered.

    b.   **Type of Boat.** The question of whether the vessel is a multihull or a monohull is very relevant. The requirements for each have implications in the planning of the vessel. Essential differences to consider are as follows:

        (1)   **Multihulls.** Weight distribution is more important in multihulls than monohulls. This is particularly relevant for batteries and their locations. Additionally, the larger overall size of catamarans entails far greater cable runs, with consequently greater cable weights and voltage drop problems.

        (2)   **Cable Lengths.** Longer cable runs with the associated voltage drop problems raise the issue of voltages. It makes sense for multihulls to go to 24 volts, instead of 12. The voltage drops are no longer a problem, the battery weights and sizes for a given capacity are less, and the weight and size of 24-volt motors and equipment is generally lighter.

        (3)   **Accommodation.** A multihull generally has a greater level of accommodation, and therefore more people are often aboard (the parties are longer!), putting greater demands on batteries for lighting, electric refrigeration, and the like, with consequentially increased requirements on charging. This lifestyle factor is largely overlooked by multihull builders, but it is significant.

    c.   **Boat Size.** Boat size is important for planning power requirements. While most boats have similar requirements concerning electronics equipment, on a larger boat, the radar usually has a higher range and output, the autopilot is larger, more lights operate, the water pump is a larger output model, cable runs get longer, and the number of circuits increases. With the increase in size and current consumption come larger cables, and implications with respect to system voltages and voltage drops.

d. **Wiring Summary.** I cannot overemphasize the importance of adopting a systems approach to preparing your vessel for electrical and electronics equipment. Do not think it is easy because it is 12 volts, like for a car. Nothing could be further from the truth. Twelve-volt systems can cause fires, and burn your boat to the waterline. Look only at quality equipment. You must select equipment that is marine grade and is rated for DC electrical systems, not AC. Look carefully at your requirements, and allow for every possible upgrade so that your electrical system will not be stressed with the addition of new equipment. Above all, do not try to reinvent the wheel. Electricity is governed by very basic, physical laws; obey those rules, and you will have a system that functions. Start experimenting and overcomplicating things, and you will join that far too large a group of boaters who spend half their time trying to resolve electrical problems that would never have occurred had they planned things properly at the outset. Do not treat wiring as a subject of mystique and complexity; it isn't.

6.4 **DC System Voltages.** Three voltages used to be common, but the 32-volt system that was common among American vessels is now nonexistent due to the lack of voltage-compatible equipment.

a. **Voltages.** The most common are as follows:

(1) **12-Volt Systems.** The 12-volt system is the most common system. This is because of automotive influences, which have led to a large range of equipment being available. Most electronics are powered by 12 volts. It is also possible to purchase virtually any appliance rated for 12 volts.

(2) **24-Volt Systems.** This system is prevalent, especially in commercial applications. It has the advantage of lower physical equipment sizes, cabling, and control gear. Additionally voltage drops are not as critical. Because most equipment is commonly 12 volts a DC-DC converter must be used to step down to 12-volt equipment. Although complicating the system a little this does isolate sensitive electronics equipment from the surge- and spike-prone power system.

b. **Mixed Voltage Systems.** It is quite common to see vessels having both 12- and 24-volt systems in use. They should be treated as two entirely separate entities with no electrical interconnection. This will mean two alternators and two battery banks. The merits of 24 volts for heavy current consumption equipment such as invertors and windlasses are obvious, because the cables are half the size and weight of 12-volt systems. In many cases electronics will be able to operate on 24 volts without modification.

6.5 **Wiring Configurations.** Most cruising yachts have a centralized distribution system based at a single switch panel, while larger vessels (and, increasingly, smaller ones, too) are using a system of subpanels. There are two basic wiring configurations used on vessels regardless of the system.

      a.   **Two-Wire, Insulated Return Systems.** This is the preferred system, and that includes the various classification societies. In this configuration, no part of the circuit, in particular the negative, is connected to any ground or equipment. The system is totally isolated, and this includes engine sensors, starter motors, and alternators. This system must be installed on steel and alloy vessels.

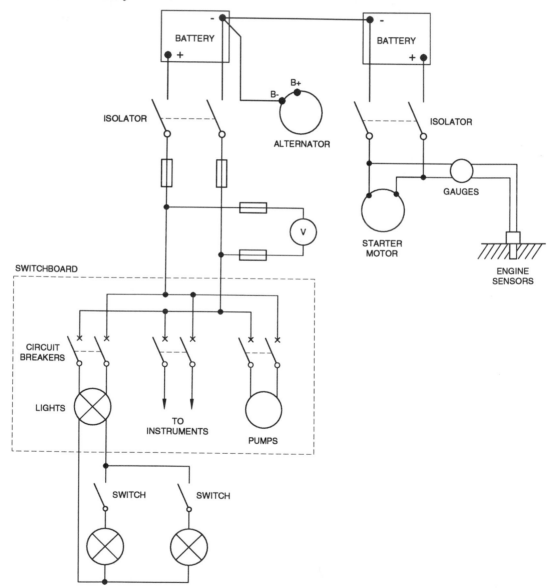

Figure 6-1 Insulated Two-Wire Return Systems

b. **Insulated Return, One Pole Grounded.** This is also called a polarized system. The most common configuration, it holds the negative at ground potential by connection of the battery negative to the engine block. The block in this case should be electrically connected to vessel ground, such as through shaft and propeller to seawater. Protection is only required in the positive conductor of circuits.

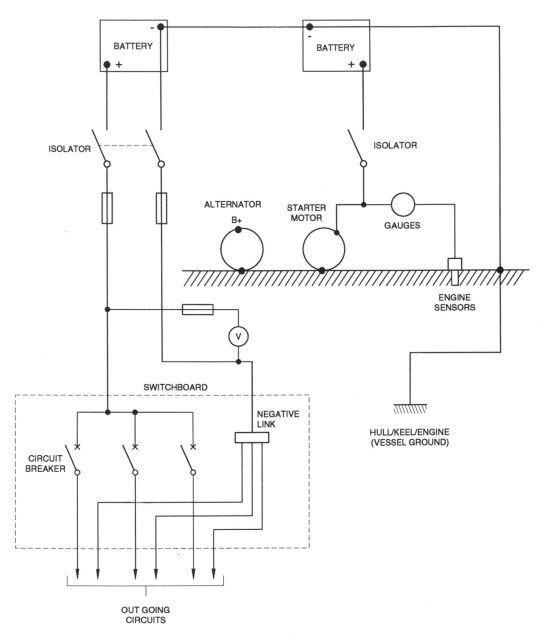

Figure 6-2 Insulated One Pole Return Systems

c. **Distributed Systems.** These systems are typically broken down into a system of subpanels. With the growth in the use of electrical equipment, distributed systems are becoming the preferred approach. There are a number of significant advantages over a centralized system, including the separation of potentially interactive equipment such as pumps and electronics, which can cause radio frequency interference (RFI). Separation also permits a reduction in the number of cables radiating from the main panel to areas of equipment concentration, which again reduces potential RFI and the need for cable. Most distributed systems run all the subcircuits from the central panel, with each circuit having a circuit breaker. The illustration below shows the preferred breakdown of subcircuits and panels. It is based on successful installations on a number of vessels. Only essential services and metering are kept on the main panel. The lighting panel can be located anywhere practicable; once the circuits are on, lights are switched locally. Electronics are ideally connected to a smaller panel located at the nav station (see Chapter 14, Navigation Station Design). The pump panel should be in an accessible location. In most cases, the greatest concentration of pumps is midships to forward.

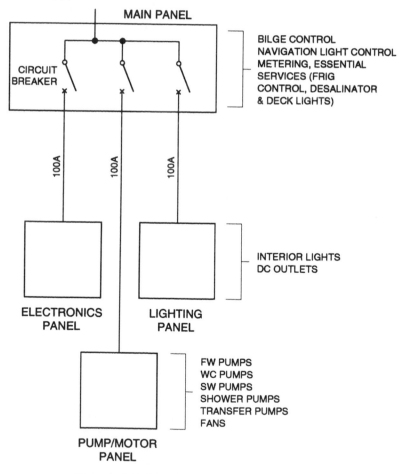

Figure 6-3 Distributed Power Systems

6.6 **Wiring Installation.** Cables are often badly installed. With planning and correct procedures, you can get a high quality job that will not cost more.

a. **Cable Types.** There are a number of important factors related to cable selection, which are as follows:

(1) **Tinned Conductors.** The installation of tinned copper conductors is essential. When untinned copper is exposed to salt water spray or moisture, it will quickly degrade and fail. The only argument used against the installation of tinned copper is cost.

(2) **Insulation.** Double-insulated cables should be used on all circuits to ensure insulation integrity. Most insulation is temperature rated, which has important implications with respect to ratings. In most cruising vessels, PVC-insulated and PVC-sheathed cables rated at 75°C are used. Classification societies specify butyl rubber, CSP, EPR or other insulating materials, which have higher temperature ratings and therefore higher current carrying capacities.

b. **Nominal Ratings.** All cables have nominal cross-sectional areas and current carrying capacities. The ISO-10133 specifies nominal capacities for a range of cross-sectional areas and temperature ranges. Temperature reference is typically 20°C. Table 6-1 illustrates typical current ratings for equivalent cable sizes. I recommend using standard cable sizes. This reduces cable types and sizes to two, which is cheaper and simpler to calculate.

Table 6-1 Typical DC Cable Nominal Ratings

Conductor Size (AWG)	Conductor Size (mm^2)	PVC Insulation, Heat-Resisting	Butyl Rubber, Lloyds 100A1	Resistance (Ohms/100m)
	1.0	11 Amps	12 Amps	1.884
	1.5	14	16	1.257
	1.8	15		1.050
14	2.5	20	22	0.754
12	4.0	27	30	0.471
10	6.0	35	38	0.314
8	10.0	49	53	0.182
6	16.0	64	71	0.1152
4	25.0	86	93	0.0762
2	35.0	105	119	0.0537
1	50.0	127	140	0.0381
0	60.0	150	160	0.0295
	70.0	161	183	0.0252

c. **Derating Factors.** All cable current carrying capacities are subject to the following derating factors:

(1) **Temperatures.** All cables have nominal ratings temperatures. In any installation where the conductors exceed that temperature, the current carrying capacity of the cable is reduced. This is important in engine spaces.

(2) **Bunching.** Where cables are bunched together in a large loom, derating also occurs.

d. **Duty Cycles.** Cables carrying heavy current loads, such as those used on windlasses, winches, and starter motors, can be smaller because there is little chance for heat buildup over the short durations they are under load. The table shows battery cables which are rated at 60% duty.

Table 6-2 Battery Cable Ratings

Conductor Size (AWG)	Conductor Size (B&S)	Conductor Size Metric	Current Rating (60% Duty)
8	8	8	90 Amps
6	6	15	150 Amps
4	3	26	200 Amps
2	2	32	245 Amps
1	0	50	320 Amps
00	00	66	390 Amps

6.7 **Voltage Drop Calculations.** Voltage drop must always be a consideration when installing electrical circuits. Unfortunately, many voltage drop problems are created by the poor practice of trying to install the smallest cables and wiring sizes possible. I do not support the practice of using tables to find cable sizes based on voltage drop. The maximum voltage drop in 12-volt systems is ideally 3% or 0.36 volt with a maximum of 0.5 volt. The voltage drop problem is prevalent in starting and charging systems, in windlasses, and in long runs to mast equipment, notably navigation lights, which can cause reduced light output. There are many methods of calculating voltage drop with respect to choosing cable sizes. The following formula is that specified in ISO Standard 10133, Annex A.2, and should be used to verify that cables are able to support load with minimal voltage drop at load.

$$\text{Voltage Drop at Load (volts)} = \frac{0.0164 \times I \times L}{S}$$

where S is conductor cross-sectional area, in square millimeters

I is load current in amperes

L is cable length in meters, positive to load and back to negative.

a.   **Current.** The current value for protection purposes is the allowable continuous current rating for 30°C ambient temperature, and normally I standardize on a 15-amp 2.5-mm² rated cable. In most cases the connected load will be significantly less than this.

b.   **Tricolor.** Load current = 2 amps, cable run = 40 meters, CSA = 2.5 mm².

$$\text{Voltage Drop} = \frac{0.0164 \times 2 \times 40}{2.5}$$

$$= \quad 0.53 \text{ volts}$$

c.   **Anchor Windlass.** These cable sizes must be calculated at working and peak loads. As the calculations show, a larger cable size ensures less voltage drop and fewer line losses. Working-load current = 85 amps, cable run = 12 meters, CSA = 35 mm², rating = 125 amps.

Voltage Drop at 85 amps   = $\dfrac{0.0164 \times 85 \times 24}{35}$

=   0.96 volts (35 mm²) 0.67 volts (50 mm²)

Voltage Drop at 125 amps   = $\dfrac{0.0164 \times 125 \times 24}{35}$

=   1.41 volts (35 mm²) 0.98 volts (50 mm²)

6.8   Cable Installation. Electrical cables in a vessel can be fastened in a number of ways. The emphasis must be on accessibility, both for initial installation and for adding circuits later. Under no circumstances should you fiberglass in cables as some vessel manufacturers recklessly do. AC and DC cables must be kept separated *(ISO 7.7)*. Install cable as follows.

a.   **Conduit.** If it can be done during the construction phase, install PVC electrical conduits to isolated areas so that cables can be easily pulled in, replaced, or added to. These offer good mechanical protection to cables. In such cases, single-insulated tinned cables can be used if the conduit runs back to the switchboard. Do not install large bunches of cables in flexible conduits as they tend to move around and chafe. Do not use PVC conduits in engine spaces.

b.   **Saddles.** Cables can be neatly bunched together and secured with PVC or stainless saddles. Saddles should be placed no more than 450 mm apart *(ISO 7.3)* to prevent cable loom sagging and movement during service. I prefer PVC-conduit saddles, which come in a variety of sizes. Ideally, I run a central cableway down one side of the vessel. This is normally a wooden panel approximately 4 inches (20mm) wide that extends forward and aft of the switchboard. The panel is run through the backs of cupboards and suitable transit holes are made where necessary. I cover the panel with a ply cover to prevent damage in lockers. Cables are then separated into signal or instruments and DC supply, and plastic saddled.

Where instrument cables must cross over power cables, this should be at right angles to avoid induced interference. In new vessels, the wiring can then be left until the fitting out is nearly completed. For circuits to the other side of vessel, provide one or two easily accessible areas to install these cables.

c.   **Hot Glue.** A hot glue gun is a useful way to fasten small or single cables above headliners, or in corners behind trim and carpet finishes. It is useful where there is no risk of cables coming loose. It must not be used on heavy or exposed cable runs.

d.   **Cable Ties.** The PVC cable tie (trade name Ty-Rap) is universal in application, and should be used where looms must be kept together, or where any cable can be securely fastened to a suitable support. Do not use cable ties to suspend cables from isolated points; this invariably causes excessive stress and cable fatigue. For internal cable ties, you only require the white ones; any external cable ties should be the black UV-resistant type.

e.   **Spiral Wrapping.** PVC spiral wrapping is an extremely useful method for consolidating cables into a neat loom. If a number of cables are laying loose, consolidate them into some spiral wrap, and then fasten the loom using cable ties.

f.   **Cable Marking.** Always mark cable ends to aid in reconnection and troubleshooting. A simple, slide-on numbering system can be used, as can some of the labeling systems for use with nylon cable ties. These simply require a permanent marker pen. The practice of color-coded wiring has diminished. Now that all cables use red for positive and black for negative, polarity identification is easy.

6.9   DC Circuit Protection. The purpose of circuit protection is to limit overload and fault currents to the rated capacity of the supply cable. Circuit protection is not normally rated to the connected loads, although this is commonly done on loads which are considerably less than the cable rating, such as VHF radios or instrument systems. The two most common circuit protection devices are the fuse and the circuit breaker. Recent developments have seen the introduction of electronic tripping and reset devices, especially in conjunction with touchpad electrical panels.

a.   **Fuses.** Fuses are still widely used, and although cheaper than circuit breakers, they have many disadvantages. They use either simple fuse holders or a combination fuse switch from Heinemann. In my opinion, fuses have no advantages except for a much lower initial cost. From my own experience, and those of many other vessel owners, there is no place for fuse systems on yachts, unless you enjoy that adrenalin rush as your navigation lights go out or the autopilot stops and you feverishly try to locate and install a failed fuse in the middle of the night in a force 9 gale off a lee shore, You know about Murphy's Law, and they say he was an optimist!

(1)   **Rating Variations.** The typical fuse is not very accurate and can rupture as much as 50% above or below nominal current rating.

(2)   **Service Fatigue.** Fuse elements fatigue in service, which alters the fuse's rated value. Vibration also commonly causes the glass to break. Worse, when you're really in trouble you can't find a spare fuse.

(3)   **Voltage Drop.** There is added contact resistance in the fuse holder between each contact and the fuse ends which commonly causes voltage drops, supply interruptions, and heating.

(4)   **Troubleshooting.** When a circuit has a fault, you can go through a box of fuses on a trial-and-error troubleshooting exercise. A circuit breaker allows simple resetting.

b.   **Circuit Breakers.** The circuit breaker is the most reliable and practical method of circuit protection. They are available in press button aircraft, toggle, or rocker switch types. They are used both for circuit isolation and protection, which saves switchboard space, installation costs and time, and improves reliability. Single-pole circuit breakers are fitted to most vessels. However, classification societies only allow these in grounded pole installations because a fault arising on the circuit provides a good ground loop and the large current flow ensures proper breaker interruption. Double-pole breakers are recommended for all circuits, as they will totally isolate equipment and circuits. This is a requirement of many classification societies or survey authorities.

c. **Circuit Breaker Standards.** Install only circuit breakers that are approved by UL, CSA, or Lloyd's. Approvals for small vessel breakers categorize them as supplementary protectors. On my switchboards, I use either Heinemann or ETA breakers; makes such as Carling are also good. All breakers are manufactured to high standards and are suitable for the demands of marine systems.

d. **Circuit Breaker Selection.** Circuit breakers must be selected for the cable size they protect. The rating must not exceed the maximum rated current of the conductor. The cable sizes in Table 6-3 give recommended ratings for single cables installed in well ventilated spaces. Bunching of cables and high ambient temperatures require derating factors. Ratings are given according to IEC Standard 157.

Table 6-3 Circuit Breaker Selection

Conductor Size	Current Rating	Breaker Rating
1.5 mm^2	7.9 - 15.9 A	8 Amps
2.5 mm^2	15.9 - 22.0	16 Amps
4.0 mm^2	22.0 - 30.0	20 Amps
6.0 mm^2	30 0 - 39.0	30 Amps
10.0 mm^2	39.0 - 54.0	40 Amps
16.0 mm^2	54.0 - 72.0	60 Amps
25.0 mm^2	72.0 - 93.0	80 Amps
35.0 mm^2	93.0 -117.0	100 Amps
50.0 mm^2	117.0 -147.0	120 Amps

e. **Discrimination.** The principle of discrimination in a circuit is extremely important but, regrettably, is rarely considered or installed on the electrical systems of cruising yachts. A circuit normally should have two or more over-current protective devices, such as the main and auxiliary circuit breakers installed between the battery and the load. The devices must operate selectively so that the protective device closest to the fault operates first. If that device does not operate, the second device will operate to protect the circuit against overcurrent damage and possibly fire:

(1) Use circuit breakers with different current ratings. This effectively means that at a point on the time delay curve (Figure 6-4), the first breaker will trip. If it does not and the current value increases, the next one will. A point is reached called the limit of discrimination. At this point, the curves intersect and both breakers trip simultaneously.

(2) Use circuit breakers with different time delay curves to achieve the same result as above.

(3) Use circuit breakers with different time delay curves, current ratings, and of different types. Using all of the above ensures discrimination.

f. **Tripping Characteristics.** These are normally provided by breaker manufacturers in a curve of current against time.

(1) The greater the current over the nominal tripping value, the quicker the circuit breaker will trip. In the event of a short circuit, tripping is rapid due to the high current values.

(2) Where a small overload exists, tripping can occur some seconds or even minutes after switching on. This happens as the current levels gradually increase.

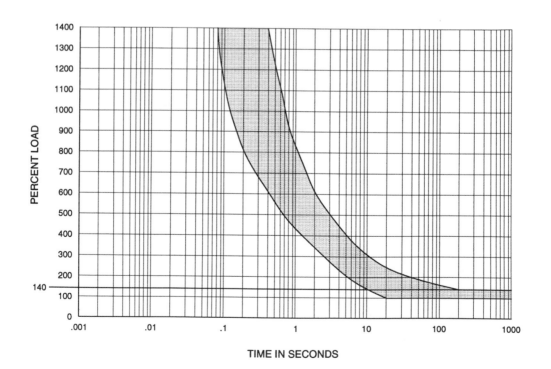

Figure 6-4 Circuit Breaker Time-Delay Curve

6.10 **Supply Circuit Isolation.** Individual circuits are isolated either by the circuit breaker or a switch. Main DC supply to the switchboards must also have isolation. In many installations, this is performed by the notoriously unreliable battery-selector switch. Better alternatives are as follows:

a. **Single-Pole Switches.** If a system is designed and installed as I have recommended, this will be replaced by a single-pole isolator rated at 100 amps.

b. **Double-Pole Switches.** In steel and alloy vessels, the isolation should be a double-pole switch normally rated at around 300 amps. This is a good idea in all vessels because it eliminates feedback into the system from lightning strikes. Double-pole switches are also required by many survey and classification societies.

c. **Isolator Location.** Isolation switches should be installed as closely as possible to the battery bank. They should also be mounted as high as possible above bilge and flooding levels.

d. **Short Circuit Protection.** Survey authorities require short circuit protection mounted next to the battery, but it should not be able to cause an arc or ignite gas from batteries. I normally install two 100- or 125-amp, DC circuit breakers as close as practical to the batteries; one is for the windlass and one is for the panel supply.

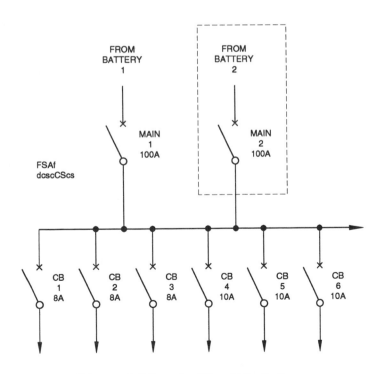

Figure 6-5 Supply-Circuit Isolation

6.11   **DC Cable Connections.** Cable connections are the single greatest cause of electrical problems on a vessel. The following practices should be used to ensure optimum reliability:

    a.   **Cable Ends.** Cable ends should have the insulation removed without nicking the cable strands. Prepare the ends as follows:

        (1)   Bare cable strands should be twisted, and inserted in the terminal block or connector of a similar size.

        (2)   Make sure that there are no loose strands. If you are terminating into an oversize terminal block, twist and double over the cable end to ensure that the screw has something to bite on.

        (3)   When connecting a cable to a screw, do not use crimped cable-pin connectors. They add contact resistance to the circuit. The holding clamps on most terminals are designed for cables, not flat connectors.

    b.   **Soldered Ends.** Do not solder the cable ends. This practice is widespread because of a misconception that soldering will make good connections and prevent cable corrosion. I have yet to discover any internal cable that failed due to corrosion, except bilge pump connections in direct contact with salt water. From experience, I find that solder causes many of the following problems:

        (1)   Solder travels up the conductor causing stiffness. This imposes greater vibrational loads at the terminal, with the resultant fatigue and failure. In most cases, the soldering is poorly done, making a high resistance joint.

        (2)   A soldered cable end also prevents the connector screw from spreading the strands and making a good electrical contact. This causes high resistance and heating. Use connectors of the correct size for the cable.

6.12   **Solderless Terminals.** Solderless terminals or crimp connectors are the most practical method for connecting cables. They are color coded according to the cable capacity. Stakon-type terminals are designed and manufactured according to NEMA standards, which include wire pullout tension tests, and voltage drop tests. Quality terminals will meet UL and CSA standards. Important points when using connectors are as follows:

    a.   **Crimping Tool.** Only use a quality, ratchet-type crimping tool, not a cheap pair of squeeze types, which do not adequately compress and "capture" the cable. Insufficient crimping pressure may cause the cable to pull out of the connector sleeve.

    b.   **Crimping.** A good joint requires two crimps. Always crimp both the joint and the plastic behind it and ensure that no cable strands are hanging out.

    c.   **Solder Reinforcement.** A crimp joint can be improved by lightly soldering the wire end to the crimp connector. Avoid excessive heat.

Table 6-4 Standard Cable Connectors Table

Color	Cables Sizes	Current Rating
Yellow	3.0 to 6.0 mm^2	30 Amps
Blue	1.5 to 2.5 mm^2	15 Amps
Red	0.5 to 1.5 mm^2	10 Amps

d.   **Spade, Tab, Lucas Connectors.** These are the most commonly used connectors. When using them, observe the following:

   (1)   **Connector Sizes.** Always use the correct spade connectors for the cable size.

   (2)   **Connector Security.** Spade connectors are easily dislodged. Since they tend to slip off the back of circuit breakers, ensure they are tight to push on. Make sure that the spade actually goes on the tab, and not between the insulation sleeve and the connector. In switchboards, I like to apply a dab of solder or a drop of silicone sealant to prevent the connector from working loose.

e.   **Ring Connectors.** Ring connectors are used on all equipment with screws, bolts, and nuts. They should also be used on any equipment subject to vibration or where accidental dislodging can be critical, particularly switchboards.

   (1)   **Connector Hole.** To get good electrical contact, always make sure that the hole fits closely to the bolt or screw used on the connection. Use spring washers.

   (2)   **Creepage.** One practical method for preventing nut creepage is to dab on a spot of paint.

f.   **In-Line Cable (Butt) Splices.** Where cables need to be connected and a junction box is impracticable, use insulated, in-line butt splices. These are more reliable than soldered connections where a bad joint can cause high resistance and subsequent heating and voltage drop. Use heat shrink insulation over the joint to maintain waterproof integrity. When heated, some connectors form a watertight seal by the fusing and melting of the insulation sleeve. These are ideal for bilge pump connections.

g.   **Pin Terminals.** Pin terminals can make a neat cable termination into connector blocks. However, I have found these to be unreliable because vibration and movement work them loose. Also, in most cases they do not precisely match the connector block terminal and make inadequate electrical contact.

h.   **Bullet Terminals.** These are useful when used in cabin lighting fittings. I often use them on all cable ends: female on the supply and male on the light fitting tails. This makes it easy to disconnect and remove fittings, especially where they are permanently installed in the headliner.

111

6.13   DC Junction Boxes. Junction boxes are the most practical way to terminate a number of cables, especially where access is required to disconnect circuits. The following are virtually standard in any installation.

   a.   Mast Circuits. Mast circuits should all have a junction box in a dry location under the deck. This will include a box for lighting circuits, a box for masthead wind instruments, a VHF coaxial cable junction box or in-line connector, and a radar junction box. These can be easily disconnected for mast removal and troubleshooting. The Index (Thrudex) models illustrated below are by far the best type available and give a neat and professional job.

   b.   Lighting Circuits. To reduce the number of cables radiating back to the switchboard and also to minimize voltage drops, I use a junction box forward and aft for lighting circuits. Where several cables are paralleled, the small domestic junction boxes that incorporate three terminals are the best. They are quite suitable as long as a dry location is chosen, such as a cupboard or behind a panel.

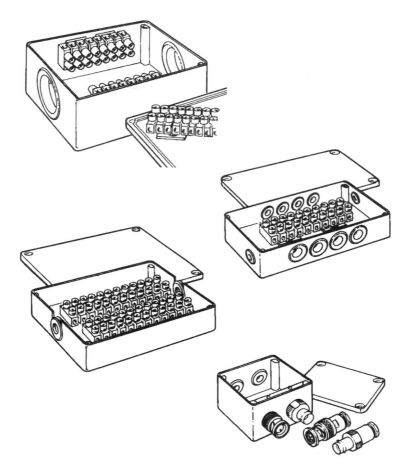

Figure 6-6 Index (Thrudex) Junction Boxes

6.14 **DC Switchboards.** A well designed and manufactured switchboard is a prerequisite for good circuit control, operation, monitoring, and protection.

    a. **Material.** Metal or plastics, this is the big question. Survey requirements and most classification societies specify a non-conductive, non-hygroscopic material, although most metal panels have gained approval. The advantages and disadvantages of each type are as follows:

        (1) **Plastics.** The multilayer boards are non-conductive and are made of traffolyte or layered plastic material. Circuit identification is engraved and cannot be rubbed off. The boards are corrosion resistant and do not scratch easily.

        (2) **Metal.** Anodized aluminum panels are generally etched with appropriate circuit identification, and are very attractive. They are conductive, however, and faults and shorting to the panel can occur. Metallic panels must always be suitably grounded. After some use, the etching can wear away and obscure the circuit names. Most off-the-shelf panels such as Marinetics, BME, and Mastervolt are anodized aluminum.

    b. **Busbars.** Fuses or circuit breakers should have a common supply busbar at the rear. My own practice is to put a separate busbar for each row of breakers and run a separate feed to each from the main positive link or from the discharge ammeter shunt. Circuit cables to the back of breakers should consist of one or more flexible looms sufficiently long to safely place the entire panel out from the mounting frame to facilitate access.

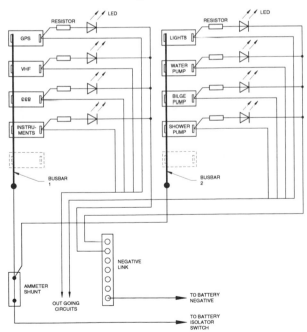

Figure 6-7 Switchboard Rear Connection Layout

c. **Fireproofing.** Survey authorities specify that the internal part of the switchboard must be lined with a fire-resistant lining. Lining all interior walls with an appropriate sheeting will help contain any fire that may arise in the event of a severe failure.

d. **Circuit Indicators.** Circuit breaker status indicators normally consist of two light types:

   (1) **LED.** Circuit status is generally a simple red LED. Green is rarely used. Although green seems the logical color, green LEDs are less bright and more difficult to see in daylight. An LED requires a resistor in series and this is typically valued at 560 ohms for 12-volt systems.

   (2) **Filament Lamp.** Red filament lamps are also commonly used. The one disadvantage is that they consume around 40 milliamps (mA). If there are 20 circuits, this adds up to a reasonable load on the system and a needless current drain. If you have a very large switchboard, allow for the current drain. In many cases, people assume they have a current leakage problem, when in fact the switchboard indicators are causing the drain.

e. **Voltmeters.** A good quality voltmeter is essential for properly monitoring battery condition. Accuracy is crucial as a battery has a range of approximately one volt from a full charge to a discharged condition.

   (1) **Analog Voltmeters.** These are the most common. The sense cable should go directly back to the battery, although on service battery connections most connect directly to the switchboard busbar. Direct connection gives greater accuracy and less influence from local loads. Voltmeters should be of the moving iron type and should also have a fuse installed on the positive input cable. Switching between batteries to voltmeter is through a double-pole, center-off toggle switch or a multiple battery rotary switch. Meters must be zeroed properly, and a check made against a digital multimeter to verify error. A half-volt error is quite common. It is prudent to switch off the meter after checking.

   (2) **LED Indicators.** These devices are often used as a voltmeter substitute, but are not recommended as they do not give the precise readings required. Some units have a high- and low-battery voltage alarm. Auxiliary output on the alarms can also switch off the power or the charging system. This sounds fine, but in practice can be a nuisance.

(3)   **Digital Voltmeters.** Digital voltmeters are far more accurate, though they are susceptible to voltage spikes and damage. Many have maximum supply voltage ranges of just 15 volts, so they should have some form of over-voltage protection and power supply voltage regulation. There are a number of types, including Liquid Crystal Displays (LCDs) and Light Emitting Diodes (LEDs). LED types look attractive and consume more power; an LCD meter consumes much less electricity and is more practical.

(4)   **Battery Level Alarms.** These relatively simple monitoring devices are connected to the main switchboard busbars. They are set to activate at both high and low voltage levels with both an audible and visual indication. The activation levels are typically 11.8 volts for a low alarm, and 15.5 volts for the high alarm. If you have no mute switch, the alarm will annoy you to the point that you have to charge the batteries, which is not a bad thing.

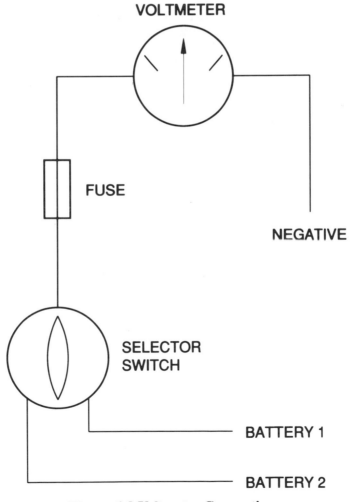

Figure 6-8 Voltmeter Connection

f.   **Ammeters.** Ammeters are essential on the switchboard's positive input to monitor the service battery's discharge levels. Although an ammeter on the charging system indicates that current is flowing, I rarely install them. (When you see the price of a quality 80-amp shunt ammeter, you will probably omit it as well). A voltmeter will tell you if the battery is charging at the correct level. Ammeter options are similar to those found in voltmeters.

   (1)   **Analog Ammeters.** Analog ammeters should be selected for the calculated operating range. A switchboard load meter should be scaled to read 0-40 amps, and the charging system ammeter should be scaled to read 90 amps. This enables the ammeter to tolerate overcurrents without being destroyed or damaged. Cheaper ammeters are of the in-line type. The cable under measurement passes through the meter. The major failing of these ammeters is that considerable cable runs are often required, which results in voltage drops. Additionally, if the meter malfunctions, damage can occur. Always use a shunt ammeter.

   (2)   **Ammeter Shunt.** A shunt allows the main current to flow while monitoring and displaying a millivolt value in proportion to the current flowing. The advantage is that only two low current cables are required to connect the ammeter to the shunt, and the risk of damage is reduced. Do not run the main charging cables to the meter; that defeats the purpose. Instead, install a shunt in the line wherever practical and run sense wires back to the panel-mounted meter.

   (3)   **Digital Ammeters.** Digital ammeters are relatively new devices that have what is called a Hall Effect sensor on the cable under measurement, instead of a shunt. The Hall Effect transducer generates a voltage proportional to the intensity of the magnetic field it is exposed to. For vessel applications, a 0-10 volt transducer output corresponds to a 0-200 amp current flow. Sensitivity is increased, and range is reduced by increasing the number of coils through the transducer core.

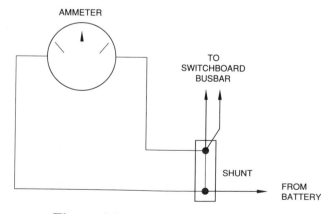

Figure 6-9 Ammeter Connection

6.15 **Digital Circuit Monitors.** While voltmeters and ammeters are a good method of monitoring circuit conditions, there are now a number of systems on the market that enable more accurate appraisal of power status. While voltage monitoring is simple, shunts are required for current measurements.

a. **Digital Circuit Monitors.** These units consist of a single monitor panel, capable of monitoring up to 4 separate circuits, either voltage or current. Some also incorporate an automatic low voltage alarm on all channels with visual and audible indication.

(1) **DCM Mk III. (Adverc BM).** This unit is a selectable, multi-circuit monitoring device. Either charge or discharge currents can be selected, as well as voltages. An adjustable, low voltage warning function is also incorporated. The alarm is both visual and audible.

(2) **Battery Monitor (Index Marine).** This unit allows either voltage or both charge and discharge current to be selected. The display is LED.

b. **Consumption Monitors.** These are "intelligent" devices that monitor current consumption and charging current, allowing the battery net charge deficit to be displayed. For many yachtsmen, they offer a simple way to diagnose battery condition without trying to "guesstimate" the actual level based on voltages and electrolyte densities. The newer units are far more reliable and sophisticated than earlier units, and what is more, they are affordable.

(1) **Bank Manager II. (Ample Power Co)** These units permit a number of monitoring functions, that include voltage and current, high and low voltage, amp-hours used and amp-hours remaining, charging current, and battery temperatures for the principal battery, with voltage monitoring and alarms on battery 2.

(2) **Amp-Hour + 2 Meter (Cruising Equipment Co).** This unit monitors and displays voltage, as well as the amps consumed and charged back to batteries. This is calculated in amp-hours. The system also maintains accuracy by taking into account charging efficiency. The efficiency factor is nominally set at 87% and automatically adjusts after each recharge cycle. Sensibly, a low battery alarm is incorporated which activates at 50%.

(3) **Battman II (VDO).** The VDO unit has a multifunction display indicating battery capacity in amp-hours, actual capacity consumed, and total amp-hours put back in through charging. Additionally, it has an accurate digital voltmeter.

(4) **Link 2000 (Heart Interface).** This unit may also be integrated with Heart inverters, enabling remote control of the inverter and charger.

6.16 **Switchboard Troubleshooting.** There are a number of faults that routinely occur on switchboards and their protective devices. The following faults and probable causes should be checked first. It is assumed that batteries are fully charged and that power is on at the switchboard.

a.   **Circuit Breaker Trips Immediately When Power Is Switched On.** In most cases, the ammeter shows an off-the-meter, full-scale deflection that indicates a high fault current.

(1)   **Load Short Circuit.** Check the appropriate connected load and disconnect the faulty item before resetting.

(2)   **Connection Short Circuit.** If after disconnecting the load the fault still exists, check out cable connections for short circuits, or cable insulation damage.

b.   **Circuit Breaker Trips Several Seconds After Power Is Switched On.** The ammeter shows a gradual increase in current to a high value before tripping off.

(1)   **Motor Seizure.** This fault may arise if the electric motor has seized or, more probably, its bearings have seized.

(2)   **Load Stalling.** This fault is usually due to a seized pump.

(3)   **Insulation Leakage.** This fault is usually due to a gradual breakdown in insulation, such as a pump connection in a wet bilge.

c.. **No Power After Circuit Breaker Is Switched On.** If power is absent at the equipment connection terminals, check the following:

(1)   **Circuit Connection.** Check that the circuit connection has not come off the back of the circuit breaker. Also check the cable's connection to the crimp connection terminal.

(2)   **Circuit Breaker Connection.** On many switchboards, the busbar is soldered to one side of all distribution circuit breakers. Check that the solder joint has not come away. In some cases, breakers have a busbar that is held under breaker screw terminals. Check that the screws and connection are tight.

(3)   **Circuit Breaker.** Operate the breaker several times. In some cases, the mechanism does not make proper electrical contact and several operations can solve the problem by wiping the contacts.

(4)   **Circuit Negative.** If all tests verify that the positive supply is present, check that the circuit's negative wire is secure in the negative link.

d.   **Circuit Power On But No Indication Light.** The LED may have failed, or in some cases, the resistor. Also check the soldered connection to the circuit breaker terminal.

6.17   Mast Cabling. Mast cabling is a common source of failure. Many problems can be avoided if the cables are installed properly. Since masts are generally wired by mast manufacturers and riggers, vessel owners rarely take the opportunity to supervise or specify requirements. There are three major areas of concern in any mast installation:

a.   **Mast Base Junction Boxes.** The most common area of failure is the junction box. If mounted inside the vessel, a good water-resistant box should be installed. If mounted externally, and this should only be a last resort, a waterproof box is required. Always leave a loop when inserting cables into the box. If water does travel down the loom, this will drip off the bottom of the loop and will not enter and corrode the junction box terminals or connections.

b.   **Deck Cable Transits.** Cable glands are designed to prevent cable damage and ensure a waterproof transit through a bulkhead or deck. A significant number of problems are experienced when water gets in through deck fittings, and I have seen some amazing systems utilizing pipes, hose, and the like. If figure 8 type cable is used, or small, single insulated cables are installed, it is virtually impossible to adequately seal them in cable glands. To overcome this problem, use circular, multicore cables if possible, or use the consolidation procedure described below (6.17. e.) to make a cable loom that can be put through a deck gland. The Index (Thrudex) cable glands illustrated below are by far the best on the market. You need to take deck material into account before selecting a gland. Steel decks require a different gland type than fiberglass, foam-sandwich decks.

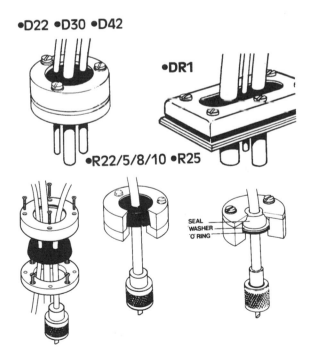

Figure 6-10 Deck Cable Glands

119

c.   **Cabling.** The following factors should be noted when installing electric cable:

(1)   **Cable Types.** The major problem is the use of single insulated untinned cables, generally of an under-rated conductor size. Small conductor sizes cause many voltage drop problems with unacceptable low light outputs as a result. Use 15-amp-rated cable for each circuit.

(2)   **Negative Conductors.** Masthead tricolors are normally connected to a dual anchor light fitting. These use a three-wire, common negative arrangement. The same arrangement is used for combination masthead and foredeck spotlights. Never use the mast as a negative return, as I have found on some vessels. Always install a negative wire to each light fitting.

(3)   **UV Protection.** All exposed cables should be covered in black, UV-resistant spiral wrapping to prevent rapid degradation of insulation. Small cracks in the insulation allow water to penetrate, which subsequently anneals the copper.

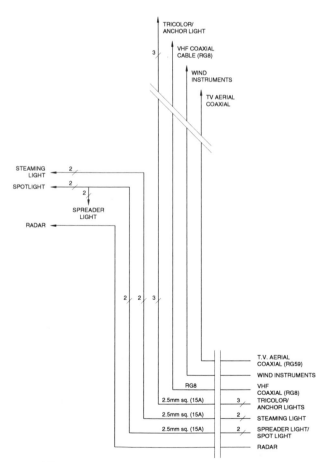

Figure 6-11 Mast Cabling Diagram

120

d. **Mast Cable Support.** Cabling must be properly secured within the mast. The weight of a cable hanging down inside a mast causes fatigue through stretching. If the cables are not enclosed in conduit (still a common practice), the internal halyards can whip against them and severe the conductors in multi-core instrument cables or severely damage the insulation. There are a number of methods for securing mast cables; a combination of all three is best.

(1) **Cable Glands.** Where a cable enters the mast base and exits at the masthead, it should pass through a cable gland. The ideal glands for this are the Thrudex DR1 rectangular units. Once cables have been placed through the neoprene, the gland is tightened and compression around the cables takes the strain. The cables are protected from chafe against the mast entrance hole.

(2) **Messenger Line.** A small messenger line can be installed with the cables and supported at the masthead. The messenger should be tied or taped to the cable loom and then fastened to take the load off the cable ends. The messenger serves as a pull-through for adding or replacing cable. However, once the line is taped to the loom over its entire length, it is impossible to remove and replace single cables.

(3) **Cable Ties.** Where possible, use cable ties to fasten and support cables. The ideal place to do so is where cables come out of the mast to connect lights, radar, etc., which usually gives 3-4 fastening points. There is generally sufficient space to insert a tie around the cables. A second hole large enough for a tie is required next to the main cable entry to enable tie to be supported. Always use black, UV-resistant cable ties.

e. **Mast Cable Consolidation.** In most cases, the mast is wired with single insulated cables. To put these cables through deck cable glands, you need to consolidate them into a single loom. One method is as follows:

(1) Neatly make a cable loom and hold it in place with cable ties. Keep the loom as circular as possible.

(2) Apply silicone sealant to the loom, and work it through all cables. This will ensure that a solid core is made. If done properly, it will prevent water from traveling down the cable loom.

(3) Apply a layer of black, UV-resistant spiral wrap to the loom. Again, spaces between the wrap should have silicone compound applied to fill any voids. The spiral wrap gives the cable loom a circular shape.

(4) Slide on a length of heat shrink tubing and shrink it in place. This forms the outer sheath.

(5) Use a suitable deck gland, pass the cable through the deck, and connect into a suitable junction box.

f. **Deck Plugs.** Instead of deck glands and junction boxes at a mast base, deck plugs are sometimes used. They can also provide outlets for hand spotlights, or other equipment commonly used. Many are of inferior quality and fail prematurely, often when you need them most. Don't use the cheap and nasty chrome plugs and sockets—they aren't waterproof. The best units on the market are either the Bulgin-type units from Index or those from Dri-plug. When using deck plugs, observe the following:

(1) **Deck Seal.** Ensure that the seal between deck and connector body is watertight. Leakage is very common on wet decks up forward where the plugs are usually located.

(2) **Plug Cable Entrance.** Make sure the cable seal into the plug is watertight. It is of little use to have a good seal around the deck if the water seeps through the cable entry and shorts out terminals internally.

(3) **Connector Seals.** Most connectors have O-rings to ensure a water-tight seal. Check that the rings are in good connection, are not deformed or compressed, and seat properly in the recess. A very light smear of silicone grease assists in the sealing process.

(4) **Connection Pins.** Ensure that the pins are dry before plugging in and that pins are not bent or showing signs of corrosion or pitting. Do not fill around the pins with silicone grease, as this often creates a poor contact. Keep plugs and sockets clean and dry.

g. **Mast System Maintenance.** Basic maintenance tasks will reduce mast wiring problems:

(1) **Mast Base Cable Exits.** Regularly examine cables where they exit the mast for signs of chafe . If the cable loom has not been protect-ed with a UV-resistant sleeve, carefully examine insulation for cracks.

(2) **Masthead Cables.** Regularly examine masthead cable exits for chafe. Ensure that coaxial, wind instrument, and power cables have a reasonable loom to allow for shortening and repair.

6.18   **Mast Cabling Troubleshooting.** Mast wiring faults are common because the mast subjects cables to the worst damaging factors, such as vibration, exposure to salt water, stretching, and mechanical damage. Fortunately, mast wiring is easy to troubleshoot.

  a.   **Tricolor/Anchor Lights.** If a light does not illuminate, lamp failure is the usual cause. If the lamp is replaced and it still does not illuminate, perform the following tests:

  (1)   **Test Supply.** Open the mast connection box and locate the appropriate terminals. Using a multimeter on the DC-volt range, check that voltage is present at the terminals with the power on. Many failures are due to poor contacts within terminal blocks, or corrosion of the terminal and cable.

  (2)   **Continuity Test.** Turn the power off, and with a multimeter set on the resistance x1 range, test between the positive and negative terminals. The reading should be approximately 2-5 ohms with a good lamp installed. If the reading is above that range, the light fitting or connection has failed or the cable has been damaged. The mast cable entry and exit points should be examined first. Internal breaks only occur in masts without wiring conduits. Many tricolor/anchor lights have a plug and socket arrangement, which is an occasional source of trouble.

  b.   **Spreader Lights.** The above tests are also valid for spreader lights. On many vessels, spreader lights are a sealed beam unit in a stainless steel housing. It is very common to have shorts to the mast as cables chafe through on sharp edges. This problem is notorious for causing circuit leakages and increased corrosion rates on steel vessels:

  (1)   **Mast Short Circuits.** With a multimeter set on the resistance ohms x1k range, check between the mast and both positive and negative wires. The reading should be over-range. If you have any reading, you have either a short or a leakage from cable insulation breakdown.

  (2)   **Check Supply.** Open the mast connection box and locate the appropriate terminals. Using a multimeter on the DC-volt range, check that voltage is present at the terminals wiht the power on.

6.19   Grounding Systems. The following chapters on lightning, corrosion, AC-power systems, radio systems, etc., all make reference to grounding systems. Therefore, it is crucial to understand what the various so-called grounds are and their importance within respective circuits as well as to each other. Invariably, confusion as to function is a key cause of system problems.

a.   **DC Negative.** The DC negative is a current carrying conductor within a two-wire system. It carries the same current flowing within the DC positive conductor. It is a recommended practice in the most common wiring configuration for the negative terminal of the battery supply to be bonded to a grounded point. In many cases, this point is the engine block. This is done to polarize the DC electrical system (that is, to hold one side at ground potential).

b.   **Lightning Ground.** A lightning ground is a point at ground potential that is immersed in sea water. It only carries current in the rare event of a lightning strike and its primary purpose is to ground strike energy. It is not a functional part of any other electrical system.

c.   **Corrosion System Ground.** The corrosion system ground is an equal potential point that connects all underwater parts to be protected and bonds them to the anode.

d.   **AC Power Ground (or Earth).** The AC ground is a point at ground potential that is immersed in sea water. Under normal operating conditions, it carries no voltage or current. In the event of a fault, its primary purpose is to carry current to the ground and hold all connected metal to ground potential, thereby reducing the risk of an electric shock from exposed metal parts.

e.   **Radio Frequency Ground.** The radio frequency ground is an integral part of the aerial system and is sometimes also termed the counterpoise. It only carries RF energy and is not a conductor as such.

Lightning Protection

7.0 **Lightning Protection.** Virtually all classification societies and national marine authorities, the ABYC, etc., lay down recommendations for lightning protection. Very few boaters bother to adhere to them, despite the startling statistic that over 10% of fatalities on cruising yachts are the result of lightning strikes.

7.1 **Lightning Physics.** Within a cloud formation, strong updrafts and downdrafts generate high electrical charges. When the voltage reaches a sufficiently high level, both cloud to cloud and ground discharges occur.

a. **Negative Cloud to Ground.** These strikes occur when the ground is at positive polarity and the cloud's negative region attempts to equalize with ground.

b. **Positive Cloud to Ground.** The positively charged cloud top equalizes with the negative ground.

c. **Positive Ground to Cloud.** The positively charged ground equalizes with the negatively charge cloud.

d. **Negative Ground to Cloud.** The negatively charged ground equalizes with the positively charged cloud top.

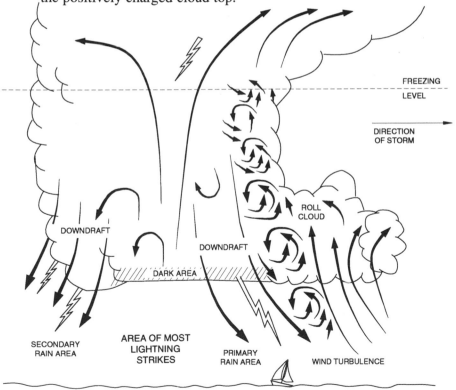

Figure 7-1 Cumulo-Nimbus Storm System

7.2   **Lightning Components.** Lightning consists of a number of components which form a multidirectional flow of charges exceeding 200,000 amperes at over 30,000°C for a matter of milliseconds. The positive ions rise to the cloud top, and the negative ions migrate to the cloud base. Regions of positive ions also form at the cloud base. Eventually, the cloud charge levels have sufficient potential difference between ground or another cloud to discharge.

a.   **Leader.** The leader consists of a negative stream of electrons comprising many small forks or fingers that follow and break down the air paths offering the least resistance. The charge follows the fork, finding the easiest path as each successive layer is broken down and charged to the same polarity as the cloud.

b.   **Upward Positive Leader.** A positive charge rises some 50 meters above the ground.

c.   **Channel.** When leader and upward leader meet, a channel is formed.

d.   **Return Stroke.** This path is generally much brighter and more powerful than the leader, and travels upward to the cloud, partially equalizing the potential difference between ground and cloud.

e.   **Dart Leader.** In a matter of milliseconds after the return stroke, another downward charge takes place along the same path as the stepped leader and return stroke. Sometimes it is followed by multiple return strokes. The movements happen so fast that it appears to be a single event. This sequence can continue until the differential between cloud and ground is equalized.

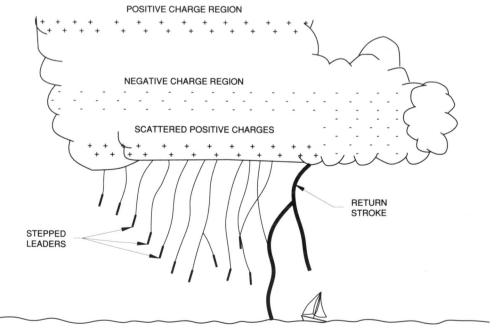

Figure 7-2 Lightning Process

7.3   **Lightning Protection Zone.** The most reliable protection system is one that grounds any strike directly. The principles are as follows:

    a.   **Grounding.** The primary purpose of a grounding system is to divert the lightning strike discharge directly to ground through a low resistance circuit suitably rated to carry the momentary current values. This reduces the strike period to a minimum, and reduces or eliminates the problem of sidestrikes as the charge attempts to go to ground. Electricity follows the path of least resistance to ground, therefore little goes down the stays.

    b.   **Cone of Protection.** The tip of the mast, or more properly a turned spike clear of all masthead equipment, gives a cone of protection below it. The cone base is the same diameter as the mast height. This protective cone prevents strikes to adjacent areas and metalwork, including stays, rails or other items lower than the masthead.

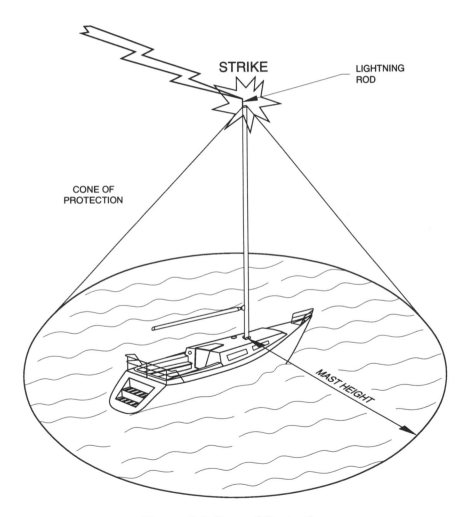

Figure 7-3 Cone of Protection

c.   **Electromagnetic Pulse.** Though insurance companies don't like to accept claims on damage unless you can show total damage to masthead systems, a vessel can have its equipment damaged by a strike within a few hundred meters. A strike sends out a very large electromagnetic pulse, which is a strong magnetic field. This field induces into wiring and systems a high voltage spike that does just as much damage as a direct hit. If you suspect damage from an induced electromagnetic pulse, check with vessels adjacent to yours and get statements to support your contention. Generally all the electronics will be out if this is the case because the mast and any wiring act as a large aerial.

d.   **Sidestrikes.** It is common among closely moored vessels and in crowded marinas to have a lightning strike literally jump from vessel to vessel as it attempts to find ground. Usually the strike exits from stays, chainplates, and spreaders. In many cases, the strike goes to water from the chainplates, causing serious damage to hull and fittings.

e.   **St. Elmo's Fire (Brush Discharge).** When this phenomenon occurs, it usually precedes a strike, although the effect does not occur all the time. The vessel becomes a large ground mass. The discharge is characterized by ionized clouds and balls of white or green flashing light that polarize at vessel extremities. The discharge of negative ions reduces the potential intensity of a strike. St. Elmo's Fire is more common on steel vessels. Damage to electrical systems is usually induced into mast wiring, as the steel hull itself acts as a large Faraday cage. For amusement, tell the insurance company that your damage was caused by St. Elmo's Fire!

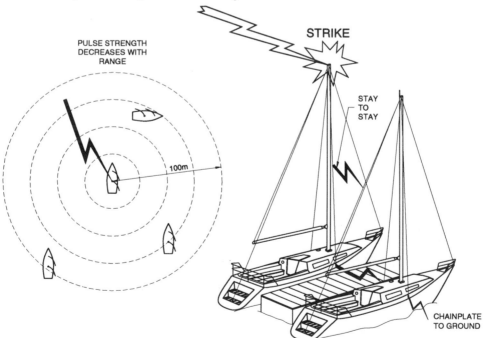

Figure 7-4 Electromagnetic Pulse Effect and Sidestrike

7.4 **Lightning Protection Systems.** Most classification societies, the ABYC, and other advisory bodies generally recommend lightning protection in the form of a directly grounded mast and spike. Other devices have come on the market, and their effectiveness has yet to be conclusively proved. Protection methods are as follows:

a. **Mast.** Lightning will generally strike the highest point and take the path offering the least resistance to ground. The mast is usually the strike point. Note that a stainless steel VHF whip does not constitute any protection. Masthead systems are as follows:

(1) **Mast Spike.** The mast spike ideally should be a copper rod with pointed end. To avoid metal interaction, stainless rods are commonly used but should be of a thicker section than the more conductive, lower resistance, copper. The spike should be at least 6 inches higher than any other masthead equipment, including VHF aerials. Many commercial units (Dynarod and Seaground) have an offset in the rod, which should be satisfactory. The point is sharp to facilitate what is called point discharge. Ions dissipating from the ground through the point effectively reduce the potential between the cloud and the sea. In many cases, the strike may be of lower intensity or not occur at all.

(2) **Lightning Protection Device (LPD).** This is an Italian invention that consists of a high-performance varistor. The device is designed to interact with the electrical charges of the initial stepped leader, when current values are relatively low, and avoid the return strokes. Charges accumulate on the atmospheric electrode and varistor poles. The varistor conducts and the charge condition on the electrode alters. These charges leave when some streamers form to meet the leader.

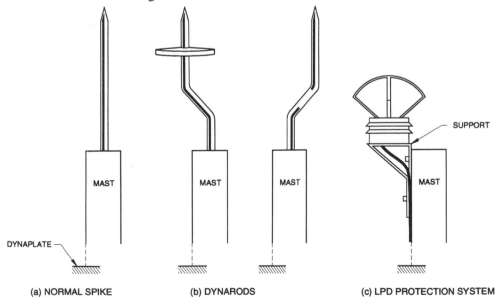

Figure 7-5 Masthead Protection Systems

b. **Mast Cable.** Much of the damage in a strike results from heat, as the large current flow into a resistive cable makes the cable act like a large heating element. The chapters on voltage drop are relevant here. The following factors must be observed:

    (1) **Cable Sizes.** It is essential that the cable has a sufficient cross sectional area, at least 4 AWG but preferably much larger.

    (2) **Cable Connectors.** Never use soldered joints alone, as they will melt during a strike and cause further havoc. Always crimp connections and ensure that all bonded connections are clean, tight, and securely bolted.

c. **Grounding.** A good ground requires direct and permanent immersion in sea water. It must also have sufficient area to adequately dissipate the strike energy. Through-hull fittings must never be used as a primary ground point, unless you want to sink the vessel. The bonding cable from the mast base to the ground plate should be as straight as possible. Sharp corners may encourage side discharges—called corona discharge—to occur. Similar side discharges can occur from boat to boat in crowded marinas. Normally, I enclose the cable in high quality electrical conduit to reduce the possibility of side-strikes, as electrical insulation frequently breaks down under high voltage conditions. Connections should be as follows:

    (1) **Steel/Alloy Vessels.** Connect the mast base to the hull or mast step with a large, low resistance bonding strap.

    (2) **Fiberglass Vessels.** A keel acts as a good ground and is sufficient. Bridge out with a stainless link at least two keel bolts to spread the contact area. Multihulls require a large, separate ground plate, such as a radio ground shoe (Dynaplate, Wonderbar or Seaground). This will ensure that there is a large and efficient ground area. Do not use the radio's RF ground plate as the lightning ground. Never bond the lightning system to the corrosion system bonding, machinery, or electrical system negatives or grounds. Never bond the lightning system to bronze through-hull fittings.

    (3) **Wooden Vessels.** Wooden vessels normally have a metal mast track which should be properly grounded. If possible, a copper strap can also be run, although this is not always practical. The same grounding method as on a fiberglass boat should be used to directly bond a ground plate or the keel. Some owners have installed gold-plated ground plates. By looking at the metal nobility table (Table 8-1) you can see that they may be inviting a corrosive situation to occur.

    (4) **Emergency Ground.** A heavy-gauge copper cable can be clamped to a stay to cover about half a meter. The other end should be clamped to a ground plate, and hung over the side. Do not use chains and anchors as they are ineffective.

d. **Corrosion Factors.** Considerable care must be taken when bonding various equipment into a lightning protection bonding system.

    (1)   On steel and alloy vessels, the hull is the same ground plane. All equipment and all grounds are therefore held at the same potential.

    (2)   In fiberglass and timber vessels, bonding can be more complicated. Problems may arise where through-hull fittings and other items are bonded indiscriminately. It is easy to cause differences of potential between various items creating a corrosion nightmare.

    (3)   After connecting a lightning system, monitor the corrosion rate of anodes and observe any items bonded underwater.

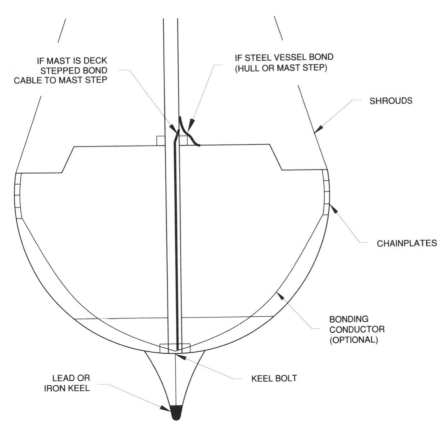

Figure 7-6 Bonding and Grounding Arrangement

e.   **Bonding.** Most authorities recommend that stanchions, chainplates, and large metal equipment such as stainless water tanks be bonded to the lightning ground. Bonding considerations are as follows:

(1)   **Stay Grounding.** I do not subscribe to the practice of chainplate and stay grounding. My reasoning is that if a good, low resistance path is installed from mast to groundplate or keel, the strike energy will be directed that way. Grounding chainplates offers alternative parallel high resistance paths. This has the effect of distributing the strike energy to other areas, which contributes to sidestrike activity. My greatest concern as a yacht owner is that large current flows in rigging components can also cause crystallization and damage to stays and fittings sufficient to degrade or damage the rig.

(2)   **Corrosion.** Any bonding must be undertaken with care. Dissimilar metals such as an aluminum mast, copper straps, and steel hulls and keels must all be considered within the context of galvanic corrosion. Ensure all connections are in dry areas where no water or moisture can cause a problem. Also consider the effects of grounding the lightning system to other grounds as described elsewhere.

(3)   **Internal Bonding.** It is only necessary to bond internal metallic items within 6 feet of the mast or bonding connections. While water tanks built under bunks are isolated, under-sole tankage should be connected.

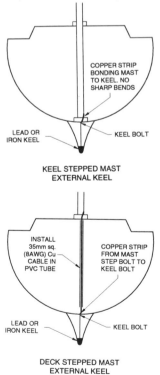

Figure 7-7 Mast Grounding Arrangements

f.   Surge Protection. Ideally, all electrical systems should have surge suppression devices fitted. Surge protection methods are as follows:

(1)   Radio Antennas. Aerials can draw a strike or cause induced current to flow through the coaxial conductor to the radio. To prevent this, all antennas should have arrestors fitted, although this is rare. Antenna cables can be fitted with a two-way switch: one side to the radio, one to ground. During a storm, or if the vessel is left unattended, place the switch to ground position. An arrestor (Hy-Gain or Dynapulse), or spark gap device can be used. Coaxial cable surge protectors (Dynadiverta or Polyphase Corp) can also be used.

(2)   DC Power Supplies. Power supplies should have isolation on both positive and negative supplies. Additionally, surge suppression units can be installed which will reduce any overvoltage condition to a safe value, typically around 40 volts. All equipment will benefit from what is called a transient protection device installed across the input power supply connections. These are generally metal oxide varistors, and are available from electronics suppliers.

(3)   AC Power Supplies. There are lightning arrestors available which can be incorporated in the switchboard. They consist of varistors that shunt excess voltage to ground.

(4)   Compasses. Compasses should be rechecked and deviation corrections made after a strike. In some cases, complete demagnetization may occur.

7.5   Lightning Safety. In an electrical storm, the following precautions should be taken to avoid any shock or something more serious:

- Stay below decks at all times.

- Stay well away from mast, boom shrouds, chainplates, and the mast compression post or mast below deck.

- Take a position and plot it prior to shutting down, in case all electronics equipment is blown.

- Turn off all electronic gear and isolate the circuit breakers if at all practical. Disconnect aerials also, if practical.

- Do not operate radios until after the storm, unless in an extreme emergency.

- After a lightning strike, be aware that the compass may be incorrect.

- Check all running rigging and fittings after a strike, as damage can occur that may seriously effect the vessel's capacity to sail.

- Check all through-hull fittings for damage, if you have decided to risk bonding them. If they are damaged or gone, you will see water over the cabin sole.

Corrosion

8.0   **Corrosion.** When two dissimilar metals (metal hull and underwater hull fittings) are placed in seawater (an electrolyte), the differing potentials between the metals cause current to flow. In effect, a battery has been created. The term *corrosion* is often improperly and simplistically called electrolysis or stray current corrosion. Corrosion with respect to yachts and basic electrical systems falls into two main categories: *galvanic corrosion* and *electrolytic corrosion*. Both corrosion processes are a result of electric current flow between the two metals in an electrolyte. The result is corroded hulls, propellers, shafts, rudders, stocks, and skin fittings.

  a. **Paint Systems.** Although a vessel's hull is protected by an extensive paint program, isolating metal from the seawater, the incorrect assumption is often made that corrosion cannot occur and cathodic protection is unnecessary. But air holes, or small areas of paint imperfection, occur along weld seams, and paint coatings are damaged due to abrasions from chains, piers, tenders, etc. Cuprous oxides used in antifouling paints can convert to copper sulfide and create a galvanic cell. And these problems can occur before we even begin to consider metal differences and electrical factors.

  b. **Galvanic Corrosion.** Where two different metals with differing potentials are interconnected and placed within proximity of seawater, a galvanic cell is created that significantly accelerates the corrosion of the base metal. Corrosion can also occur if a metal hull contains microscopic impurities, which can form local cathodes and anodes. This process generates a measurable current flow between the two metals and forms a galvanic cell (or galvanic couple). The part of the cell that corrodes is termed the anode, and is the more positively charged metal, and the other is the cathode, which is negatively charged with respect to the anode. Corrosion rates are directly proportional to the corrosion current levels.

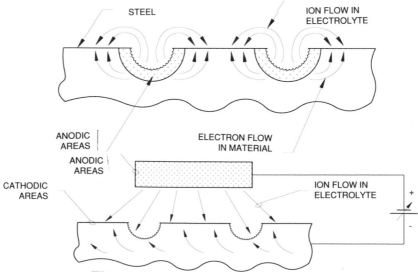

Figure 8-1 Galvanic Corrosion Process

c. **Metal Nobility.** The metals with higher negative potentials will corrode faster than metals having lower potentials.

Table 8-1 Metal Nobility Table

Metal	Voltage
Magnesium and Alloys	- 1.65 V
Zinc Plating on Steel	- 1.30 V
Zinc	- 1.10 V
Galvanized Iron	- 1.05 V
Aluminum Alloy Castings	- 0.75 V
Mild Steel	- 0.70 V
Cast Iron	- 0.70 V
Lead	- 0.55 V
Manganese Bronze	- 0.27 V
Copper, Brass, and Bronze	- 0.25 V
Monel	- 0.20 V
Stainless Steel (passive)	- 0.20 V
Nickel (passive)	- 0.15 V
Silver	- 0.00 V
Gold	+ 0.15 V

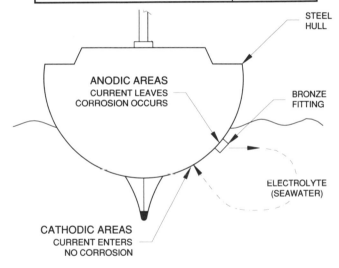

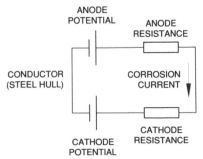

Figure 8-2 Vessel Galvanic Corrosion

135

8.1 **Galvanic Protection.** Ideally a vessel should be constructed so that most metallic items are compatible. If they are different, they must be either isolated or protected. Anodes are the normal protection method. Anodes are also called sacrificial anodes because they are sacrificed instead of the hull or fittings. Because they are high on the nobility scale, they tend to corrode quicker than other items such as mild steel, alloy, etc. The zinc anode generates an electric current and because the hull effectively has a higher potential, the anode allows current flow through it and bonded items to the seawater and back to the hull. Figure 8-3 illustrates the galvanic corrosion process. The process corrodes the anode proportional to the level of current flow present, while preserving the hull and fittings.

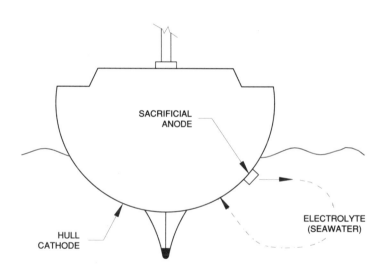

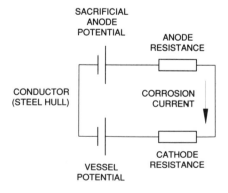

Figure 8-3 Galvanic Corrosion Protection

8.2 **Anode Systems.** It is essential for the anodes to be of the correct size, in the correct location, and of the correct number for the area being protected. It is quite possible to overprotect the hull and fittings. If your vessel is in warm highly saline waters, you must make more frequent inspections of zinc anodes. The following illustrates typical arrangements recommended by corrosion specialists M.G. Duff Marine for steel, aluminum, fiberglass, and timber vessels. Note that metal and fiberglass hulls are treated separately. Anode position is not critical, but they must be able to "see" the parts to be protected. Anode fixing must be above the bilge line internally, and there must be a minimal internal bonding cable run length. Anode systems are only as good as the paint and antifouling on the hull. Good corrosion protection starts with this. Don't believe you can bypass this by using an anode system. Anode systems are as follows:

a.   **Class One Vessels.** These are generally single-screw vessels with a small propeller shaft and mild steel rudders or wood/fiberglass rudders with mild steel hangings. Normally, one anode is required for propeller and shaft protection, and two for rudder protection. The main anode should be located on the main hull below the turn of the bilge equidistant from the gearbox and the inboard end of the stern tube.

b.   **Class Two Vessels.** These vessels have long, exposed propeller shafts with mild steel rudders or rudders of wood and fiberglass with mild steel hangings. One anode is required to protect each propeller and shaft, with separate anodes for rudder protection.

c.   **Class Three Vessels.** Class Three vessels are the same as Class One except for having bronze or stainless steel rudder hangings. The general rule is one anode to protect propeller, prop shaft, and rudder.

d.   **Class Four Vessels.** These are similar to Class Two, but have bronze or stainless steel hangings. One anode can provide protection for one propeller, shaft, shaft strut (bracket), and rudder. Anodes are located similarly to Class Two vessels.

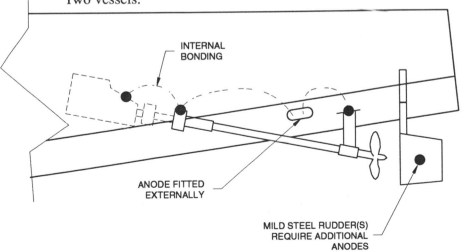

Figure 8-4 Class 2 Anode Arrangements

8.3   **Anode Mass Selection.** Table 8-2 and Table 8-3 offer guidelines recommended by M. G. Duff for selecting anode sizes. Rudders, skegs, and bilge keels are covered separately.

  a.   **Anode Purity Standards.** Zinc alloy anodes should conform to US Mil Spec MIL-18001J, or in Australia AS2239-1979. If they do not have a standard quoted, don't use them.

Table 8-2 Anode Mass Table

Class	Prop Size	Prop Size
Class 1	up to 14 in	up to 29 in
Class 2	up to 11 in	up to 21 in
Class 3	up to 12 in	up to 26 in
Class 4	up to 10 in	up to 19 in
	1 x 1 Kg	**1 x 2.2 Kg**

  b.   **Rudder, Skeg, and Bilge Keel Anodes.** Anodes for mild steel rudders, skegs, and bilge keels are normally installed directly to steelwork. In most cases, the best solution is to bolt the anodes back-to-back, or they may be welded on if required.

Table 8-3 Rudder, Skeg, and Keel Anodes Table

Protection Area	Anode Size
Up to 10 Sq ft Steelwork	2 x 1.35 Kg Strip Anodes
Up to 30 Sq ft Steelwork	2 x 0.90 Kg Anodes
Up to 70 Sq ft Steelwork	2 x 2.22 Kg Anodes

8.4   **Anode Number Calculations.** Calculations are normally based on wetted surface area. The main vessel dimensions used are waterline length, waterline beam, and mean loaded draft. Area is calculated using the formula:

Waterline Length (LWL) x (Waterline Beam + Draft)

This formula suits most heavy-displacement sailing vessels and motor cruisers. For medium-displacement vessels, multiply the calculated sum by 0.75. For light-displacement vessels, multiply by 0.5.

Table 8-4 One-Year Anode Selection Table

Wetted Area	Stud Fixed Anodes	Twin Screw
Up to 28 m^2	2 x 4.0 Kg	2 x 1.0 Kg/rudder
28.1 - 56 m^2	4 x 4.0 Kg	2 x 1.0 Kg/rudder
56.1 - 84 m^2	6 x 4.0 Kg	2 x 1.0 Kg/rudder
84.1 - 102 m^2	4 x 6.5 Kg	2 x 2.2 Kg/rudder
102.1 - 148 m^2	6 x 6.5 Kg	2 x 2.2 Kg/rudder

8.5 **Anode Bonding.** There are a number of factors to consider when fitting and connecting anodes. These are as follows:

a.   **Anode Stud Connections.** Anode fixing studs should be connected to bonded parts by the shortest practical route to minimize resistance. It is critical that bonding be resistance free, therefore a heavy-gauge conductor is necessary. Use 11 AWG (4 mm^2) cable as a minimum.

b.   **Bonding Through-Hull Fittings.** Don't do what many vessel manufacturers do, which is to connect every metal item, including through-hull (skin) fittings, with stainless wire and hose clamps. It is only advisable to bond the main raw sea water inlet fitting. Any others connected with rubber or PVC hoses need not be bonded. The current flow in a bonding circuit is very small; any resistance introduced into the circuit from bad connections and cable resistances creates a difference in potential that will cancel any protective measures and may actually create problems.

c.   **Bonding Straps.** Most recommendations call for a bonding loop. In fact, it is better to connect bonded items in a radial arrangement back to the anode bonding bolt to minimize resistance. If one bonding wire is accidentally broken, the majority of the bonding network will not be lost.

d.   **Shaft Collar Anodes.** When fitting collar anodes to propeller shafts, make sure that the shaft is clean and not covered with antifoulant. I have frequently seen this done around launching ramps (slipways). The collars must be mounted as close as possible to the shaft strut (bracket), typically a clearance of 4-10 mm. Do not put bottom paint on the anode!

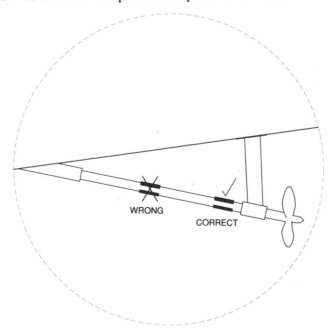

Figure 8-5 Shaft Anode Installation

e.   **Anodes for Fiberglass and Timber Vessels.** There are a few facts to remember with fiberglass or timber vessels:

(1)   **Connection.** Anodes on fiberglass and timber hulls must have the internal bonding system connected to them. This is a common omission. An anode is working only when some corrosion is visible on it. I have frequently seen anodes mounted and not connected, and heard those same vessel owners proudly proclaim that there was no corrosion problem.

(2)   **Shaft Bonding.** Slip rings are not the ideal solution for short shafts. It is better to bridge the coupling to the engine block and use a collar anode or separate anode bonded directly to the engine block.

(3)   **Seal Anode Bolt Holes.** Always seal the wood around the anode bolt holes as this can prevent wood electrolysis if an overprotection situation exists.

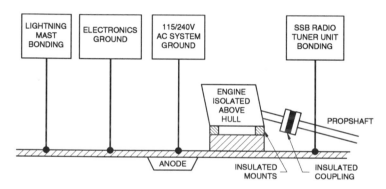

(a) STEEL/ALLOY BONDING CONNECTION

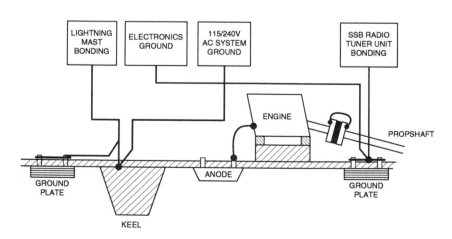

(b) GRP/TIMBER HULL BONDING CONNECTION

Figure 8-6 Corrosion Bonding Arrangements

f.   **Temporary Anodes.** Some alloy and steel vessels also use a zinc anode (guppy) on a wire over the side while in a marina or on a mooring. This must be properly grounded to the hull and have a low resistance copper cable connected to the anode. M.G. Duff manufactures a hanging anode with stainless steel wire. The drawback with homemade units is that the copper cable quickly deteriorates in salt water and becomes ineffective.

g.   **Shaft Coupling Bonding.** Many engine installations incorporate flexible couplings to the propeller shaft. The coupling must be electrically bridged to ensure proper continuity of the system where the engine is not maintained electrically isolated above the bonding system.

h.   **Propeller Shaft Bonding.** The usual method for bonding propellor shafts, both commercially and in small vessels, is to install a brush system. M.G. Duff's system, illustrated below, is called the Electro Eliminator. Essentially, it is a brush system connected to the cathodic bonding system. If such a system is used, the shaft must be kept clean and free of oil, grease, and water.

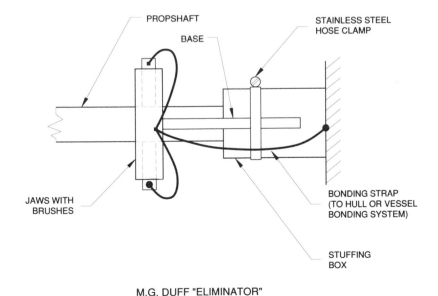

M.G. DUFF "ELIMINATOR"

Figure 8-7 Propeller Shaft Bonding

141

8.6 **Galvanic Isolators.** These devices are designed to galvanically separate an AC ground conductor from the DC negative conductor where they are connected. They are designed to eliminate small DC currents arising on the AC ground that could then pass to the DC and bonding system, which can increase corrosion rates. These devices were developed mainly to combat the not inconsiderable corrosion problems encountered in alloy stern drive legs.

a. **Device Types.** There is much controversy in the U.S. regarding UL listed devices versus those that are unlisted, the unlisted devices allegedly being substandard. While questions relate to technical design matters, the principal factors revolve around the location of the devices in an installation, and the use of two paths to ground, with one using a capacitor in one of the paths. It would appear that only the Quicksilver type is UL listed, although the Newmar device also complies with NFPA/ABYC design recommendations. A typical connection for the Newmar isolator is illustrated in Figure 8-8.

b. **Installation.** When installing an isolator, it is important to follow installation instructions very carefully; in fact, boaters should employ a qualified marine electrician. Ensure that isolators are installed in front of all grounding connections within the vessel. Under no circumstances should you install a device in the AC to DC bonding conductor.

c. **Safety warnings.** In some countries it is a violation of electrical standards to insert any device into a main grounding (safety) conductor, and use of an isolator may therefore invalidate insurance policies. The heating effects of devices operating under AC fault conditions can create a fire hazard if located next to flammable materials. The dockside receptacle grounding circuit must be good or the device is unable to protect against an electrical fault current.

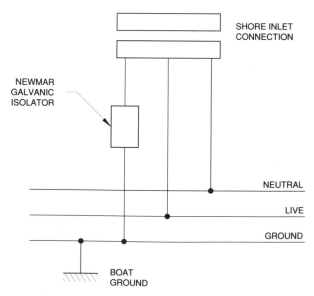

Figure 8-8 Galvanic Isolator System

8.7   **Impressed Current Cathodic Protection.** These systems are generally installed on larger steel vessels or on some outboard engines.

    a.   **Theory.** Essentially, impressed current systems use an on-board power source to transmit a protective counter current through the electrolyte to the areas under protection. Protected areas are thereby converted from anodes into cathodes, which inhibits metal corrosion. Zinc anodes have very low and non-variable driving voltages with reduced effectiveness.

    b.   **Anodes.** In an impressed current cathodic system, the anode is made of a relatively inert material such as silicon iron, silver/lead alloys, tantalum, or platinum. The driving voltage and current outputs can be adjusted at the power source to precisely control the process. Corrosion is prevented as long as the protective potential is applied. In normal operation, an insulative layer of sea salts will form over damaged or porous hull areas in response to the current flow. A typical impressed current system is illustrated below. Some systems are available for small vessels, but the big disadvantage is the constant need for power, uneconomical on a vessel with only batteries. A steel vessel permanently in port with a marina power source may find this method both economical and workable.

    c.   **Cathodic Protection Problems.** It is critically important not to overprotect using too high a potential. Traditional paint systems will soften and blister as hydrogen bubbles form under the paint surface. Chlorinated rubber paint systems are used to counter this characteristic.

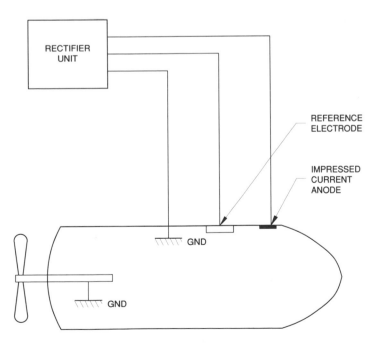

Figure 8-9 Impressed Current Protection System

8.8 **Electrolytic (Stray Current) Corrosion.** Electrolytic (stray current) corrosion is caused by externally generated DC electrical currents that pass through a metal item (anode) in an electrolyte (seawater) to another metal item (cathode). Protective measures against galvanic corrosion are only partially effective against electrolytic corrosion. Electrolytic corrosion will significantly increase corrosion rates. If faults are undiagnosed, the rapid degradation of anodes, followed by stripping of antifouling paint, will occur. In many cases the problems are cumulative, and only serious analysis reveals a number of differing contributing factors.

    a. **Electrolytic Corrosion Sources.** Electrolytic corrosion is caused by an external DC current source.

        (1) **DC Circuit Leakage Currents.** The most common DC leakage currents are (a) leakages across condensation or conductive salt deposits in DC circuit connections or junction boxes and (b) tracking or surface leakages across the top of a battery to the positive terminal, caused by moisture and dust accumulations.

        (2) **DC Ground Faults.** Ground faults on DC conductors occur where the cable insulation has been damaged and contact is made with the hull or connected metalwork. In many cases, the fault may not be sufficient to activate protective devices and can remain unnoticed for a considerable, possibly damaging, period of time. The most common areas causing faults are where cables enter stanchions and mast cabling exits to light fixtures.

        (3) **AC Shore Power Systems.** A problem can occur when vessel grounds are coupled to shore grounds through the ground conductor. Any impressed DC component on the AC will cause corrosion. When power is switched off, the ground is still connected if left permanently plugged in, allowing any stray currents to feed back through. Another major cause of problems is the transposition of neutral conductors and grounding conductors, which allow stray currents to pass through in polarized DC installations.

        (4) **Water Current Gradients.** DC potential gradients may exist in the water around a vessel. This will contribute to corrosion, and is caused by variations in salinity and temperature. If paint is chipped off under the bow, a circuit may be created with anodes or hull fittings in another part of the vessel with an area of water of differing potential. This can occur in small marinas with reduced tidal flows to flush out water heated during the day.

        (5) **AC Ground System Potentials.** Variations can exist within potentials of grounding connections at various shore power supply locations within a marina complex.

    b. **Corrective Measures.** Install a DC leakage test unit so the hull can be monitored continuously, with any problems identified and rectified promptly. This is standard practice on commercial ships.

        (1) **DC Leakage Currents.** All connections, and ideally there will be none in wet areas, should be in proper water-resistant junction boxes. They should be placed in dry locations away from any metalwork liable to conduct any leakages to the hull. Install a monitor on steel and alloy vessels.

(2) **DC Ground Faults.** Ensure that all cables are double insulated. Check that all transits through metal bulkheads or stanchions have additional mechanical protection or grommets to prevent grounding.

(3) **AC Shore Power.** Steel and alloy vessels should have an isolation transformer on the shore power supply. This electrically separates the vessel from the shore supply, breaking the circuit. A separate vessel ground is used, connected in a grounded neutral configuration. Another measure is to install a galvanic isolator to prevent leakages of DC stray currents. See the section on galvanic isolators.

(4) **AC Shore Power Polarity Tester.** A polarity indicator will indicate transposed neutrals and grounds. On some switchboards a switch is installed to change over to correct polarity. Do not connect shore power until you have corrected the problem.

8.9 **Steel/Alloy Hull Leakage Inspections.** It is always difficult to maintain a hull above electrical ground. Moisture and oil residues mixed with salt lower the isolation level. It is important to regularly examine isolation values to ensure that isolation is maintained.

a. **Passive Insulation Test.** This test simply measures the level of resistance between the hull and both positive and negative. A multimeter set on the ohms scale is required. Perform the test as follows:

(1) Turn main power switch off.

(2) Turn on all switches and circuit breakers to ensure that all electrical circuits are at equal potential or are connected in one grid.

(3) Connect the positive meter lead to the positive conductor, and the negative to the hull. Observe and record the reading.

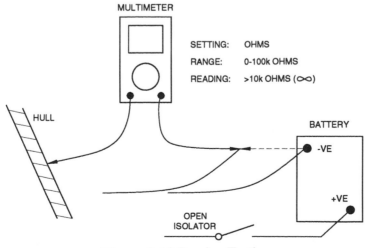

Figure 8-10 Passive Testing

(4) Connect the positive meter lead to the negative conductor, and the negative to the hull. Observe and record the reading.

b. Passive Test Results. The test results can be interpreted as follows:

(1) 10k ohms or above indicates that isolation above the hull is acceptable.

(2) A reading in the range of 1k ohm to 10k ohms indicates that there is leakage, and that isolation is degraded. While not directly shorted to hull, leakage can be through moisture or a similar cause. With meter connected, systematically switch off each circuit to localize the fault area and rectify the problem. A common area is the starter motor connections.

(3) A reading less than 1k ohm indicates a serious leakage problem which must be promptly rectified or serious hull damage can result.

c. Voltage Insulation Test. While a passive meter test can show that all is satisfactory, the voltage of a system in use can break down resistances and cause leakage. To properly test the electrical isolation, a voltage test should be performed. With 220/115-volt power systems, this test must be performed using a 500-volt insulation tester. All results must exceed 1 megOhm. This is not recommended for low voltage installations as the insulation values of cables are not rated this high. A low voltage DC tester set at 100-volt DC should be used. Another easier test is as follows:

(1) Turn on all electrical circuits so that all are "alive."

(2) With a digital multimeter set on DC volts, place the positive probe on the supply positive. Place the negative probe on the hull.

(3) There should be no voltage at all. If there is a small voltage, a leakage may exist on the negative.

(4) With a digital multimeter set on the DC volts, place the negative probe on the supply negative. Place the positive probe on the hull.

(5) There should be no voltage at all. If there is a small voltage, a leakage may exist on the positive.

(6) Systematically turn off electrical circuits to verify that there is a leakage, and that with all power off the difference in potential is zero.

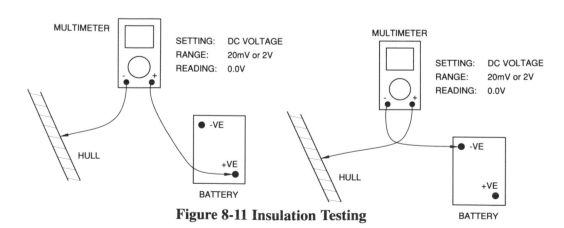

Figure 8-11 Insulation Testing

8.10   Corrosion Protection Recommendations. The following basic recommendations should be implemented. I have encountered an increasing number of corrosion problems with steel vessels using copper-based antifouling paint. These antifoulings rapidly degrade the anodes performance, and in most cases I have found corrosion and pitting where the paintwork has been chipped off the hull. Shaft struts (brackets) and propellers have suffered damage also. Wherever possible, use copper-free antifouling. When in doubt, you should always consult a corrosion specialist.

a.   **Fiberglass/Wood Vessels.** As a general guide, the following measures should be taken and used in conjunction with the previous chapters:

(1)   **Bonding.** Bonding straps should be installed above the bilge line and connect all metallic items to be protected. All connections must be made with at least a 4-mm^2 conductor and be bolted to the main bonding connection. Do not bond bronze or other through-hull (skin) fittings as they are normally isolated since their connecting hoses and pipes are PVC or rubber and offer no conductive path and therefore no circuit. When the vessel is hauled, use a multimeter set on the 1-ohm range and check the resistance between anode and propeller; the maximum reading should be 0.2 ohm.

(2)   **Negative Cables.** Install a separate negative return from the alternator to the battery and bond the starter battery negative as close as possible to the starter, if not to one of the holding bolts itself. This reduces the stray currents floating around and though the engine block.

(3)   **Lightning Bonding.** Do not bond the lightning conductor to the anode bonding system. As explained earlier, this is a separate circuit with a separate function.

b.   **Steel Vessels.** Steel vessels present the most concerns about corrosion; the following precautions must be observed to reduce galvanic and electrolytic corrosion. Good protection on steel is a function of a well planned and applied painting program. A paint system should consist of 3-5 coatings of an epoxy paint, followed by a suitable antifouling. Use the technical services of the paint manufacturer—they all give assistance—and bond as follows:

(1)   **Bonding.** Although it is common to simply bond to the hull, I would advise to install a bolt next to each anode and to have all anodes bonded internally by a large, insulated conductor of 11 AWG (4 mm^2) and not to the nearest hull point. Crimp and solder all connections to ensure that no resistance is introduced into the circuit. It is essential that no difference in potential arises between any part of the bonding system. This method ensures that bonding is direct to the anode area. When the vessel is hauled, use a multimeter set on the 1-ohm range and check the resistance between anode and propeller. The maximum reading should be 0.2 ohm. The reading between the anode and the hull should be zero.

(2)   **Keel Anodes.** If a steel keel is fitted, an anode may be installed on each side. Follow the calculated wetted surface guidelines (Chapter 8.4) so that overprotection does not occur.

(3)   **Negative Cables.** Install isolated negative return starter motors, alternators, and monitoring gauge sensor units. These ensure that no electrical items are connected to the block. Use double-pole, engine starter isolators. If you do not have a fully isolated engine, make sure that the engine is isolated above hull, with insulated coupling and engine mounts.

(4)   **AC Ground.** The AC ground can be bonded directly to hull. This normally has no voltage flowing in it, except under fault conditions. It is essential that the main hull be part of the AC ground because in a fault condition the hull could become partially live, up to rated voltage. This will not cause premature corrosion of anodes. Connect the AC ground to the same point as other grounds. See notes on galvanic isolators (Chapter 8.6)

(5)   **Isolation Transformers.** Install an isolation transformer on the shore power supply. This is probably the single greatest protective measure.

(6)   **Vessel Interaction.** Avoid mooring adjacent to any copper sheathed or aluminum vessels. Do not use steel cables to tie up to shore.

c.   **Aluminum Vessels.** Aluminum hulls have different requirements from steel vessels, and it is essential that they be correctly protected. Unlike steel vessels, an overprotected aluminum hull doesn't simply lose paint, it is eaten away by a caustic attack. The recommendations for steel hulls are also valid for the electrical systems on an aluminum vessel.

(1)   **Material Compatibility.** Insulate or use compatible through-hull fittings. In fact, insulate any equipment made of metals above aluminum on the metal nobility scale (Table 8-1). Avoid bronze fittings if at all possible. I have come across some who are using aluminum and plastic fittings, which resolves many problems.

(2)   **Vessel Interaction.** Avoid mooring next to steel or copper sheathed vessels for extended periods. The interaction can be very severe with aluminum.

d.   **Ferro-Cement Vessels.** Forget the cement component of ferro-cement vessels and treat them as steel vessels. Make sure bronze through-hull fittings are isolated from reinforcing mesh.

8.11 **Corrosion Leakage Monitoring.** Leakage to the hull on steel and alloy vessels can be monitored using suitable systems.

    a. **System Monitors.** Mastervolt have a small AC and DC light indicator and there is a French device that has an LED-based monitor. This system monitors in a range of approximately 0.2-1 milliamps. Additionally, if a direct short occurs to the hull, a flashing LED indicates the condition. One unit uses a row of LED indicators to indicate the leakage level.

    b. **Portable Equipment.** EC Smith in the U.K. sells both a portable digital and an analog corrosion meter. These involve the use of a reference cell dropped into the water around the hull and a clamp to the steel hull. The potential differences can then be found. I have used similar devices on oil rigs and found them very useful.

8.12 **Corrosion System Maintenance.** The following maintenance procedures should be undertaken every 6 to 12 months.

    a. **In-Water Examinations.** Perform the following basic examinations:

        (1) **Main Anodes.** Do an underwater check of anodes at 6 months to determine if any increases in corrosion rates are present. If rates increase, it may be because the vessel has moved into warmer or more saline conditions. Otherwise, examine the electrical system for hull leakages.

        (2) **Shaft Anodes.** Check that shaft anode is still on the shaft. Check the anode corrosion rates.

    b. **Haul-out Examinations.** Perform the following examinations when the boat is hauled:

        (1) **Anode Replacement.** Replace depleted anodes if reduced more than 80%, and check connections. Check that the replacement zincs are of the correct grade and size. Check and replace studs if they are deteriorated.

        (2) **Shaft Anodes.** Replace anode if necessary. Check the mating surface of the shaft anode and check that it is correctly located.

        (3) **Bonding Connections.** Inspect the bonding system connections to see that they are sound and clean. If not, remove and clean them so that contact resistance is zero.

        (4) **Check Bonding System Resistances.** Check bonding resistances between the propeller and anodes and the anodes and hull.

Table 8-5 Corrosion System Troubleshooting

Symptom	Probable and Possible Faults
Anode corroded 80% or more	Replace anode
Rapid anode corrosion	Hull electrical leakages Increased water salinity Increased water temperature Degraded bonding system Copper based antifoulants Moored adjacent to aluminum or copper sheathed vessel Marina electrical problems No isolation transformer on boat Moored over metallic debris on seabed
Paint stripping off keel and hull	Hull overprotected (too many anodes) Severe electrical leakage to hull Copper based antifoulants
Paint stripping around anode studs	Anode stud connection defective
No anode corrosion	Anode hull connections defective Bonding wires broken Impure zinc anode
Propeller and shaft pitted	Inadequate protection Degraded bonding system Shaft anode missing Shaft anode incorrectly fitted Shaft anode fitted over antifouled shaft Copper based antifoulants Cavitation corrosion Improper grade of stainless

Lighting Systems

9.0   Lighting Systems. Yacht lighting systems are one of the most frustrating, as the selection of suitable lights is always a problem. Aesthetic considerations are of obvious importance, but there are other facts to consider.

a.   **Illumination Area.** The size of the area to be illuminated is one important consideration. Where specific areas are to be illuminated, the factors to consider are as follows:

(1)   **Spot Lighting.** Spot lighting in areas such as bunk reading lights and spreader lights require special attention. Projected light applications require a reflector or a special lamp. Factors such as beam power and beam angle are important.

(2)   **Large Area Illumination.** When lighting deck areas or the saloon, consider beam angles and light output power.

b.   **Illumination Level.** The level of light reaching the working areas on deck or the overall light level below must be sufficient to perform tasks safely. There are a number of factors that must be considered:

(1)   **Background Lighting.** This is generally low power lighting and uses interior surfaces and upholstery to reflect light for unobtrusive and shadowless illumination.

(2)   **Low Level Lighting.** This is localized illumination that does not require levels sufficient to perform work. Typical are night lighting, courtesy lights, and general saloon lighting.

(3)   **High Level Lighting.** This lighting is used in any application where safety or ease of work is important. It includes deck spotlights, hand-held spots, saloon lights, bunk lights, engine space lights and targa/transom lights, to name a few. Ideally, such lights should give shadowless illumination without excessive glare.

c.   **Light Colors.** The color-rendering properties of a light source play a significant part in effective lighting. Using lights with the right color-rendering properties can significantly alter the apparent richness of woods, for instance.

(1)   **Warm or Soft Colors.** Fluorescent tubes are generally warm soft. The newer, low energy lights that use Philips and Thorn tubes have a softer light that strikes a balance between good illumination levels and good color rendering.

(2)   **Cold or Hard Colors.** Halogen lamps and some fluorescent tubes have a cold, hard, intense white light.

d. **Power Consumption.** Electrical power consumption is the very first factor to consider. Compare the main light types and make your decision based on the most satisfactory light for a given power consumption. To date, low energy tube lights have the best light-per-amp ratio and I have had great success with them.

9.1 **Internal Lights.** Lighting systems for cabins may consist of a number of light types. Different lights may be used for different functions, and one of the main criteria is gaining maximum light output for a given power consumption. There are four main types available. Before deciding on lights for below, consider light reflectivity.

a. **Reflectivity.** The level of brightness and the contrast with background must be considered. In a teak-lined cabin, reflected light will be minimal, while a cabin with painted surfaces or light timbers will increase overall illumination levels. I have seen some beautiful wood-lined cabins with large numbers of lights fitted in the headliner and additional corner spots. Yet even with many lights on, they are still gloomy with low light levels. Interior schemes that are efficient mean fewer lights with less cable, and much lower power consumption for a given light level. Reflectivity is usually expressed as a percentage. The following range of interiors are typical:

Woods

- Maple and birch: 60%
- Light oak: 40%
- Walnut and teak: 15-20%

Paints

- White and light cream: 70-80%
- Pale yellow: 55-65%
- Sky blue/pale grey: 40-45%
- Beige: 25-35%

b. **Fluorescent Lights.** Fluorescent lights, now one of the most common lights, do have drawbacks that must be considered. DC tubes have a built-in inverter that raises the voltage to a higher AC value. Their elongated shape provides a good lumen/watt ratio at a relatively low power consumption—80% less than incandescent for the same light output. Typical output is 65-90 lumens. They also withstand vibration and shock well, and their working life is 5-8 times that of incandescent lights. Components are as follows:

(1) **Inverter.** The inverter in low voltage DC fittings is generally the main cause of failure. In most cheaper light fittings, the quality of the electronics is poor. They also fail in relatively small overvoltage conditions such as when charging voltages rise to 14 volts. Always install fluorescent lights with a voltage input up to 15 volts.

152

(2) **Tube**. The fluorescent tubes for household use function quite satisfactorily with good quality inverters. If the electronics are of poor quality, the tubes will show blackening in a short period. Tube output varies with temperature. Peak output is normally at 25°C. If hotter or colder, output is reduced.

(3) **Radio Frequency Interference.** Fluorescent lights have a notorious reputation for radio frequency interference. This is due to the quality of the inverter electronics. High quality inverters, such as those from Aquasignal, are suitably suppressed to international standards. Additionally, fluorescent units with high quality inverters are far more reliable.

c. **Incandescent Lights.** Incandescent lights are the oldest and most common light types. The following factors should be considered:

(1) **Power Consumption.** When switched on, power consumption can be 15 times normal (hot) power consumption. The basis of the incandescent lamp is the heating of a filament, therefore much of the energy is dissipated as heat.

(2) **Life Expectancy.** Incandescents are power hungry for the available light output, are subject to damage by vibration and overvoltage, and suffer rapid filament degradation.

(3) **Voltage Limitations.** Overvoltage conditions significantly reduce incandescent lamp life expectancies. Operating at lower voltages extends service life, but seriously reduces light output. For every 5% voltage drop, light reduces by 20%. Many of you are familiar with that yellow glow as the battery voltage decreases. The secret to operating incandescents, especially navigation lamps, is to minimize voltage drop.

d. **Halogen Lighting.** Halogen lighting is being seen in many vessels due to its higher light output, typically around 20 lumens. Halogen lights have relatively long service lives. Certain provisos have to be kept in mind:

(1) **Life Expectancy.** Halogen lights belong to the incandescent light category, and are designed for use in commercial installations on a stable 12/24-volt AC power source. When used in DC installations, their life expectancy is significantly reduced; the higher voltages generated during battery charging also reduce life.

(2) **Voltage Limitations.** Vibration resistance is relatively poor. Resistance to overvoltage situations is also poor. Normally, a halogen lamp is operated in commercial applications with a very stable 12-volt AC supply, with maximum life being at around 11.8 volts. Operating on DC, with charging voltages up to 14.5 volts, bulb life can be seriously reduced.

(3) **Installation.** Under no circumstances must a halogen bulb be touched as salts and impurities from the fingers will degrade the pure silicon glass and shorten life. The bulbs are also subject to some degradation through interaction with salt air. Allowances must be made for the high temperatures these lights generate—up to 700°C in normal operation. Most halogen fittings have high-temperature wiring, but good ventilation is required to prevent lamp holder or wire from reaching a maximum of 250°C.

e. **Low Energy Lighting.** Low energy lights operate on a principle similar to fluorescent lights and give a very high output for a relatively small power draw. These are now my favorite lights. For cruising, they are incomparable. Leisure Lights in the U.K. makes a light with an output only marginally less than a 100-watt household bulb but with a power consumption of just 16 watts. Most vessels I have installed these on now run just one light for the entire saloon.

(1) **Life Expectancy.** Life expectancy is greater than standard fluorescent lights.

(2) **Voltage Limitations.** Similar to other lights, they are intolerant to overvoltage conditions. Fortunately, some manufacturers have designed power supplies on their lights that accept up to 17 volts, which solves this problem.

f. **Red Night Lights.** It can take up to 45 minutes for normal night vision to return if the eye is subjected to a white light, which is why red night lights are used. Typical locations for night lighting are at the helm, by the navigation station, in the pilot house, at the galley (for late night hot drinks), and in the head. There are a number of ways to install red lighting:

(1) **Separate Fitting.** Companies such as Aquasignal manufacture incandescent fittings with a red diffuser. These can be mounted adjacent to a normal fitting.

(2) **Dual Tube/Lamp Fittings.** These light fittings have a painted red tube or lamp on a separate switch. This offers a single fitting with a dual function.

(3) **Red Navigation Lights.** I use a small Hella or Aquasignal port navigation light—one at the steering position, and one in the galley—with a minimum-rated lamp of around 5 watts; a large light level is not required. The color-rendering properties of the light are ideally suited to night vision. Make sure that the steering position light faces down toward the deck and cannot be seen or construed as a port navigation light by anyone outside the vessel. If you have a coach house, a red-and-white unit can be mounted and switched locally.

g.   **Courtesy Lights.** Courtesy lighting in the cockpit and transom areas is very useful, but many of the lights available are of very poor quality and quickly degrade:

    (1)   **Manufactured Fittings.** While useful in cockpits, courtesy lights do tend to leak and should only be installed where they back into lockers, not below decks. On transoms, especially stepped ones, they are very useful for night boarding. These lights use a festoon-type bulb. Vibration frequently causes a poor contact at lamp ends.

    (2)   **Navigation Lights.** I recommend fitting a couple of stern navigation lights facing downwards off the stern pulpit (pushpit) or the stern arch. They provide satisfactory low level illumination, are weatherproof, and are a valuable safety feature when retrieving the dinghy or a crewmember.

h.   **Safety and Working Lights.**

    (1)   **Targa/Stern Arch Lights.** Lighting fixtures installed under arches are an essential aid when retrieving crewmembers or the dinghy or when boarding at night.

    (2)   **Anchor Light.** Because anchor problems are common, foredeck spotlights do not illuminate properly, and it is difficult to hold a flashlight while anchoring, I have devised my own solution. A small, white navigation light is installed face down under the step or seat at the bow pulpit. If there is no step, mount it directly under the bicolor or another convenient location. I also installed another white navigation light on the center rail of the pulpit facing down and inwards to illuminate the anchor well. These lights, switched from the cockpit, are not too bright, but they work and are in the right area.

9.2   Lamp Bases. Lamp bases are extremely varied and designations are often confusing. The illustrations below show many of the more common lamp bases and their designations.

    a.   **Halogen Lamps.** Lamp socket types include E14, E27, E40, R75, BA95, B15D, G4, G6, and 35.

    b.   **Incandescent Lamps.** Lamp socket types include E14, E27, E40, B15D, B22D, P28, Candle base E12, Medium base E26.

    c.   **Fluorescent Lamps.** Lamp socket types include G5, G13, G23, G24, and G32.

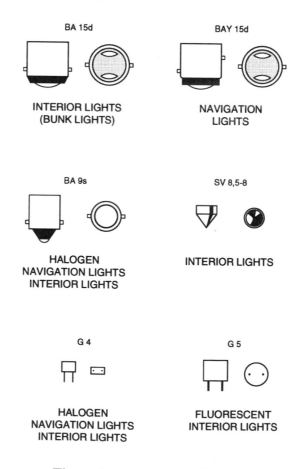

Figure 9-1 Lamp Base Chart

9.3 **External Lights.** External lights are generally confined to spreader and foredeck spot lighting. Always use the best quality available because they are subject to all kinds of weather and you always need them under difficult conditions.

    a.   **Spotlights**. Spotlights, especially on the foredeck, are very useful, but fittings must be of high quality if they are to survive. Lights are as follows:

        (1)   **Foredeck.** Light output must be sufficient to ensure good illumination at deck level, and typically this is the anchor windlass area. When there is a problem with anchors, you really need good illumination. Use sealed beam units with 35-50 watt ratings, such as those from Aquasignal.

        (2)   **Hand Spot.** Handheld spots are an essential item on board, but some are average and some are good. Spotlights should have a clearly defined beam pattern without scattering at the sides. The illustration below shows the different beam distributions and light ranges for Optronics Blue Eye spotlights. The ranges shown are for clear conditions and a reflective target. If you want increased power for less-than-ideal conditions choose a higher candlepower rating. Always select a light with a switch for signaling.

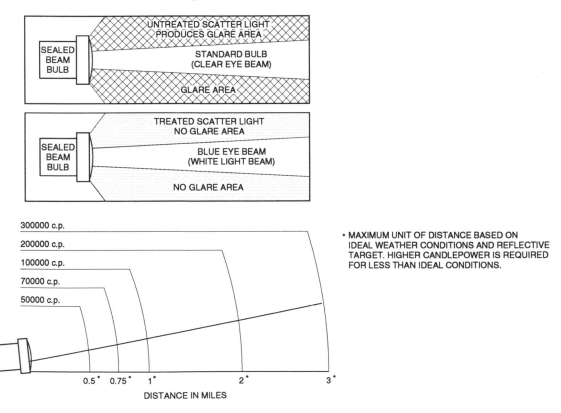

Figure 9-2 Spotlight Characteristics

157

b. **Spreader Lights.** Spreader lights are invaluable safety equipment. When severe problems are encountered on deck, good lighting allows for safer, faster work, and this reduces deck exposure time. The following must be considered when installing spreader lights:

(1) **Illumination Levels.** Lights are designed to facilitate on-deck safety without excessive shadows. Do not use navigation lights under the spreaders; their deck level illumination is generally very poor. Use high quality, sealed beam halogen lights rated around 35-50 watts.

(2) **Construction.** Use fittings made of plastic to avoid corrosion. Stainless units are prone to shake apart at the spot welds.

(3) **Installation.** Spreader lights are exposed to weather and subject to severe vibration. It is essential that lights are mounted securely in a location where these factors are minimized. Cables should be of sufficient length and connections should be wrapped with self-amalgamating tape. Make sure that you can change burned-out lamps.

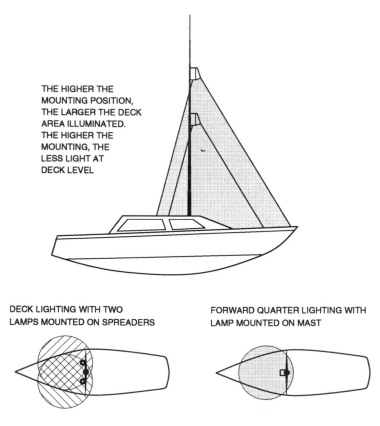

Figure 9-3 Mast Lighting Arrangements

9.4 **Navigation Lights.** Navigation lights are of the utmost importance, both for safety and for legal, rules-of-the-road reasons. It is amazing how few sailing vessels display the correct lights. My personal survey shows that only about 40% of vessels have the correct lights displayed. It is not sufficient to simply say you have lights installed and turned on, they must be mounted at the correct locations. It is all very well to blame merchant vessels for running over pleasure craft, but if your correct lights are missing, nobody will be able to identify your vessel and status.

a. **Legal Requirements.** All vessels are required by the International Regulations for Preventing Collisions at Sea to display the correct lights. Failure to comply may void insurance policies in the event of a collision:

(1) **Navigation Lights.** Lights should be displayed in accordance with the provisions in Part C, Lights and Shapes.

(2) **Lights.** Lights should be of an approved type and conform with the provisions of Annex I with respect to positioning and technical details of lights and shapes.

b. **Tricolor. (Under Sail Only).** For yachts under 20 meters, the combination port, starboard, and stern light mounted at the masthead is the best solution. Because only one lamp is burning, it does not consume too much battery power. It must not be used under power, as is commonly done, or in conjunction with any other light.

c. **Anchor.** The anchor light is an all-round white light. It should not be masked at any point. See Annex I, 9(b) regarding horizontal sectors. Vessels should install a combination tricolor anchor light for simplicity. Always use it if you are anchored where traffic is possible. If you do not and a vessel collides with or sinks you, it's your fault.

d. **Port and Starboard Lights. (Sidelights).** The port light (red), and the starboard light (green) must display an unbroken light over an arc of $112\frac{1}{2}°$, from dead ahead to $22\frac{1}{2}°$ abaft the beam. On a vessel under 20 meters, the light can be combined into a bicolor fitting. On many yachts, these lights are installed on the bow pulpit, but there is often a section of the pulpit that partially obscures the light. Ensure that the light is visible over the prescribed arc, otherwise you are displaying a light that is technically illegal.

e. **Stern Light.** This is a white light placed at or near the stern, preferably on the centerline. Its arc of visibility must total $135°$, from dead astern to $67\frac{1}{2}°$ each side:

(1) **Display.** Stern lights must always be displayed when vessel is under power, along with the sidelights and masthead light.

(2) **Mounting.** Do not mount stern lights on angled transoms without mounting plates that ensure they are vertical. Lights angled skywards are very difficult to see and aren't legal.

f.   **Masthead Light. (Steaming Light).** This is a white light that must be visible over an unbroken arc of 225°, from dead ahead to 22½° abaft the beam on each side. The light must be fixed on the centerline of the vessel, typically on the top of mast. There are also vertical mounting requirements for the masthead light. See Annex I.2, Vertical Positioning and Spacing of Lights:

(1)   **Vessels 12 meters LOA or less.** A minimum of 1 meter above the sidelights.

(2)   **Vessels 12 to 20 meters LOA.** A minimum of 2.5 meters above the gunwale.

STARBOARD LAMP	112.5 DEGREES
PORT LAMP	112.5 DEGREES
MASTHEAD LAMP	225 DEGREES
STERN LAMP	135 DEGREES
ANCHOR LAMP	360 DEGREES

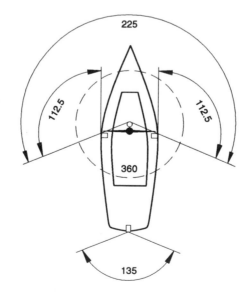

Figure 9-4 Navigation Lighting Plan

9.5   **Navigation Light Technical Requirements.** Regarding (chromacity) color, these are covered in Annex I.7: Color specification of lights and Annex I.8: Light intensities.

    a.   **Color.** Color or chromacity are defined by international collision regulations. By purchasing approved light fittings, you know that they meet the requirements.

    b.   **Lamp Ratings.** Lamp ratings are generally given by the manufacturers and are designed to give the required range and luminosity for which the light is granted approval. Do not increase the lamp rating to increase the brightness or decrease it to save power. If you do alter the lamps and have an accident, your insurance may be invalidated and you could be sued for damages because technically you were not displaying approved navigation lights:

        (1)   **Sockets.** Special sockets are used to ensure that filaments are correctly aligned to the lens and horizontal shades systems.

        (2)   **Light Outputs.** Light output and wattage are designed for a high lumen-per-watt ratio.

        (3)   **Light Consistency.** The lights are designed to emit an even output through a 360° azimuth.

    c.   **Visibility.** The required minimum range of visibilities are as follows:

        (1)   **Stern Light.**   <12m = 2 NM,   12-20m = 2 NM.

        (2)   **Sidelights.**   <12m = 1 NM,   12-20m = 2 NM.

        (3)   **Masthead Light.**   <12m = 2 NM,   12-20m = 3 NM.

        (4)   **Tricolor Light.**   <12m = 2 NM,   12-20m = 2 NM.

        (5)   **Anchor Light.**   <12m = 2 NM,   12-20m = 2 NM.

    d.   **Approvals.** Navigation lights should all be approved. Most manufacturers issue a certificate with each fitting:

        (1)   **National Approvals.** It is important to note that some fittings are only approved by a national port or marine authority and may be illegal in other countries.

        (2)   **Approval Certificates.** Always keep the numbered approval certificate with your vessel's files in case of litigation.

    e.   **Maintenance.** Check lights regularly. Any defects may cause failure or be illegal. Check the following:

        (1)   **Moisture.** Check the light's interior for moisture that can degrade lamp contacts or cause a short circuit.

        (2)   **Diffuser.** Check the light diffusers for cracks or crazing that will alter the light's characteristics.

DC Electrical Equipment

10.0   Electrical Standards and Ratings. For reliability and performance, the major requirements of any vessel equipment, it is essential to understand the various approvals attached to equipment. It must be noted that approvals are really only valid if the equipment is installed or used in the prescribed application. If not, the approval and warranty may be invalid. Approvals are as follows:

a.   **Class Society Approvals**. Type approvals are given to a wide range of equipment. Essentially it indicates that the designated equipment has been exhaustively tested and approved for shipboard installation. Most equipment is approved for large commercial installations; however, the marks will be seen on circuit breakers, fuses, and other equipment on smaller vessels.

b.   **National Approvals.** Most countries have national testing bodies which frequently test and approve equipment for installation. The various approvals for a range of countries is often seen on equipment.

c.   **UL Standard.** (Underwriters Laboratory). This body is an independent, non-profit American organization which publishes product-safety standards and specifications, as well as tests and approves a wide range of equipment. UL approvals are considered the benchmark standard, and equipment without approval is generally deemed substandard.

d.   **CSA Standard.** This is the mark of the Canadian Standards Association. In many cases, electrical equipment available in Canada must bear the mark by law.

e.   **VDE Standard.** (Verband Deutscher Electrotechniker) This is the mark of the German Electrical Technicians Association. While the law doesn't require the approval to be carried, if equipment bearing the mark causes a fatality or fire, the manufacturers are exempted from prosecution. VDE standards are regarded as the desired safety standards.

10.1   Refrigeration Systems. Iceboxes and cool boxes are rapidly being replaced by both refrigerators and freezers. Cruising in comfort entails a well–found galley, and an occasional steak on the barbecue. Freezer capacity to store a good catch is also a desirable element of a comfortable cruising lifestyle. A refrigeration system must be properly installed and selected, and this chapter illustrates the basic principles of eutectic systems, the most common and practical on cruising vessels. I was fortunate enough to serve a number of times on some of the finest refrigerated cargo vessels afloat—MV Polar Uruguay and MV Polar Colombia. We carried bananas from Costa Rica, Honduras, Ecuador, and Colombia to the USA and Europe, Chilean apples and grapes to the U.K., Australian lamb to Iran and Syria, as well as frozen chicken and beef from Brazil and Uruguay to Iraq. On one trip from Morocco to Europe, we carried zucchinis and tomatoes, which in the event of a collision and fire would have created the world's biggest ratatouille. On cruising yachts, the decision is usually for one of two refrigeration systems, and the big question is, should they be electric or engine driven?

a.   **Electric Refrigeration.** The principal reason given for choosing electric systems is the intent to operate them off wind- and solar-energy sources. In practice, this is not entirely successful, and some engine charging is often necessary, at least every second day. The facts are as follows:

(1)   **Battery Demand.** Electric refrigeration systems are power hungry. No matter how many systems put forward attractive consumption figures (most are often optimistic), average usage is at least 50 amp-hours for a refrigerator, and around 100 amp-hours for freezers on a 50% duty cycle. On a Glacier Bay system, the quoted figures over 24 hours are a very economical 20.5 amp-hours and 39.5 amp-hours for refrigerator and freezer respectively.

(2)   **Battery Charging.** A far greater run time is required to restore battery capacity than for an equivalent engine driven system. You will definitely require a higher output alternator, and a fast-charging device is essential. The average vessel recharging time with electric systems is typically around one hour, morning and night. Remember that you have to replace 120% of the power used.

(3)   **Efficiency.** The majority of electric systems use hermetically sealed, Danfoss-type compressors. Glacier Bay uses reciprocating units. The reciprocating compressor system is far more efficient, more reliable, and robust. It is almost universally found on engine driven systems. An engine driven compressor applies a greater load to the engine, which along with an alternator and a fast-charge device, allows reasonably economical engine use instead of damaging, light load conditions. There is, however, a more intangible efficiency gain with an electric system because it keeps temperatures stable, so the actual run times to pull down temperatures are relatively small.

(4)   **Economics.** The engine driven system is generally more expensive to install, requires more engineering, pipework, etc. Engine maintenance is lower than simple battery charging duties because the run times have greater loads and are for considerably shorter periods. Electric systems are initially cheaper to buy and install, but they do require much greater battery capacity, and thousands can be spent on solar and wind systems, high output alternators, etc. Also, longer engine run times are often required when wind and sun do not deliver, generally costing more in maintenance and fuel.

b.   **Engine Driven Eutectic Systems.** The engine driven compressor is probably the most efficient and is able to pull down temperatures quickly. Selection factors are as follows:

(1)   **Economics.** Engine driven compressors make more economical use of the engine by imposing a substantial load, which reduces maintenance costs. If you have to run the engine for battery charging, it makes good sense to fully utilize the energy source. The extra load also gets the water hot if you have a calorifier.

(2)   **Dual Circuit Systems.** An engine driven system enables both refrigerator and freezer to run off the same refrigeration plant. There is a growing trend to incorporate engine driven compressors with small electric systems. The main refrigerator space can be pulled down initially and every second day using the engine compressor. The electric unit, sustained by alternative energy sources, can then maintain the temperature for a significantly increased period.

(3)   **Disadvantages.** The capital cost of installation is relatively high, as are the installation time and work involved. If an installation is not properly done, gas leakage problems are common.

10.2 **Refrigeration Principles.** The fundamental principle is that when a high-pressure liquid or gas expands, temperature reduces. A compressor pumps the refrigerant, normally Freon, around the system. The typical cycle of a system is as follows:

a. **Compression.** The compressor increases the refrigerant gas pressure, which becomes hot. The high–pressure, hot gas then passes through to the condenser.

b. **Condensation.** The condenser is a heat exchanger, either air cooled by natural convection or a fan, or by water passing through coils. The hot gas passes through the condenser, condenses into a hot liquid, and passes through to the expansion valve.

c. **Thermostatic Expansion Valve.** The liquid passes through the expansion valve, where the liquid is allowed to expand. This pressure reduction causes the liquid temperature to fall. The cold liquid then passes to the evaporator.

d. **Evaporator.** The cold liquid passes through to the evaporator cooling surfaces (or eutectic tanks). Heat within the refrigerator space is absorbed by the cold refrigerant, causing the air to cool. The absorption of the heat causes the refrigerant liquid to evaporate into a gas.

e. **Recycle.** The cold gas is suctioned back into the compressor to repeat the cycle.

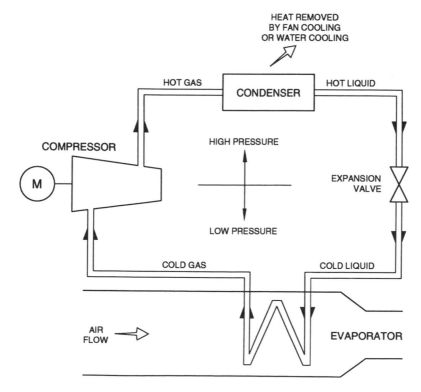

Figure 10-1 Basic Refrigeration Cycle

10.3   **Eutectic Refrigeration Systems.** This is the most common and efficient method of vessel refrigeration. The evaporator is replaced by a eutectic plate or tank. Operation is as follows:

    a.   **Eutectic Principles.** A eutectic system uses brine or a fluid that freezes at what is called eutectic temperature. Originally, brine solutions were used, but systems now have an ethylene glycol/water mixture or a similar solution. The mixture has a much lower freezing point than water. Once the mixture is frozen completely (the eutectic point) and refrigeration is removed, the tank will cool the refrigeration space as it gradually thaws out.

    b.   **Holdover Period.** The time that the space remains within required temperature ranges before refrigeration is required is called the holdover period. When specifying a system, the holdover time and the temperature required are critical to the size of the plates or tanks and the type of eutectic solution required. The typical eutectic system is based on the basic refrigeration system, but has a number of additional components.

    c.   **Engine Driven Compressors.** Most eutectic systems use an engine driven compressor. Compressors are always belt driven by the engine and the drive pulley has an electromagnetic clutch for operating the compressor. The compressors usually fall into two groups:

        (1)   **Swash Plate Compressors.** These are typified by automotive air-conditioning compressors, which are satisfactory where temperatures down to approximately -15°C are required. For most average cruising applications, these are suitable. These compressors are not really designed for eutectic refrigeration systems and although they work well, failure rates are higher than with reciprocating units.

        (2)   **Reciprocating Compressors.** Where refrigeration of seafood and other foodstuffs require long-term storage temperatures of -18°C, the more robust and suitable reciprocating compressors are required. If you are doing serious, long-term liveaboard cruising, then the reciprocating compressor offers greater reliability and efficiency.

    d.   **Lubrication.** The lubricants in refrigeration systems are miscible, wax-free oils. They do not degrade under low temperatures or high pressures. Lubricating oils are carried around the system with the refrigerant and eventually return back to the compressor sump. Only reciprocating compressors have an oil sump, swash plate units do not.

e. **Condensers.** In the majority of engine driven installations, water cooled condensers are used. The engine's salt water cooling pump usually supplies the same system. Other units have a fan cooled condenser where good ventilation ensures good performance.

f. **Pressure Switches.** Pressure switches have very important functions within a refrigeration system:

(1) **High Pressure Cutout.** The purpose of the high pressure cutout is to protect against high pressures caused by the loss of cooling water, a plugged condenser, or at worst, serious contamination of the refrigerator system with water and air. The cutout is usually wired in series with the clutch.

(2) **Low Pressure Cutout.** The low pressure switch monitors suction line pressure. The cutout operates when gas discharge from the evaporator is too low. A cutout indicates a low refrigerant charge.

g. **Receivers.** A receiver is essentially a pressure vessel which maintains the refrigerant in a liquid state before passing it through an expansion valve.

h. **Clutch Engine Interlocks.** Most electromagnetic clutches are operated from a dedicated circuit breaker on the main switch panel, giving protection to the clutch coil and cabling. It is common for the switch to be left on inadvertently, causing the batteries to flatten (typical current draw is around 3-4 amps). On some occasions, the operating coil can burn out. To prevent this, an interlock should be installed into the ignition system so that the clutch is de-energized when the engine is shut down. The recommended circuit is illustrated below.

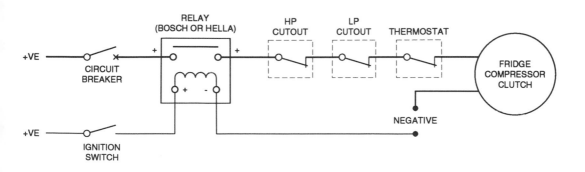

ELECTRIC FRIDGE COMPRESSOR INTERLOCK

Figure 10-2 Refrigeration Clutch Interlock

i. **Drier.** There will always be a small amount of water vapor remaining in a system regardless of purging and evacuation. Water causes ice to form at the expansion valve, creating either total blockage or bad operation. A drier installed in the liquid line between the receiver and expansion valve serves both as a filter and to remove water.

j. **Sight Glass.** A sight glass allows visual inspection of the liquid. Bubbles indicate low refrigerant levels. All indicators also incorporate a moisture indicator.

k. **Evaporator.** The evaporator absorbs heat. In eutectic systems, this is a coil within the tank. Where evaporators are simply plates or finned coils in the refrigerator, they must be ice free for good cooling.

l. **Expansion Valve.** The thermostatic expansion valve (TX valve) regulates the rate of refrigerant liquid flow into the evaporator in exact proportion to the rate of liquid leaving the evaporator. Flow is regulated in response to both pressure and temperature within the evaporator. A bulb and capillary, normally located on the suction line, are connected to the TX valve, which should be located as close as possible to the evaporator. Valves can normally be adjusted for optimum temperature.

10.4 Refrigeration System Installation. There are kits for refrigerator installations; however the best practice is to get a good refrigeration mechanic to install the system. There are a number of factors that can be controlled:

a. **Insulation.** If a refrigerator system is to be effective and reliable, it must be of sufficient size to meet the expected needs, and it must be well insulated.

(1) **Insulation Thickness.** Insulation thicknesses should be at least 4 inches. Inadequate insulation levels cause the majority of inefficiencies in vessel refrigerator systems. Install as much as you can.

(2) **Insulation Types.** Each insulating material has varying degrees of thermal conductivity. The ideal insulating material is urethane foam, followed closely by fiberglass (glassfibre wool) and then polystyrene foam. In many installations, insulation is done by foaming in place a two-part urethane mix. Great care must be taken, as failure to have the correct mix will produce inadequate results without the closed cell finish required for good insulation. Preformed urethane slabs are much more reliable and any voids can be filled with foam mix. The whole insulation block should be surrounded with plastic to prevent the ingress of moisture, and with a layer of reflective foil (such as that used in house construction) to minimize heat radiation. A two-layer system of foam slabs and foil is the ideal combination.

b. **Refrigeration Size.** Do not build refrigeration spaces larger than you need. Far too many oversized boxes remain half empty, which wastes energy and increases installation costs for a larger and more powerful system.

c. **Compressor Brackets**. The compressor mountings and brackets must be extremely robust to prevent vibration. Over engineer this to ensure that vibration will not fracture it.

d. **Compressor Drive Belts.** The compressor and engine drive pulleys must be correctly aligned to ensure the proper transfer of mechanical loads. Belts are usually dual pulley arrangements. Ensure that both belts are tensioned correctly.

e. **Refrigeration Components.** Ensure that all components are located in an easily accessible location. Adopt a modular approach like Glacier Bay's systems.

    (1) **Modular System.** All components should be installed using compression fittings to facilitate replacement, in particular the driers.

    (2) **Compressors.** Ensure that compressors all have good quality service valves so that they can be removed ashore easily for overhaul and repair without serious loss of refrigerant.

10.5   Electric Refrigeration Systems. Where there is sufficient charging capabilities or AC power, it is quite feasible to install electrically powered systems. There are two primary electrical configurations in use:

a.   **Electric.** There are a number of freestanding, or self-contained refrigerators in use. These are DC powered and have eutectic holdover plates. Insulation on the units is reasonable, but where installed, the surrounding area should be insulated further. A typical cycle is illustrated for the Italian Indel units, with which I have had great success on vessels needing only a small refrigerated capacity.

(1)   **Refrigerator Size.** Unit sizes tend to be in the range of 40 to 120 liters.

(2)   **Power Consumption.** The great fear has always been the power consumption factor: these units average around a 35 amp-hour capacity per day, depending on ambient temperatures, and frequency of opening. The Indel technology has been derived from the space shuttle systems. Other makes include Engel.

(3)   **Installation Factor.** Good ventilation must be provided to carry away heat from the compressor unit. Many units do not function properly as a result of this omission.

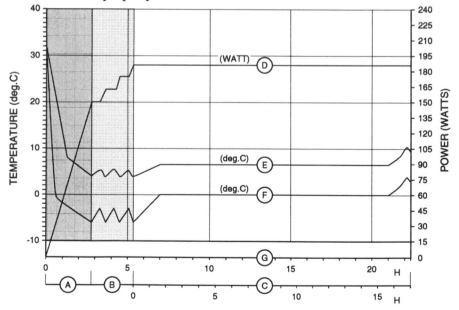

A = COLD BUILD-UP
B = CYCLING OPERATION
C = AUTONOMY IN HOURS
D = ABSORBED WATTS
E = COOL CELL TEMPERATURE
F = EVAPORATOR TEMPERATURE
G = TIME IN HOURS

AMBIENT TEMPERATURE AT 32 deg.C

Figure 10-3 Indel Electric Refrigerator Characteristic

b. **Electric Compressor Systems.** These are typified by the following:

(1) **DC Motor Direct-Driven Electric Systems.** Units like the Sea Frost DC5000 have a heavy-duty DC motor and compressor. Like all new systems, they use 134a gas and are very compact. Cooling is accomplished by using a water jacket to remove condenser, compressor, and motor heat.

(2) **DC Motor Belt-Driven Electric Systems.** These are typified by the Glacier Bay system. Belt tension must be regularly checked. This system also has a thermostat bypass system so that during engine runs, maximum pull-down is achieved. A similar circuit is shown below.

(3) **DC Motor Driven System Maintenance.** Every 3 months, check and clean the DC motor commutator, use a vacuum cleaner to remove dust, and wash brush-gear with CRC ElectraClean. Ensure that brushes move freely within brush holders. Tighten all electrical connections. Check anode and clean.

(4) **Hermetic Compressor Systems.** The Isotherm Magnum ASU unit is a hermetically sealed, precharged 134a system. Having installed a 4201 unit on my boat I am pleased with the performance. The units are easy to install and have water cooling, although it is only a low 1.5 liters a minute. An important innovation is the automatic compressor motor speed function. On detection of a higher voltage on the supply, from alternator or battery charger, the electronics module operates the motor at double speed, ensuring a quick pull-down of the holdover plate while power is available, and then reverts to economy mode. With a small refrigerator/freezer compartment, I opted for a freezer model with spillover plate and stainless butterfly vent to adjust cooling in the refrigerator space. Note that the seawater cooling system anode must be removed every 6 months and cleaned, or it will shed enough material to clog the pump suction lines. My own solution is to install a separate valve in the seawater inlet with a small 2-liter bottle similar to a car screen wash bottle. When shutting down for any period, simply flush the system with fresh water. In cold climates, remember to add antifreeze.

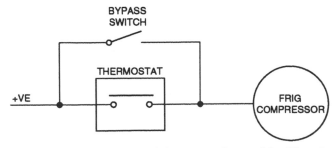

Figure 10-4 Electric Refrigerator Over-ride Circuit

c. **Energy Saving Measures.** There are a few energy saving, efficiency increasing measures that can be implemented:

(1) **Void Spaces.** Fill any empty spaces in the refrigerator compartment with blocks of foam or inflated empty wine-cask bladders. This will decrease the refrigerator space and reduce energy requirements.

(2) **Food Covers.** If all frozen goods are placed at the bottom of the compartment, place a mat over the food so that cold air is retained within the food below the mat.

(3) **Battery Voltages.** Ensure that battery voltage levels are maintained. Low battery levels will cause inefficient compressor operation. Do not let the battery level sink to the normal minimum level of 10.5 volts. It takes far more energy and engine running time to charge a nearly flat battery than one that is half charged.

(4) **Ventilation.** See that the compressor unit is well ventilated. Installing a small solar fan will ensure positive ventilation.

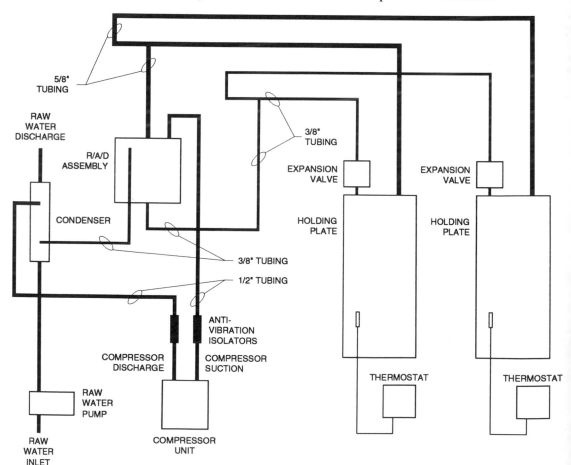

Figure 10-5 Glacier Bay Refrigerator System

d. **Chilled Air Systems.** These innovative systems, marketed by Glacier Bay, are called Frostmaster Blast Chiller systems. I have worked with similar systems in commercial shipping, and find them very efficient, with high heat transfer. The systems are relatively cheap and easy to install. The system available uses 100-volts AC so an inverter, generator, or shore power is required. For cruisers, they are probably better suited to the larger yachts. The quoted power consumption is 2.1 amps, and has a similar daily average to holding plate systems.

e. **Refrigerants.** Freon 12 (R12) and R22 have been the most commonly used gases in marine refrigeration systems. Unfortunately Freon 12 and 22 are harmful to the ozone layer, and like all CFC gases will be replaced under the Montreal Protocol. HFC-134a is becoming the standard system gas replacement. Auto air conditioning systems are all using the same gas. All the major manufacturers, including Technautics, Glacier Bay, Sea Frost, Grunert, and Isotherm offer 134a systems.

    (1) **Recovery and Servicing.** Many countries now require all servicing and recovery of CFCs to be done by suitably qualified and licensed persons. With R12 systems, many cruisers carried spare gas to recharge systems; however, in most countries doing this will violate what are normally very stringent environmental protection laws, resulting in very large fines. It is suggested that you convert your system to 134a prior to any long voyage.

    (2) **Spares.** Because many countries still have limited service capabilities and suitable parts and gas supplies, you should carry appropriate refrigerant oil, gas, dryers, and an uncontaminated charge manifold/gauge set.

f. **Refrigeration Updates.** New systems are constantly appearing, as well as advice on getting the most out of your system.

    (1) **Electric Fan Compressor Cooling.** Fan kits are being marketed that can be retrofitted. These will improve heat transfer from air-cooled compressor units.

    (2) **Water Cooling.** Isotherm has developed an innovative new system, called the self-pumping (SP) cooling system. A special integrated condenser and through-hull fitting have been developed that replace the galley sink fitting. The movement of the vessel causes water to "pump" in and out and remove waste heat. This is a great idea because pumps and fans are eliminated with far greater efficiency in heat transfer.

    (3) **Box Cooling.** Another useful idea is to install a small fan unit in the box. (I used a 3-inch Attwood unit.) This should be connected into either the DC compressor circuit or a separate switch. This will enable more rapid displacement of warm air within foodstuffs, and more rapid cooling.

10.6   Refrigeration System Troubleshooting. There are very few cruising yachts around that carry vacuum pumps, bottles of refrigerant, gauge sets, and appropriate spare parts. I used to work as a refrigeration mechanic repairing shipping container systems, where all repairs were done in filtered clean areas. It is highly unlikely that conditions will be suitable for you to properly overhaul and repair compressors. The first way to avoid problems is have the system properly installed in the first place. If after checking the basics you are unable to rectify the problems, call a reputable serviceman. I do not recommend that you dismantle and check compressors, or purge and recharge a system, because you are more likely to do further damage. The Glacier Bay systems make user servicing reasonably easy. This is a part of their systems design philosophy, and should be a primary purchase factor.

a.   **Refrigerant Loss.** Refrigerant loss is the most common fault. It causes a gradual reduction in cooling efficiency, eventually trips the low pressure cutout (if fitted), and the system fails. Low refrigerant levels can be observed in the sight glass; bubbles will be seen. An empty sight glass indicates no refrigerant at all. If all the gas has escaped, after the leak has been located, the system must be purged of air and moisture before being recharged. Normally, you should get a qualified and reputable refrigeration mechanic to do this.

b.   **Leak Detection.** Leak detection is carried out by pressurizing the system and checking all possible leakage locations at joints and fittings. Do not use a torch with HFC-134a refrigerants.

(1)   **Halide Torch.** The most common test requires the use of a halide torch. Air is drawn to the flame through a sampling tube. Small gas leakages will give the flame a faint green discoloration, while large leaks will be bright green.

(2)   **Soapy Water.** A simple method is to apply soapy water, generally dishwashing liquid, to all piping joints with the system running. If a pressurized leak is in the joint, a bubble will form.

c.   **Reduced Holdover Times.** This is by far the most common problem. Causes are as follows:

(1)   **Warm Foodstuffs.** A refrigerator or freezer system pulled down to the required temperature and then loaded with unfrozen food or warm drinks will not remain cold for as long as a system where the contents are pre-cooled.

(2)   **Climate Change.** More often than not, the system works well in a temperate climate, but the first extended cruise to tropical waters results in a dramatic reduction in apparent efficiency. A liveaboard opens the refrigerator sparingly, while the people new to the liveaboard lifestyle are probably opening it far more than is necessary and far more than they did on a normal weekend cruise. Keep access to a minimum.

(3)   **Mechanical Causes.** Engine drive belts are not retensioned. Belt slippage under load causes decreased refrigeration.

Table 10-1 Refrigeration Troubleshooting

Symptom	Probable Fault
No Cooling	Electric clutch switched off
	Clutch connection broken
	Interlock relay (if fitted) faulty
	Clutch coil failure
	High pressure cutout
	Low pressure cutout
	Low refrigerant level
	Drive belt broken
	Drive belt slipping
	Thermostat faulty
Slow Temperature Pull Down Times	Drive belt slipping
	Low refrigerant level
	Compressor fault
	High cooling water temperature
	Condenser plugged
	Low battery voltage
	Refrigerator space seals damaged
	High ambient temperature
	Insulation failure
	Thermostat faulty
	Clutch coil failure
Clutch Circuit Breaker Tripping	Clutch cable shorting out
	Compressor bearing failure
Noisy Compressor	Compressor fault
	Compressor mounting loose
	Low cooling water flow
High Pressure Cutout	High water temperature
	Condenser clogged
	Electric condenser fan failure
	Insufficient ventilation
	Incorrect setting
Expansion Valve Icing Up	Capilliary or bulb damaged
	Expansion valve faulty
	Pump impeller failure
No Cooling Water	Drive belt loose
	Drier requires replacement
Moisture in System	Condenser leaking
	Compressor gasket failure
Gas Leakage	Compressor bearing failure
	Pipe compression fitting
	Condenser leak
	Isolation valve leak
	Damaged piping

10.7 **Air-Conditioning Systems.** Air conditioning is becoming a common feature on larger vessels; I have installed systems on cruising vessels up to about 50 feet. Like refrigeration, air conditioning cools a cabin by transferring heat out. In most marine installations, sea water is used for condenser cooling. Most modern marine systems are reverse cycle so that winter heating can also be obtained. There are two types of marine air-conditioning systems: the single stage type and the tempered water, two-stage type. The majority of smaller vessels will have a single stage system. System factors are as follows:

a.   **Single Stage System.** These units are ideal on vessels up to about 80 feet. They can be either self contained or have a remote condensing unit in a machinery space. The self-contained system is normally a small module that can be hidden away under a bunk or other suitable location. It is precharged at the factory. The remote system requires installation of the cooling unit only in the cabin; only a grill is seen. Refrigerant is carried to the cooling unit in a manner similar to a refrigerator installation.

b.   **Electrical Power Requirements.** The power requirements of air-conditioning systems are as follows:

(1)   **AC Systems.** A system normally requires a constant AC power source to operate, so the generator must run continuously. Cruisair quotes as a guide at 117 volts, at 1 amp per 1000 BTU/hour. If an air-conditioning system is to be installed on the new vessel, the generator must take account of the expected loads. AC induction motors on the compressor have a significant start-up current surge that must be allowed for in generator load calculations.

(2)   **DC Systems.** HFL Marine International have a 12-volt system in their "Ocean Breeze" series. It draws a rather large 40 amps for a 6000 BTU unit, so the engine must run to supply the power.

(3)   **Dual Refrigerator Systems.** Glacier Bay has introduced Arctic Air. This sensible idea utilizes the refrigerator system and a separate evaporator. For cruising yachts, it is a low cost way to cool down in extreme heat.

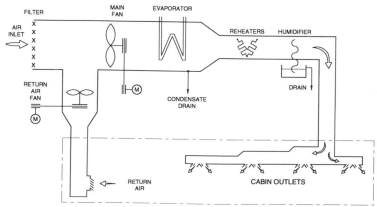

Figure 10-6 Typical Air–Conditioning Schematic

10.8 **Ventilation Fans.** Good ventilation is essential in many areas of the vessel, especially the galley, the engine space, and the cabins. There are a number of ventilation fan options, and all have uses in particular applications. Fans can be classified either as extraction fans or as blowers.

    a.   **Extraction Fans.** Extraction fans take air out of a space, either to increase natural ventilation flow rates and air changes or to remove excessive heat or fume concentrations.

        (1)   **Solar Fans.** Solar fans are an excellent accommodation ventilation option. They simply have a small solar cell powering the fan motor. Newer models have a small, solar-charged battery so that the fan can operate at night, the period when it is most required.

        (2)   **Engine Extraction Fans.** These are used to extract heat from engine spaces. In warmer climates, it is preferable to leave the fan operating for half an hour after the engine stops to reduce heat buildup and stop the increase in lower deck temperatures from radiated heat.

        (3)   **Ventilators.** The most familiar of these types are the Ventair and Ventilite static ventilators. The latter allows natural light from the outside to come into the cabin. These units have two speeds and are reversible, allowing them to be adapted to the conditions inside. At 25 cfm (cubic feet per minute), air displacement is very good, which suits normal cabin environments. Power consumption is also relatively low at only 1.7 amp on the fast setting. The two-speed Vetus units are a more economical option; they utilize an electronic, brushless motor with a current draw of only 0.2 amp. Air extraction rates are a reasonable 36 cfm.

    b.   **Blowers.** Blowers push air into a space, and are used either to displace existing air such as in bilge blower applications, or in most cases to direct air in large volumes over specific areas, such as in alternator cooling applications.

        (1)   **In-Line Fans.** In-line fans are commonly used in bilge blower applications. These types simply install into the ventilation ducting tubes. Air flow rates are typically around 100 cfm and have a power consumption of around 4 amps.

        (2)   **Bilge Blowers.** Blowers used in areas where hazardous vapors are concentrated must be ignition proof. They are often used to ventilate engine spaces. Typical air flows are in the range of 150-250 cfm. Power consumption ranges from 4 to 10 amps, which is quite high. In most cases, though, they are run with the engine operating. It is a good practice to interlock the fan to the engine start with a relay to ensure that it always operates and switches off at engine shut-down.

10.9   Diesel Heater Systems. Power consumption figures, heat outputs, and fuel consumption rates for typical Eberspacher models are illustrated in Table 10-2. Heaters have the following operational cycles:

a.   **Starting.** Cold air is drawn in by an electric fan to the exchanger/burner.

b.   **Ignition.** Fuel is drawn at the same time by the fuel pump, mixed with the air, and ignited in a combustion chamber by an electric glowplug.

c.   **Combustion.** The combustion takes place within a sealed exchanger and gases are exhausted directly to atmosphere.

d.   **Heating.** Heat is transferred as the main air flow passes over a heat exchanger to warm the air to the cabin. A thermostat in the cabin shuts the system down and operates the system to maintain the set temperature.

Table 10-2 Diesel Heater Data Table

BTU Output	Fuel (liters/hour)	Power Draw
6,100	0.21	40 watts
11,000	0.38	45 watts
15,000	0.57	70 watts
28,000	1.05	115 watts
41,000	1.40	190 watts

e.   **Power Consumption.** Typical power consumption is 40 watts (3.33 amps) during running. At start up, the draw can be up to 20 amps for a period of 20 seconds during the glowplug ignition cycle.

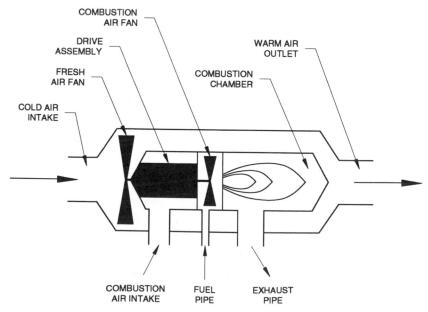

Figure 10-7 Diesel Heater System

f. **Heater Maintenance.** The following maintenance tasks should be carried out to ensure optimum operation:

(1)   Check that all electrical connections are tight and corrosion free.

(2)   Check exhaust connections and fittings for leaks. Leakages can cause dangerous gases to vent below deck.

(3)   Remove and clean the glowplugs. Take care not to damage glowplug spiral and element. Use a brush and emery cloth and make sure all particles are blown out afterwards.

(4)   At 2000 hours, take the unit to a dealer for a decoke of the heat exchanger and replacement of the fuel filter.

Table 10-3 Diesel Heater Troubleshooting

Symptom	Probable Fault
Heater Will Not Switch Off	Temperature switch fault
Heater Smokes and Soots	Combustion pipe clogged
	Fuel metering pump fault
	Blower speed too low
Heating Level Too Low	Hot air ducts clogged
	Fuel metering pump fault
	Blower speed too low
	Temperature switch fault
Heat Will Not Start	Supply fuse blown
	Low battery voltage
	Blower not operating
	Fuel-metering pump fault
	Thermal cutout tripped
	Fuel filter clogged
	No fuel supply
	Glowplug fault
	Control unit fault
Heater Goes Off	Fuel-metering pump fault
	Thermal cutout tripped
	Fuel filter clogged
	Fuel supply problem
	Control unit fault

10.10   Anchor Windlass. It is crucial that anchor windlasses are properly selected and installed. Unfortunately, they are rarely maintained properly and subsequently fail at critical periods. This chapter explains the process and the factors to consider when selecting and installing a windlass.

> a.   **Windlass Selection.** Choose the windlass based on the weight of anchor chain and the vessel size.
>
> b.   **Electrical Installation.** Install correctly rated cables and protective systems.
>
> c.   **Electrical Control.** Install a reliable control system.

10.11   Anchor Selection. If it is a new system, it is prudent to select the correct anchor for the vessel. The CQR, manufactured by Simpson-Lawrence (U.K.), is one of the most useful and common anchor types, and this will be used as a yardstick. Simpson-Lawrence's selection chart should be used as correct weight selection is critical. Finding the right windlass chain is more fraught with difficulty than can be imagined. The principal problem is that chain types do not always match the windlass chain lifter.

10.12   Anchor Windlass Selection. Windlass selection is based on the weight of an anchor and the chain weight. Table 10-4 illustrates a selection of short link chain sizes for a variety of vessel lengths.

Table 10-4 Anchor Chain Weight Selection Table

Vessel Size	10 Meters	12 Meters	14 Meters	16 Meters	18 Meters
Chain Size	8 mm	10 mm	10 mm	13 mm	13 mm
All Chain	40 m	50 m	70 m	80 m	90 m
Rope/Chain	12 m	14 m	16 m	18 m	20 m
Chain Wt	1.42 kg/m	2.22 kg/m	2.22 kg/m	3.75 kg/m	3.75 kg/m

> a.   **Winch Loading Calculation.** Minimum windlass capacity is derived from the following formula, after working out the chain weight for your vessel size:
>
> Windlass Capacity = (Anchor Weight + Chain Weight) x 2
>
> eg., 12-meter vessel has CQR of 35 kg.
>
> Chain Weight 111 kg + 35 kg = 146 kg x 2 = 292 kg
>
> b.   **Rated Output.** The windlass in this instance must have a rated pull of at least 292 kg. Manufacturers have selection charts to assist in selection. Always add at least a 25% margin to the calculated figure.
>
> c.   **Recovery Speeds.** Speeds are typically designed around a figure of 10 meters/minute at a 100-kg load. The higher the load, the slower the anchor retrieval rate.

d. **Anchor Loading.** A windlass is not designed to take the entire load when riding to anchor, especially in large swells or heavy conditions. As a safety precaution, always transfer the load to a bollard using a rope snubber.

e. **Operational Notes.** When operating the windlass, observe the following:

(1) **Engine Running.** Always operate the windlass with the engine running. The alternator supplies part of the motor load and keeps the motor from impressing a large voltage surge on the electrical system. More importantly, running the engine keeps the voltage from dropping too low.

(2) **Run Times.** In cases where the windlass is used without the engine running, the voltage drop is such that a severe drop in windlass power occurs after a few minutes. A further problem is that the motor may overheat due to the lower voltage, causing winding damage or burn-out. Always pause for 20-30 seconds every few minutes and allow the voltage to recover. If you are having a problem with anchor retrieval, do not continue to load the anchor windlass until it stalls. Stop every five minutes and allow the motor to cool down.

10.13 **Anchor Electrical Installation.** Anchor windlass performance is frequently reduced by the installation of incorrectly rated cables. Anchor windlass electrical supplies should run the most direct route to the engine starting battery, via the appropriate isolator and protective devices. At full-rated load, significant voltage drops can develop, with a corresponding decrease in rated lifting capacity. The following system components must be specified and installed correctly. The practice of installing a separate battery, either at the machinery space or forward next to the windlass, is not recommended. Use the engine starting battery; it has a high cranking amp rating and is more able to deliver the currents required by a windlass at maximum loads. A deep-cycle service battery cannot cope with these loads without being damaged.

a. **Cabling.** Cabling must be able to cope with large currents over an extended distance. Voltage drop should not exceed 5%. Table 10-5 gives recommended cable sizes for length of cable run, not for vessel length.

Table 10-5 Windlass Cable Rating Table

Cable Length	Current Rating	AWG	Metric	B & S
up to 6 meters	200 amps	4/0	5 mm^2	3
up to 8 meters	245 amps	2/0	35 mm^2	2
up to 10 meters	320 amps	1/0	50 mm^2	0
up to 12 meters	390 amps	0	70 mm^2	00

b. **Circuit Protection.** Current ratings vary depending on the manufacturers. Many windlasses have converted DC starter motors on the entire powered range. Typical current loadings are given as 55 amps at no load, 110 amps at half load, and 180 amps at full rated load. Protective devices are as follows:

(1) **Circuit Breakers.** A circuit breaker should be installed on the supply reasonably close to the battery, and easily accessible. Typically, 100- and 125-amp circuit breakers are used, and those from Heinemann are ideally suited to this application. Use DC-rated circuit breakers, not AC ones as many commonly do.

(2) **Automatic Thermal Cutouts.** I would caution against using automatic thermal circuit breakers. They trip automatically in overload conditions and reset; the problem is that you have to wait until they reset, which is usually when you desperately need the windlass.

(3) **Slow Blow Fuses.** ABYC and USCG require a slow blow fuse be installed on the system, and many manufacturers integrate this within the control box. The fuses are normally rated above the windlass' rated working current, typically 200 amps for 12-volt systems. Make sure you carry a spare.

c. **Connections.** Connections are a common cause of failures. The following points should be observed:

(1) **Connector Types.** Always use heavy-duty crimp connectors. Do not solder connections as dry joints are commonplace and solder can melt under maximum load. Soldered joints also stiffen up the cables, causing fatigue.

(2) **Insulation.** Put on a section of heat shrink tubing over the entire crimp connector shank and cable to prevent the ingress of moisture.

(3) **Connections.** The lug terminal hole should always fit neatly to ensure maximum contact. Use a spring washer on the nuts to prevent loosening and subsequent heating and damage under load. Coat terminals with a light layer of petroleum jelly.

d. **Performance Curves.** The following curves for Lewmar windlasses graphically illustrate the effect load has on power consumption and hauling speed.

(1) The higher the load, the higher the current, until a point is reached where the motor overloads and stalls. The higher the load when the windlass is operated, the shorter the operation time allowed on the motor.

(2) The higher the load, the slower the recovery speed. Hoisting the anchor can take less time and cause less wear and tear on the windlass if you motor up over the anchor and remove chain tension.

A: LOAD/CURRENT CURVE
B: LOAD/SPEED CURVE

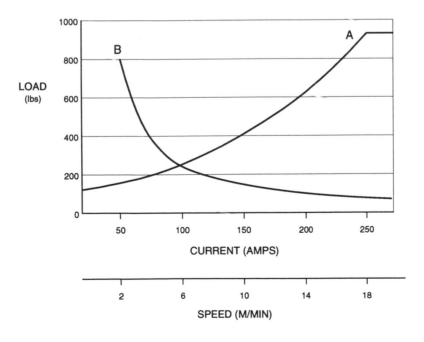

Figure 10-8 Anchor Windlass Performance Curve

10.14 **Anchor Windlass Electrical Control.** One of the most common failure points in an anchor windlass is the control system. Controls come in the following configurations:

a. **Single Direction Foot Switch.** A foot switch is connected directly in the positive supply to the windlass motor. Foot switches are notorious for filling with water, and usually in this type of control a short develops, or the contacts and spring corrode. Shorting can result in brief, uncontrolled windlass operation and a burned-out switch.

b. **Single Direction Solenoid/Foot Switch.** The foot switch is used to control a heavy-duty solenoid located below decks, which closes the main power supply to the motor.

c. **Pneumatic Deck Foot Switch.** These units have a PVC tube connecting the switch to the control solenoid box. Air pressure from the switch operates a microswitch. There have been reports of spontaneous start-ups or shut-offs in extremely hot conditions, which in one case caused serious injuries. The problems were caused by pressure build-up in the air system. Evidently, earlier units are the most prone to trouble and major suppliers such as Lewmar already have a safety air bleed to correct the problem. Carefully follow the proper depressurizing procedures when installing switches.

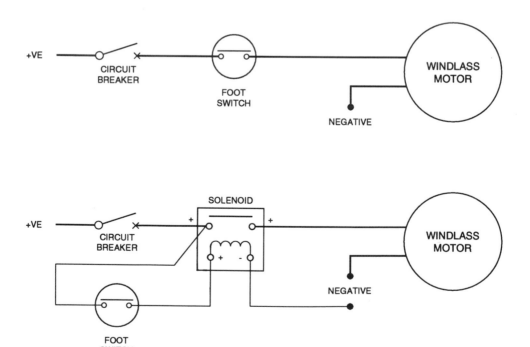

Figure 10-9 Windlass Control Systems

184

d. **Dual-Direction Solenoid Control.** A control box consisting of two or four solenoids is used for reversing the motor for both hoisting and lowering. Control is usually by a pair of foot switches and/or a remote panel.

   (1) **Power Consumption.** Solenoids typically consume 1 amp each.

   (2) **Caution.** Never operate both foot switches together. In fact, many manufacturers specify only the "up" foot control be fitted.

   (3) **Protection.** Some control boxes incorporate fuse protection. Fuse failure is rare, but make sure that a spare is in the box for emergencies.

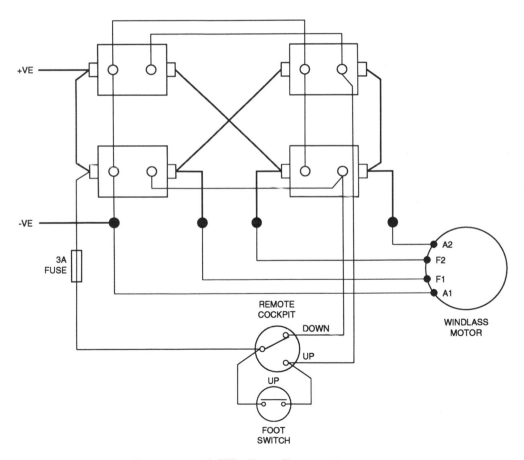

Figure 10-10 Windlass Control Systems

185

e.   **Remote Controls.** Remote control devices take a variety of forms:

(1)   **Portable Controls.** These are usually weatherproof control modules that can be plugged into prewired socket-outlet stations. Ensure that the socket remains watertight.

(2)   **Radio Controls.** These devices are relatively new and innovative, and work like TV controls. How efficient they are, I am unable to verify.

(3)   **Touchpad Panels.** These are touch panels covered with a waterproof membrane. Their reliability is low—I have removed every unit that I installed—and they tend to complicate things as well. Normally, control is achieved through the positive side of relays or solenoids. Many touchpad controls switch the negative so that other foot switch controls on solenoids must also be converted to negative or have relays inserted in the circuit.

(4)   **Switch Panels.** The basic, weatherproof pushbutton or toggle-switch remote system has proved to be the most reliable remote-station system. The switches must be waterproof and be spring loaded to off.

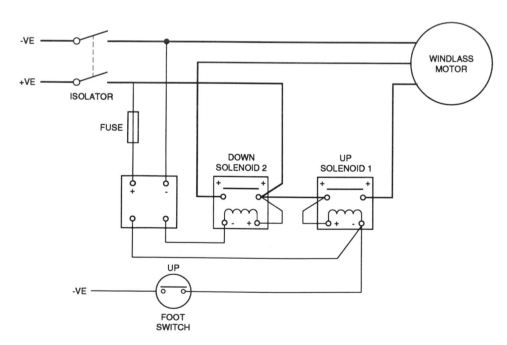

Figure 10-11 Windlass Remote Control Systems

Table 10-6 Anchor Windlass Troubleshooting

Symptom	Probable Fault
Windlass Will Not Operate	Foot switch fault (most common cause)
	Circuit breaker switched off
	Isolator switch off
	Foot switch connection loose
	Solenoid connection fault
	Solenoid fault
	Solenoid fuse blown (if fitted)
	Motor connection loose
	Motor fault (sticking brush is common)
	Motor fault (winding failure)
	Motor internal thermal cutout tripped
Windlass Stalls Under Load	Slow blow fuse ruptured
	Excessive load
	Low battery voltage
	Motor connection loose
	Motor fault (brushes sticking)
Windlass Operates Slowly	Battery terminal loose
	Excessive load
	Low battery voltage
	Motor connection fault (hot)
	Motor fault (brushes sticking)
	Battery terminal loose
Circuit Breaker Trips During Operation	Motor fault
	Windlass seizing
	Windlass overloading
Circuit Breaker Trips at Switch On	Motor fault
Control Fuse Ruptures	Fault in solenoid
	Fault in control circuit
	Fuse fatigue
Solenoid "Chatters"	Low voltage
	Fault in control switch
	Control switch connection loose
	Solenoid connection loose

10.15   Electric Furlers and Winches. Deck winches and furling gear are rapidly being electrically powered and are taking a lot of the muscle out of cruising for the short-handed crew and older husband/wife cruising teams. They are generally treated in the same way as anchor windlass circuits, requiring good circuit protection and correctly sized cables. Winches may be powered from an electric motor or hydraulic power pack. Most furlers operate from an hydraulic power pack. Electrical loads are considerable and for 12-volt systems the following cable sizes are required. Electric winches generally consume far more power than windlasses and careful power supply planning is required. The power source should be a starting battery—the engine start battery can be paralleled with another of equivalent size. Install the battery with the largest possible cold cranking rating.

Table 10-7 Winch Cable Rating Table

Cable Length	Current Rating	AWG	Metric	B & S
up to 10 meters	320 amps	1/0	50 mm²	0
10 to 15 meters	390 amps	0	65 mm²	00
15 to 20 meters	500 amps	00	85 mm²	000

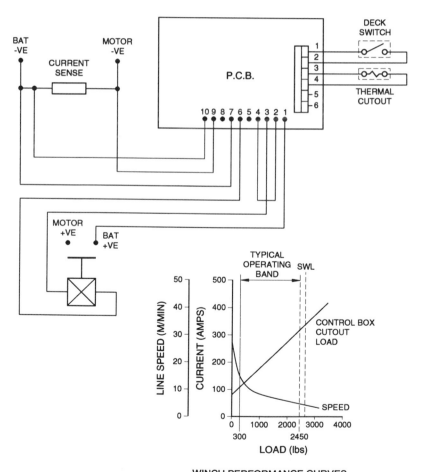

WINCH PERFORMANCE CURVES

Figure 10-12 Lewmar Winch Control

188

10.16   DC Motors. Most installed pumps and machinery have DC motors, and most are maintenance free. However, where larger motors are in use (windlasses, winches, refrigeration compressor drives, starter motors, and motor-driven generators), the question of proper maintenance becomes paramount. I started my commercial seagoing career on 220-volt DC systems, and quickly learned the key to motor performance and reliability is preventive maintenance:

a.   **Shunt Wound DC Motors.** This motor operates at a constant speed, irrespective of the loads applied to it. It is the most common motor used in industrial applications and is suited to applications where starting loads are not excessive. Motor speed may be varied by two methods:

   (1)   **Armature Resistance.** Inserting resistance in the armature circuit decreases speed.

   (2)   **Field Resistance.** Inserting resistance in the field circuit increases speed.

b.   **Series Wound DC Motors.** In this type of DC motor, the speed varies according to the load applied, i.e., speed increases as the load decreases.

c.   **Compound Wound DC Motors.** This is a combination of both shunt- and series-wound motors. It is generally used where high starting loads and constant speeds are required.

10.17   Commutators. The state of a DC motor can often be ascertained by observing the condition of the commutator. Look for the following:

a.   **Good Commutator Surfaces.** Good commutators have a copper surface patina or surface markings. An overriding desire to grab an emery cloth and polish the commutator till shiny will severely shorten the life and performance of the motor.

   (1)   **Light Tan Film.** This condition indicates a machine is performing correctly.

   (2)   **Mottled Surface.** This condition is characterized by random film patterns on commutator segments and is also normal.

   (3)   **Slot Bar Marking.** Film is slightly darker, and occurs in a definite pattern that corresponds to the number of conductors per slot.

   (4)   **Heavy Film.** This condition is acceptable if uniformly spread over the entire commutator.

b.   **Commutator Deterioration Signs.** The following signs and causes indicate that the motor performance is degrading and require attention:

   (1)   **Streaking.** Surface streaking on the commutator indicates the start of metal transfer from commutator to brush. The condition can be caused by light brush pressures, a light electrical load, an abrasive or porous brush, or contamination by dust.

(2)   **Threading.** Fine line threading on the commutator surface happens when an excessive quantity of copper transfers to the brushes. If severe, the commutator will require resurfacing and brush wear will be rapid. The condition can be caused by light electrical loads, light brush pressures, porous brushes, or dust contamination.

(3)   **Grooving.** Grooves in the brush path are caused by abrasive brushes and contamination by dust.

(4)   **Copper Drag.** A build-up of copper material at the trailing edge of a commutator segment is caused by light brush pressures, vibration, abrasive brushes, and contamination.

(5)   **Pitch Bar Marking.** Low or burn spots on the commutator surface are caused by poor armature connections, unbalanced shunt fields, vibration, or abrasive brushes. The number of marks equates to all or half the number of poles.

(6)   **Heavy Slot Bar Marking.** Etching of the trailing edges of the commutator segment is caused by poor electrical adjustment, electrical overloads, or contamination. The pattern relates to the number of conductors per slot.

c.   **Commutator and Brush Maintenance.** Perform the following checks:

(1)   **Commutators.** Check commutators every 6 months and blow and wash them clean with an electrical solvent. If possible, use a small brush and clean out any dust build-up between commutator segments. Dust build-up has the effect of shorting out the insulation between the commutator segments.

(2)   **Brushes.** Check brushes every 6 months and blow and wash them clean with an electrical solvent. In addition, ensure that brushes move freely within the brush holders. Check that spring pressure is correct by pulling the brush back and snapping it against the commutator. Check that the brush tail connections are secure.

(3)   **Brush Replacement.** Get the correct brush for the machine. If brush replacement becomes necessary, use a very fine strip of sandpaper slightly wider than the brush. Place the abrasive surface under the brush and move it back and forth around the commutator so that the carbon brush is shaped to the commutator. Use a vacuum cleaner and extract all the dust out of the machine to prevent accumulation of abrasive materials. Never use emery cloth; it will scratch the commutator surface and will shed conductive particles that lodge in the commutator segments, causing shorts and arcing.

Table 10-8 DC Motor Troubleshooting

Symptom	Probable Fault
Windings Overheating	Motor overloading
	Run time excessive
	Ventilation insufficient
	High ambient temperature
Excessive Commutator Sparking	Motor overloading
	Oil on commutator
	Brushes sticking
	Brush pressure too low
	Brushes worn
	Commutator dirty
	Commutator damaged
	Excessive brush dust buildup
Motor Overloading	Excessive mechanical load
	Bearings binding
Excessive Current Draw	Excessive mechanical load
	Bearings binding
	Valve closed (if a pump load)
	Electrical connection fault
Excess Motor Noise and Vibration	Bearing failure
	Motor hold down bolts loose
	Motor load transmitting vibration
	Misaligned coupling
	Coupling damaged and out of balance
	Brushes bouncing on commutator

Water Systems

11.0   **Water Systems**. Water systems cover a number of different areas:

- Pressurized Water Systems

- Desalination Systems

- Bilge Pump Systems

- Sewage and Shower Drain Systems

11.1   **Pressurized Water Systems.** Water is the one essential, where water is everywhere but none is fit to drink. A system is easy to install, but certain basics must be considered.

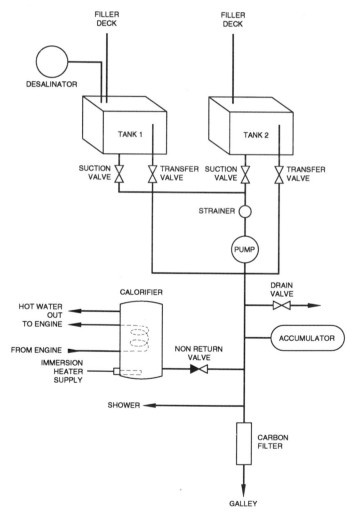

Figure 11-1 Water System Schematic Diagram

11.2   Water Tanks. It is good practice to have two separate tanks for water stowage. Before filling a tank, transfer remaining water to one tank. The new water can be put in the tank without contaminating water you know to be good. Then, if the water is of poor quality and you have to dump it, you do not lose the whole lot. Toxic by-products from bacteria are characterized by unpleasant smells. Cleaning regimes should be undertaken at least twice a year to ensure the integrity of your water.

   a.   **Cleaning.** The tank should be scoured by hand with a brush, but do not use excessive quantities of detergent.

   b.   **Flushing.** Fill and flush out the tank at least three times.

   c.   **Disinfection.** New water and the tank must be disinfected to prevent bacterial growth. Water chlorination is easily accomplished by adding a solution of household bleach in the quantities of 5 to 100 of tank contents. Let some amount run though all outlets to disinfect all parts of the system. Then top off the tank and allow to stand for four hours. Re-flush the system another three times. Now add vinegar in the ratio of 1 liter to 50 liters of system capacity and allow to stand for two days. Refill with fresh water and flush three times again. The tank is then ready for use and will maintain potable water quality for several months. An easier and quicker way is to use Puriclean or Aquatabs or a similar brand, which will clean and purify the tank. After filling tank and adding the cleaning solution, always let it stand a few hours before flushing.

11.3   Water Pressure Pumps. The primary purpose of the pump is to supply and pressurize the water from the tank. A pump is selected based on the number of outlets to be supplied and the flow rate required. If the pump is incorrectly rated for the system, the flow will drop off when another outlet is opened.

   a.   **Diaphragm Pump.** These units are the most robust and are designed for multi-outlet systems. They are self priming, are more tolerant of dry running conditions, are relatively quiet in operation, and have built-in hydraulic pulsation dampening.

   b.   **Impeller Pump.** These units normally have a pump with a bronze casing and a nitrile or neoprene impeller. They are also self priming, but are less tolerant of running dry.

Table 11-1 Water Pump Data Table

Model	Current	Flow l/min	Max. Head	Cut-in	Cut-out
Jabsco					
44010	4.0 amps	9.5	1.2m	10psi	20psi
36800	6.0 amps	12.5	1.5m	10psi	20psi
Flojet					
143-12 V	3.9 amps	12.5		20psi	35psi
143-12 V	6.0 amps	17.0		20psi	35psi
Whale					
EF 2.0612	3.9 amps	7.0		16psi	32psi
EF 2.1012	4.2 amps	10.0		16psi	32psi

11.4 **Water System Strainer.** The strainer installed in the water suction line to the pump protects the pump from damaging sediment and particles from the storage tank. Observe the following:

    a. **Element Cleaning.** It is essential to clean regularly the stainless steel strainer. Blockages are most frequent when commissioning a new vessel or after refilling a totally empty tank. I have seen a number of vessels where the element has been removed because the owners were tired of cleaning blockages. The result will be early pump failure. Better to clean the system and eliminate the cause.

    b. **Bowl Seals.** After cleaning the element, make sure that a good seal is made with the transparent inspection cover. Imperfect seals can cause air and contamination to be drawn into the system. Ensure that the seal is in good condition. A smear of silicone grease often helps.

11.5 **Water System Accumulators.** An accumulator is an essential part of any water system. It is designed to be a pressure buffer in the system, absorb flow from the pump at low demand, and smooth the outlet pressure. The immediate benefit of an accumulator is extended pump life as the accumulator eliminates the need for the pump to operate immediately after an outlet is opened. The larger the accumulator fitted, the less often a pump is required to operate. The larger the proposed water demand, the larger the accumulator required. Accumulators come in two main types:

    a. **Non-pressurized.** These units are typically plastic cylinders, which are installed upright within the system. They also have a cock at the top to vent air from the water system.

    b. **Pressurized.** These accumulator types have an internal membrane and can be externally pressurized with a bicycle pump or factory pressurized with nitrogen. At installation, the following procedure must be performed:

        (1) Turn pump off.

        (2) Open all outlets and release system pressure.

        (3) Using a car tire pressure gauge, release nitrogen until pressure falls to 5 psi below pump cut-in pressure.

        (4) If too much pressure is relieved, use a bicycle pump to increase the pressure.

11.6 **Water Filters.** Filters should be fitted to all drinking water outlets. A filter will remove small particles, off tastes caused by tank-water purification chemicals, as well as some bacteria. Always install a filter with easily replaceable filter elements and replace them promptly when stated service life is completed. The Whale types simply require a unit replacement. Filters are generally manufactured of activated carbon. Filters that use porous ceramic, which removes all particles and detectable bacteria, will provide better water quality. A good filter should always come with a test report issued by an appropriate authority. It should be rated for the expected flow rate and should be renewed at the due date. Always clean the water system before installing a new filter. A filter can never substitute for clean tanks. If you rely only on the filter, you risk the safety and health of all on board.

11.7 **Hot Water Calorifier.** Hot water is one of those hard-to-do-without luxuries. They are easy to install or incorporate into a water system. The old term *calorifier* is still used because most marine hot water systems still heat from in-built coils (calorific transfer) supplied from heated engine cooling water or, on the old tramp ships I once served on, steam. It makes economic sense to utilize all the available waste energy of the auxiliary engine:

a. **Heat Transfer.** Calorifiers are usually fitted with a single copper heating coil. Beware of the cheap units, because the coils are often small and only have one or two coil turns. Quality calorifiers are often able to quote heat transfer data; for instance, Allcraft quotes a copper bronze heat exchanger of 2 square feet surface area that is able to heat water to 190°F in 15 minutes. Isotemp heaters quote that water will reach engine water temperature within 30 minutes. Heating coils use 316 stainless steel, which suits those of us who still have older raw seawater-cooled engines. Isotemp also has the innovative Magic models. which have a eutectic heat accumulator. The accumulator consists of a block of special salt type that melts at 58°C. The stored energy required to liquefy the salt slowly cools and solidifies, releasing the stored heat to the water. This results in smaller units, with higher heat transfer efficiencies, and is ideal for short engine run periods.

b. **Electric Elements.** Calorifiers should also incorporate an electric element for heating via the shore power connection or generator. The rating should not exceed 1200-1800 watts due to supply limitations of both shore power outlets and generators. The thermostat is essential for proper temperature control, limitation of overheating, and conservation of energy. Don't set it too high.

c. **Calorifier Valves.** The water inlet should have a non-return valve fitted to prevent the heated and expanding water in the tank from syphoning back and pressurizing the cold water system. Isotemp Magic units also have a thermostatic regulated mixing valve on the outlet side that is adjustable to ensure stable hot water temperatures that conserve hot water. Some systems also incorporate a manual inlet shutoff valve, and a drain tap for draining down the heater in cold climates and lay-ups. A pressure relief valve is also essential, but make sure that you manually operate it every few months to clear away debris, insects, etc.

d. **Insulation.** Good insulation is essential to prevent thermal leakage and heat wastage. Isotemp uses polyurethane foam and quotes a 0.5°C loss per hour. These units also have increased insulation layers at the top where water is hottest. Good insulation allows hot water maintenance over 24 hours from the daily engine run time.

e. **Installation.** The calorifier should be mounted on the same level as the engine cooling water source or below, if possible. Keep interconnecting hoses to a minimum length so that no unnecessary resistance is introduced into the engine cooling water circuit. Use good heat-resistant hoses and double-clamp connections. Ensure there are no air locks within the water system, which can cause engine cooling problems.

11.8   Diesel Hot Water Heaters. The diesel hot water system is now becoming commonplace on vessels. This unit can also be part of a central heating system. Companies such as Eberspacher and Webasto have very efficient systems. The Webasto is illustrated below. The typical operational cycle is as follows:

a.   **Starting.** Cold air is drawn in by an electric fan to the heat exchanger/burner. This is normally from the engine area.

b.   **Ignition.** Fuel is drawn in at the same time by the fuel pump from the main tank and mixed with the air. The fuel is ignited by an electric glowplug in a combustion chamber.

c.   **Combustion.** Combustion takes place within a sealed exchanger and the exhaust gases are expelled to atmosphere.

d.   **Heating.** An integrated water pump circulates the water through the heat exchanger and subsequently to the calorifier and heating radiators. A thermostat in the cabin shuts the system down and operates to maintain set temperature. Eberspacher has developed an automatic quarter heat control to reduce unnecessary cycling, thereby improving fuel economy.

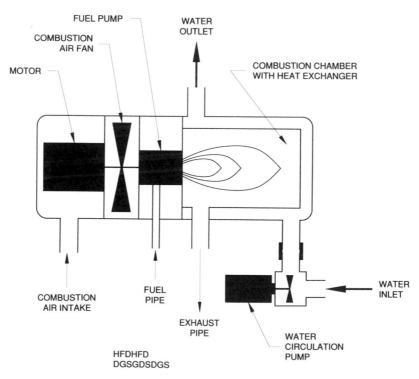

Figure 11-2 Diesel Hotwater System

11.9   **Water Pipes and Fittings.** Water pipes should be of a high quality material that is suited to both hot and cold water. Observe the following when selecting and installing piping:

a.   **Pipe Standard.** The piping should be non-toxic, suitable for potable water systems, and must not be able to support microbiological growth. There are two types:

(1)   **Semi-Rigid Piping.** Whale offers a color-coded, semi-rigid pipe system. Ensure that pipe is not kinked. Where tight bends are required, install a bend.

(2)   **Flexible Hose.** Hose is the most common piping. Ensure that it meets required standards. Hose is prone to kinking, so installations should be done with care.

b.   **System Pressures.** Piping must be able to withstand the water system pressures. Whale piping is rated at 60 psi and 90°C. When installing piping over longer runs, larger pipe diameters are required to reduce the friction losses. Table 11-2 illustrates pipe diameters.

c.   **Fittings.** Fittings must be able to withstand system pressures. Nuisance leakage can be avoided. Where plastic hoses are used, generally PVC tee-joints are installed with clips. The Whale or Acorn systems are excellent, and they are easy to install and service.

d.   **Outlets.** There are many different taps, valves, and shower heads on the market. Always choose good quality items, and choose only those that are compatible with the whole plumbing system. This makes finding spare parts easier. Reputable names include Whale and Jabsco. If you are using a non-flexible, permanent shower head, opt for one of the domestic, low water consumption fixtures. See Chapter 11.17 for information on shower drain pumps and water conservation.

e.   **Connections.** Ensure that all piping or hose connections are double clamped. Acorn and Whale fittings should be firmly tightened.

Table 11-2 Recommended Pipe Diameters

Pump Port Diameter	Hose Diameter
6 mm	13mm ID
10 mm	13mm ID
13 mm	16mm ID
19 mm	25mm ID
25 mm	25mm ID
38 mm	38mm ID
50 mm	50mm ID

Table 11-3 Water System Troubleshooting

Symptom	Probable Fault
Will Not Prime (No Discharge)	Restricted inlet
	Restricted outlet
	Air leak in suction line
	Pump diaphragm ruptured
	Debris under flapper valves
	Pump housing fractured
	Strainer clogged
	Valve closed
	Kink in water pipe or hose
	No water in tank
	Clogged one-way valve
	Discharge head too high
	Low battery voltage (pump slow)
Pump Will Not Operate	Circuit breaker tripped off
	Pump connection loose or broken
	Pressure switch fault
	Motor fault
	Pump seized
Pulsating Water Flow	Restricted pump delivery
Pump Cycling On and Off Excessively	System pressure leak
	Water outlet leaking
	Accumulator problem
Pump Will Not Switch Off	Water tank empty
	Pump diaphragm ruptured
	Discharge line leaking
	Pressure switch fault
	Debris under valves
Low Water Flow and Pressure	Air leak on pump inlet
	Strainer clogged (common)
	Pump impeller worn
	Pump diaphragm ruptured
	Pump motor fault
	High discharge head
	Pump improperly rated

11.10 **Water System Winterizing.** In colder climates, proper winterization is essential to prevent damage from freezing. Perform the following protective measures:

      a. **Remove Pump.** If possible, remove the entire pump and store in a dry place.

      b. **Drain System.** The most practical precaution is to totally drain the water system, including the pump and accumulator. Do not use antifreeze solutions in the potable water system.

11.11 **Shore Water Systems.** There has been a rapid increase and improvement in marina facilities worldwide, enabling vessels to connect with shore electrical power, telephones, and water supplies. Water connections pose some problems in that shore water pressures are significantly higher than onboard system pressures. Med Aqua Marine Systems in the U.K. has developed a new system, The shore water system is filtered, and regulated down to system pressure. The system can incorporate a solid-state bilge sensor that will automatically close an inlet solenoid, and should the bilgewater level rise, will activate an alarm as well as the bilge pump. This ensures that should the system leak there is minimal flooding. The system is illustrated below.

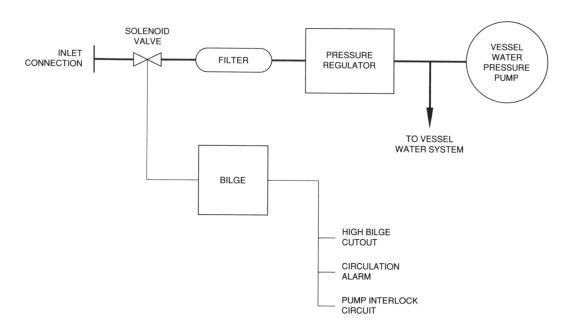

Figure 11-3 Shore Water Systems

11.12   **Desalination Systems.** Cruising to foreign places is half the fun, but unfortunately when you get there, the water is often scarce or not fit to drink. As a result, watermakers are becoming more popular on many vessels as they give you a greater degree of freedom. Onboard water resources are limited, and this affects maximum cruising ranges. The most practical system is the reverse-osmosis desalinator, as evaporative systems require long-term engine use for reasonable economy. It must be stressed that water should not be made within 10 miles of a coastline or within inhabited atolls in the Pacific. These are generally polluted to levels well above World Health Organization (WHO) recommendations and this pollution can be carried into the tanks with product water. Principles are as follows:

a.   **Reverse-Osmosis Principles.** In natural osmosis, when fresh and salt water are separated by a semi-permeable membrane, fresh water flows through to the salt water side. To reverse this process, salt water is pressurized to force the fresh water out through the membrane. Sea water is pressurized by a priming pump and filtered to remove particles. Then pressure is increased with a high-pressure pump, which forces fresh water through the membranes. The membranes are housed in a high-pressure casing. The illustration below shows the basic principles of operation for the Seafresh system.

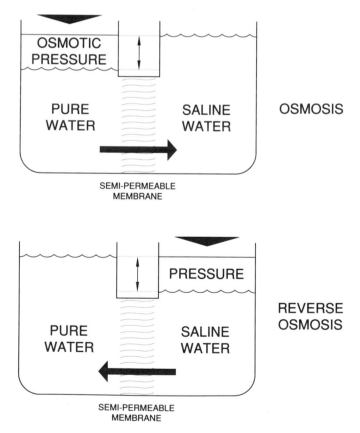

Figure 11-4 Reverse-Osmosis Process

b. **System Components.** The osmotic membranes are the heart of any system. Membrane quality is the key to a good unit; cheaper units with poor quality membranes usually cost considerable sums because of the high maintenance and replacement costs. Pumps can either be engine driven or AC-shore power driven. Power consumption can be up to 2 kilowatts. Seafresh specifies a minimum generator capacity of 3 kilowatts for starting currents and approximately 1.5 kilowatts for running currents. Well-designed systems incorporate prefilters for the salt water. Prefilters typically have a rating of 50 microns, followed by a second filter of 5 microns.

c. **Monitoring and Control.** Salinity is monitored constantly and excess saline product is automatically dumped. The SeaFresh system is typical and its operation is as follows:

(1) Raw sea water enters the system through strainer.

(2) Raw water is pressurized by primer pump.

(3) Water passes through 50 micron prefilter.

(4) Water passes through 5 micron prefilter.

(5) Water is pressurized to 900 psi by high-pressure pump.

(6) Pressurized water enters the reverse-osmosis membrane, which filters out the salt and minerals.

(7) Product water is monitored. If good, it is sent to tanks. If below quality, it is dumped.

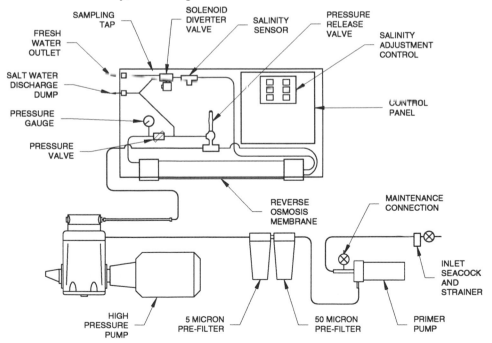

Figure 11-5 SeaFresh Desalination System

d. **Installation.** Space considerations are always of critical importance. The SeaFresh Spacesaver and Ocean models have resolved this problem. Through-hull fittings are required for the raw sea water intake and the overboard brine discharge. It is not a good practice to take the input from auxiliary engine or generator water inlets.

e. **Outputs and Membrane Correction Factors.** In a good system, salt rejection rates are typically 99% in the pH ranges 4 to 11 at operating pressures of 700-900 psi. In these conditions, output is unaffected by pressure and temperature. Where temperatures and pressures change, correction factors must be applied to ensure improved production rates.

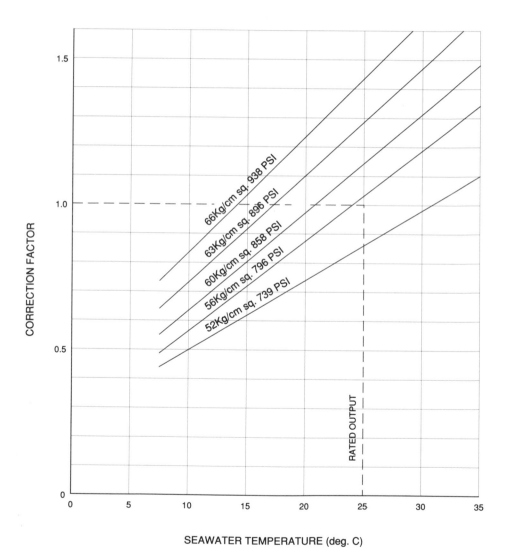

SEAWATER TEMPERATURE (deg. C)

Figure 11-6 Desalinator Temperature Correction Factors

f. **Maintenance.** The following maintenance tasks are recommended for Seafresh desalinators:

(1) Clean inlet strainer at the same time as the engine strainer.

(2) Prefilters can be washed 5 or 6 times before replacement. This equals approximately 80 hours operation in clean ocean waters.

(3) For shutdown periods exceeding 14 days, disinfect membranes to prevent biological fouling. Failure to do this will significantly reduce output and damage membranes. Never allow membranes to dry out or they will be ruined.

(4) Check high pressure pump oil levels and renew every 500 hours.

(5) Check and retension rubber drive belts every 6 months.

(6) Membrane cleaning should be undertaken whenever output drops below 15% of normal rated output or whenever product salinity increases. This occurs through the build-up of grime, biological material, and mineral scale. Do not open the pressure vessel to do this. Cleaning should be done according to manufacturers' recommendations and usually entails the use of alkaline and detergent cleaners to remove organic material, and acidic cleaners to remove mineral scale.

Table 11-4 Desalinator Troubleshooting

Symptom	Probable Fault	Corrective Action
Low Water Flow	Blocked strainer	Clean strainer
	Blocked prefilter	Clean or replace filter
	Membranes fouled	Clean membranes
	Pump belts loose	Tension belt correctly
No Product-Water Flow	Pump stopped	Check circuit breaker
		Check drive belts
Circuit Breaker Tripping	Circuit breaker tripped	Clutch coil fault
	Pump clutch coil failed	Replace winding
	Clutch wire grounding out	Repair connection/wire
	Pump seizing	Repair pump
Low Working Pressure	Relief valve leaking	Overhaul valve
	Pump fault	Overhaul pump
	High pressure loss	Examine for leaks
	Dump valve jammed open	Repair valve
Product Water Salty	Fouled membranes	Clean membranes
	Excess working pressure	Decrease pressure

11.13 **Bilge Pump Systems.** Bilge pumps play a crucial safety role in any vessel, yet many owners tend to get the cheapest units and install them improperly. Bilge pumps should be of the highest quality available, and they should be installed correctly and regularly maintained. The following factors should be considered when selecting and installing electric bilge pumps. There are basically two types, the submersible pump and the centrifugal pump. Submersible pumps are notoriously unreliable and cannot be maintained or repaired.

    a.   **Head.** Head pressure is related to the height that water must be lifted to. All pumps have maximum head figures for a particular model.

    b.   **Flow Rate.** Most bilge pumps are listed with flow rates, which are designated as gallons (or liters) per hour or per minute. Electric pumps with bronze housings are rated up to a maximum of 11 gal/min (50 l/min).

    c.   **Impellers.** Pump impellers come in a number of different compounds. Choose the correct type for optimum life and efficiency. Centrifugal pumps should never be operated dry for more than 30 seconds; they are designed to be lubricated by the pumped liquid. Operating without liquid generally means a ruined impeller. Impeller types are as follows:

        (1)   **Neoprene.** These are typically found in bronze pumps (Jabsco) and are suitable for bilge pumping in temperatures ranging from 4°C to 80°C. Use at the outer temperature limits reduces performance and service life. They must not be used to pump oil-based fluids as the neoprene impeller can absorb oil compounds and expand. On the next start-up, the binding impeller is destroyed. Always flush out a line if oily fluids are used.

        (2)   **Nitrile.** These are designed for pumping fuel, but they are also suited to pumping oil- and fuel-contaminated engine bilges in temperatures from 10°C to 90°C. Use at the outer temperature limits reduces performance and service life. Nitrile impellers have a flow rate 30% lower than neoprene impellers, so they should not be used in any high temperature applications.

    d.   **Submersible Pumps.** These pumps are by far the most common. It is important to always buy and install the very best quality you can. Pumps have the following general characteristics:

        (1)   **Motor Rating.** Motors are rated continuously, but the bilge water normally assists motor cooling while pumping.

        (2)   **Motor Type.** Motors generally use a permanent magnet motor, which means no brushes.

        (3)   **Dry Running.** Pump impellers are not damaged by dry running, though motors require water to cool them.

e. **Automatic Systems.** Automatic bilge pumps are now very common. There are a number of important considerations to keep in mind when putting in any automated control:

   (1) **Pollution.** There are heavy fines for those who willfully or accidentally discharge oily wastes into harbors and coastal waters. It is the environmental responsibility of all boaters not to discharge any waste into the sea. A bilge capable of having oil in it must never be fitted with an automatic pumping system.

   (2) **Controls.** Automatic switches are notoriously unreliable. If the float switch stays on, the bilge pump will probably be burnt out and ruined and a set of batteries will be totally flattened. There are a number of activation devices; these are explained below.

f. **Float Switches.** Float or level switching devices may use a number of different operational principles:

   (1) **Mechanical Floats.** This is by far the most common device and probably the most reliable, if the float switch is of high quality, if it cannot be fouled by the pump cable, and if the bilge is free of debris. This circuit diagram, provided for steel vessels, isolates the positive supply to the float switch. This minimizes the common and serious risk of corrosion problems if a leakage occurs.

   (2) **Solid State Devices.** These include ultrasonics, conductive probes, etc. While some appear to work well, there are a great number of failures. Some cheaper units can cause electrolytic corrosion problems. If the probes are fouled or coated with oil, they often don't work. Some have a delay feature that requires the presence of water for 15 to 20 seconds before they activate. This prevents the pump from start-and-stop cycling in rough water. I have not found any of these devices to be too reliable.

   (3) **Optical Devices.** These devices are quite new and resolve many of the problems normally encountered with units using probes. The pump units are controlled by an innovative optical fluid switch that emits a light pulse every 30 seconds. If the lens is immersed in water, the light beam refracts and the beam's change in direction is sensed by a coating inside the lens. This triggers the pump. Time delay circuits can be adjusted for periods of 20-140 seconds so that the pump will continue draining the bilge after water clears the sensor. I have tried some of these devices and I find them very good.

(4) **Vacuum Devices**. These are relatively old but simple devices which work reliably. They depend on the pressure of water in a tube to activate a switch via a diaphragm.

(5) **Ultrasonic Devices.** In practice, these devices have had limited success and I would not recommend them.

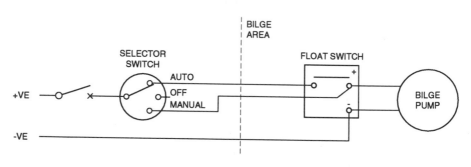

STANDARD BILGE CONTROL

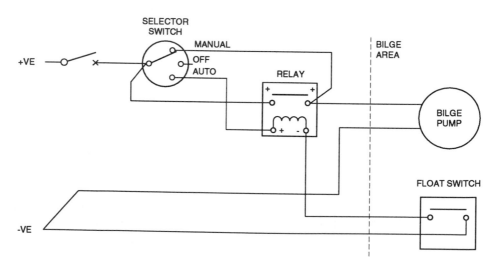

ISOLATED SYSTEM FOR STEEL/ALLOY VESSELS

Figure 11-7 Bilge Control Schematics

11.14   Bilge Pump Installation. Bilge pumps must be installed as follows to operate correctly and reliably:

    a.   **Location.** Mount the pump or suction line in the lowest part of bilge. It is best to keep this a short distance from the bottom to avoid drawing in bilge sediments.

    b.   **Strainer.** Always install a strainer on the suction side of centrifugal pumps. Submersible pumps have a strainer as an integral part of the base, but these are rather coarse. It is quite common for bilge debris to jam the impeller .

    c.   **Discharge Piping.** Select flexible hose that will not kink. Many pumps are rendered ineffective due to kinks or constrictions in the discharge line. Always use two hose clamps on every hose connection as a safety precaution. The discharge should be as far above the waterline as possible so it will be clear even when heeled.

    d.   **Electrical Connections.** If the cable is long enough, make connections above the maximum bilge water level. I recommend to solder each connection, to cover the joint with heat shrink insulation, and to cover the entire cable with heat shrink insulation or wrap it in self-amalgamating tape. This will generally prevent the joint from interacting with salt water and failing. The circuit must be fused on a circuit breaker rated for the cable size, typically 15 amps. Always run the pump after installation to ensure that pump rotation is correct.

11.15   Bilge Pump Maintenance. Regular maintenance is essential for reliable pump operation. Regularly clean bilges of sediment and debris. Run pumps every month with water in the bilge. Many bilge pumps can seize after months or even years of disuse.

Table 11- 5 Bilge Pump Troubleshooting

Symptom	Probable Fault
Low Water Flow	Strainer blocked with debris
	Pump impeller fouled
	Suction hose kinked
	Suction hose blocked with debris
	Suction line has air lock
Pump Will Not Operate	Circuit breaker tripped
	Float switch fouled (usually with debris)
	Float switch connections corroded off
Pump Will Not Switch Off	Float switch jammed
	Float switch fouled by debris
	Float switch mounted too low
	Float switch connection short circuited
Circuit Breaker Tripping	Pump impeller seized
	Bilge area connections short circuited
	Pump winding fault

11.16 **Sewage Systems**. Many sewage systems are being altered as electrical fixtures replace hand-pump toilets, and stringent requirements for holding tanks and pump-out systems are legislated. This requires careful consideration in systems planning.

a.   **Toilets**. Many electric toilets or manual units with conversion systems have an integral, self-priming, water flushing pump and macerator.

b.   **Electric Devices.** One of the biggest problems with toilets is the failure to install adequately sized cables to the units or to allow for voltage drop. The PAR unit consumes 18 amps and requires a heavy-duty cable rated at around 30 amps. As toilets are always located in wet shower areas, ensure that all electrical connections are covered with waterproof, self-amalgamating tapes. Always use enough cable so you can pull the toilet out. Otherwise, the motor will be difficult to disconnect. Check the motor connections monthly to ensure no corrosion is occurring and lightly coat the terminals with silicone grease or petroleum jelly. I now respray motors with an additional layer of paint to prevent water from seeping into the motor housing flanges where corrosion easily occurs. Before installation, remove each bolt and apply an anti-seize grease.

c.   **Waste.** It is essential that only normal waste be put through the toilet. To quote the plaque for marine heads, "Don't put anything in the bowl that you haven't already eaten and digested". Macerator cutter plates are easily jammed or damaged by cigarette or cigar butts, rags, and sanitary towels. Cleaning macerators is the number one most unpleasant task on a vessel, so it is well worth making the effort.

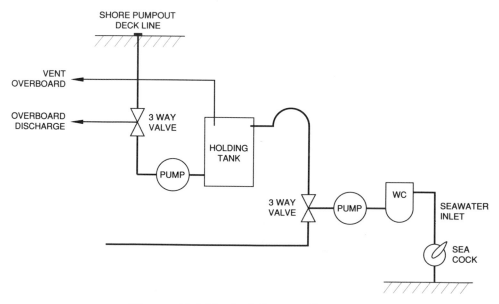

Figure 11-8 Typical Sewage System

d. **Macerators.** Macerator pumps are usually connected to the holding tank discharge and are used to pump out waste to shore facility tanks or overboard. Units grind waste to 3 mm, and are self priming. Remember that pumps are not rated continuously, so run times should not exceed 10 minutes. Heavy-duty models are available for larger systems and have greater pump-out capabilities. Jabsco Models are given in Table 11-6. Flow rates are given at maximum and normal heads. After pumping out tanks, flush out the macerator pump with clean water to expel any debris that may cause bacterial build up.

Table 11-6 Jabsco Macerator Pump Specifications

Pump Type	Port Size	Current	Flow Rate
21950 -1603 (12 mins rated)	Inlet 1½-2" Outlet 1"	10 amps	36 l/min @ 1.5m 19 l/min @ 6.1m
22140 - 1421 (60 mins rated)	Inlet 1½-2" Outlet 1"	25 amps	40 l/min @ 1.5m 30 l/min @ 9.8m

e. **Operation Periods.** On some vessels, in particular larger multihulls, I have installed a timing system, a press-and-forget feature, that gives either a long or short flush time. This eliminates the need to hold buttons in and saves water. The circuit is illustrated below.

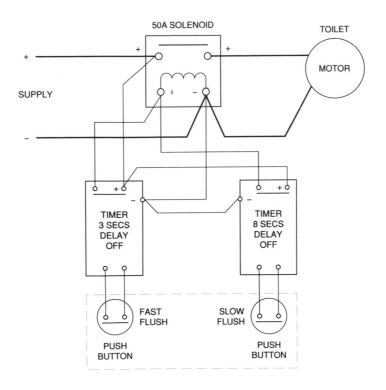

11.17   **Shower Drain Systems.** Shower drain systems are required in all shower drain sumps. Variations and options are described as follows:

    a.   **Diaphragm Pumps.** Jabsco and Whale offer shower waste diaphragm pumps that do away with a submersible sump pump and float switch. The pump is connected directly to the drain outlet and simply has a strainer in-line on the suction side. The pumps are self-priming to 12 ft, will run dry, and can pump air and water mixtures. I have a Whale Gulper installed and it has performed extremely well. Pumps typically consume 4 amps at full load with water output of 12 liters/min. They are reliable and easily repaired. In the interests of redundancy and standardization, the Whale Gulper pump is identical to the same Whale models used for Gulper bilge pumps and Gulper toilet holding tank pumps.

    b.   **Submersible (Bilge) Pumps.** These units are the most common type. Rule manufactures an integrated sump, filter, pump, and float switch.

    c.   **Centrifugal Pumps.** Flojet and Jabsco make a self-priming pump, similar to water pumps. Typical rating is 3.3 gpm at 2.8 amps.

    d.   **Water Conservation.** This water-saving shower idea has worked well on many vessels, including my own. It allows long showers, with low water consumption. The options are that either Solarbag water can be recycled through a water-saving shower head or come directly from the hot water system. The sump suction has a filter to strain suds and hair, and then recycles water back through the system. When finished, water is diverted overboard and you rinse off using the same procedure.

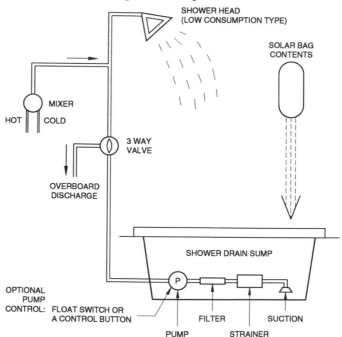

Figure 11-10 Shower System

Engine Electrical Systems

12.0   Engine Electrical Systems. Engine electrical systems are not complex, but do require proper understanding. Most manufacturers have standard control practices, although there are a number of variations, often within the same engine make.

a.   **Starting Circuits.** The starting control system is the cause of many troubles. One of the most frequent problems is the starter solenoid push on control wires that comes from start/stop buttons falling off starter motor solenoid connections.

b.   **Starter Motors.** The starter motor is in effect a large DC motor with appropriate gearing to turn the engine over. Preventive maintenance is essential for reliable performance. The most common problems encountered on starter motors are as follows:

(1)   **Shaft Corrosion.** This is a common problem, especially on little used vessels. Surface corrosion builds up on the shaft, causing the sliding assembly to seize and not engage. The location of the starter can cause problems, too, as water left in bilges can be picked up by the flywheel and sprayed under pressure against the starter. Remove the starter every 6 months and lightly oil the components according to the manufacturers' recommendations.

(2)   **Check Brushgear.** Many problems occur with seized brushes. Always manually check that the brushes are moving freely in their holders and that the commutator is clean. Wash out dust with a quality electrical spray cleaner. Follow the DC motor maintenance procedures. Under no circumstances should you clean and polish the commutator with abrasive materials.

12.1   Engine Starting System Diagrams. The following are simplified wiring diagrams for a variety of engines. Always check the diagrams supplied in the operator's manual for your specific engine model. Make sure that you have the correct circuit diagram for the installed engine and laminate a copy. Wiring varies considerably, even between older and newer engine models. The following table gives equivalent color codes for various manufacturers.

Table 12-1 Engine Wiring Colour Codes

Purpose	US Codes	Yanmar	Bukh	Volvo	Perkins	Nanni
Ignition Start	yell/red	white	blue	red/yell	white/red	brown
Ignition Stop	black/yell	red/black	black	purple	blk/blue	white
Preheat		blue	yellow	orange	brown/red	orange
Negatives	black	black	black	black	black	black
Alternator Light	orange	red/black	green	brown	brown/yell	green
Tachometer	grey	orange	yellow	green	blk/brown	blue
Oil Press. Gauge	light blue	yellow/blk	green	light blue	green/yell	grey
Oil Warning Lt.		yellow/wh	brown	blue/wh	black/yell	grey/red
Wtr. Temp. Gauge	tan	white/blk	brown	light brn	green/blu	yellow
Wtr. Temp. Lt.		white/blue	yell/green	brown/wh	blk/lt green	yell/red

a.   **Yanmar Starting System.** The simplified circuit diagram for the starting system of a typical Yanmar engine is illustrated below.

Table 12-2 Yanmar Troubleshooting

Symptom	Probable Fault
Engine Will Not Start	Start button fault
	Key switch fault
	Starter solenoid connection off
	Stop solenoid seized
	Stop button jammed in
	Negative connection fault
Engine Will Not Stop	Stop solenoid seized
	Stop solenoid connection fault
No Preheating	Air heater connection broken
	Key switch fault
	Negative connection fault
	Glowplug connection fault

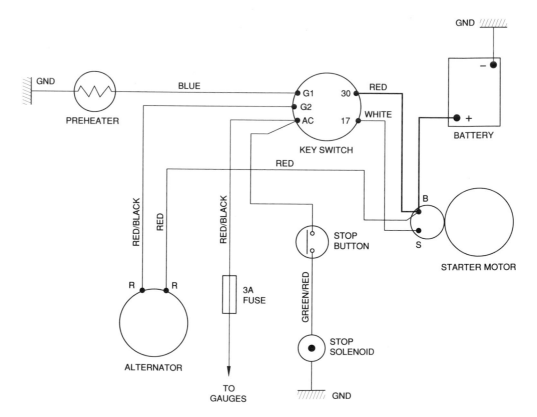

Figure 12-1 Typical Yanmar Engine Starting System

b.   **Nanni Starting System.** The simplified circuit diagram for the starting system of a typical Nanni engine is illustrated below.

Table 12-3 Nanni Troubleshooting

Symptom	Probable Fault
Engine Will Not Start	Start button connection off
	Start button fault
	Control fuse failure
	Starter solenoid connection off
	Stop solenoid seized
	Stop button jammed in
	Negative connection fault
	Loom connector fault
	Stop solenoid connection fault
Engine Will Not Stop	Stop solenoid seized
	Loom connector fault
	Fuse failure
No Preheating	Key switch fault
	Negative connection fault
	Glowplug connection fault
	Glowplug timing relay fault
	Fuse failure

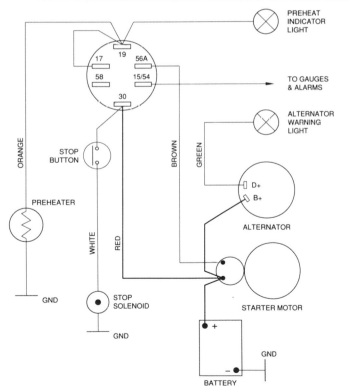

Figure 12-2 Typical Nanni Engine Starting System

c.   **Perkins Prima Starting System.** The simplified circuit diagram for the starting system of a typical Perkins Prima engine is illustrated below.

Table 12-4 Perkins Troubleshooting

Symptom	Probable Fault
Engine Will Not Start	Start button connection off
	Start relay fault
	Starter solenoid connection off
	Stop solenoid seized
	Stop button jammed in
	Negative connection fault
	Stop solenoid connection fault
	Stop solenoid seized
	Stop solenoid connection off
	Loom connector fault
Engine Will Not Stop	Diode failure
	Earthing relay fault
	Key switch fault
	Negative connection fault
	Glowplug connection fault
No Preheating	Relay fault
	Earthing relay fault

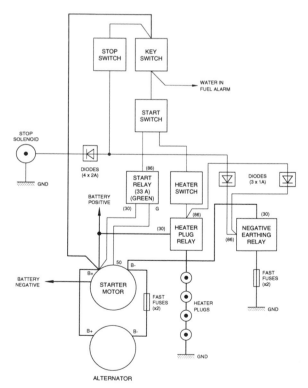

Figure 12-3 Typical Perkins Engine Starting System

d. **Bukh Starting System.** The simplified circuit diagram for the starting system of a typical Bukh engine is illustrated below.

Table 12-5 Bukh Troubleshooting

Symptom	Probable Fault
Engine Will Not Start	Start button connection off
	Start button fault
	Control fuse failure
	Starter solenoid connection off
	Stop solenoid seized
	Stop button jammed in
	Negative connection fault
	Loom connector fault
Engine Will Not Stop	Stop solenoid connection fault
	Stop solenoid seized
	Loom connector fault
	Fuse failure
No Preheating	Key switch fault
	Negative connection fault
	Glowplug connection fault
	Fuse failure

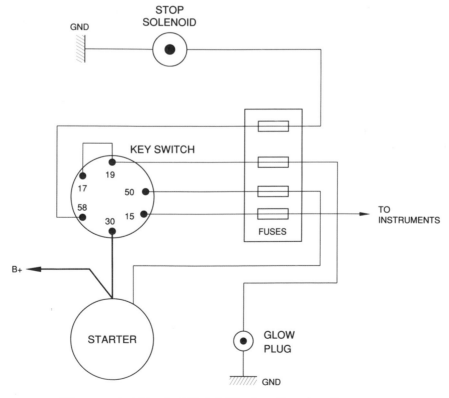

Figure 12-4 Typical Bukh Engine Starting System

215

e.   **Volvo Starting System.** The simplified circuit diagram for the starting system of a typical Volvo engine is illustrated below.

Table 12-6 Volvo Troubleshooting

Symptom	Probable Fault
Engine Will Not Start	Start button connection off
	Start button fault
	Control fuse failure
	Starter solenoid connection off
	Stop button jammed in
	Negative connection fault
	Loom connector
	Stop solenoid connection fault
Engine Will Not Stop	Stop solenoid seized
	Loom connector fault
	Fuse failure
No Preheating	Key switch fault
	Negative connection fault
	Glowplug connection fault
	Fuse failure

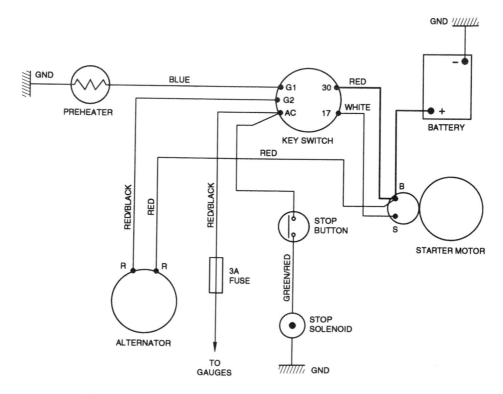

Figure 12-5 Typical Volvo Engine Starting System

12.2 **Preheating Circuits.** Preheating systems are mainly designed to ease starting in cold weather, although many engines will not start even in mild temperatures. Some engines simply will not start without preheating. Preheating reduces excessive engine turnover, which can overheat and damage starter motors.

    a. **Glowplugs.** Most engines have glowplug heaters installed in each cylinder. They heat the air in the cylinder to facilitate starting. In cold weather, this reduces the electrical power needed to start the engine.

        (1) **Activation.** Before the engine starts, the plugs can be activated for an operator selected time period or interlocked to a timer, typically in the range of 15 to 30 seconds.

        (2) **Power Consumption.** Glowplugs draw large current levels for a short time. Therefore, if batteries are at a low charge level, it is best to wait a few seconds after preheating before starting the engine. This enables the battery voltage to recover from the heater load.

    b. **Air Intake Heaters.** These heaters are installed in the main air intake of the engine. Normally, there is only one heating element.

    c. **Preheater Control.** Many preheating circuits have relays, either timed or untimed. From experience, timed relays are a common cause of failures. I recommend having a straight relay with a separate switch, which lets you preheat manually for 15 seconds and then start.

    d. **Preheater Maintenance.** The following maintenance tasks should be carried out:

        (1) **Electrical Connections.** Preheater glowplug connections must be regularly checked if they are to function properly. Clean and tighten the connections every 6 months.

        (2) **Cleaning.** The insulation around the glowplug connections must also be cleaned using a suitable electrical spray cleaner. It is common to have tracking across oil and sediment to the engine block with a serious loss of preheating power.

        (3) **Glowplug Cleaning.** The plugs should be removed and cleaned every 12 months. Take care not to damage the element.

    e. **Preheater Troubleshooting.** The following faults are typical on preheating systems:

        (1) **No Preheating.** This is invariably due to the relay malfunctioning, or to a broken supply cable leading to the first series-connected glowplug. Where the system is fused, check that the fuse has not ruptured.

        (2) **Low Preheating.** This is generally caused by tracking across dirty insulation or across connections to the block, or by a defective glowplug.

12.3   **Engine Tachometers.** Monitoring engine speed provides important information about fuel consumption and vessel performance. There are a number of tachometer types based on the way they detect engine revolutions.

a.   **Generator Tachometer.** This type of tachometer receives a signal from a mechanically driven generator unit. The generator produces an AC voltage proportional in amplitude to the engine's speed. This is decoded in the tachometer. Changes in speed give proportional changes in output voltage, which changes the meter reading. The most common fault on these units is a damaged driveshaft mechanism.

b.   **Inductive Tachometer.** These tachometers have an electromagnetic pick-up that "counts" the teeth on a flywheel or camshaft and sends a pulse that it is decoded and displayed on the tachometer. Make sure the sensor unit is properly fastened. One common cause of failure is that the flywheel damages the sensor head if it is adjusted too close.

c.   **Alternator Tachometer.** This type of tachometer derives a pulse from the alternator AC winding. The alternator output signal frequency is directly proportional to engine speed. The pick-up is from the star point or one of the unrectified phases. Typical connections for VDO tachometers are illustrated. If the alternator is faulty, there is no reading.

d.   **Alternator Tachometer Output Terminals.** There are a number of different alternator terminal designations used by various manufacturers. The main ones are W, STA, AC, STY, SINUS. If there is no output terminal, make the connection shown in the diagram when you install this tachometer.

e.   **Alternator Frequency Calculation.** The frequency value for meter set at full-scale deflection is calculated using the following formula. Tachometers have range switches and fine adjustment potentiometers that need calibration. Give this information to your instrument agent and the tachometer can be calibrated on the workbench as follows:

$$\text{Hertz} = \frac{\text{CSPD x FSD x P/R x 0.98}}{\text{APD x 60}}$$

CSPD	= Crankshaft Pulley Diameter.
FSD	= Meter Full-Scale Deflection (scale).
P/R	= Number of Pulses/Revolution of Alternator Rotor.
APD	= Alternator Pulley Diameter.
0.98	= Correction Factor for Belt-Driven Alternators.

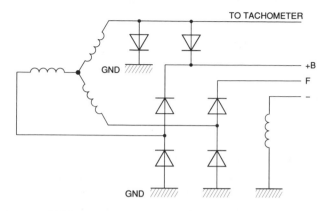

STAR WINDING, SINGLE PHASE

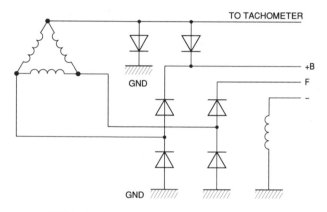

DELTA WINDING

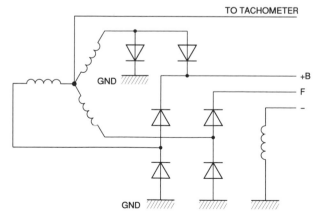

STAR WINDING, MULTI PHASE

Figure 12-6 Alternator Tachometer Circuits

12.4   Pressure Monitoring. There are a number of pressures that require monitoring:

a.   **Oil Pressure Monitoring**. The oil pressure sensor unit is a variable resistance device that responds to pressure changes. When the alarm goes off, check the following causes of low oil pressure before you say the meter is wrong:

(1)   Faulty fuel pump.

(2)   Cogged oil filter.

(3)   Higher oil temperatures caused by an increase in engine temperature.

(4)   Higher oil temperatures caused by an oil cooler problem.

b.   **Oil Pressure Alarm**. A pressure alarm is either incorporated into a sensor gauge or is separate. The alarm consists of a pressure-sensitive mechanism that activates a contact when a factory set pressure is reached. Like most sensors, it is grounded to the engine block on one side. Activating it grounds the circuit, setting off the panel alarm. To test the alarm circuit, simply lift off the connection and touch it to the engine block.

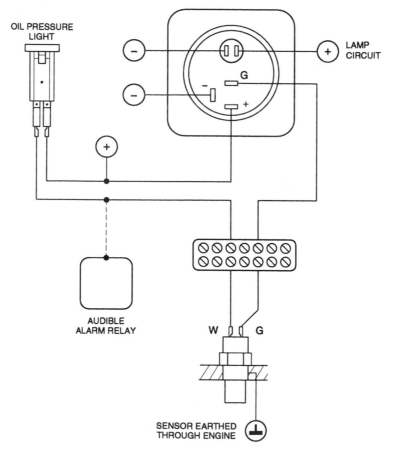

Figure 12-7 Oil Pressure Alarm and Monitoring

12.5 **Temperature Monitoring.** There are two main temperature monitoring points utilizing the same sensor types:

   a.   **Water and Oil Temperature Gauges.** Monitoring water temperature is essential to safe vessel operation as temperature extremes can cause serious engine damage or failure. Sensors are resistive in proportion to temperature; resistance within the sensor unit changes in a non-linear curve. If the gauge readings are not correct and a gauge test shows it to be good, check the sensor. Before you check the sensor unit, the main causes of high water temperatures are as follows:

   (1)   Loss of fresh water cooling can be caused by water pump problems, a loose rubber drive belt, low water levels, or increased combustion temperatures.

   (2)   Loss of salt water cooling can be caused by a blocked intake or strainer, a faulty water pump, or a leak in the suction side of pump (aeration).

   (3)   Increased engine loadings caused by adverse tidal and current flows.

   b.   **Water Temperature Alarms.** These stand-alone alarms have a bimetallic element that closes when the factory set temperature is reached. To test, simply remove the connection from the sensor terminal and touch it on the engine block to activate alarm. The sensor has two terminals, "G" is used for the meter, "W" is used for the alarm contact. In many yachts, damage occurs because the alarm does not function or is not noticed. The first reaction is often "What's wrong with the alarm?" instead of "What's wrong with the engine?" It is good practice to add a loud audible alarm. Some engine panel alarms are difficult to hear over engine noise.

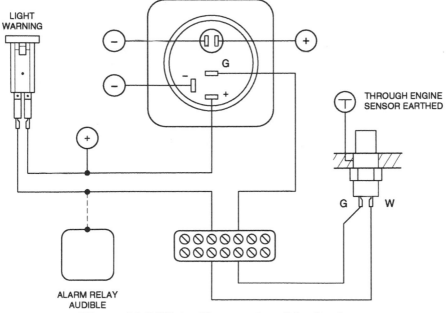

Figure 12-8 Water Temperature Monitoring

221

12.6. **Tank Level Monitoring.** Monitoring onboard fuel or water stocks is an essential task. A simple electrical gauge can be installed that provides the necessary information.

a. **Resistance Sensor.** Most tank sensors operate by varying a resistance proportional to tank level. The two basic sensor types are:

(1) **Immersion Pipe Type.** This sensor consists of a damping tube with an internal float that moves up and down along two wires. These units are only suitable for fuel tanks. The big advantage of these sensors is that they are well damped, which eliminates fluctuating readings.

(2) **Lever Type.** The lever type system consists of a sensor head on the end of an adjustable leg. The sensor head comprises a variable resistance and float arm pivot. As the float and arm move relative to fluid levels, the resistance alters and the meter reading changes. Typical resistance readings are in the range 10-180 ohms. Lever type units should be installed fore-and-aft, as an athwartships orientation will have serious problems when a vessel rolls. In water sensor units, the variable resistance is located outside of the tank to avoid water problems, while the fuel unit has its resistance unit in the tank.

b. **Capacitive Sensors.** This type of transducer operates on the principle that the value of a capacitor depends on the dielectric between plates. The sensor unit measures the capacitance difference between air and the liquid.

(1) **Output Values.** The sensing circuit outputs a voltage proportional to the level, typically in the range of 0 to 5 volts.

(2) **Faults.** The most common fault in these systems is water damage to the circuit board, usually because of tank condensation.

c. **Pressure Sensors.** These sensors are considerably more expensive, but very accurate and less prone to damage. The transducers are placed either at the bottom of the tank or on a pipe to one side of the tank bottom.

(1) **Output Values.** The sensors output either 4-20 milliamps or 0.6-2.6 volts proportional to the pressure of the fluid in the tank. The pressure is proportional to the tank volume.

(2) **Faults.** If the sensor is located on a small pipe, it may become clogged.

12.7   Exhaust Gas Temperature Monitoring. Exhaust gas temperature monitoring is not all that common on cruising yachts, but it is highly recommended. Commercial shipping uses temperatures as an accurate guide to engine loading; many of my old Chief Engineers watched them faithfully. It generally shows problems quicker than water temperature and oil pressure monitoring.

a.   **Operating Principle.** Exhaust temperature sensors are thermocouples that generate a voltage proportional to the heat applied to the sensor.

b.   **Location.** On large vessels, both individual cylinder exhausts and main exhaust are monitored. On smaller vessels, a sensor on the exhaust manifold is sufficient.

c.   **Causes of High Temperatures.** High temperature readings can be caused by:

(1)   Engine overloads due to adverse tidal and current flows.

(2)   Air intake obstructions due to clogged air filters or blocked air coolers.

(3)   Combustion chamber problems due to defective injectors.

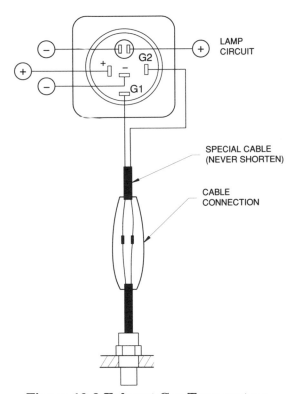

Figure 12-9 Exhaust Gas Temperature

223

12.8   Electrical System Monitoring. There are a number of parameters for monitoring electrical systems and methods for installing instruments.

a. **Charging Voltmeters.** Many instrument panels incorporate a voltmeter to indicate the state of the battery's charge. Voltmeters are fairly coarse, and not useful in precisely assessing battery voltage, but they are a useful indicator on the charging system. Most voltmeters have a colored scale for rapid recognition of battery condition.

b. **Charging Ammeters.** Charging ammeters are reasonably popular and are an easy guide to the level of charge current from the alternator. There are basically two types of ammeters:

(1) **In-Line Ammeter.** This ammeter type has the main charge alternator output cable running through it. In many cases, the long run to a meter results in unacceptable voltage drops and undercharging. Another problem with locating such ammeters on switch panels is that the charge cables invariably run with other cables and cause radio interference. If you are going to install this type of ammeter, make sure that the meter is mounted as close as possible to the alternator. If these ammeters start fluctuating at maximum alternator and rated outputs, this is generally due to voltage drops within the meter and cable. Undersized connectors are also a major cause of problems.

(2) **Shunt Ammeter.** The shunt ammeter overcomes the voltage drop problem. The shunt is essentially a resistance inserted in the charging line. Sense cables are connected across the output cable and can be run to any meter location without voltage drop problems because ammeter output is in millivolts. Always ensure that meter cables are at least 16 AWG (1.5 mm²) to avoid any voltage drops that can cause meter inaccuracies. The ammeter must always be rated for the maximum alternator output. Many installations do not do this, which can damage the shunt or meter or create big voltage drops in the charging line.

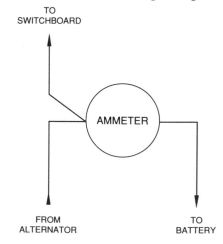

Figure 12-10 Ammeter Connections

12.9 **Hour Counters.** An hour counter is essential for keeping a record of engine maintenance intervals. Essentially, it is a clock activated only when the engine is operating. Both methods are illustrated below.

   a.   **Ignition Switch.** This is the easiest and most practical method. The meter is simply connected across the ignition positive and a negative so that it operates when the engine is running.

   b.   **Alternator.** In many installations, the counter is activated by output from the alternator's auxiliary terminal D+ or 61.

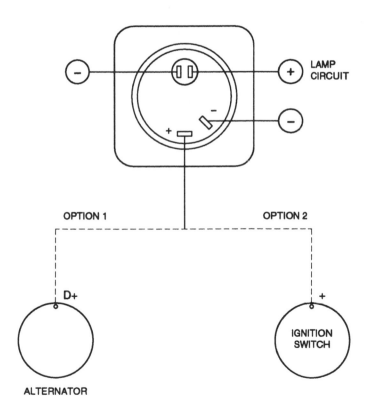

Figure 12-11 Hour Counter Connections

225

12.10   Acoustic Alarm Systems. Acoustic alarms are generally connected to warning light circuits and the buzzer is activated by a relay. Acoustic warnings are activated along with the lamp from sensor contact "W". An acoustic alarm should be activated through a relay, not through a sensor contact which is not rated for such loads.

a.   **Buzzer Test.** Using a lead, connect a positive supply to the buzzer positive terminal, and check that a negative one is also connected. If buzzer operates, remove the bridges. A test function should be inserted into the circuit so that alarm function can be verified.

b.   **Operating Test.** With alarm lights on, put a bridge from negative to buzzer negative; sometimes a "lost" negative is the problem. Connect a positive supply to the relay positive, typically numbered 86. If the relay does not operate and the buzzer works, then the relay is suspect. After removing it, verify using the same procedure. Note that sometimes a relay may sound like it is operating, but in fact the contacts may be damaged and open circuited. If a buzzer is not operating along with the lights, either a cable or connection is faulty or the operating relay is defective.

c.   **Mute Function.** On many home-built engine panels, it is essential to silence the alarm. This entails placing a switch in line with the buzzer. The lamp remains illuminated to indicate the alarm status.

d.   **Time Delays.** When starting the engine, a time delay is necessary to prevent the alarm from sounding before the oil pressure has reached a normal operating level. Time delays are typically in the range of 15 to 30 seconds.

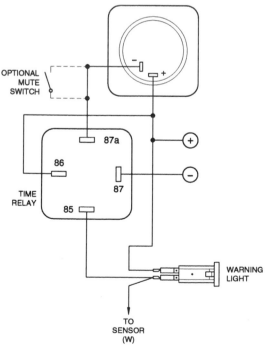

Figure 12-12 (a) Acoustic Alarm System

e. **Combination System.** The illustration below shows the use of both a switching relay and a time delay relay. The system functions as follows:

(1) **Switching Relay.** On ignition, the switching relay energizes. This illuminates the warning light and normally the oil pressure will activate the alarm.

(2) **Time Delay Relay.** The time delay relay is energized by the switching relay. The contacts that activate the acoustic alarm do not operate for 15 to 30 seconds. If oil pressure has risen to normal within that period, the alarm will not activate.

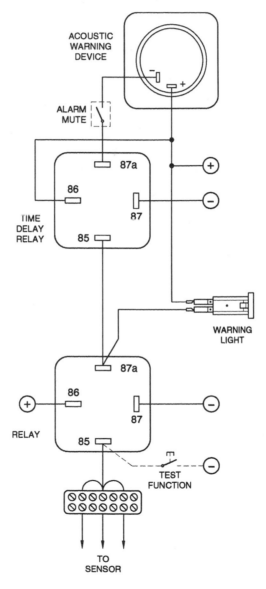

Figure 12-12 (b) Acoustic Alarm System

12.11 **Instrumentation Maintenance.** Maintaining instruments is relatively simple.

a. **Electrical Connections.** A regular check of all sensor unit terminals and connections, along with a test of alarm functions, is all that is required.

b. **Oil Pressure Sensors.** Oil pressure sensors should be removed every year and any oil sludge cleaned out of the fitting. Sludge-clogged sensors may be inaccurate or show no reading.

12.12 **Gauge Testing.** If gauges are suspect, use the following testing procedures:

a. **Open Sensor Test.** Remove the sensor lead marked "G" from the back of the gauge. Switch on meter supply voltage. The gauge needle should now be in the following positions:

(1) Temperature Gauge: left-hand, hard-over position.

(2) Pressure Gauge: right-hand, hard-over position.

(3) Tank Gauge: right-hand, hard-over position.

b. **Sensor Ground Test.** This test involves bridging the sensor input terminal "G" to negative. Remove the sensor lead and turn the meter supply on. The gauge needle should now be in the following positions:

(1) Temperature Gauge: right-hand, hard-over position.

(2) Pressure Gauge: right-hand, hard-over position.

(3) Tank Gauge: left-hand, hard-over position.

12.13 **Sensor Testing.** Disconnect the cable from the sensor. Using a multimeter (digital or analog), set the resistance (ohms) range to approximately 200 ohms. Place the positive (red) meter probe on the terminal marked "G" on the sensor. If it has a dual alarm-and-sensor output, the alarm output is marked "W". Place the negative (black) meter probe on the sensor thread.

a. **Temperature Sensors.** These approximate readings should be observed:

(1) 40°C = 200-300 ohms.

(2) 120°C = 20-40 ohms.

b. **Pressure Sensors.** These approximate readings should be observed:

(1) High Pressure = 10 ohms.

(2) Low Pressure = 180 ohms.

Table 12-7 Instrument Troubleshooting

Symptom	Probable Fault
Gauge Does Not Operate	Power off
	Gauge supply cable off
Temperature Gauge Needle Hard Over	Sensor fault
	Cable fault
Pressure/Tank Gauge Needle Hard Over	Sensor fault
	Cable fault
Alternator Tachometer No Reading	Alternator fault
	Lead off alternator terminal
	Alternator not "kicked in"
	Meter fault
Generator Tachometer No Reading	Broken drive mechanism
	Meter fault
	Generator fault
	Cable fault
Inductive Tachometer No Reading	Sensor mechanically damaged
	Sensor clearance excessive
	Meter fault
Low Gauge Readings	Negative connections to engine block and sensors degraded
Oil Pressure Alarm Activated	Low oil pressure (oil pump fault)
	Low oil level
	High oil temperature (cooling fault)
	Blocked sender unit
	Sender fault
	Cable fault
Water Temperature Alarm	High water temperature
	Low cooling water level
	Saltwater cooling inlet blocked
	Cooling water pump fault
	Loose drive belt
	Sensor fault
No Audible Alarm	Relay fault
	Audible alarm fault
	Connection fault
No Visual Alarm	Lamp failure
	Lamp connection fault
	Alarm circuit board fault

AC Power Systems

13.0   AC Power Systems. The need for power away from the marina is increasing due to the growing use of domestic appliances such as microwaves and power tools. The sources for AC power on vessels consist of the following, which are illustrated in Figure 13-1.

- Shore Power Installations

- AC Grounding and Circuit Protection

- AC Cable Installation

- Diesel Generators and Alternators

- Static Inverters

- Engine Driven Alternators

- Hydraulic Alternators

- Rotary Converters

- Gasoline Gensets

- AC Machinery

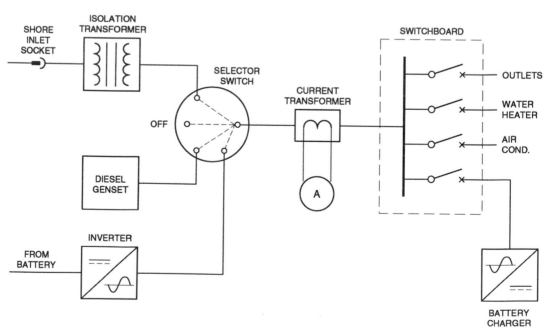

Figure 13-1 AC Power Systems

13.1 **AC Power Safety.** AC is potentially lethal, and every precaution must be made to ensure that systems are correctly selected and installed. Where possible, always consult an AC-qualified, licensed marine electrician, or a shore-based, licensed industrial electrician. The following safety precautions must be undertaken at all times when undertaking any work:

WARNING

a. **Never work on "live" equipment. Always isolate equipment before opening.**

b. **Never work on AC equipment alone. Always have someone ready to assist if you accidentally receive a shock.**

c. **Always remove shore plug before checking anything on the switchboard. No power source should be on the system.**

d. **Learn artificial respiration and CPR techniques.**

13.2 **AC Voltage Systems.** There are two voltage systems in use worldwide:

a. **115-Volt, 60-Hertz System Configuration.** This voltage (also stated as 110 or 120 volts) is used primarily in the United States. The lower voltage significantly reduces the risks of fatal electric shock but requires proper installation to ensure safety. Cables used in these lower voltage installations are double the size of high-voltage systems, as are the equipment's current ratings.

b. **220/240-Volt, 50/60-Hertz System Configuration.** This voltage is used in the U.K., Europe, Australia, and New Zealand.

13.3 **Shore Power Installations.** Marinas have become far more sophisticated facilities in recent years and most marina berths are now able to supply single- and three-phase power. Connecting the vessel to a marina power system imposes certain obligations on the owner. A vessel must comply with national or other electrical standards. Marina outlets may be one of several on a circuit or have a dedicated and protected circuit. Many also incorporate earth leakage circuit breakers, which impose other considerations. This chapter looks at the deceptively simple subject of shore power systems and the considerations required when installing them.

a. **Standards.** Each country has national standards, as do the various classification societies. The recommendations in this chapter should ensure compliance with most of them. Standards are as follows:

(1) U.S. National Electrical Code and the American Boat and Yacht Council (ABYC) have set a number of sensible requirements and recommendations.

(2) U.K. Institute of Electrical Engineers.

(3) Standards Association of Australia.

b.   **Cabling.** Inlet cabling should be heavy-duty and meet marine standards. It is good practice to also have a strain relief grip over the cable to prevent unnecessary strain, particularly where the plug into the supply pedestal has a screw ring fitting. The flexible cable should permit normal movement of the vessel without stress, prevent water from traveling along it to the inlet receptacle, and be secured so that immersion is unlikely. Additionally, provision must be made to prevent the plug from falling into the water if it is accidentally disconnected.

c.   **115-Volt Systems.** Normally, 30-amp supply requires 11 AWG (4 mm^2) supply cable. The following circuit illustrates a typical shore power system. In this configuration, only one wire in the power inlet is "hot" or energized.

(1)   Black wire is "hot"

(2)   White wire is neutral

(3)   Green wire is ground or earth

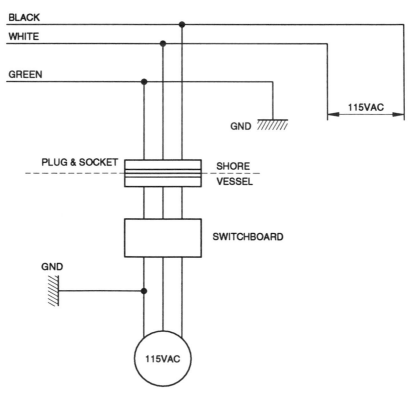

Figure 13-2 115-Volt AC Shorepower Systems

d. **115/230-Volt Systems.** The following circuit diagrams and color codes are for typical American dual-voltage shore supply systems. Observe the following:

(1) Red wire is "hot"

(2) Black wire is "hot"

(3) White wire is neutral

(4) Green wire is ground or earth

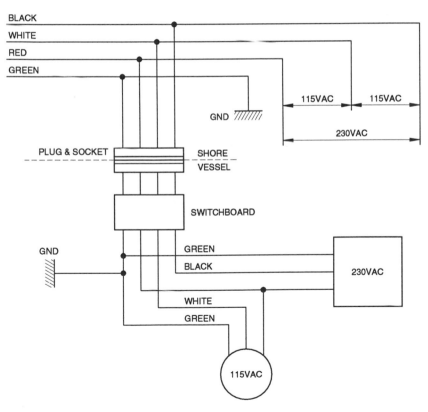

Figure 13-3 115/220-Volt AC Shorepower Systems

e. **220/240-Volt Systems.** The following circuit diagrams and color codes are for typical systems using IEC standard color codes, and incorporating an isolation transformer. Normally, a minimum 15-amp supply rating requires supply cable of 13 AWG (2.5 mm²). Many marina supplies only have a 10-amp supply. The cable should be approximately 12 meters long, but anything over 15 meters brings on voltage drop problems at the rated load. In regard to grounding isolation transformers, you should under no circumstances connect the shore and vessel grounds. The transformer should be insulated from the case on rubber mounts (or similar) and the core should be connected to shore ground. The case can then be connected to boat ground. Test with a multimeter that isolation between the two grounds is above 1 megOhm.

(1) Brown wire is "hot" (used to be red)

(2) Blue wire is neutral (used to be black)

(3) Green/yellow stripe wire is ground or earth (used to be green)

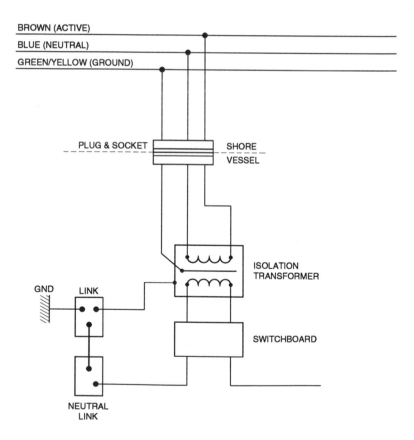

Figure 13-4 220/240-Volt AC Shorepower Isolation Systems

f. **Shore Power Inlet Receptacles.** Inlet receptacles should be weatherproof in accordance with the international protection standards, IP56 rating, which require protection against heavy seas, rain, and splash. Do not use receptacles designed for mobile homes, trailers, or recreational vehicles as they do not meet the required standard. Suppliers such as Marinco and Hubble can supply good quality equipment. The requirements are as follows:

(1) Receptacles must have spring-loaded, self-closing, locking covers. The receptacles must also have a male-type connector only.

(2) Rating must be a minimum of 15 amps for 240-volt systems, 30 amps for 115 volts.

(3) The receptacles should be in an accessible location, well ventilated, and as high as possible above the deck line. They must be placed so there is no risk of mechanical damage.

(4) The receptacles should be shielded so that driving rain at a 45° angle will not enter plug or socket.

g. **Plugs.** Plugs must be double insulated and be made of impact-resistant material. If a plug has accidentally been immersed, do not use it. Disconnect and dismantle it for cleaning and drying first.

13.4 **Isolation Transformers.** Isolation transformers are essential on all steel, alloy, or ferrocement vessels. By eliminating the ground path ashore, they galvanically isolate the vessel from the shore power system, which reduces electrolytic corrosion. They are useful on fiberglass vessels, too, but less necessary. Transformers are heavy and take up space, so they may not be desirable on small vessels.

a. **Ratings.** Most marina outlets rarely exceed 15 amps/240-220 volts or 30 amps/115 volts. The table below show kVA and KW ratings at 0.8 power factor.

b. **Dual Inputs.** If you cruise to foreign countries, it is best to have a dual-input transformer with two primary inputs of 220 and 115 volts. Frequency may vary; an altered frequency will slow down electric motors, but for simple battery charging, domestic appliances, and resistive loads, this is not a major problem. Transformers do not alter frequency.

Table 13-1 Isolation Transformer Rating Table

Output (kW)	Output (kVA)	Current 115 V	Current 220 V
3	3.74	34 Amps	17.0 Amps
4	5.00	45 Amps	22.7 Amps
5	6.25	57 Amps	28.4 Amps
7	8.75	80 Amps	39.8 Amps

13.5   AC Grounding. It is important that standard electrical industry practices be followed when installing and connecting AC grounds. The requirements and purpose are frequently misunderstood. At all times, it is recommended that an AC licensed electrician be used to ensure that installations are done correctly.

    a.   Legal Obligations. Any fault arising on an ungrounded or improperly grounded piece of equipment may cause exposed metal to be "alive" up to rated voltage. Any person coming in contact with that equipment may suffer severe electrical shock, injury, or even death. If an investigation shows that the system was not installed in accordance with recognized electrical standards, or by a qualified person, then it is almost certain that charges of criminal negligence or manslaughter may be instigated, with subsequent litigation for damages. In many countries, this may lead to immediate arrest and imprisonment and the confiscation of your vessel. Your vessel's insurance policy may also be invalidated.

    b.   Protection Principles. Grounding provides a low resistance path for any fault current arising on the bonded metal. During fault conditions, extremely high currents may flow. This high current usually ruptures fuses or trips circuit breakers. Improper grounding, or a high resistance ground may cause excess conductor heating, fire, and unacceptably high voltage levels on equipment.

13.6   AC Grounding (Earthing) Practices. The primary purpose of grounding is to protect against electric shock and to safely ground fault current. It also ensures that the protective devices operate correctly. Grounding has absolutely nothing to do with corrosion protection, and a properly grounded AC-power system will not adversely affect electrolytic corrosion rates. A grounding system must never be installed with prevention of corrosion as one of the design criteria. To modify grounding systems to correct corrosion problems is misguided and dangerous.

    a.   AC Ground to DC Bonding. The only reason such bonding should exist is where the DC negative is grounded in a normal polarized DC system, and the AC ground is connected to the same ground point. This does not mean AC grounds should simply be connected to a battery negative. This ground point should be connected to an immersed ground point. The idea that connections are made to provide an alternate ground path is flawed and dangerous. In practice, the preferred DC configuration is a two-wire insulated DC system, where no polarizing ground is required, and is recommended in all steel and alloy boats.

    b.   Lightning Protection. It is important that a lightning ground be kept separated from AC grounds, DC negatives, and bonding systems. In a strike, high voltages will be impressed on all connected systems, providing many parallel paths, and destruction or damage to all connected equipment. This is a common scenario. Proper grounding as described in Chapter 7 and surge suppression will offer the best solution and minimize the buildup of high voltages within AC and DC circuits.

c.   **Common Bonding.** Bonding of AC grounds, DC negatives, lightning protection system, RF grounds, and bonding systems can cause serious hazards. In the event that the AC ground is damaged or disconnected, and a fault arises, the DC system, mast, and every "safe" DC item on board can be "alive" up to rated voltage. In a boat electrical system, in some situations equipotential bonding of all electrical circuits can hold these systems at full rated AC voltage rather than ground potential, and this does occur. Consider the purpose of each ground before performing indiscriminate bonding.

13.7   Earth Leakage Protection. A much more reliable and acceptable way to protect circuits and people, both ashore and afloat, is to install earth leakage protection devices. Many marinas now have these on each circuit. Earlier units were voltage operated and prone to nuisance tripping. New devices called residual current devices (RCD) are considerably more advanced and reliable. The following should be observed:

a.   **Installation Requirements.** The selection and installation of an RCD is based on the tripping values, and therefore the level of protection. The values are as follows:

   (1)   **30-mA Value.** This value is for quick tripping and protection against personal shock.

   (2)   **100-mA Value.** This level is designed to provide fire protection.

b.   **Nuisance Tripping.** Earth leakages are commonplace, and nuisance tripping is common at marina berths. The principal causes of nuisance tripping are as follows:

   (1)   Connection of a neutral and ground (earth) downstream of an RCD.

   (2)   A crossed neutral between protected and unprotected circuits.

   (3)   Deterioration of cable insulation.

   (4)   Water and moisture in terminal boxes.

   (5)   Cumulative leakages from many sources with small leakage paths.

   (6)   Absorption of moisture into heating elements including steam irons, refrigerator defrost elements, stove and hot-water elements, and electric kettles. This problem disappears if the element operates for a half hour or more.

   (7)   Tracking across dirty surfaces to ground.

   (8)   Intermittent, internal arcing in appliances.

   (9)   High voltage impulses caused by switching off inductive motor loads.

   (10) High current impulses caused by capacitor start motors.

c.   **RCD Operation.** The RCD units work on an electromagnetic principle illustrated below:

    (1)   A toroidal transformer detects magnetic fields created by current flow in the active and neutral conductor of the protected circuit.

    (2)   Under normal conditions, the vector sum of the currents, known as residual current, is effectively zero and the magnetic fields cancel.

    (3)   If a condition arises where current flows from active or neutral to ground, the residual current will not be zero and the magnetic field will send a tripping signal to the protected circuit.

d.   **Installation Checks.** Installation should be performed by an AC-licensed electrician and should be tested using test equipment made for the purpose. The following tests must be performed using a 500-volt (Megger) tester:

    (1)   Disconnect supply, neutral, and earth. Test between active and earth. On new installations, readings must exceed 1 megOhm, and be a minimum of 250k ohms on existing systems.

    (2)   Test between neutral and earth. Readings must be a minimum of 40k ohms.

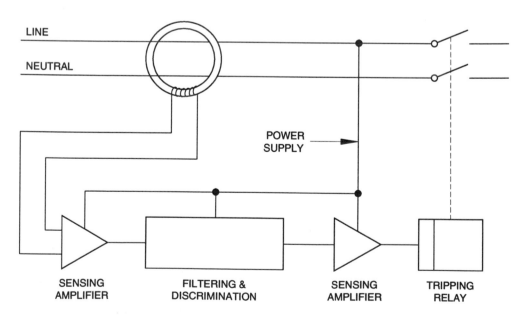

Figure 13-5 Residual-Current Protection Devices

13.8   AC Circuit Protection. Most installations are protected by a circuit breaker on the marina distribution panel or by an earth leakage circuit breaker (Residual Current Device) on later pedestals to detect and isolate leakage conditions. The main circuit protective device is the Miniature Circuit Breaker (MCB).

a.   **MCB Selection Factors.** There is more to installing circuit breakers than simply putting a breaker in. The following factors should be noted:

(1)   The device voltage must suit the system voltage.

(2)   The interrupting capacity must be able to cope with any prospective fault current levels.

(3)   The MCB current rating must hold at 100% of operating current and trip at 125% at 40°C.

(4)   The MCB must protect the cable, not the equipment.

(5)   The MCB must be rated to the maximum demand. Motor starting loads can be 4 to 6 times rated load.

b.   **MCB Principles.** An MCB combines the action of a switch, overload protection, and short circuit protection.

(1)   **Overload Protection.** This function is thermally operated. At 25°C, an MCB normally holds at 110% of rated value and trips at 137% of rated value.

(2)   **Short Circuit Protection.** This function is magnetically operated. A solenoid coil within the breaker trips when the factory set, short circuit current value is reached. Short circuit faults can generate a large arc. Breakers use the generated magnetic field to direct and quench the arc in a chute.

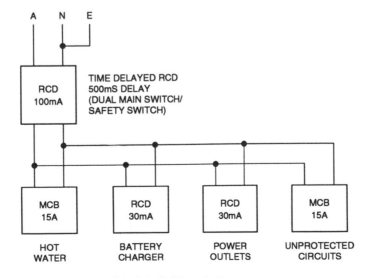

Figure 13-6 AC Circuit Protection

13.9   AC Cable Installation. AC systems are by their nature hazardous. Every precaution must be taken to ensure that the systems are properly installed so that there is no risk to people and vessel.

   a.   Cable Ratings. Cables should be carefully selected. Observe the following:

   (1)   Cable Standards. Cable ratings and insulation materials should conform to recognized national standards. Where possible, use cables classed as "Shipwiring Cables." Two-core and earth cables should be used. Typical ratings are given in Table 13-2.

   (2)   Cable Types. Shipwiring cable is expensive. If you do not want to pay the costs of such cable, install 15/30 amp, heavy-duty, orange- or yellow-sheathed extension cable. Under no circumstances should you install domestic cable.

Table 13-2 AC System Two-Core Cable Ratings

Cable Size	PVC	Butyl Rubber	EPR
1.0 mm²	8 Amps	12 Amps	13 Amps
1.5 mm²	11 Amps	16 Amps	17 Amps
2.5 mm²	14 Amps	22 Amps	23 Amps
4.0 mm²	19 Amps	31 Amps	32 Amps
6.0 mm²	25 Amps	39 Amps	40 Amps
10.0 mm²	35 Amps	53 Amps	57 Amps
16.0 mm²	40 Amps	70 Amps	76 Amps
25.0 mm²	60 Amps	93 Amps	102 Amps
35.0 mm²	73 Amps	115 Amps	120 Amps
50.0 mm²	85 Amps	135 Amps	155 Amps

   b.   Cable Installation. Cable must be installed so that there is no risk of mechanical damage. Route it well away from machinery and heat sources. Observe the following:

   (1)   Saddle Distances. The distance between saddles should be no more than 20 cm.

   (2)   Minimum Bending Radius. To avoid stress to conductors, the minimum internal radius of a bend should be approximately three times the overall cable diameter.

   (3)   Bulkhead Transits. Cables going through bulkheads should be installed so that there is no risk of insulation damage. Use suitable watertight cable glands to protect the integrity of watertight bulkheads.

c. **Cable Terminations.** Cable terminations must be properly made inside junction boxes as follows:

(1) **Machinery Spaces.** Waterproof junction boxes with proper cable glands should be used to prevent the entry of moisture.

(2) **Accommodation Spaces.** Ideally, water-resistant boxes should be used, but on smaller vessels I have found mini-junction boxes with integral terminal blocks to be practical.

d. **Circuit Protection.** Circuit protection should consist of circuit breakers rated for the maximum current carrying capacity of the cable. If protective and isolation devices are not integrated into the main panel, a domestic, consumer distribution panel may be a good alternative. These compact panels, made of plastic with a splashproof cover, have all earth and neutral conductors and main switch or RCD and MCBs within one unit.

e. **Grounding.** Earth or ground conductors must be terminated to the vessel's ground system. *The ground system must never be connected to DC system negatives.*

f. **Switchboards**. Switchboards must be made of a non-conductive, non-hygroscopic material. Where DC and AC are installed on the same panel, which is common on yachts, cover the exposed AC connections at the rear of the panel.

g. **AC System Commissioning.** The following *must* be checked before putting any circuit into service:

(1) **Earthing Resistance and Continuity.** Maximum resistance should be 2 ohms between main ground (earth) block and boat ground or between any grounded point and boat ground.

(2) **Insulation Resistance.** A 500-volt, DC-insulation tester (megger) must be used. Disconnect all electronics and appliances, turn off power, and disconnect main grounding conductor. Turn on all switches. Insulation resistance between ground and live conductors must be a minimum of 1 megOhm. Water-heater elements must be at least 10k ohms.

(3) **Polarity.** All switches, circuit breakers, outlet live pins, and equipment terminals must all be the same polarity. No transposition of neutral and actives is allowable.

(4) **Neutral and Ground Conductor Transposition.** Check that both circuits are separated.

(5) **Conductor Short Circuits.** Use an ohmmeter to check between active and neutral to ensure that only load resistances are present. With all switches on, there should be no short circuits because of cable damage or incorrect equipment connection.

13.10   Diesel Generators. The diesel generator is the most common onboard AC power source on vessels greater than 40 feet. It can be a far more economical, long-term supplier of power and virtually relegate the engine to propulsion duties. Most generators are single phase; three-phase machines are used on larger vessels. The majority come complete with sound shields and only require external connection of cooling water, fuel, electrical, and exhaust systems. Top-of-the-line units are made by Northern Lights, Kohler, and Onan.

13.11   AC Alternators. Alternators are generally robust and constructed to marine standards.

> **a.   Single Phase Alternators.** The single-phase alternator is the most common. The typical alternator is a brushless, self-excited machine with either two or four poles. Units may be single bearing machines directly coupled to the engine, or dual bearing units driven by a belt or coupling.
>
> > **(1)   Operation.** At initial start-up, there is sufficient remanent voltage left in the machine to establish the main field. Once rated speed and output are reached, the Automatic Voltage Regulator (AVR) controls the output voltage in response to system variations. Frequency is a function of speed, and stability is maintained by the engine governor.
> >
> > **(2)   AVR Operation.** The AVR controls the excitation voltage level. The control voltage is applied through the excitation winding and is fed through the rotor mounted excitation winding to the diode rectifier. The rectifier's DC output then goes to the main rotor winding rotating field and controls the field strength.

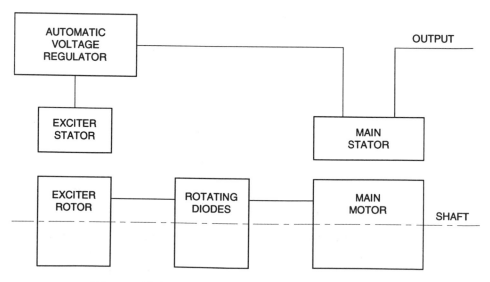

Figure 13-7 Single-Phase Alternator Diagrams

b. **Mase Generators.** A typical Mase control system and alternator electrical diagram are illustrated below. Unlike many alternators, these brushless machines do not use a voltage regulator. They are self-regulating and self-exciting with a capacitor connected across the auxiliary winding of the stator:

(1)   While rotating, the residual magnetism and permanent magnets induce a voltage into the auxiliary winding for excitation. This voltage is fed to the capacitor, which generates a capacitive current in the circuit.

(2)   The capacitive current creates a magnetic field, which is rectified by the diode, supplying a DC current to the induction winding. This generates a rotating magnetic field for generation of output. A varistor is connected across the diode to absorb transient spikes.

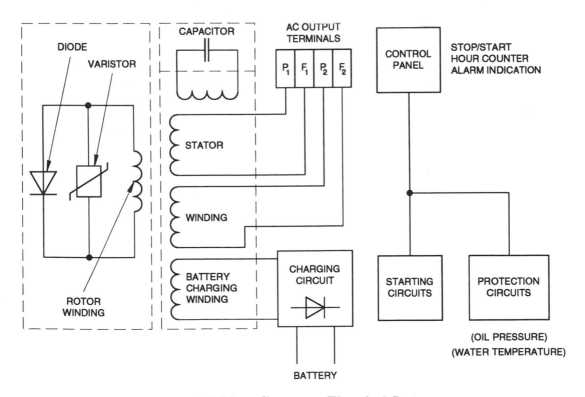

Figure 13-8 Mase Generator Electrical System

243

13.12   AC Alternator Parameters. The alternator has the following parameters:

    a.   **Voltage.** The typical rated output voltages are 115/230, or 220/240 volts for single-phase machines, and 415/440 volts for three-phase machines. Nominal output is maintained by the Automatic Voltage Regulator (AVR). The AVR is an electronic regulator that senses output terminal voltage and varies the field strength to maintain the correct value. Regulation is typically within 2% of nominal rating. The AVR must be able to control the output rapidly in response to large load fluctuations. Recovery in good machines is typically 3% of rated output within 0.25 seconds when full load is applied. Voltage is not a function of speed or frequency when an alternator is running at or near rated speed.

    b.   **Frequency.** Frequency is specified in hertz, the number of alternating cycles per second. Output frequency is a function of speed and varies in response to speed fluctuations. Stability depends on the ability of the machine to maintain a nominal frequency over the complete power output range; this is typically within 1%. Engine speed is controlled by the engine governor. When a large load is applied, such as a motor starting, the generator loads the engine, causing it to slow momentarily. The governor reacts by increasing fuel flow and speeding the engine up. When the load is removed, the reverse occurs. Stability depends on response time, and governors are factory set. A small time lag is inherent in the system and helps minimize hunting, caused by continual alterations in response to small load fluctuations. Frequency and specified engine speed depend on the number of poles within the alternator. Two-pole machines generate one cycle per revolution and require an engine speed of 3000 rev/min for 50 hertz. Four pole machines generate two cycles per revolution, and only require 1500 rev/min for 50 hertz. For the average vessel, the high-speed machines are the most reliable and do not increase maintenance costs, as is commonly asserted.

    c.   **Power.** Power output is stated in either kVA or kW ratings. These are defined as follows:

        (1)   **KVA Rating.** The kVA rating is the power output, which is the current multiplied by voltage to give voltamps, and divided by 1000 to give a KiloVoltAmp rating.

        (2)   **KW Rating.** The kilowatt rating is the kVA rating multiplied by a power factor, typically 0.8. This is the actual power output.

13.13   AC Alternator Rating Selection. Rating selection must consider a number of factors. A total expected load analysis must also be undertaken to calculate the peak loads that might be encountered:

    a.   **Starting Currents.** Starting current may be as high as five to nine times that of normal running current. These high currents are caused by the in-rush current at starting, and the energy required to overcome bearing friction and load inertia. Duration of the peaks is typically less than one second, and most alternators can withstand 250% overloads for up to 10 seconds.

b. **Power Factor.** In simplified terms, Power Factor (PF) is the ratio of useful power in watts to the apparent power (voltamps) of the circuit. Power (watts) = Volts x Amps x Power Factor. In a purely resistive circuit such as a heater, the alternating current and voltage are said to be in phase. The average power over a complete cycle is the product of the voltage and current in voltamps. When reactance is introduced into the circuit, the voltage and current become out of phase, so that during any cycle the current is negative and the voltage positive. The resultant value is less than the voltamp value. Inductive reactance causes current to lag the voltage. This will be an electrical angle between 0 and 90°. Resistive loads are said to be in phase, with no angle of difference and these are termed unity power factor. In electrical circuits, capacitive reactance cancels out inductive reactance. Capacitive reactance causes current to lead the voltage. The use of capacitors can improve unacceptably high lagging power factors. This correction is generally limited to fluorescent lighting systems in larger commercial vessels.

c. **PF Ratings.** Most machinery nameplates specify power factor ratings. Available alternator output power decreases as system power factor values decrease. On fully automated, refrigerated cargo vessels, up to 100 large electric motors are running. The inductive load requires up to four, 400-kilowatt gensets on line to meet the demand. With power factor correction capacitors in circuit, this could be reduced to two units, for a considerable saving of fuel and maintenance costs.

13.14   AC Rating Calculation. From a load analysis, the following calculations can be performed to estimate minimum alternator size:

a.   Max.   Expected   Continuous   Load   =   3600   watts
Largest   Single   Load   Value   =   2400   watts

Running Current (Ir) = $\frac{\text{Power (watts)}}{\text{Volts x PF.}}$ = $\frac{2400}{40 \times 0.7}$ = 14.2 amps

Starting Current (Is) = Ir x 4 = 56.8 Amps

b.   If alternator can withstand overloads of 250% for 10 sec. starting current (Is) must be divided by 2.5 = 22.8 amps.

c.   Rating is therefore 22.8 x 240 = 5 kVA, or 0.8 x 22.8 x 240 = 4 kW

d.   In selecting an output rating, an estimate must be made of the maximum load likely to be applied. The larger the rating, the greater the initial capital cost and the greater the weight and space required. A decision must be made about how the equipment will be used in order to reduce the generator to a suitable size. Ideally, the generator will be loaded to around 75% of maximum and running efficiently. Running large gensets on light loads significantly increases maintenance costs.

Table 13-3 AC Load Analysis Table

Equipment	Typical Rating	Actual Rating
Toaster	1000 Watts	_____
Kettle	1200	_____
Television	100	_____
Video Player	200	_____
Microwave	1200	_____
Hair Dryer	500	_____
Iron	1200	_____
Fan Heater	2400	_____
Fluorescent Light	20	_____
Incandescent Light	60	_____
Low Energy Light	16	_____
Water Heater	1800	_____
Pressure Cleaner	2400	_____
Refrigerator	1000	_____
Washing Machine	1800	_____
Battery Charger	300	_____
Food Processor	400	_____
Coffee Maker	700	_____
Hand Tools	600	_____
Air Conditioner	3600	_____
_____		_____
_____		_____
		_____
TOTAL LOAD		_____ W

e. **Appliance Ratings.** Many yachts have a genset with a rating far in excess of what is required. Oversizing problems can be resolved by carefully choosing appliances for use on board.

(1) **Kettles.** Many fast boil kettles have an element rated at 2.4 kilowatts (240 volts AC). On a 4-kilowatt generator, that is more than half load. Buy a simple kettle rated about 1200 watts.

(2) **Toasters.** Most toasters, besides being notoriously unreliable on yachts, consume large amounts of current. The older, fold down side toasters have a lower current draw and are more reliable.

(3) **Microwaves.** Get a simple, compact unit with a relatively low power rating. Some regular-size microwaves have ratings of around 1600 watts when set on "high".

(4) **Fan Heaters.** Many fan heaters on "high" settings are also rated at 2.4 kilowatts, and place a significant load on a generator.

(5) **Water Heaters.** Install a heating element of around 1.2 kilowatts instead of a 2.4 kilowatt unit.

13.15   AC Electrical Installation. It is important that electrical installations be installed to comply with relevant national standards. These standards also apply to general AC systems. Relevant standards are laid down by survey classification societies and national authorities, including:

a.   U.S. Coast Guard

b.   U.K. Institute Electrical Engineers Recommendations

c.   Lloyd's Rules for Yachts and Small Craft

13.16   Generator Cabling. Cable should meet marine standards. As an alternative, use high-grade cable such as that for underground electricity or industrial electrical installations. It has a characteristic orange outer sheath.

a.   **Protection.** Generator electrical circuits are protected with one or more of the following:

(1)   **Overload.** Some gensets have an overload circuit breaker fitted at the genset control box. Reset it, if tripped. If repeatedly tripping occurs, find and remove the cause of the overload. In many cases, the problem may be too many appliances operating.

(2)   **Short Circuit.** This is generally a circuit breaker mounted at the genset control box. If it trips after resetting, then find and correct the fault.

(3)   **Reverse Current.** This protection is usually seen only on larger installations or where two units are parallelled.

(4)   **Low Frequency.** Not all generators have this protection. Adjust only according to manufacturers' instructions.

(5)   **Undervoltage.** Undervoltage systems are used in larger installations and are normally interlocked with main circuit breakers.

b.   **Grounding.** All exposed metal able to carrying a voltage under operating or fault conditions must be grounded to an equipotential point. The generator frame should be securely connected to the common ground system, but be sure the common ground is not connected to the DC system negative. Where generator units have the starter motor negative bonded to the frame, this is a problem. Ideally, this should be isolated, although a modification may be required where a relay or solenoid is inserted in the negative conductor so that it disconnects after starting.

c.   **Neutral Connection.** In single-phase installations, the neutral is connected to the distribution system neutral, not the ground.

d.   **Parallelling of Machines.** In larger vessels with more than one generator, parallelling the units to the main switchboard busbar may be necessary. To do this, a frequency meter is required to synchronize the machines.

13.17   **AC Maintenance.** Electrical system maintenance consists primarily of the following:

a.   **Visual Inspection.** Visually inspect the connections and terminals every 6 months, and tighten where necessary. Connection boxes should be clean and dry.

b.   **Insulation Test.** Using a 500-volt insulator tester, check all active conductors to ground. Any reading less than 1 megOhm should be rectified.

13.18   **AC Generator Troubleshooting.** Faults within the electrical supply system are normally caused by bad connections at the alternator or isolation transformer. In rare cases, cables may chafe and damage insulation. The main faults that can arise on the alternator are:

a.   **Over Voltage.** The voltage regulator is faulty.

b.   **Under Voltage.** The voltage regulator or excitation circuit is faulty.

c.   **Voltage Fluctuation.** A voltage regulator is faulty. In brush machines, this occurs when a brush sticks or the slip rings are dirty and there is arcing.

d.   **Cannot Sustain Load.** Typically, a regulator is faulty, or a rotor diode is breaking down or has failed. In units with capacitors, the inability to sustain a load can also be caused by faulty capacitors or transient suppressors.

13.19   **Generator Fuel Consumption.** Table 13-4 gives approximate fuel consumption rates at full-rated loads for a number of engine (not electrical) output ratings. These will serve as a general guide in working out similar onboard consumption values.

Table 13-4 Generator Fuel Consumption

Cylinders	Capacity	Speed	Output	Fuel Rate
2	0.5 liter	3000	7.5 kW	1.5 l/hr
3	1.0	1500	7.7	2.5
4	1.3	3000	9.8	3.2
4	1.3	1500	19.4	5.9
4	1.5	1500	11.9	2.6
4	1.8	1500	13.0	4.5
3	2.5	1500	21.0	6.1
4	3.9	1500	34.0	10.2

13.20   Generator Mechanical Systems. The alternator prime mover gives the most in-service troubles. The principles involved are identical to the main propulsion engine. If the lubrication, cooling, and fuel and air quality are maintained, long-term, trouble-free operation is assured.

a.   Coolants. Genset diesels may be cooled by sea water or have a heat exchanger with a closed-circuit cooling system. The coolant provides the medium for transferring engine heat to the primary sea water coolant and for controlling the overall operating temperature of the engine. It is essential that adequate heat transfer is maintained. The coolant must remain free of salt water contamination to prevent corrosion or the formation of sludge and scale that may impede coolant flow or block coolers. A coolant which has no inhibitors, incorrect inhibitors, or improper concentrations of inhibitors will ultimately cause problems with rust, sludge, fatigued water-pump seals, and reduced heat transfer rates as engine block water passages become coated with insulating layer of scale. This will gradually result in overheating and all the damage that goes with it.

(1)   **Additives.** A number of additives are available that improve the performance of coolants, including sulfates, chlorides, dissolved solids, and calcium. Coolant should also have an antifreeze additive to prevent freezing and engine damage in cold climates. Most ethylene-glycol-based antifreeze solutions contain the inhibitors required for normal operation.

(2)   **Corrosion Inhibitors.** This is generally a water-soluble chemical compound that protects the metal surfaces within the system against corrosion. Compounds can include borates, chromates and nitrites. Inhibitors with soluble oils should never be used as a corrosion inhibitor.

b.   Lubricating Oil. Lubrication has the dual function of reducing friction between moving parts and taking away some of the heat generated during combustion. It is essential that the correct grades of oil be used for the prevailing temperature conditions, and that the filter be changed regularly along with oil. Oil viscosity must be maintained if correct lubrication is to be achieved, and this depends on the engine remaining within proper operating temperature range. Lubricating problems include:

(1)   **Fuel in Oil.** Fuel in the oil creates the risk of a crankcase explosion and is characterized by low lube oil viscosity.

(2)   **Water in Oil.** Water in the oil causes emulsification, which destroys the lubricating properties. After repairing a leak, completely flush out the system. No moisture must remain.

(3)   **Microbe Growth.** Moisture in the system can encourage microbial growth in the oil. Once the system is "infected," considerable flushing is required if it is to be eliminated.

c.   **Fuel.** Uncontaminated fuel is essential to good combustion and efficient engine operation. There has been a history of water-contaminated fuels supplied to unsuspecting yachts from bunker barges. Observe the following installation precautions:

   (1)   Filters. Install a filter and water separator (Racor), preferably with a water-in-fuel alarm. In most cases, the generator takes fuel from the same tanks as the main engine, which should have similar protection.

   (2)   Purge Fuel Tanks. Microbial growth can occur in water-contaminated fuels. Tanks must be regularly purged of water and kept topped up to avoid condensation.

d.   **Electrical System.** The electrical and monitoring system is similar to the main engine system. It consists of the following:

   (1)   Starting System. Always install a separate starting battery for the generator. Start batteries for a typical 4-6 kVA genset are recommended at 70AH/325CCA. This provides backup power for the main engine in an emergency, or alternatively ensures that the genset can be started if the main engine is out of service. Some generators have an interlock in the starting system that prevents starting if the generator is running.

   (2)   Charging System. The alternator charging system on most gensets is very small, typically around 25 amps maximum. Normally, it is only used to charge the start battery, although alterations can be made to charge main engine or house batteries. In some cases, the alternator can be uprated to 55 amps or even 80 amps, which when connected up to a cycle regulator, provides the main battery charging source, limiting the run time requirements of the main engine. Care must be taken as output shafts cannot always cope with large mechanical side loads.

   (3)   Monitoring System. Most generator units have basic control panels with alarms only for high water temperature or low oil pressure. Many newer units, such as the Mase, also incorporate an hour meter, pilot light, overload alarm, and a water warning alarm. It is generally easy to install gauges which give a clearer indication of performance.

   (4)   Preheat Systems. Many generators have a preheating system which uses a traditional cylinder glowplug in the combustion chamber. Some engines also have preheaters in the air intakes, referred to as a cold start aid.

13.21   Generator Maintenance. The maintenance tasks for the main engine are also valid for generators.

a.   **Fuel System.** Renew and clean filters every 1000 operating hours.

b.   **Lube Oil System.** Replace oil and filters every 500 operating hours. Always check oil viscosity, and for signs of water, fuel or microbial growth that may affect viscosity and quality.

c.   **Air System.** Replace filter element every 1500 operating hours.

d.   **Coolant System.** Check coolant levels monthly. Periodically check inhibitor concentrations with test kit. Check thermostat.

e.   **Cleaning.** Keep engine clean of oil and dirt.

f.   **Belts.** Check and tighten alternator and water/fuel pump drive belts monthly.

g.   **Charging System.** Using voltmeter, check that the charge voltage is approximately 13.5-14.5 volts.

h.   **Mountings.** Check rubber mountings for cracks and fatigue.

i.   **Electrical.** Check that battery and starter connections are clean and tight.

j.   **Anodes.** Sacrificial zinc anodes in the cooling system should be checked every 6 months and renewed if corroded.

13.22   Generator Operating Notes. There are certain points to consider when operating the genset:

a.   **Starting.** After starting, always check that sea water coolant is discharging overboard to ensure that coolant is passing through the engine. Don't wait for a high-temperature alarm to warn you of possible engine damage.

b.   **Operating Temperatures.** Run the genset for five minutes before putting a load on it. This gives the engine a chance to increase to a normal operating temperature.

c.   **Loading.** Do not let the generator run on light or no load for extended periods. This will cause cylinder glazing and deposits within the engine which will increase maintenance costs. If you have an electric water heater, put it on to increase load and make the most of the available energy.

Table 13-5 Generator Troubleshooting

Symptom	Probable Fault
Generator Will Not Start	Fuel supply valve closed
	Fuel filter clogged
	Flat battery
	Control power failure
	Stop solenoid jammed
	Fuel lift pump fault
Low Cranking Speed	Low battery voltage
	Battery terminal loose
	Starter motor fault
Will Not Hold Load	Fuel filter clogged
	Air filter clogged
	Air in fuel system
	Governor fault
	Voltage regulator fault
High Temperature	Air cleaner clogged
	Injector pump fault
	Injector atomiser fault
	Thermostat fault
	Heat exchanger clogged
	Water pump fault
	Water pump belt loose
	Low coolant level
	Seawater strainer clogged
	Seawater pump fault
Low Oil Pressure	Low oil level
	Oil filter clogged
	Oil cooler clogged
	Oil pump fault
	Bearing problem
	Pressure gauge fault
Exhaust Smoke Black (incomplete combustion)	Air cleaner clogged
	Low compression
	Injector pump fault
	Restricted exhaust
	Head gasket leak
	Engine cold
	Valve stuck
Exhaust Smoke White (unburnt fuel vapor)	Low compression
	Head gasket leak
	Cold start
Generator Starts and Stops	Fuel filter clogged
	Air in fuel system
	Fuel supply valve closed
Generator Misfiring	Injector pump fault
	Overheating

13.23   **Inverters.** Inverters are becoming very popular where a relatively small AC power source is required. Output ratings cover a wide range, and some units can be parallelled with an automatic synchronization module. It is quite common to have smaller units connected to various equipment such as video players and televisions. While this arrangement provides redundancy, more practical use can be made of one larger output unit connected to the AC switchboard. A number of microwaves have appeared with dedicated inverters fitted with a single outlet, but this is uneconomical for the average vessel.

      a.   **Construction.** All units have solid state electronics and price variations can be considerable. The quality of construction is a major cost consideration, with electronic design and component quality accounting for most cost variations. Problems with earlier units unfairly gave inverters a bad reputation; now technological advances have improved reliability. With the large number of units on the market, it is impossible to appraise all the different models. Nevertheless, always choose a unit from an established manufacturer with good service support.

      b.   **Output Waveforms.** Output waveforms are an important consideration when looking at proposed applications.

          (1)   **Square Wave.** The majority of inverters have a trapezoidal waveform. This is suitable for most equipment, but microwaves and some inductive loads do not operate at full output, dropping efficiency by 20% or more in some cases and making fluorescent lights slower to start. For microwaves, one solution is to use an auto-transformer to boost peak voltages. A 3-microfarad capacitor across input will improve lighting starts.

          (2)   **Sine Wave.** These units are the ideal, but are very expensive and not commonly used on smaller vessels. Some units have a modified- or quasi-sine wave output which closely resembles a pure sine waveform.

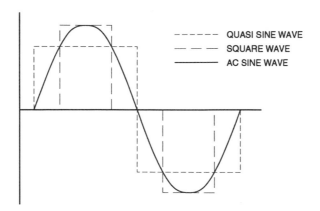

QUASI SINE WAVE
SQUARE WAVE
AC SINE WAVE

Figure 13-9 Inverter Output Waveforms

c. **DC Loads.** The typical inverter is capable of drawing large DC current loads from the battery. It is essential for battery capacity to be able to support these loads without affecting the existing electrical system and connected loads, particularly electronics equipment. The large power consumption makes mandatory the installation of a fast charge regulator to properly recharge batteries.

Table 13-6 Inverter 12-volt DC/220-volt AC Current Loads

AC Load	DC Current Draw	Peak Overload
200 W (0.8 Amps)	18 Amps	42 Amps
400 W (1.6 Amps)	37 Amps	100 Amps
600 W (2.4 Amps)	56 Amps	145 Amps
900 W (3.6 Amps)	84 Amps	180 Amps
1200 W (4.8 Amps)	120 Amps	290 Amps
2400 W (9.6 Amps)	240 Amps	580 Amps
3000 W (12 Amps)	300 Amps	750 Amps

d. **Transfer Systems.** If another AC power source is accidentally connected across the inverter output, the inverter electronics will be seriously damaged. Shore power, generator, and inverter outputs must not be paralleled at any time.

(1) **Rotary Switches.** The normal selection system is a rotary cam switch. The switch should be a center-off type with the inverter to the side opposite the generator and shore power.

(2) **Automatic Changeover Systems.** Intervolt manufactures a relay-operated module that automatically switches the power supply to the inverter when shore power is disconnected. A system of solenoids activated by an off-the-shelf electronic module is also used. The illustration shows the system recommended by Victron: an interlocked automatic changeover contactor that breaks before making each circuit.

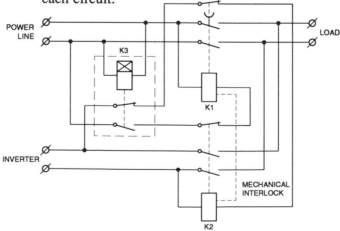

Figure 13-10 Inverter Interlocks

e.   **Efficiency.** The typical inverter is now approximately 85% efficient at rated output. Newer units such as the Mastervolt MASS 24/3000 from Intervolt in the Netherlands have raised this to a staggering 97%. This efficiency level was achieved through the use of new electronic switching technologies (Mosfets) and toroidal transformers. The illustration below shows the various output characteristics of inverters.

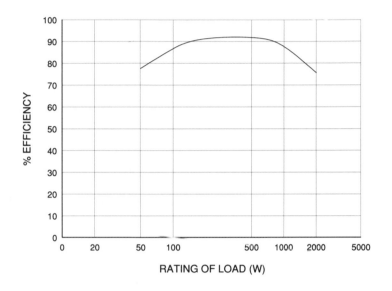

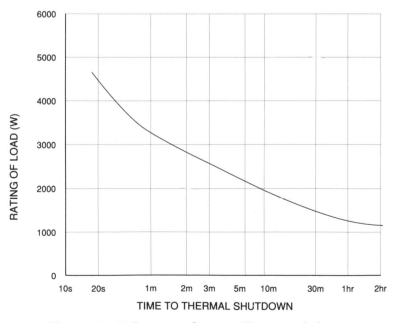

Figure 13-11 Inverter Output Characteristics

255

f. **Auto Start.** Most units now have an autostart capability. This means they can remain in a standby or idle mode until a load is switched on.

　　(1)　**Idle Mode.** Input current in idle mode is typically around 10-50 mA. This load must always be included in DC load calculations.

　　(2)　**Activation Load.** The load required to activate most inverters is approximately 6-10 voltamps or greater. If the vessel is to be left unattended for an extended period, the DC supply should be switched off. In some cases, the loads from fluorescent lights or electronics equipment may not be enough to activate the inverter; another load should be momentarily switched on to cut the inverter in.

g. **Protection.** Most inverters have an undervoltage cutout that is typically set at 10.5 volts. Units also have overload protection, a high voltage cutout, and thermal overload protection that shuts down the inverter if overheating takes place.

h. **Ventilation.** Good ventilation is essential for reliable operation and full rated outputs.

　　(1)　Install the unit in a dry, clean, and well ventilated area.

　　(2)　Allow sufficient vertical clearance for the convection of heat from the unit. Derating factors are illustrated in Table 13-7.

Table 13-7 Temperature Derating Factors

Temperature	Output Rating
+40°C to +50°C	80% Rated Output
-10°C to +40°C	100% Rated Output
-10°C to -20°C	140% Rated Output

i. **Ratings.** Units generally have a number of ratings:

　　(1)　**Output Rating.** The rating based on a resistive load for a nominal period, typically 30 minutes (e.g., 1600 watts).

　　(2)　**Continuous Rating.** The normal, continuous rating (e.g., 1000 watts).

　　(3)　**Maximum Rating.** The maximum, short duration load (e.g., 3000 watts). Most units are able to withstand the short duration and intermittent overloads that occur, especially with motor starts.

13.24 **Engine Driven Alternators.** A number of alternators have been developed to be driven off the main propulsion engine. There are two principal types, categorized according to their output waveforms.

a. **Sine Wave.** Many yachtsmen couple small gensets to the engine, either via lay shafts or belt drives. Some of the systems available include:

(1) **SeaGen.** SeaFresh of the U.K. has developed a conversion kit for Yanmar diesels that has a double belt drive off the output shaft of the engine. The alternator is conveniently mounted in the vacant space above the gearbox.

(2) **Auto-Gen.** The American-made Auto-Gen unit generates 4.5 kilowatts (19.6 amps). This unit is belt-coupled to a main crankshaft pulley, and requires up to 9 horsepower at full, rated output. It also needs a reasonable area to install the alternator and the electric clutch assembly. The units use a clutch and control system to compensate for engine speed variations and to ensures frequency stability. Units are quite heavy (64 kg).

b. **Square Wave.** These units, typified by the Waeco AC Power (a modified version of the defunct Kestrel Power AC) and Sea Power, are direct replacement alternators for the existing unit on the main engine.

(1) **Output Ratings.** Outputs are available in 110 or 240 volts and typically have a 2- to 3-kilowatt modified square wave. These units have the same limitations as static inverters but are much easier to install.

(2) **Construction and Operation.** Typical units employ a Bosch DC alternator casing with a stator having a double winding. The units generate DC, which is converted through an electronics module to AC. Both voltage and frequency are stabilized for all engine speeds. The AC power also has a selectable DC charging output of 65 amps, with a fast charge option built into the control system. Alternator speed ranges are 5000-7000 rev/min when using the correct pulley ratios.

(3) **Protection.** These units incorporate earth leakage, overload, and short circuit protection.

(4) **Recommendations.** I have installed many of the Kestrel units and encountered many reliability problems. I do not regard them as sufficiently proven, although the new French manufacturers may have solved many of the problems. With the recent advances in inverter and charging efficiency, the inverter and fast charging arrangement are a better option.

13.25 **Hydraulic Generators.** Hydraulically powered alternators are another innovative source of AC power. Hydraulic systems with larger outputs are a good proposition aboard vessels such as ferries or trawlers that have long engine run times. System outputs can be single or three phase, depending on the output required, from 6.4 kilowatts up to 120 kilowatts.

    a.   **Pump Drive.** The system uses a directly coupled or belt driven hydraulic pump.

    b.   **System Operation.** The pump delivers oil to the hydraulic motor via a valve system. Valves maintain alternator speed at rated speed irrespective of engine speed or electrical loading. Frequency and voltage are maintained to within 2.5 hertz over the full range of engine speeds. Electronic feedback options can be incorporated to reduce this to 0.5 hertz.

    c.   **Auxiliaries.** The system incorporates an oil cooler and reservoir tank. A bow thruster can be operated off the same hydraulics system. The typical system is illustrated below.

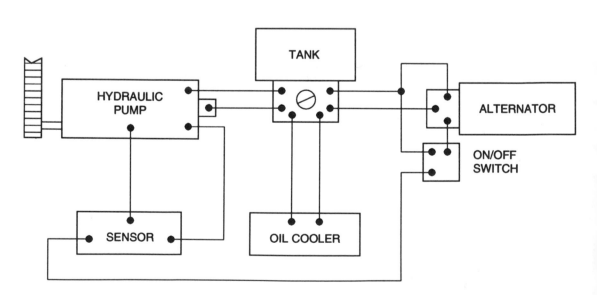

Figure 13-12 Hydraulic Powered Alternator System

13.26   Rotary DC Converters. The DC motor-powered generator is an alternative to gensets and inverters. The Redi-Line system is simply a 240-volt alternator driven by a direct coupled DC motor.

a.   **DC Power Supply.** If you intend to use the units continuously, the manufacturer specifies at least a 50 amp-hour battery capacity just for the converter, though in fact a larger capacity is essential. Like the static inverter, large current levels are required to operate the unit at full load. Therefore it is essential to have a good charging source.

b.   **Ratings.** Ratings are typically in the range of 500 to 1400 watts of continuous sine wave output. Efficiency is often low, and this is amplified with low loads or in standby conditions.

c.   **System Interference.** If units are operated as recommended off the deep-cycle house batteries, surges and voltage drops on the power supply to other equipment will be visible. Caution must be exercised so that electronics data are not corrupted. It is best to run the engine so that some load can be supplied by the alternator.

d.   **Maintenance.** The motor should be maintained in accordance with the recommendations in Chapter 10.

13.27   Gasoline Gensets. Portable gasoline gensets typically have ratings up to around 3 kilowatts. They are designed primarily for land-based applications, not for use in marine environments. There are many in use on cruising yachts, but they have significant disadvantages.

a.   **Explosive Fuel.** Gasoline is extremely volatile and good ventilation is essential to avoid potentially hazardous vapor concentrations.

b.   **Exhaust Emissions.** Gasoline gensets emit toxic carbon monoxide; belowdeck concentrations can be extremely hazardous. Good ventilation is essential to avoid any exhaust gas buildup.

c.   **Electric Shock.** As components are not designed for marine environments, the risk of electric shock does exist. Grounding is also more difficult. Grounding should be to the vessel AC ground source. A prominent boating journalist once recommended that grounding on fiberglass vessels was unnecessary due to the insulating nature of the deck it sat on. The premise was that it was difficult for anyone to ground out a fault on the unit and hence electrocute themselves. Not true! Failure to ground represents a considerable shock hazard. Don't risk it!

d.   **Installation.** The lubrication system is not designed to operate at any angle of heel, so the units must be run in a near level attitude. Because of this, multihulls may have more use for portable gensets, and since a number of fairly large multihulls are propelled by outboards, the fuel will be identical.

13.28   AC Machinery. The most common type of equipment is the electric motor. Motors are very robust and generally give years of trouble-free service. The principal problem with AC motors is the starting currents, which can be two to five times their rated load. Most starters have a Direct-On-Line (DOL) starting system. On-board repairs are generally limited to bearing replacement. Rewinding and similar repairs should be undertaken by a reputable shore repair facility. On many occasions, an AC motor may have a very low winding insulation value, due to moist air or being flooded. To undertake both repairs, the following should be undertaken to get up and running again:

  a.   **Winding Drying.** Dismantle the motor completely. If the motor has been immersed, replace the bearings and do the following:

  (1)   Wash the motor stator with fresh water.

  (2)   Place the stator in the oven at approximately 70°C for at least four hours.

  (3)   Check insulation value to case with 500-volt (megger) tester. Reading should be at least 1 megOhm.

  (4)   Recheck insulation reading after 4 hours to ensure that the reading remains high.

  b.   **Maintenance.** The maintenance requirements of AC motors are minimal and consist of the following:

  (1)   **Insulation Testing.** Every 6 months, the winding-to-ground insulation resistance should be tested using a 500-volt (megger) tester. Readings should be a minimum of 1 megOhm.

  (2)   **Terminals.** Connections should be checked and tightened.

  (3)   **Bearings.** If bearings are not sealed, they should be repacked every two years, depending on run times. If a motor is stationary for much of the time, maintain the bearings by manually turning the shaft at least once a month.

13.29   Bearing Replacement. Removing bearings and pulleys is a task that requires both care and skill. More damage is done to motors and machinery because of improperly installed bearings than nearly any other cause. A good puller set is very useful. I have a very good Proto set that caters to most pulling tasks.

Table 13-8 AC Motor Troubleshooting

Symptom	Probable Fault
Ground Fault	Insulation resistance broken down (moisture, overheating, aging or mechanical damage to winding)
Motor Overheating	Ground fault
	Mechanical overload
	Bearings seizing
Circuit Breaker Tripping	Ground fault
	Mechanical overload
	Winding intercoil short circuit
	Terminal box cable fault
Motor Overload	Stalled load
	Seized bearings
	Terminal connection loose
Bearings Hot	Bearing lubrication failure
	Drive belts overtensioned
	Bearings worn
Vibration	Coupling misaligned
	Bearing failure
	Loose frame holding bolt

13.30   Microwave Ovens. The number of onboard microwave ovens has increased rapidly over recent years. Coupled with good freezer capacity, they make meal preparation much easier, especially in bad weather. Additionally, they conserve cooking gas. Before buying or installing a microwave, consider the following factors:

a.   **Power Ratings.** Microwaves convert the AC input voltage into very high frequency energy using a magnetron. They are around 50% efficient, so a microwave rated at 650 watts, for example, would actually consume around 1300 watts at maximum output. An inverter would have to be able to supply that value.

b.   **Efficiency.** If operating off a square wave inverter, efficiency could drop by up to 30% due to the power supply waveform.

c.   **Protection.** These domestic appliances should be permanently installed to prevent moist, salt air and condensation from getting into the magnetron, which may cause corrosion and premature failure. It is a good idea to put a bag of silica gel inside the case.

SECTION TWO

ELECTRONICS SYSTEMS

Navigation Station Design

14.0   Navigation Station Design. Before you start installing navigation equipment, especially if you are fitting out a new vessel, consider carefully the following requirements that ensure reliable performance:

    a.   Aesthetic Considerations. There is a certain amount of satisfaction in having a good looking navigation station. It attests to a seamanlike attitude that is not lost on guests, and it is nice to show off. The trap is that a nicely presented navigation station is worthless if the equipment malfunctions or is unreliable because of a lack of planning or a failure to consider the technical requirements of the equipment. Make it look good, but above all make sure it all works.

    b.   Location. The nav station is invariably located at the bottom of the companionway steps where it is easily accessible. In many cases, the electronics are exposed to spray or even solid water if the washboards are carelessly left out in the event of a knockdown. Many problems are associated with this exposure. Precautions should include the following:

        (1)   Equipment Selection. Select equipment rated as splashproof so it can withstand exposed positions and intermittent spray.

        (2)   Waterproofing. Mount instruments in a panel that prevents water from getting behind to connectors and power connections. In exposed positions, protect the instruments with a clear perspex or plastic sheeting, if possible.

    c.   Ergonomics. Instruments should be positioned so they are easy to operate and monitor. Instruments should be grouped into functional blocks where possible. Keep communications equipment in one block, position fixing equipment in another. Equipment must be fitted so that access is unobstructed. Many nav stations are a jumble of systems thoughtlessly crammed into any available space. Important considerations are as follows:

        (1)   Display Visibility. Position displays at an angle that is normal to observation. Many instruments are mounted vertically for observation when sitting down, but when at sea in normal operation, they are generally monitored when standing up. Difficulties are especially pronounced with LCD displays.

        (2)   Accessibility. Make sure you can easily reach and operate controls. On some badly designed stations, you either have to stretch awkwardly or a knob is placed in such a tight corner you can't get to it.

        (3)   Lighting. Make sure that there is adequate lighting with a good deckhead light above or at the chart table.

d. **Electrical Factors.** Consider the effects the instruments can or may have on one another.

    (1)   **Cable Routing.** Route all radio transmission cables clear of signal cables. Where cable crossovers are required, make sure they are at 90°. Properly space out and secure cables with the required separation distances. Position electronic equipment so that aerial cables and inputs exit the nav station directly, without being routed behind other instruments or close to other cables.

    (2)   **Electrical Equipment Location.** Where possible, do not locate the main electrical switchboard next to the electronic equipment. In most cases, this is nearly impossible. The trend now is to install a small sub-board containing circuit breakers for the electronic equipment only. This removes a great deal of interference caused by the electrical equipment.

    (3)   **Interference Protection.** Interference sensitive equipment such as GPS, Loran, and autopilot control units should be located in a block. Construct an aluminum housing around the section and ground it.

    (4)   **Accessibility.** Make sure you have easy access to rear connections or rear fuse holders.

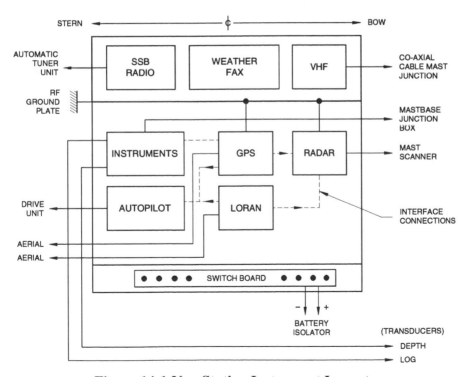

Figure 14-1 Nav Station Instrument Layout

Radar

15.0   Radar. RADAR is an acronym for RAdio Detection And Ranging. Radar is a method for locating the presence of a target, and calculating its range and angular position with respect to the radar transmitter. Good radar units make close-in navigation a lot easier for making landfalls, navigating channels, or when visibility is poor. Do not put your faith in the accuracy of GPS; its fix errors can exceed 100 meters. With the advent of GPS, some mistakenly see radar as redundant, but there is no substitute for radar as a navigational aid. Radar indicates where things are; GPS indicates where you are. Radar offers many very useful functions:

- Position fixing from geographical points.

- Positions of other vessels.

- Positions of buoys.

- Rain and squall locations.

- Land formations when making a landfall in poor visibility.

- Collision avoidance at night and in poor visibility.

15.1   Radar Theory. Radar transmits a pulse of radio frequency (RF) energy. This is radiated from a highly directional rotating transmitter called the scanner. Any reflected energy is then received and processed to form an image. The time interval between transmission of the signal and reception of reflected energy can be calculated to give target distance. The subject of radar reflection theory is complex and is covered extensively in Chapter 16. It is essential to understand how radar signals behave on various target materials if radar is to be fully utilized.

15.2   Radar Scanners. In practice, the larger the scanner, the narrower the beam width and the better the target discrimination. Of the two main scanner types, the beam widths of enclosed scanners are always larger than the open types. This factor is one of the trade-offs that has to be considered when selecting a radar unit. If it can be accommodated, an open scanner performs far better. The two scanner types in common use are as follows:

    a.   **Enclosed Scanners.** The enclosed array scanners are commonly used on yachts. There are two basic types of antenna elements in use:

        (1)   **Printed Circuit Board.** Printed circuit board, phased antenna arrays are commonly fitted to enclosed scanners. The antenna is on a circuit board instead of the more expensive slotted waveguides.

        (2)   **Slotted Waveguide.** Center fed, slotted waveguide arrays are normally used on open array antennas and larger range radomes.

b. **Open Scanners.** An open array scanner has a beam width nearly half that of enclosed units, which gives far better target discrimination. If you can tolerate an open scanner, the improved performance is worth it. The downside is that power consumption is greater. Open array scanners are more suited to power vessels.

c. **Sidelobe Attenuation.** Beam widths are not precisely cut off. There are zones outside the main beam where power is wasted and dissipated. End slotted waveguides are often used in new radars to suppress sidelobes, which generate false echoes. False echoes are more pronounced on short ranges at increased sensitivity.

d. **Frequencies.** All small boat radars operate on microwave frequencies in what is termed the X band. Frequency ranges are 9200 to 9500, a wavelength of around 3 cm.

e. **Output Power.** Power ratings are given for the actual microwave output power. A 16-mile radar is typically around 1.5 kilowatt and a 24-mile unit is 3 kilowatts. A kitchen microwave operates on the same principle. Given the effect microwaves have on food, always follow the warnings on eye protection. It is quite common on naval vessels with high power radars to incinerate any birdlife in the rigging at start-up.

f. **Range Discrimination.** Range discrimination or resolution is a function of transmission pulse length. When the distance between two targets on the same bearing is longer than the pulse length, they are shown as separate. When the distance between targets is less than the pulse length, they appear as one target. Most radar sets automatically alter pulse length with a change in range settings.

g. **Beam Angles.** Radar transmissions are similar to the light beam from a lighthouse in that a radar's beam has a defined angle in both vertical and horizontal planes. The beam width is normally defined as the angle over which the power is at least half of maximum output.

   (1) **Horizontal.** Horizontal beam widths for an enclosed scanner are around 4°. Open scanners have a more defined beam of around 2.5° and 5-6° for radomes and short antennas.

   (2) **Vertical.** Vertical beam widths are all typically in the range 25 to 30°. The greater the vertical width, the better the performance under heeling conditions. It must be remembered that there is always a blind spot around the vessel and targets inside the minimum range may not be seen.

(3)   **Heel Angles.** The heel of a vessel, and therefore of the scanner, has an adverse effect on performance. Most radars have vertical beam angles of 25 to 30°, so at a heel angle of approximately 15°, anything to windward is invisible and there is a significant blind spot to leeward. That doesn't take into account the additional masking of the signal by waves. This problem is very pronounced on stern post mounted units. One solution is to alter the attitude of the scanner using one of the several self-leveling systems available. These include gimbals systems, or manually operated hydraulic systems. The new Questus system can be mounted around a backstay, mast or stay pole and has hydraulic damping on the leveling mechanism. The cheaper alternative is to level up the boat periodically and have a look, which shouldn't be a problem on a cruising yacht.

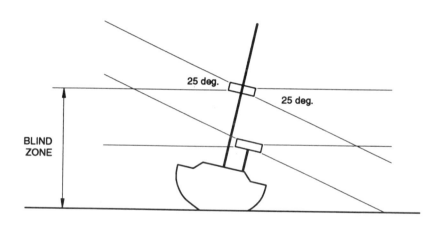

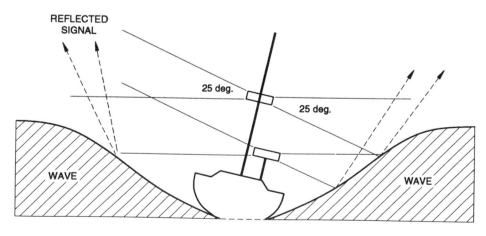

Figure 15-1 Radar Heeling Effects

h. **Target Discrimination.** Target discrimination or resolution is a function of beam width. A scanner with a narrow beam width is effectively slicing and sampling sectors of approximately 2.5° around the azimuth. Large targets will be sampled a number of times and their size quantified. A wider beam width will sample an area twice that size, but will not always discriminate between two or more targets. If a harbor entrance is narrow, the radar beam may in fact see it as part of the breakwater until the range has closed up. At longer ranges, two targets at the same distance and close together may appear as one.

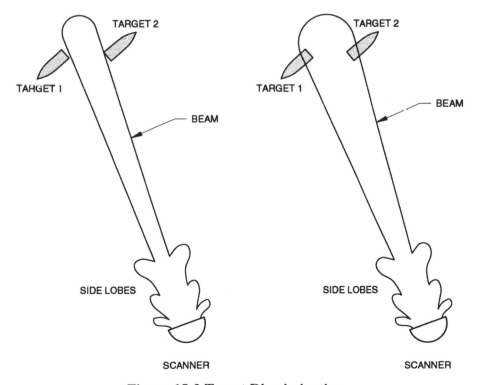

Figure 15-2 Target Discrimination

15.3   Radar Ranges. Maximum radar ranges are a function of scanner height. Table 15-1 gives the approximate horizon ranges for radar under standard conditions for targets of a known height. Conditions at sea may give better results, but it should be noted that atmospheric conditions affect the ranges as well. Radar signals travel in a straight line, but are subject to bending under normal atmospheric conditions. This bending increases the radar's horizon approximately 8% over optical horizons. Targets such as large vessels or land masses, for instance, may appear at much greater ranges, and the known height of these should be added to the scanner height. Ranges can increase or decrease depending on the prevailing atmospheric conditions.

Table 15-1 Radar Horizon Table

Target Height (meters)	Scanner Ht. 5 m	Scanner Ht. 10 m	Scanner Ht. 15 m	Scanner Ht. 20 m	Scanner Ht. 25 m
Zero	5.0 nm	7.0 nm	8.5 nm	10.0 nm	11.0 nm
5	10.0	12.0	13.5	15.0	16.0
10	12.0	14.0	15.5	17.0	18.0
15	13.5	15.5	17.3	18.5	19.8
20	14.8	17.0	18.5	19.8	21.0
25	16.0	18.2	19.8	21.0	22.3
30	17.3	19.0	20.8	22.0	23.3
35	18.0	20.0	21.8	23.0	24.3

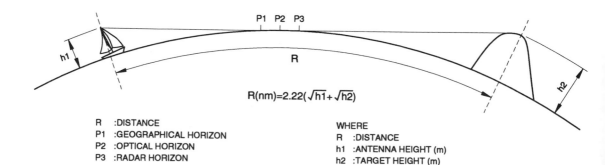

$$R(nm) = 2.22(\sqrt{h1} + \sqrt{h2})$$

R   :DISTANCE
P1   :GEOGRAPHICAL HORIZON
P2   :OPTICAL HORIZON
P3   :RADAR HORIZON

WHERE
R   :DISTANCE
h1   :ANTENNA HEIGHT (m)
h2   :TARGET HEIGHT (m)

Figure 15-3 Radar Horizons

15.4   Radar Displays. The display used to be called the plan position indicator (PPI). There are now a number of display types available on various radar systems.

    a.   **Rasterscan Displays.** These displays use the same technology as computer monitors. Essentially, the radar screen consists of many dots called pixels. The status of the pixels installed in the memory is altered in response to signal processing changes. Resolution is quoted as the number of pixels on the screen. The Koden MD-3400 has a resolution of 480 x 640 pixels. Unlike the CRT display, the rasterscan display is a result of complex digital-signal processing and allows the use of numerical information on the screen. Digitally processed signals usually have to be above a minimum level to be displayed, so weak echoes are often rejected. For this reason, proper tuning and operation are essential if all targets above that threshold are to be displayed. Manufacturers have introduced a number of processing techniques to overcome these shortcomings:

        (1)   **Single-Level Quantization.** This method displays all targets at the same intensity level, regardless of size or strength of return. The main problem is that targets, sea clutter, and rain do have to be distinguished.

        (2)   **Multi-Level Quantization.** This method of processing assigns echoes into strength categories. The stronger echoes appear bright, while weak echoes appear dim on the screen. Inconsistent or weak echoes may not be displayed. These systems are more expensive because more processing power is required.

    b.   **CRT Displays.** The cathode ray tube (CRT) was the primary display type until recent technological advances. The radial display synchronized with the scanner and effectively displayed every return with target brightness being relative to target strength. These displays required hoods for daylight operation, and consumed large quantities of power.

    c.   **Liquid Crystal Displays (LCD's).** LCD radars are the ideal solution for most average yachts. They are low on power consumption (2.5-3.5 A), are compact, low profile, and radomes are lightweight (8.8-16 lb), which means less weight aloft. Models such as the JRC 1000 are now less than a $1000, which makes radar affordable. In the 24-nm range, Raytheon, Autohelm, and Furuno all have excellent equipment. In the 16-nm range the JRC is joined by the Furuno 1621-MkII and the SI-TEX T-150. I would also invest in a Waltz RLS Radar Leveling System antenna mount to ensure maximum benefit under sail.

d. **Display Orientation**. A radar display can orient to one of three configurations. These are:

(1) **North Up**. Interfacing a gyro or fluxgate compass puts true north at the head of the screen. One of the advantages of this display is that both chart and display correspond and bearings are easily transferred for plotting purposes. Many plotting and navigating errors are made by incorrect transfers of screen information.

(2) **Head Up**. The top of the screen is the same as the vessel heading; all bearings are relative.

(3) **Course Up**. The top of the screen is aligned to the selected course using an interfaced fluxgate compass.

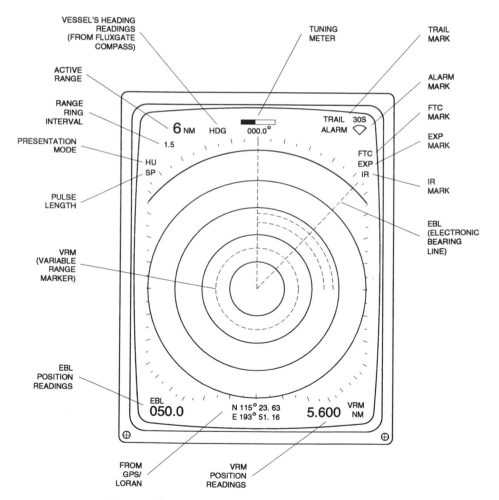

Figure 15-4 Koden 24-nm Radar Display

15.5   **Radar Installation.** The two most common scanner mountings are mast mounted, or stern post mounted. Each has advantages and disadvantages.

    a.   **Mast Mounted.** There are a number of factors affecting the mounting of the scanner on the mast:

        (1)   **Radar Range.** Mast mounting increases radar range. This is clearly illustrated in the radar horizon table.

        (2)   **Weight and Windage.** Contrary to opinion, weight and windage are very low. Six kg for a 16-mile scanner are not really a problem in cruising yachts.

        (3)   **Blind Sectors.** The position of the scanner is important. Locate the bracket above or below the spreaders to minimize obstruction. There will be a small blind sector astern. Where scanners are mounted on ketch mizzen masts, you have both forward and stern shadows.

    b.   **Stern Post Mounted.** The stern post mounting arrangement is more accessible than mast mounting and has become a very popular alternative in recent years. Some stern posts are hinged to allow easy lowering. I can never understand why 24-mile radars or above are used in these installations, as their range is limited by the post's height. It is preferable to use an open array antenna to improve the resolution.

        (1)   **Radar Range.** The radar range is reduced by a couple of miles depending on the target height. Typical height is around 3 meters, compared to around 6-8 meters for a mast mount.

        (2)   **Scanner Leveling.** When the boat heels, the scanner also tilts, leading to significant loss of performance and range. There are now some innovative self-leveling mountings available.

        (3)   **Health Risks.** There are increased health risks with stern mounted units.

    c.   **Eye Damage.** Direct exposure to an operating radar transmission can permanently damage retinas or cause blindness. Safe distances are normally given as around one meter, but recent medical research has recommended an absolute minimum of two meters. In this respect, stern post radars represent a real health hazard, especially when powerful units are installed.

    d.   **Cables.** When are manufacturers going to supply cables that come in two sections to enable easy installation or disconnection on masts? Very few options exist other than the multi-pin plugs or junction boxes available for this purpose. Always ensure that radar cables are well protected from chafing where they enter the mast.

e. **Power Consumption**. Small boat radars generally have power consumptions around 4 amps. With newer technology, consumption figures are getting lower; some are nearly down to 3 amps. Open scanners typically have a power consumption 50% greater than enclosed types because they have a heavier scanner and require a more powerful motor to rotate it.

f. **Economy Mode**. This function has been incorporated into a number of new radars and is very useful for power-conscious sailors. The radar can remain operating with guard zones activated and the display off to save power. If any target is detected within the guard zone, the alarm will sound and the display can be called up with one button. With radars, typical power consumption is 3.3 amps. The power saving mode draws only 2 amps, a significant reduction in terms of battery power.

g. **Grounding**. As a transmitter, radar requires proper grounding, usually at the scanner and the rear of the display unit. If a stern post is used, ensure that a grounding cable is attached from the base to the RF ground.

15.6 Radar Operation. Correct operation of radar is essential if you are to get the maximum benefit from it. It is prudent to attend a shore-based course as well. Don't be one of the all-too-common radar assisted casualties. A radar has a bewildering array of controls, but they all have clearly defined functions which are easily learned.

a. **Power Up**. At power up, all radars have a magnetron warm-up period. When warm-up is complete, the radar always defaults to stand-by status. If operating a new set, allow it warm up for at least 30 minutes before using it or making adjustments.

b. **Range Selection.** Always set the range you wish to work on. Typically, the 12-mile range is ideal for the average yacht given the radar's horizon. On a mast mounted scanner, a greater range will enable you to detect a large vessel on or just over the horizon. Selecting a range automatically sets the appropriate range ring intervals, the pulse length, and the pulse repetition rate.

c. **Adjust Brilliance.** Adjust the brilliance control to suit your requirements. Don't make it too bright at night or so dim that targets are not clearly displayed.

d. **Adjust Gain.** The gain control removes background "noise"—large areas of irregular speckles—from the display. Adjust the gain control so that screen speckling just starts to appear. Gain controls the signal amplification, so be very careful not to overadjust as smaller echoes can be masked, or if under the required threshold, will not appear at all. The gain is normally set high for long ranges and reduced for low ones.

e. **Adjust Anti-Clutter.** This control is often referred to as the Sensitivity Time Constant control. Sea clutter, most apparent at the screen center in that region closest to the vessel, is interference caused by rough seas or wave action where some of the transmitted signal is reflected off wave faces. Most 3-cm radars transmit at a very low signal angle which grazes the water surface. On short ranges, clutter can mask targets, especially weak ones. The effect decreases at long ranges. Sea clutter always appears stronger on the lee side of the vessel because vessel heel in that direction exposes the beam to larger water areas.

f. **Tuning**. The majority of radars are self-tuning, and adjustment will be indicated on a small bar readout on the screen. Most radars can be manually tuned, but this should be done carefully and according to your manual.

g. **Pulse Length Selection.** Pulse length selection is automatic with range changes on modern small boat radars. At short ranges, pulses are at 0.05 microsecond to give better target resolution. At long ranges, they increase to 1.0 microsecond.

h. **Pulse Repetition.** Repetition rates vary across ranges from 200 to 2500 per second. Rates determine the size of the area around the vessel where there is a dead zone. At 0.05 microsecond, this is around 150 meters. At 1.0 microsecond, this reduces to 30 meters.

i. **Fast Time Constant (FTC).** This control reduces rain clutter. Rain clutter is proportional to the density of the rain, fog, or snow. Although the control is useful in tracking squalls and rain, caution should be used so that targets are not obscured. Heavy rain may cause total loss of target definition and cannot be adjusted for.

j. **Interference Rejection (IR).** Interference can come from a number of sources:

   (1) **Other Radars.** Other radars operating in the area can cause interference on the display. This is particularly apparent near major shipping routes where powerful commercial vessel radars operate. Use the IR function to remove these unwanted signals.

   (2) **Mast Clutter.** When a radar is installed, there will be a blind spot abaft the scanner due to the mast. No targets will be detected in this area at close ranges. On a stern post or mizzen mast mounted radar, the area in front will be masked for the same reason. Caution must be exercised as this is the normal collision risk sector.

15.7   Radar Plotting. The main purpose of a radar is to detect stationary and fixed targets. A number of basic features facilitate this:

a.   **Range Rings.** The range rings are self explanatory. They change with the selected radar range.

b.   **Variable Range Maker (VRM).** This function uses the range rings and the marker. The readout appears on the screen, but as with all navigation exercises, make sure you are measuring the correct target. Many errors are made this way, which is why radar should be used in conjunction with other position keeping systems, principally the charts and eyeball.

c.   **Electronic Bearing Line (EBL).** The most commonly used function in conjunction with the VRM enables easy plotting of a target, but be careful, many unfortunate incidents occur because a bearing was taken without checking which headup display was being used.

d.   **Target Expansion.** This function on many radars allows short or long range contacts to be expanded. It is useful when reaching low altitude landfalls such as atolls and islands.

e.   **Off Centering.** A number of radar sets have an offset function which alters the screen center (the vessel) 50% down the screen. This makes forward long range observations possible in the same radar range.

f.   **Guard Zones.** Guard zones offer real safety advantages. They can be set for complete circular coverage or for specific sectors. It is a big error to rely on this function when sailing shorthanded; proper observations still should be regularly made. On some newer radars, an economy mode saves power by letting the guard zone and alarm function operate without the screen being on.

g.   **Target Plotting.** This feature, now part of a number of radar models, allows a trail of targets to be plotted. Target plotting is time related and can be continuous or set at a number of seconds. A clear plot of the target is invaluable for ensuring that collision risks do not arise. What a change from plotting aids and chinagraph pencils!

15.8   Radar Maintenance. There is not much maintenance required on a radar unit, but taking the following steps will ensure long term reliability:

a.   **Connections.** Once a year, open the scanner and tighten all the terminal screws.

b.   **Clean Scanners.** Clean the scanner with warm soapy water to remove salt and dirt. Do not scour or use harsh detergents.

c.   **Scanner Bolts.** Check and tighten the scanner holding bolts.

d.   **Gaskets.** Check that the scanner's watertight gaskets are in good condition and seal properly.

e.   **Scanner Motor Brushes.** Some scanner motors have brushes. Check these every 6 months. Manufacturers sometimes provide a spare set taped to the motor (Well done, Koden!).

f.   **Display Unit.** Clean the screen with a clean cloth soaked in an anti-static agent. Do not use a dry cloth as this can cause static charging which attracts and accumulates dust.

15.9   Radar Troubleshooting. The following table gives typical faults that can be investigated and rectified before calling a technician.

Table 15-2 Radar Troubleshooting

Symptom	Probable Fault
Scanner Stopped	Motor brush stuck (if fitted)
	Bearing seized
	Scanner motor failure
	Scanner motor control failure
No Display	Power switched off
	Brightness turned down
	Fuse failure
	Loose power plug
	Incorrectly tuned
Display On, No Targets	Scanner stopped
	Local scanner switch off
	Scanner plug not plugged in
Low Sensitivity	Ground connection loose
	Radome salt encrusted
	Open array salt encrusted

Radar Reflectors

16.0   **Radar Reflectors**. The subject of radar reflection has sparked continuing controversy over the years. There has also been a constant stream of so-called reflective safety devices launched upon unsuspecting yachtsmen. Not to have an effective reflector mounted at all times is, in my judgement, negligent in the extreme.

    a.   **Merchant Vessel Visibility.** If you have never been on the bridge of a fast merchant vessel steaming up the English Channel at 24 knots, dodging yachts that are invisible to radar, I can assure you that it is not a deck officer's favorite pastime. In deep ocean waters, there is still a requirement to be seen. While the shipping lanes may constitute areas of heavy commercial traffic, commercial vessels ply waters everywhere. The attitude commonly adopted—that no one is keeping a look-out anyway, so why bother—is fatally flawed. Most, if not all, vessels these days have the radar set with collision avoidance tracking and alarm systems, so if the vessel's radar cannot lock onto a good, consistent signal, it cannot identify and track a target. I have sailed under many flags commercially, including the much-maligned "flags of convenience" such as Liberia and Panama, and the officers were all qualified, contrary to popular opinion. With large and fast vessels, the earlier you are detected and your course and collision risk assessed, the earlier action can be taken to change course and avoid a close quarters situation.

    b.   **Search and Rescue.** Besides the collision risk problem, the reflector's important role during search and rescue (SAR) operations cannot be overstated. Many SAR operations are called off at night. Much valuable air time and fuel are wasted in aerial search patterns under poor conditions and low cloud cover simply because no effective reflector is hoisted. Reaction times, rescues, and survival prospects even in spite of EPIRBs are decreased in the localization and visual identification phase of the operation.

    c.   **Mast Weight and Windage.** One of the main reasons given for not having a reflector hoisted is that reflectors are too bulky, cause windage, or are too heavy up the mast; yet the mast will carry a radar and lights.

    d.   **Mast Shadowing.** Wherever you mount your reflector, there will be some shadowing from the mast. When a reflector such as a Blipper 210-7 is mounted directly in front of the mast, there is typically a 10° blind spot directly aft, the lowest collision risk sector of all. A yacht's track is far from straight, whether under autopilot or hand steering. Typically variation is in the range of 10 to 25°. Even though some reflective surface will be "seen" overhanging the mast, this movement will expose a substantial number of reflective corners, enough to offer a reasonably consistent return at a range of at least 5 miles.

16.1 **Reflector Theory**. To understand reflectors, a basic understanding of radar signal behavior is required.

a. **Radar Beam Behavior.** When a radar beam reaches a target, in theory it reflects back on a reciprocal course to be processed into a range and bearing for display on the screen. In practice, a beam does not simply bounce back off an object. Some materials are more reflective than others, while others absorb the signal.

b. **Reflective Materials.** The best reflective structures are made of steel and aluminum. Materials such as wood, fiberglass, and sailcloth do not reflect at all. In fact, fiberglass absorbs some 50% of a radar signal. There will almost always be some reflection, but the direction of the reflected beam will be erratic and so minimal that no consistent return can be monitored on the screen.

c. **Reflection Consistency.** Consistency is one of the major requirements of a good reflector. A good reflector consists of a metallic structure, normally aluminum, with surfaces placed at 90° to each other. If a beam is directed to the center of a re-entrant trihedral parallel to the center line, it will reflect on a reciprocal course back to the scanner. A re-entrant trihedral is simply a corner with three sides, such as the corner made up of two walls and a ceiling. The center line of the corner points in a direction approximately 36° to each of the sides making up the trihedral. The more the angle increases away from the center line from a radar beam, the less radar signal returns back. This simple fact forms the basis of radar reflectors.

d. **Radar Reflection Standards.** The basic standards include a number of specifications. Never buy a reflector that does not comply. A peak echoing area of 10 m^2 is defined as the equivalent of a metal sphere of approximately 12-feet diameter. International requirements and standards are as follows:

   (1) **ISO (8729).** This is an IMO sponsored standard. It specifies an RCS of 2.5 m^2 as the minimum threshold of radar visibility.

   (2) **USCG.** A standard is set for survival craft reflectors. Manufacturers are required to demonstrate a range of 4 nautical miles in a calm sea.

   (3) **DOT (U.K.).** Set down in the Marine Radar Performance Specification, 1977, it requires that reflectors have an equivalent echoing area of at least 10 m^2.

   (4) **RORC (U.K.).** A documented equivalent echoing area of not less than 10 m^2 is required.

   (5) **AYF (Australia).** A minimum equivalent echoing area of at least 10 m^2 is required.

e. **Reflector Types.** There are a variety of reflectors on the market. See the illustrations below. The illustrations are to scale and show the various sizes of the devices, indicating relative effectiveness.

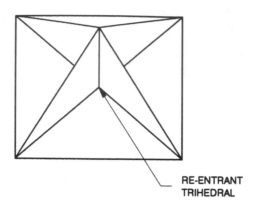

RE-ENTRANT
TRIHEDRAL

18" OCTAHEDRAL IN CORRECT "CATCHRAIN" POSITION

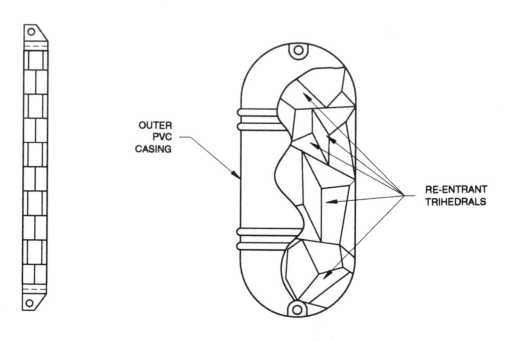

OUTER
PVC
CASING

RE-ENTRANT
TRIHEDRALS

MOBRI S2 REFLECTOR

BLIPPER 210-7 REFLECTOR
(CUT AWAY)

Figure 16-1 Radar Reflector Types

f. **Octahedrals.** The standard octahedral is a structure consisting of eight reentrant trihedrals. It was developed in the early 1940's, when radar was under development. For maximum effect, the octahedrals must be mounted in the proper orientation, which is called the "catchrain" position. It is amazing how many are hoisted up by a corner; one magazine survey had a figure approaching 70%, and my survey was closer to 80%. The structure, in fact, has only 6 effective corners, pointing alternately up and down, the remaining corners being of little use. The effectiveness of the radar reflector is shown in the polar diagram. On the typical 18-inch octahedral polar diagram, the lobes where peak reflection occurs are clearly visible. The peaks clearly exceed the peak echoing area of 10 m². A big problem, however, is created by the large areas between the lobes, where no reflection occurs, or it is so minimal that they are under the minimum standards set down by IMO of 2.5 m². The total blind spots on the correctly hoisted octahedral total nearly 120°, which is not ideal. The small peaks do not affect the result much. The bad news is that when heeled to 15°, the blind spots increase to nearly 180°. So, under sail, you have a 50-50 chance of being seen on a radar, in most cases intermittently, so the radar will reject the inconsistent signal. This can be further reduced when part of the signal, after reflecting off the sea surface, cancels out another beam traveling directly to the reflector. If you are using an octahedral, anything under 18 inches is a waste of time.

g. **Optimized Arrays.** The Marconi-Firdell Blipper 210-7 is representative of these reflectors. The Blipper consists of an array of precisely positioned reentrant trihedrals designed to give a consistent 360° coverage, and through heel it angles up to 30°. As a vessel moves around in a typical three-dimensional motion, each of the corners moves in and out of 'phase' to the radar signal, with one corner sending back signal directly, and others giving partial returns, resulting in a consistent return at all times. The units are rotationally molded inside a radar invisible plastic case, and the windage is only 15% of an 18-inch octahedral, and the unit weighs less than 2 kilograms. These reflectors have a reputation of meeting and exceeding all published standards. This can be seen by the numbers mounted on masts; my own survey at a major British marina was marginally over 50%. The Blipper 210-7 has been recently awarded a NATO stock number, which indicates the effectiveness of the unit.

h. **Stacked Arrays.** These are typified by tubular reflectors that resemble a fluorescent tube or rolling pin such as the Mobri and Slim Jim units. I have seen many of these taped to a backstay or stay, sometimes three or four on a yacht. They consist of an array of tiny reflectors housed in a see-through plastic case. These reflectors are purchased because they are cheap and small, not for the visibility factor which is the primary safety requirement. If you sit back and analyze the unit, you will see that it can only effectively return the amount of signal required in a perfectly vertical position. At any angle of heel, at 1° or more the unit return falls away to virtually nil. At best tabulated positions, at 0° azimuth, the RCS is 6.05, heeled to 1° it falls to 1.46, and at 2° to 0.18. So you can draw your own conclusions; if you have one taped to a backstay, it simply doesn't do anything.

i. **Luneberg Devices**. These devices resemble two half spheres mounted back to back; they are typified by the Visiball. They are normally fitted to the masthead in a fore-and-aft configuration. They are very heavy. The main criticism of the reflector is that the returned echo is only fore-and-aft and not athwartships, permitting a large and dangerous blind sector. More importantly, the return does not meet the minimum standards of the IMO or RORC, having an RCS of only about 0.8 m^2.

j. **Foil Devices.** I have read several articles and I have also heard many people advocating filling the mast with foil, or simply hanging a pair of stockings full of foil in the rigging. A recent case was heard in the courts in the U.K. regarding the loss of a catamaran in a collision with a coastal vessel during the 1986 Round Britain Race. The skipper did not hoist a reflector because he feared windage would reduce sailing performance; he inserted instead a foil filled stocking into the mast. The Admiralty judge included the following in his decision against the catamaran skipper: "To leave an anchorage and proceed without radar into a shipping lane when the visibility is less than 75 yards, so that the navigator is blind, and without a radar reflector so that the yacht is invisible, is in my judgement seriously negligent navigation." That statement sums up the issue of radar reflectors and the necessity for having them.

k. **Others.** The quantity of products launched, discredited, and withdrawn from the market illustrates the lack of technical understanding by the manufacturers concerned, and the vulnerability of yachtsmen. Some of these products are listed below:

 (1) **Radar Flags**. These devices are constructed of two layers of cloth with a metallized fabric in the middle. They were claimed to be U.S. Coast Guard tested. This was apparently incorrect; they do not meet required performance standards.

 (2) **Mast Steps**. Engraved mast steps were a popular method for improving the reflective qualities of a mast. This method has been largely discredited.

 (3) **Cyclops**. This is a more recently launched product that operates on the Luneberg Lens principle. It uses concentric shells of material to reflect and refract radar signal. Two lens assemblies plus an additional two trihedrals are used to give full coverage around the azimuth and at heel. The polar diagram claims RCS of 10.5 m^2 and average of 4 m^2 all round. The problem is that it is large for intended masthead mounting, and weighs some 4 kilograms. Additionally it is expensive and has been the subject of some criticism.

 (4) **High Gain Rotation.** These devices have been shown to have a best RCS of 3-4 m^2. They are being sold in the U.S., with claims that they are better than all others, but RCS values are not stated. Supposedly North Atlantic port authorities use them, but I could not find out which authorities. Buyer beware.

16.2   **Radar Reflection Polar Diagrams.** Polar diagrams are the usual way manufacturers represent the performance of radar reflectors. There are two types of polar diagrams:

   a.   **Horizontal Polar Diagrams.** Polar diagrams are essentially signal returns plotted for all points around the azimuth for a reflector in the vertical position. This is crucial to the understanding of test claims and actual onboard performance of the reflector. The various polar diagrams for the 18-inch octahedral reflector and the Mobri tubular reflector are illustrated below. The Firdell Blipper 210-7 reflector now only has three-dimensional polar diagrams and is therefore not included.

   b.   **3D Polar Diagrams.** The more accurate test of a radar reflector is a three-dimensional polar diagram, which indicates performance under actual heel conditions. These are illustrated below: they are derived from computer generated results and give a close image of actual performance. The white space is the area of no radar visibility. Given that performance under heel is the critical requirement, I would caution purchasers against buying a product that cannot produce such data, or verifiable proof that it works under the normal heeled sailing conditions of a yacht.

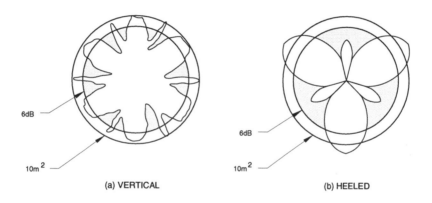

(a) VERTICAL   (b) HEELED

18" OCTAHEDRAL

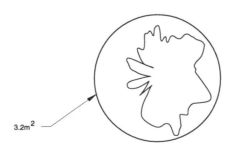

MOBRI S2

Figure 16-2 Horizontal Polar Diagrams

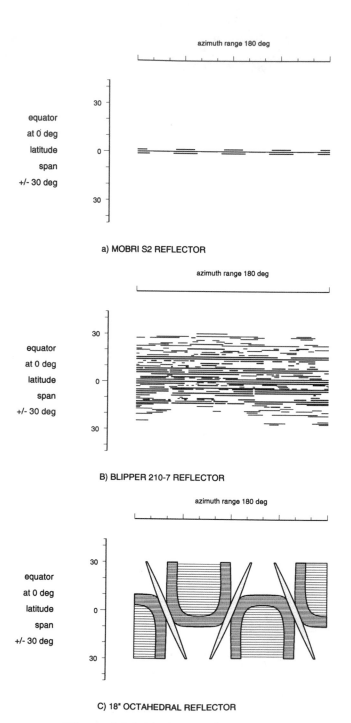

a) MOBRI S2 REFLECTOR

B) BLIPPER 210-7 REFLECTOR

C) 18" OCTAHEDRAL REFLECTOR

Figure 16-3 3D Polar Diagrams

16.3 **Radar Fresnel Zones.** In some cases radar signals self-cancel, either in the transmission or return path. This problem is related to a variety of factors including radar height, target height, sea and earth surface conditions, and radar range. The regions where cancellation occurs are called fresnel or extinction zones; they can be up to a mile-wide. In such conditions the radar signal reaching the radar reflector may be relatively weak, with a weak return. The result is no return to the radar, or a return so weak that it is not processed.

    a.   **Reflector Mounting.** It is apparent from the fresnel tables that the masthead is not the ideal place to put your reflector, as a relatively large cancellation zone exists. Reflectors are best mounted around the spreaders, or about 4 to 5 meters high.

    b.   **Fresnel Tables.** The following fresnel tables are published courtesy of Marconi-Firdell, and cover the first Fresnel Zone for 12- and 16-feet radar heights, and 4- to 22-feet target heights. The tables are based on a radar frequency of 9.4 GHz and for the range of 0.1 to 10 nm which is typical for cruising yachts.

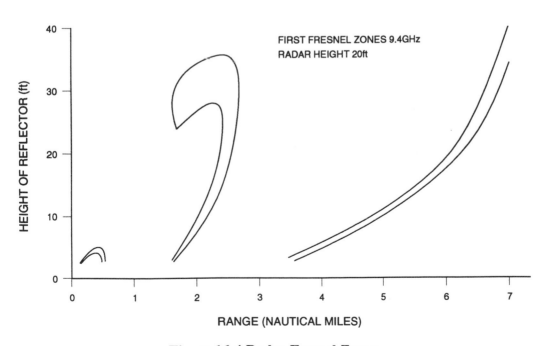

Figure 16-4 Radar Fresnel Zones

285

Table 16-1 First Fresnel Zone Tables Radar Height 12 Feet

Target Height	Zone (nm)	Zone (nm)	Zone (nm)
4 m	0.140-0.457	1.536-1.578	3.626-3.692
6 m	0.212-0.481	1.692-1.741	4.086-4.166
8 m	0.288-0.487	1.814-1.868	4.440-4.529
10 m	0.393-0.453	1.906-1.965	4.708-4.805
12 m	1.978-2.041	4.915-5.016	
14 m	2.033-2.102	5.078-5.182	
16 m	2.077-2.150	5.209-5.316	
18 m	2.122-2.190	5.318-5.427	
20 m	2.141-2.224	5.410-5.521	
22 m	2.164-2.253	5.492-5.604	
24 m	2.183-2.279	5.565-5.678	
26 m	2.199-2.301	5.632-5.747	
28 m	2.211-2.321	5.695-5.811	
30 m	2.221-2.339	5.755-5.872	

Table 16-2 First Fresnel Zone Tables Radar Height 16 Feet

Target Height	Zone (nm)	Zone (nm)	Zone (nm)
4 m	0.188-0.469	1.626-1.673	3.824-3.891
6 m	0.290-0.473	1.775-1.828	4.271-4.351
8 m	1.898-1.958	4.648-4.740	
10 m	1.997-1.064	4.957-4.058	
12 m	2.077-2.150	5.209-5.316	
14 m	2.140-2.220	5.414-5.526	
16 m	2.189-2.276	5.583-5.700	
18 m	2.227-2.322	5.723-5.844	
20 m	2.256-2.359	5.842-5.966	
22 m	2.276-2.389	5.944-6.071	
24 m	2.288-2.413	6.033-6.162	
26 m	2.292-2.532	6.112-6.243	
28 m	2.288-2.447	6.183-6.316	
30 m	1.574-2.457	6.248-6.382	

Autopilots

17.0   Autopilots. The autopilot is one of the few indispensable electronic items. It is often referred to as the non-complaining, non-eating extra crewmember. The real advances in autopilot technology are powerful microprocessors and equally complex software algorithms that give "intelligent" control. Most autopilot problems occur because of incorrect installation, improper matching to the vessel, or improper operation, rather than personality conflicts. The basic function of an autopilot is to steer the vessel on a predetermined and set course, to a position or waypoint, or to wind angle. The pilot makes course corrections at an amount corresponding to the course error, usually correcting to eliminate any overshoot as the course is met. Virtually all autopilots are microprocessor based, and use the proportional rate system of operation. Correction is based on the amount of course deviation and the rate of change. Autopilots vary depending on the type of steering system used. The factors affecting autopilot selection are as follows:

   a.   **Autopilot Selection.** An autopilot is selected on the basis of a number of important criteria:

   (1)   The steering system installed, either tiller or wheel hydraulic, wire or direct drive.

   (2)   The loaded vessel displacement, as it is more valid than length, which has wide variations, and beam, draft and displacement. Autohelm recommends that 20% be added to design displacement to get realistic cruising displacement.

   (3)   Type of sailing is also important. For cruising you must base all factors on worst weather possible, which means power ratings must be capable of coping with prevailing conditions.

   b.   **Power Consumption.** Always compare the current consumption at full-rated load, not average consumption. Many find that the pilot uses far more power than expected, although much of the heavy consumption relates to excess weather helm activity and overworking of the pilot. There is no significant difference between the average consumption of the various drive types for a specific vessel size.

   c.   **Factors Affecting Performance.** The following factors must be considered when selecting an autopilot:

   •   The speed of rudder travel

   •   The rudder size

   •   The required number of turns lock to lock

   •   The expected wind and sea conditions

   d.   **Autopilot Torque.** Torque is the force required to hold the rudder in position due to the pressure of water on the rudder, and to overcome the steering gear resistance of bearings and steering system drives. The vast majority of people underestimate this, and while the pilot works well in average conditions, it fails to keep course in bad weather.

e.   **Sail Trim**. Overloading and burn-outs are almost always due to excessive weather helm. If the helm is constantly held over by the pilot, trim the sails. The following can be done to improve performance, and reduce electrical and mechanical loads:

   (1)   **Reduce Vessel Heel.** Minimize vessel heeling, ease the mainsheet, or traveler to leeward.

   (2)   **Reef Early.** It is a good idea to reef the first time you think about it. The power saving is worth the effort.

f.   **Trim and Load Monitoring.** One more innovative suggestion is to insert an ammeter in the autopilot supply scaled to the full load rating. This enables the current consumption to be used as a trimming guide.

17.1   Autopilot Drive Systems. The choice of pilot is obviously based on the steering system in use. These systems are summarized as follows:

a.   **Hydraulic**. A reversible pump must be installed in the system, and controlled by the autopilot. Hydraulic steering systems consist of a steering wheel pump and steering cylinder. The wheel pump forces oil into the cylinder from either end, depending on the direction required. The system should have a lock valve to prevent the rudder driving the wheel pump. Hydraulic systems are inherently more reliable than mechanical drives. Pump types are as follows:

   (1)   **Constant Running**. Pumps are usually dual speed to save power in lighter conditions. Solenoid valves control oil pressure for directional activation of the hydraulic ram.

   (2)   **Reversible Motor**. These pumps are the most common. They have a low overall power consumption with the pump operating under autopilot command. Typical power consumption is in the range of 2-4 amps on units for vessels up to around 45 feet but will have a maximum of approximately 20 amps. On larger vessels, this moves up to 4-8 amps. The pump unit consists of an electric permanent magnet motor, valve block, reversible gear pump, and non-return valves on the directional outlets.

b.   **Hydraulic Steering Types.** There are three basic types of hydraulic steering systems.

   (1)   **Two Line System.** Pressurized fluid is pumped into the ram from either end, depending on the direction required.

   (2)   **Two Line Pressurized System.** This system has an external pressurized reservoir.

   (3)   **Three Line System.** Pressurized fluid flows in one direction only. A uniflow valve is installed within the system to direct all fluid back to the reservoir.

c. **Installation.** There are a number of important considerations when installing pumps:

(1) The pump must be mounted in a horizontal position. I have seen units mounted in the vertical as it was more convenient.

(2) The pump should be mounted adjacent to the steering cylinder.

(3) The pump must be securely mounted to prevent vibration.

(4) Non return valves must be fitted to the helm pump to prevent the autopilot pump from driving it instead of the ram.

d. **Pump Maintenance and Testing.** Perform maintenance and testing as follows:

(1) **Test Rudder Operation.** Drive the rudder lock-to-lock, using the pilot control unit. Ensure that the rudder moves to the same side as the required command signal. If reversed, the motor terminal connections require reversal at the autopilot control box. The oil expansion reservoir, if fitted, may require topping up. Make sure the rudder stops before reaching the mechanical stops.

(2) **Maintenance.** Dismantle the pump after 1000 hours operation. Examine oil seals and replace them (I always do this regardless of the condition). Check the motor brushes, and replace if excessively worn. Clean the brushgear with CRC or similar electrical cleaner, and make sure that they move freely in the brush-holders.

e. **Hydraulic System Troubleshooting.** The following faults and symptoms are applicable to most pump systems:

(1) **Spongy Steering.** This is the most common; it is caused by air trapped in the hydraulic system. The system must be bled according to the manufacturers' instructions. When bleeding, ensure that the steering is operated stop-to-stop to expel air in the pump and pipework. This problem will greatly affect the performance of the autopilot.

(2) **System Cleanliness.** The system must be absolutely clean, and no particles of dirt should be introduced into it. This means clean hands, clean tools, and clean oil. Particles commonly lodge in check valves, causing loss of pressure and back driving of steering wheel.

Table 17-1 Autopilot Hydraulic System Troubleshooting

Symptom	Probable Fault
Excessive Pump Noise	Air in hydraulic system
No Piston Movement on Command	Oil valve closed
	Pump sucking in air
	Non return valve leaking
Rudder Moves Back to Amidships	Non return valve leaking
Wheel Moves with Pump Operation	Lock valve leaking
Piston Moves Erratically	Air in hydraulic system
Rudder Movement Stops with Increase	Pump underrated
in Rudder Load	Low pump motor voltage

f.   **Wheel Drive**. Wheel pilots are usually located on the steering pedestal. The drive unit is mounted in line on a cockpit side; it consists of an integrated gearbox and motor, rotating the wheel via a belt. Vessel steering characteristics can be programmed into the control system, and a simple clutch lever enables instant changeover to manual steering. The trend in wheel pilots is now towards an enclosed belt drive system. Belts must be correctly tensioned to avoid premature breakage or wear.

g.   **Linear Drive**. The linear drive unit is either an integrated hydraulic ram and pump system, or a motor and gearbox drive directly connected to the rudder quadrant.

   (1)   **Advantages.** The linear drive has a minimal effect on helm "feel". It is relatively low cost, and the hydraulic units are very reliable. There is also the advantage of a backup steering if some part of the steering drive or pedestal fails.

   (2)   **Power Consumption.** Typical power consumption is relatively low, in the range 1.5-3 amps and 2.75-6 amps for larger vessels.

h.   **Rotary Drives.** These drives are usually fitted on vessels where linear drives cannot be installed, where there are space restrictions, or an inaccessible or small quadrant cannot accommodate any other drive. The motors on these systems consist of an electric motor coupled to a precision manufactured epicyclic gearbox. Whitlock has developed its own drive motor integrated into the steering system for connection to the pilot. Power consumption is typically in the range 2-4 amps, and 3-8 amps for larger vessels.

i.   **Windvane**. The windvane allows steering to wind and is locked into the existing wind angles. The pilot will alter and follow a course to hold the same relative wind angle. Averaging is often used to account for wind shifts and side gusts so that unneccessary alterations are eliminated, saving power. Older pilots used to carry a separate windvane, usually on the stern pulpit, but in most cases the information can now be taken directly from the masthead unit information via an interface. Obviously the monitored wind direction can be different between the two vanes.

17.2   Autopilot Installation. There are a few fundamental points to observe when installing autopilots. Appraisals and post-mortems of the recent BOC race revealed that many problems were directly attributable to improperly installed autopilots. The following factors should be considered, as they are the major causes of problems:

a.   **Anchoring**. Always ensure that the drive units are mounted and anchored securely. It is sensible to mount a strong pad at anchoring points, as it is quite common on fiberglass vessels to see the hull flexing because the inadequate mounting points are unable to take the applied loads.

b.   **Wiring**. There are a number of important points to consider:

(1)   **Power Cables.** Make sure that power cables to drive units are rated for maximum current demand and voltage drops, as cable runs are normally long. As standard, I install a minimum 6 mm² twin tinned copper cable to the motor and computer unit.

(2)   **Radio Cables.** Make sure that all wiring is routed well away from radio aerial cables since interference is a major cause of problems during radio transmission. Ensure that a ground cable is run from the computer unit to your RF ground. In rare cases you may have to put on a foil shield to SSB tuner unit interconnecting cables as well.

c.   **Fluxgate Installation**. There are a number of important points to remember:

(1)   **Location in Fiberglass and Timber Vessels.** The fluxgate compass should be installed in an area of least magnetic influence, and close to the center of the boat's roll to minimize heeling error. Turning errors can arise if the compass is not properly compensated. The southerly and northerly turning errors increase as distance from the Equator increases. This causes slow wandering and slow correction; normally compensation reduces this problem.

(2)   **Location in Steel Vessels.** Steel vessels pose problems due to the inherent magnetic field in the hull. Autohelm recommends to mount the fluxgate sensor at a minimum of 5 feet above the deck. Note that, as this is often on the mast, it may become disturbed when radar or radio cables passing through the mast are carrying current or signal.

(3)   **Cables.** Ensure the compass is mounted clear of any cable looms or any other metallic equipment. As fluxgates are invariably installed under saloon bunks, do not store any metallic items such as tool boxes or spares there, as often happens.

d.   **Course Computer Location.** This should be located clear of magnetic influences and away from radio aerial cables. While older units were prone to induced interference, newer units are generally made to strict international noise emission standards.

17.3 **Autopilot Controls.** Many adjustments can be made to achieve optimum autopilot operation. As a note of caution, do not use in any channels, confined areas or heavy traffic zones, as VHF and SSB operation can cause sudden course changes. The various controls are as follows:

a. **Deadband.** This is the area in which the heading may deviate before the pilot initiates a correction.

b. **Rudder Gain.** This relates to the amount of rudder to be applied for the detected heading error, and must be calibrated under sail. It is inextricably linked to proper compass set-up and damping.

c. **Rudder Feedback.** Rudder feedback provides instantaneously the precise rudder position information to the pilot. It is essential that the feedback potentiometer is properly aligned. Most new pilots have a high resolution potentiometer that offers more precise feedback than earlier and coarser units.

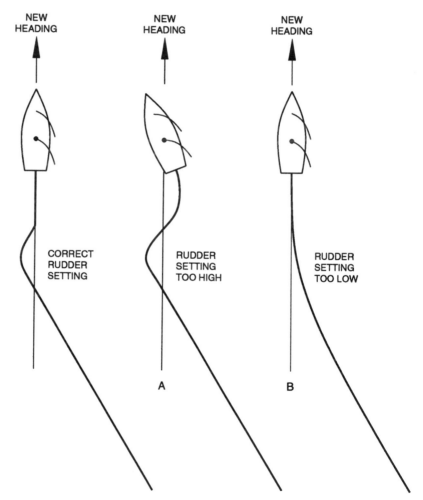

Figure 17-1 Rudder Gain Effect

d.   **Rudder Limits.** This controls the limit of rudder travel. The autopilot must stop before reaching the mechanical stops or serious damage may result.

e.   **Rudder Damping.** This calibration is used where a feedback transducer is installed and minimizes hunting when the pilot is trying to position the rudder.

f.   **Rate of Turn.** The rate of turn limitation is typically 2° per second.

g.   **Tack and Gybe Function.** Automatic tack and gybe functions are ideal for shorthanded sailing. With a one-button command, the pilot will take the vessel through to the same apparent wind angle on the opposite tack.

h.   **Dodge Function.** This function usually operates in a 10° step with automatic return to original course. The function is useful for dodging containers, debris, etc.

i.   **Off-Course Alarms.** All autopilots have an off-course alarm, which activates when the course error exceeds typically 15°. Specific alarm angles can be programmed in.

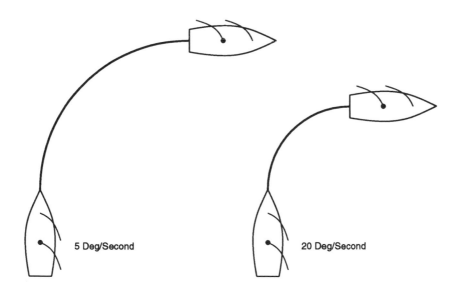

Figure 17-2 Rate of Turn

j. **AutoTrim and AutoSeastate.** These functions were pioneered by Autohelm and are as follows:

    (1) **AutoTrim.** (Autohelm) This function automatically compensates for alterations in weather helm, and applies the correct level of standing helm.

    (2) **AutoSeastate.** (Autohelm) This function enables the pilot to automatically adapt to changing seastate conditions and vessel responses. It alters automatically the deadband settings. It is controlled by the pilot software. The pilot does not respond to repetitive vessel movements, but only to true course variations.

k. **Magnetic Variation.** The variation must be entered into the autopilot. Newer units have automatic compass linearization to correct for compass deviation errors.

l. **Compass Damping.** The basis for good autopilot performance is proper setting of compass damping. You should start with minimum damping and increase according to conditions. Failure to get this right will cause either lagging or overshooting as rudder is applied to maintain course. This of course has detrimental effects on power consumption rates, as well as making you sail a lot farther than you have to.

m. **Heading Error Correction.** This correction compensates for northerly and southerly heading errors. Failure to do this will cause amplification of rudder responses on northerly and southerly headings. Autohelm calls it AutoAdapt.

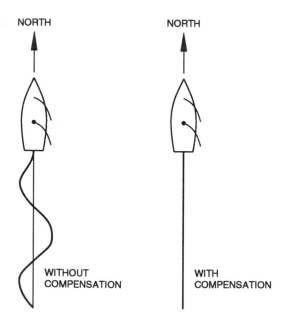

Figure 17-3 Heading Error Correction

n. **Autopilot Interfacing.** Interfacing of compasses and navigation receivers is now standard.

(1) **Navigation Receivers.** Input from SatNav, Loran, Decca and GPS will enable steering to a position or waypoint. Most manufacturers will list the NMEA 0183 recognized sentence headers. It is important to remember that position fixing systems are subject to errors, sometimes extremely large. This will have obvious effects on the steering, so it is important to keep a regular plot as the autopilot will not be able to recognize the errors.

(2) **Fluxgate Compass.** Input from fluxgate compass gives accurate heading data to course computer.

(3) **Rate Gyro (Autohelm GyroPlus).** This recent development allows rapid real time sensing of vessel yawing prevalent in light weight vessels and multihulls in following and quartering seas. The data input supplements the fluxgate signal and allows fast correction to counter the rapid heading changes which the fluxgate cannot compensate for.

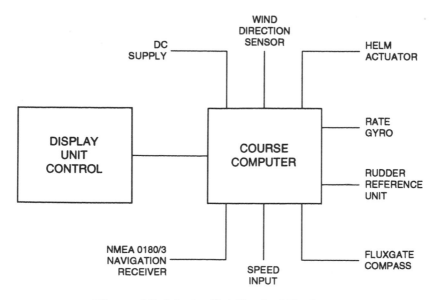

Figure 17-4 Autopilot Control System

o. **Track Control.** Track control enables a pilot to steer from waypoint to way-point in conjunction with a navigation receiver. The autopilot effectively adjusts to take account of tide and leeway. To do so it takes cross track error (XTE) data and uses it to compute and initiate course changes to maintain the required track.

(1) **Limitations.** Most pilots will keep within 300 feet of desired track. Track control is less effective at lower speeds, as tidal stream effect has a greater impact. Differences are noticeable where flow speed exceeds 35% of vessel speed, and careful plotting is essential.

(2) **Waypoint Advances.** Many pilots will advance to next waypoints at a single command. This depends on reception of valid NMEA headers that are the waypoint numbers and bearing to waypoint.

(3) **Cautions.** You must be aware that, if a navigation receiver passes incorrect or corrupt position data, the pilot may alter course and put the vessel in danger. Never use unsupervised autopilot steering to position or waypoint close to the coast or in enclosed waterways. It can happen that a large error occurs on a GPS, and by the time you realize it, you are aground.

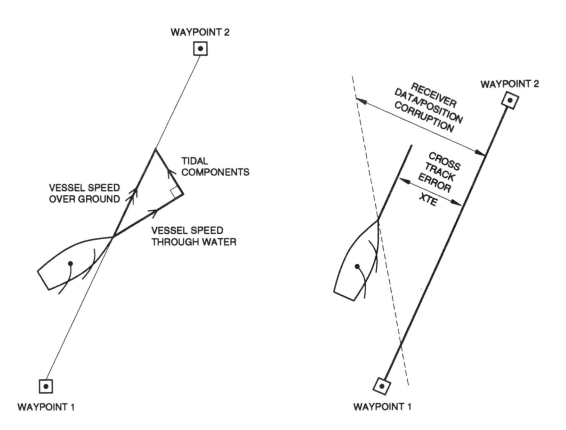

Figure 17-5 Autopilot Track Control

17.4 **Autopilot Maintenance.** A number of basic measures can be undertaken to ensure reliability.

    a. **Electronics Temperature.** This mostly applies to tiller units which incorporate processors. Install the electronics away from the sunshine if at all possible, and keep them cool. Manufacturers make units with black plastic to facilitate heat transfer from components inside, as well as to resist the effects of UV rays. While heat generated inside may be more easily dissipated by the black casing when exposed to atmosphere, the casing will absorb heat. To reduce heat absorption, cover the unit with a light weight white sail cloth cover in hot sunny weather; use Velcro for easy removal.

    b. **Corrosion Control.** Ensure that systems are not exposed to excessive salt water and that seals are intact. Exposed units will be protected by the additional cover.

    c. **Plugs and Sockets.** Regularly check plugs and sockets for water and moisture. Make sure they seal properly.

    d. **Cleaning.** Clean using a damp cloth. Do not use any solvents or abrasive materials. Do not use a high pressure hose.

Table 17-2 Autopilot Troubleshooting

Symptom	Probable Fault
No Rudder Response	Loss of power
	Autopilot fuse failure
	Rudder jammed
	Plug/connection fault
	Control unit fault
Rudder Drives Hard Over	Radio interference
	Loss of feedback signal
	Rudder limit failure
	Fluxgate compass failure
	Radio nav data corruption
	Control unit failure
	Wind data corruption
Wandering Course	Calibration settings incorrect
	Overdamped compass
	Rudder gain setting incorrect
	Feedback transducer linkage loose
	Control unit fault
	Drive unit fault
North/South Headings Unstable	Incorrect setup
Display & Compass Headings Different	Deviation correction incorrect
Rudder Angle Display Incorrect	Incorrect rudder offset setting
Condensation in Display	Turn on illumination to dry

Position Fixing Systems

18.0   Electronic Position Fixing Systems. The rapid advances in satellite positioning systems in recent years have been nothing short of spectacular. Most yachts carry a GPS, given that handheld units are only a few hundred dollars. Many rapid changes have occurred in terms of systems upgrades and commissioning, and obsolete systems have been shut down.

    a.   **Navigation Systems Status.** Many cruisers are curious about the status of the various systems, given the rapid integration of GPS-based systems.

        (1)   **Transit Satellite Navigation System.** This system, which served boaters so well, is no longer operational. It was switched off on December 31, 1996, and its receivers cannot be converted for use with GPS.

        (2)   **Decca.** This system is in decline and is expected to be maintained until around the end of 1998, although this cutoff date is not definite.

        (3)   **Radio Direction Finding (RDF).** Although RDF is still in use, there has been considerable reorganization of both stations and beacon frequencies, with fewer stations and frequencies now available. There are recommendations in the U.K. to terminate the service in 2000.

        (4)   **Loran.** Although there has been pressure to shut down the Loran system (and some chains have been shut down), some system expansion has occurred. A new European system has been commissioned (NELS) for which receivers will require reprogramming

    b.   **Navigation System Accuracy.** It is important to define accuracy.

        (1)   **Repeatable Accuracy.** This is the ability to return to a position or waypoint previously stored within the receiver. Consider the example of a man overboard situation. If you lost crew over the side, will the displayed position be the one you should steer back to, or will the error be 100 meters from that position several minutes later?

        (2)   **Predictable Accuracy.** This is the difference between the position indicated on your position fixing equipment and the position indicated on the chart (where you are plotting your position at regular intervals!). These errors can be attributed to datum variations, inaccuracies in the electronically derived position, etc.

    c.   **Chart Datum Variations.** Plotting a position on a chart has inherent errors. These errors can be caused by the GPS fix error or the transformation between GPS datum and chart datum. There may be a discrepancy that requires correction, and many charts carry appropriate notes. A wide variety of datums are used around the globe, and new charts are generally being compiled on WGS84 datum, the same datum used by GPS. Of the 3337 current British Admiralty charts, 65 datums are used, and a typical error is a 140-meter offset in Dover Strait. Recently an official warning was issued not to rely on any position within 3 nm of land in the Caribbean. Note that Datum NAS83 on U.S. charts is same as WGS84 (GPS) datum on U.K. charts.

18.1 **Global Positioning System (GPS).** The NAVSTAR system is operated by the US Department of Defense (DoD). The system consists of 24 satellites in 6 polar orbits; 4 will always be visible above the horizon at any time. Twenty one are in operation, with 3 used as spares. Position fixing involves triangulation of position from a number of satellites, satellite ranging to measure the distance from the satellites, accurate time measurement, the location of all satellites, and correction factors for ionospheric factors. Operation of a GPS set is as follows when the power is on:

a. **Initialization.** Turning the power on initializes with the closest satellite and ephemeris data (relating to the orbital parameters of the satellites) being downloaded into memory. A period of at least 20 minutes is required to stabilize a position and verify the status of satellites, availability, etc. After a GPS is switched off, the last position is retained in memory. If your position remains within 50 nm, a position will generally be available within approximately 3-5 minutes next time the power is turned on.

b. **Acquisition.** The receiver collects data from other satellites in view. Based on the data, it locks on to a satellite to commence the ranging process.

c. **Position Fix.** Based on the data on position and time, the receiver triangulates the position with respect to the positions of satellites. Normally this will be displayed in two decimal places. Some units give three decimal places, but such accuracy is highly suspect and should be treated with caution. If typical accuracy is 100 meters with Selective Availability (where the accuracy of the signals is deliberately degraded), relying on a position fix with an accuracy of approximately 3 meters or less is not as accurate as you would like to believe.

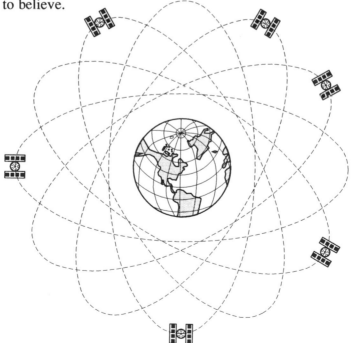

Figure 18-1 GPS Satellite Matrix

18.2   GPS Accuracy. GPS accuracy is the subject of widespread debate and controversy. The inaccuracies currently inherent in the system due to governmental policies have initiated expensive and technologically advanced solutions to improve accuracy.

a.   **Precise Positioning Service (PPS).** This service is primarily for military use and is derived from the Precise (P) code. The P code is transmitted on the L1 (1575.42MHz) and L2 (1227.60MHz) frequencies. PPS fixes are generally accurate within 16 meters spherical error.

b.   **Standard Positioning Service (SPS).** This service is for civilian use and is derived from the Course and Acquisition (C/A) code. Accuracy levels have been degraded to within 141 meters 95% of the time.

c.   **Selective Availability (SA).** This is the process of degrading positional accuracy by altering or introducing errors in the clock data and satellite ephemeris data. SA is characterized by a wandering position, and often a course and speed over the ground of up to 1.5 knots while actually stationary.

d.   **Horizontal Dilution of Position (HDOP).** Accuracy is determined by what is called (Geometric) Horizontal Dilution of Precision (HDOP), which indicates the dilution of precision in a horizontal direction. The cause is poor satellite geometry, which is due to poor satellite distribution. It is generally measured on a scale of one to 10; the higher the number, the poorer the position confidence level.

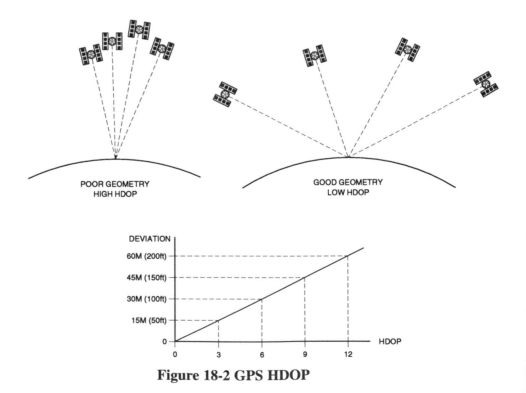

Figure 18-2 GPS HDOP

18.3   **GPS Error Sources.** The GPS that is considered by many cruisers to be an accurate navigation source has inherent errors that decrease accuracy. These errors are in addition to the HDOP and SA errors mentioned in Section 18.2. It is important to understand them.

a.   **GPS Clock Errors.** Each GPS satellite has two rubidium and two cesium atomic clocks. These clocks are monitored against terrestrial atomic clocks. Based on this information, the entire GPS system is continually calibrated against UTC.

b.   **GPS Rollover Week.** Another time-related problem area is coming up on August 21, 1999. This is called *GPS Rollover Week.* The GPS time system operates on a cycle of 1024 weeks. The reference point for this is the date and time the system was initialized. In this case Week 1 started on January 6, 1980. When that limit is reached on the nominated date, the GPS week count will reset to zero. If your system is prone to disruption, then the next morning could prove to be a surprise. The problem occurs because the time information stored within the almanac of your GPS receiver will conflict with that on the satellites, which could result in data corruption and incorrect positions. The problem will probably require a cold manual start initialization as you would a new GPS, that will take time to calculate position and download new ephemeris from satellites. Most manufacturers report that no problems are expected. Contact your supplier to confirm this.

c.   **Ionosphere Effects.** Like radio signals, both ionospheric and tropospheric conditions can affect GPS accuracy. Errors occur in signal transmission times that can impose signal propagation delays. This signal refraction introduces timing errors that cause positional inaccuracies. Like radio propagation it alters given changes in atmospheric conditions, solar activity, etc. Errors can be as great as 20-30 meters during the day and 5 meters at night.

d.   **Multipath Effects.** This occurs when signals from a satellite traveling to a receiver arrive at slightly different times due to reflection or alteration. The effect is that positions may be derived off the "bad" signal, resulting in an inaccuracy.

e.   **Satellite Integrity.** If the signal being transmitted from a satellite is corrupt due to a malfunction, it will have subsequent effects on position computations.

18.4   **The Millenium Bug.** Many cruisers are asking how the end of the century date change or *"millenium bug"* will affect GPS operation. Given that GPS units are essentially signal processing computers that are highly dependent on time for accurate calculations, the answer is simply that GPS receiver internal clocks may have to be reset. Most manufacturers report that no problems are expected. Contact your supplier to confirm this.

18.5   **GLONASS Positioning System.** The Russian system is now up and running with a 24-satellite system. The claims are that the system is more accurate than GPS, and this has been proven in higher latitude locations such as the U.K. and Europe. It is also supposed to be more reliable because it is not subject to experimental shutdowns or position degradation.

Receivers are a little more expensive than current GPS units. You can get details from Russian Space Forces, P.O. Box 543, Moscow 119021, Russia, or look them up on the Internet at http://www.rssi.ru. Another development is a move to incorporate both GLONASS and GPS within a common unit to improve accuracy and overcome the SA problem. Some U.S. manufacturers have systems on the market already.

18.6   Differential GPS (DGPS). This system is designed to overcome the position errors with respect to Selective Availability. DGPS is a subject of great controversy as well as considerable expense. It does enable monitoring of the GPS system, resulting in rapid identification of problems.

a.   **DGPS Operation.** DGPS uses a shore based reference station located in an accurately surveyed location. The position is compared with the GPS derived position to produce an error or position offset. These errors may be due to SA or others previously covered. A correction signal to satellite range data (pseudorange differential) is then broadcast by radio beacon (285-325 kHz in standard format RTCM SC104)) which is then received by a radio beacon receiver, then incorporated into the vessel GPS receiver position computation to derive a final and more accurate position. The accuracy has come down to around 2 meters in some instances.

b.   **DGPS Coverage.** There has been construction and implementation worldwide of DGPS networks. Some are operated commercially on user pays subscriber systems. Others are now becoming free-to-air systems. The USCG system is virtually complete and operational. The U.K. is to commission 12 stations in 1997/98. A free DGPS service is available in Sweden and Finland.

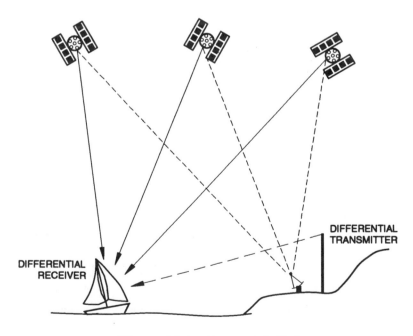

Figure 18-3 Differential GPS

c.   **Wide Area Augmentation.** It is expected that the United States Federal Aviation Administration (FAA) will introduce what is called Wide Area Augmentation System (WAAS) in 1998. This effectively offers global DGPS. The system operates by the transmission of ground base calculated correction signals being uploaded back to a satellite and rebroadcast.

18.7   GPS Satellite Acquisition Modes. The various methods of satellite acquisition are explained below.

a.   **Single Channel, Sequential.** A single-channel receiver reduces receiver costs. Position updates are made every 10-15 seconds because a single-channel receiver must search for, interrogate, and acquire satellites in sequential order. This method is slow and in bad weather can cause some problems. In rough weather, when the vessel is subject to considerable movement, the receiver has problems acquiring and locking onto satellites, with resultant position degradation. These types of receivers generally take some time to acquire their first fix, typically from 10 to 20 minutes and longer.

b.   **Dual Channel, Sequential.** These common types of receivers use two channels to track several satellites and they process two channels sequentially. Accuracy is very good and the time-to-first-fix (TTFF) is generally very fast, typically around 5 minutes. On some two-channel units, one channel ranges, which speeds up position processing, while the other channel downloads ephemeris.

c.   **Multiple Channel, Parallel Processing.** Multiple-channel units are the most expensive, incorporating up to 12 receivers. This powerful processing capability enables the monitoring and tracking of up to 12 satellites and the parallel processing of all those satellites in view simultaneously. These units increase position accuracy, reduce errors, and improve the HDOP. The TTFF in these units is very fast; in fact, TTFF can be achieved in several seconds. Many handheld receivers now incorporate parallel processing, and it is by far the better system to choose. In rough weather conditions, fix integrity and accuracy will generally be very high.

d.   **Multiplex Processing.** Multiplex systems use one or two channels to sequentially handle satellites at high processing speeds. They are sometimes referred to as pseudo-multichannel systems because performance under ideal conditions is nearly as fast and accurate as that of true multiple-channel systems. The high speed sampling and processing of ephemeris occurs concurrently with the ranging function.

18.8   GPS Trivia. A severe meteor shower called the *Leonid Storm* is expected to reach earth on November 17, 1999. This consists of at least 150,000 stones from the tail of a comet named *Temple-Tuttle*. All GPS satellites are at risk, and at least one is expected to be destroyed. Information is that three spares are in place. At the time one or more satellites may fail, causing some temporary position variations. Should be a great light show though, don't miss it!

18.9   GPS Installation and Troubleshooting. The reliability and accuracy of your GPS system depends on a proper installation. Now that most cruisers use GPS as their primary navigation source, it is essential that the system be properly installed.

a.   **Aerial Installation.** Aerials should be sited so that they are clear of spars, deck equipment, other radio aerials and insulated backstays used for single sideband. Where possible the aerial should have as wide a field of view as practicable, while being located as low as possible. In installations that utilize a stern arch or stern post with a mounted radar, ensure that the GPS aerial is not within the beam spread of the radar antenna. It is common to mount GPS aerials on the stern rail using one of the many commercially available rail base mount systems. Ensure that the location is not prone to fouling by ropes and halyards or other equipment that may damage the aerial.

b.   **Cabling.** Many GPS problems are a result of cabling problems. Power supply cables should be routed as far away as possible from equipment cables carrying high currents. Aerial cables should also be routed well clear. It is extremely important for the aerial cable not to be kinked, bent, or placed in any tight radius. This has the effect of narrowing the dielectric gap within the coaxial cable, which may cause signal problems. All through-deck glands should be of high quality to properly protect the cable and keep water from going below. Thrudex (Index) makes cable glands that enable the plug to be passed through along with the cable. Do not shorten or lengthen an aerial cable unless your manufacturer approves it.

c.   **Connectors.** All connectors must be properly inserted into the GPS receiver. Ensure that screw retaining rings are tight, because plugs can work loose and cause intermittent contact. The coaxial connector from the aerial into the receiver should be rotated properly so that it is locked in. External aerial connections should be made water resistant where possible. Use of self-amalgamating tape is a useful method for doing this. If you have to remove and refit an aerial connector, ensure that you use considerable care and assemble the connector in accordance with the manufacturer's instructions. Use a multimeter on the resistance range, and check the center pin to shield resistance. Low resistance generally means a shorted shield strand. Resistance is typically 50-150 ohms.

d.   **Grounding.** The ground connection provided with the system must be connected to the RF ground system.

e.   **Power Supplies.** A clean power supply is essential to proper operation. Use either an in-line filter or install suppressors across "noisy" motors and alternator. The power supply should not come from a battery used for engine starting, or used with any high current equipment such as an anchor windlass or electric toilet. Note that many cheaper unsuppressed fluorescent lights also create interference that may cause data corruption.

f.   **GPS Maintenance.** Perform the following routine maintenance checks. Many problems can be identified and rectified before the system fails.

(1)   Check the aerial to make sure the connections are tight and the plugs in good condition. Ensure that it is mounted vertically and has not been pushed over, a common problem.

(2)   Ensure that all connectors are properly inserted. In particular, examine the external aerial connector for signs of corrosion, especially the outer shield braiding.

(3)   Many earlier GPS units have internal lithium batteries with a life span of only around 3 years so ensure that the battery is renewed prior to any voyage.

g.   **GPS Troubleshooting.** You should attempt some basic troubleshooting before you call a technician or remove a GPS unit for repair by the manufacturer. Many problems are related to peripheral equipment rather than the unit, and simple checks may save considerable sums of money.

(1)   **Large Fix Error.** The GPS system may be down, or a satellite may be shut down. Check your NAVTEX transmissions or other navigation information source for news of outages. SA may be activated, or the HDOP may simply be excessive due to poor satellite geometry in your location. With sequential receivers, loss of signal may be a problem in heavy sea states.

(2)   **Small Fix Error.** Errors that are not significantly large but consistently outside normal accuracy levels are attributable to a number of sources. The signal may be subject to an excessive amount of atmospheric disturbances, such as periods of extensive solar flare activity. This may be confirmed by similar HF reception difficulties, which also suffer propagation problems. The aerial connections and part of the installation may have degraded, so check the entire system. Make sure aerial orientation is vertical and not partially pushed over. Check that some aerial shadowing has not been introduced, and if possible vary the aerial position.

(3)   **No Fix.** This is often caused in sequential receivers by loss of a satellite view or when a satellite goes out of service. Another common cause is the aerial being pushed over to horizontal, so check that it is vertical. Aerial damage from having been struck by equipment is another major cause of a sudden fix loss. Check all cables, connections. etc. If these areas show no defects, a check of all initialization parameters may be necessary; if those check out, then the receiver and aerial may require shore servicing.

(4)   **Data Corruption.** This error is often caused by power supply problems. Check whether the incident coincides with engine or machinery run periods. Radiated interference is also a possibility, often from radio equipment. A lightning strike with resultant electromagnetic pulse can also cause similar problems. Another quite common cause of data corruption is that caused by "fingers." Has another person unfamiliar with operating the GPS altered configuration parameters such as time settings or altitude? This is a common problem!

18.10 **Loran-C.** Loran-C (Long Range Aid to Navigation) is a pulsed, low-frequency hyperbolic radio aid. The basic theory relies on the accurate measurement of the time difference of radio signals received from a master and slave transmitters to derive a hyperbolic position line. With two position lines or more, a position fix can be made based on the intersection on lines of position. There are a number of excellent books available on the subject, and Loran-C users should invest in one. Most Loran-C receivers such as my Dart have a very good manual as well. The following factors affect Loran-C operation:

a.   **Transmitter Chains.** Transmitter chains are always grouped according to their geographical location. A transmitter group consists of the following:

(1)   A master station designated as M.

(2)   From 2 to 5 secondary stations designated as V (Victor), W (Whiskey), X (X-ray), Y (Yankee), Z (Zulu).

b.   **Time Differences.** Loran calculates a Line of Position (LOP) from signals transmitted from a master and a secondary station. The receiver measures the difference in time signal arrival which is in microseconds. For every Time Difference (TD), there is a line between master and secondary station where the TD is constant and therefore where your vessel location may be. A second set of signals enables calculation of position based on intersection of two LOP's.

c.   **Group Repetition Intervals.** As all chains operate at 100 kHz, differentiation can only be achieved as each chain is identifiable from a Group Repetition Interval (GRI). Each chain therefore has a unique GRI. Essentially the GRI is a variation in timing of pulses.

d.   **Accuracy.** Accuracy is the fundamental reason behind any navigation system. Like all systems, Loran-C has errors that must be accounted for when using it for navigation:

(1)   **Absolute Accuracy.** Absolute accuracy is the ability to uniquely determine position using the receiver. Typical accuracy can be around 0.1 to 0.25 nm. Errors are caused by signal anomalies and conversion of TD's to latitude/longitude.

(2)   **Repeatable Accuracy.** This is typically in the range of 50-500 feet. The accuracy in Loran-C is best where TD lines are close and cross at 90°. Accuracy is obviously worst at the limit of the coverage area of about 1200 miles where signal strength is weak. At these ranges, the angles of intersection are low and accuracy is poor. For a given position the plotted positions can wander around and usually vary up to a 100 meters, and tend to align with the TD lines. A problem in European areas is interference caused by excessive radio transmissions. Good Loran-C sets have high quality filters to minimize this.

e. **Secondary Station Selection.** The following criteria should be used in secondary station selection.

    (1) **Signal Strength.** Always select a secondary station with a strong signal. Weak signals are often distorted by skywaves.

    (2) **Crossing Angles.** Selected LOP's should cross as near to perpendicular as possible. Shallow crossing angles increase plotting errors.

    (3) **Time Difference Gradients.** The spacing of Loran lines is called the TD gradient, and the closer they are together, the better the gradient. Being hyperbolic, Loran LOP's are not a constant distance apart. Avoid any secondary station that requires operation near the baseline extension.

f. **Fix Errors.** Loran-C is prone to a range of errors which are caused by the following:

    (1) **Skywave and Groundwave Effect.** Loran signals travel via a ground wave which is the shortest path. Other paths also occur, including several skywave types. Depending on time of day, skywaves may be even stronger than groundwaves, but they always arrive after groundwaves. At chain extremities, the stronger skywaves may be stronger than weak groundwaves giving errors up to 10 nm.

    (2) **Lightning Impulses.** Pulses from lightning can distort or corrupt signals.

g. **Installation.** Like most electronic equipment, correct installation is the key to optimum performance.

    (1) **Antenna and Coupler Location.** Correct installation away from electrical equipment and other antennas is necessary. Install away from spars and masts. Clearance is ideally a minimum of 6 feet. On cruising yachts either a separate whip antenna or alternatively an insulated backstay can be used (but not the SSB backstay).

    (2) **Grounding.** The grounding factor is as important as the antenna. This can be the RF groundplate used by other electronic equipment. The grounding wire should be at least 12 AWG.

    (3) **Interference.** Interference is the major cause of fix errors. Loran-C is sensitive to noise in the 90-110 kHz spectrum. Common causes are fluorescent lights, alternators, tachometers, and radars. Suppression methods are outlined in Chapter 21; they should all be installed. Generally you can test for noise problems using receiver diagnostics to check Signal to Noise Ratio (SNR).

18.11   Loran Transmission Chains. It is surprising to many that Loran is being expanded and augmented while GPS is being implemented.

a.   Chain Closures. The following chains have been decommissioned:

- Norwegian Sea Chain (Rate 7970)

- Icelandic Chain (Rate 9980)

- Labrador Sea Chain (Rate 7930)

b.   New Chains. Must be programmed into Loran receivers.

- Ejde Chain (Norway) (Rate 9007)

- Bø Chain (Norway) (Rate 7001)

- Sylt Chain (Norway) (Rate 7499)

- Lessay Chain (France) (Rate 6731)

- Newfoundland East Coast Chain (Rate 7270)

c.   Existing Chains

- Southeast USA Chain (Rate 7980)

- Northeast USA Chain (Rate 9960)

- Great Lakes Chain (Rate 8970)

- Canadian East Coast Chain (Rate 5930)

- Saudi Arabian North Chain (Rate 8830)

- Saudi Arabian South Chain (Rate 7030)

- Russian American Chain (Rate 5980)

- North Pacific Chain (Rate 9990)

- Gulf of Alaska Chain (Rate 7960)

- Canadian West Coast Chain (Rate 5990)

- USA West Coast Chain (Rate 9940)

- Northwest Pacific Chain (Rate 8930)

- India (Bombay) Chain (Rate 6042)

- India (Calcutta) Chain (Rate 5543)

18.12. Chart Plotters. Chart plotters are making a rapid transition into both commercial shipping and yachts. Although a very useful aid to navigation, they should always be used along with paper charts, *never* instead of. Standards are under development for Electronic Chart Display and Information Systems (ECDIS). Much debate is going on at the International Maritime Organization (IMO) level, and at the recent 43rd session of the IMO Sub-Committee on Safety of Navigation, a delay was requested for the acceptance of performance standards for Raster Scan Chart Display Systems (RCDS). The standard is close to being accepted by all maritime organizations as a "legal" navigation chart. Obviously the debatable issues surround questions of accuracy and reliability. Another issue is that of what constitutes a proper backup should the system fail. Organizations such as the U.K. Hydrographic Office have developed very good systems such as the Admiralty Raster Chart System (ARCS), which, when fully approved, will provide very accurate electronic charts. The criteria are that electronic charts be exact reproductions of existing paper charts, be correctable, and be officially approved. With a trend toward integrated GPS/plotters, remember that they inherit the inaccuracies of both charts and GPS, so prudence is recommended at all times, otherwise you may join an ever increasing number of grounded vessels, both commercial and yachting.

a. **Chart Plotter Basics.** The chart plotter is essentially a computer with a monitor. The computer "reads" chart data from a map cartridge or CD-ROM disk, displaying the information on the screen. Screens are either high resolution color or monochrome, or high resolution LCD. Plotters generally have a range of screen manipulation functions and route planning aids. Features include extensive waypoint storage, storage of actual routes traveled, zoom in and out, multi-screen chart displays, seamless chart changes, track-up displays, printing of screens, and more.

b. **Map Cartridge Systems.** This system is used in dedicated plotters. The market is dominated by C-Map (new CF-95 format), and Navionics (PCM-CIA). Information is stored in EPROM (Electronically Programmable Read-Only Memory) devices. The latest Geonav systems utilize a 32-bit high speed processor (400% faster in just 12 months). Both manufacturers have very large chart portfolios available for most sailing areas, and seamless cartography is now the norm. The large processor power increases are allowing the introduction of databases of tidal predictions, global light lists, multiple datum points, port services guide (Geonav), and other important databases.

c. **CD-ROM Systems.** Again there are major players such as Maptech and Mentor. This is probably where technology will go, with NOAA charts in the USA being sold under the format name BSB Charts. CD chart storage is ideal in that compressed files enable massive data storage and are incorruptible.

d. **Chart Corrections and Updates.** Monthly disks with corrections are issued, and plans are under way for commercial vessels to download corrections weekly over INMARSAT, straight into the plotter or disk.

Communications Systems

19.0   Global Maritime Distress and Safety System (GMDSS). February 1, 1999, is an important date for the world's maritime community. On this date all commercial vessels 300 GRT and above must comply with the provisions of the Global Maritime Distress and Safety System. GMDSS was defined at the International Convention for the Safety of Life at Sea (SOLAS) in 1974, and called for a phase-in period for the new requirements over the period February 1992 to February 1999. The provisions of GMDSS have widespread ramifications for the cruising yacht. How will GMDSS affect cruising yachts? If you use VHF Channel 16 or 2182 kHz to make a distress call, or simply call up a merchant vessel bearing down on you, there is a reasonable chance that they will not be listening. Listening watches are not required under GMDSS on either VHF 16, or 2182 kHz, because its use has effectively been replaced by Channel 70. Channel 16 has been abused and congested for so long that an alternative secure channel was inevitable. The stated watch-keeping cutoff date in Europe is being stated as between 2001 and 2003 on VHF 16, depending on the country.

19.1   GMDSS Principles. The primary function of GMDSS is to coordinate and facilitate Search and Rescue (SAR) operations, by both shore authorities and vessels, with the shortest possible delay and maximum efficiency. It also provides efficient urgency and safety communications, and broadcast of Maritime Safety Information (MSI) such as navigational and meteorological warnings, forecasts, and other urgent safety information. MSI is transmitted via NAVTEX, International SafetyNet on INMARSAT C, and some NBDP radio telex services.

19.2   GMDSS Operational Details. Worldwide communications coverage is achieved using a combination of INMARSAT and terrestrial systems. All systems have range limitations that have resulted in the designation of four sea areas, each defining the type of radio equipment required on the vessel operating in that particular area.

    a.   **Area A1.** Within shore-based VHF range. Distance in the range of 20-100 nm. Radio required is VHF operating on Channel 70 for DSC, and Channel 16 radiotelephone. EPIRB required is 406 MHz or L-band unit (1.6 GHz). After February 1999 VHF-EPIRB is required. Survival craft require a 9-GHz radar transponder and portable VHF radio (with Channel 16 and one other frequency).

    b.   **Area A2.** Within shore-based MF range. Distance in the range of 100-300 nm. Radios required are MF (2187.5 kHz DSC) and 2812-kHz radiotelephone, 2174.5 NBDP, and NAVTEX on 518 kHz. Also needed are the same VHF requirements as A1. EPIRB required is 406 MHz or L-band (1.6 GHz). Survival craft requirements are the same as in A1.

c.   **Area A3.** Within geostationary satellite range (INMARSAT). Distance in the range of 70°N-70°S. Radios required are MF and VHF as above and satellite (with 1.5-1.6 GHz alerting), or as per Areas A1 and A2 plus HF (all frequencies). Survival craft requirements are the same as in A1.

d.   **Area A4.** Other areas (beyond INMARSAT range). Distance north of 70°N and south of 70°S. Radios required are HF, MF, and VHF. EPIRB required is 406 MHz. Survival craft requirements are the same as in A1.

19.3   GMDSS Radio Distress Communications Frequencies. The frequencies designated for use under the GMDSS are as follows:

- VHF   DSC Channel 70, radiotelephone Channel 16, Channel 06 intership, Channel 13 intership MSI

- MF   DSC 2187.5 kHz, radiotelephone 2182 kHz

- HF4   DSC 4207.5 kHz, radiotelephone 4125 kHz

- HF6   DSC 6312 kHz, radiotelephone 6215 kHz

- HF8   DSC 8414.5 kHz, radiotelephone 8291 kHz

- HF12   DSC 12577 kHz, radiotelephone 12290 kHz

- HF16   DSC 16804.5 kHz, radiotelephone 16420 kHz

19.4   Digital Selective Calling (DSC). DSC is a primary component of the GMDSS and is used to transmit distress alerts and appropriate acknowledgments. The automation of VHF is an inevitable result of the chaos and misuse that occurs along with the plethora of hoax distress calls. DSC will improve accuracy, transmission, and reception of distress calls and eliminate the false alerts that occur under the VHF Channel 16 regime. Channel 70 is the nominated DSC channel, and has been reserved since 1985. Under no circumstances is Channel 70 to be used for voice broadcasts.

a.   DSC has the advantage that digital signals in radio communications are at least 25% more efficient than voice transmissions, as well as significantly faster. A DSC VHF transmission typically takes around a second, and MF/HF takes approximately 7 seconds, both depending on the DSC call type.

b.   DSC requires the use of encoders/decoders, or additional add-on modules to existing equipment. A dedicated DSC watch receiver is required to continuously monitor the specified DSC distress frequency. A problem with this implementation phase is the lack of a suitable receiver for yachts and small craft. In the U.K. a technical standard has been defined (MPT1279). Affordable DSC radio equipment is a priority for small vessels and Navico is set to launch a GMDSS-compliant SelCall VHF radio. These radios will incorporate a watch-keeping circuit and be compatible with a retrofitted (Class D) DSC controller.

c. DSC equipment enables the transmission of digitized information based on four priority groupings, which are Distress, Urgency, Safety, and Routine. The information can be selectively addressed to all stations, to a specific station, or to a group of stations. To perform this selective transmission and reception of messages, every station must possess what is called a Maritime Mobile Selective-call Identify Code (MMSI). Note that Distress "Mayday" messages are automatically dispatched to all stations. A DSC Distress alert message is configured to contain the transmitting vessel identity (the MMSI nine-digit code number), the time, the nature of the distress, and the vessel's position. After transmission of a distress alert, it is repeated a few seconds later to ensure that the transmission has been successful. Individuals should not acknowledge a distress transmission; this action should be performed by the land-based rescue authorities.

19.5 GMDSS Distress Call (Alert) Sequence. It is important to explain the various elements of GMDSS in an emergency situation, and these are summarized as follows:

a. **Distress Alert.** This is usually activated from a vessel to shore; for yachts, it is usually via terrestrial radio, whereas larger vessels use satellites. Ships in the area may hear an alert, although a shore-based Rescue Coordination Center (RCC) will be responsible for responding to and acknowledging receipt of the alert. Alerts may be activated via an INMARSAT A, B, or C terminal, via COSPAS/SARSAT EPIRB (243/406 MHz), or via an INMARSAT E EPIRB. Alerts can also be activated by DSC VHF or MF/HF.

b. **Distress Relay.** On receipt and acknowledgment of alert, the RCC will relay the alert to vessels in the geographical area concerned, which targets the resources available and does not involve vessels outside the distress vessel area. Vessels in the area of distress can receive appropriate alerts via INMARSAT A, B, or C terminals, DSC VHF or MF/HF radio equipment, or via NAVTEX MSI. On reception of a distress relay the vessels concerned must contact the RCC to offer assistance.

c. **Search and Rescue.** In the SAR phase of the rescue, the previous one-way communications switch over to two-way for effective coordination of both aircraft and vessels. The frequencies used are as outlined in the previous chapter.

d. **Rescue Scene Communications.** Local communications are maintained using short-range terrestrial MF or VHF on the specified frequencies. Local communications take place using either satellite or terrestrial radio links.

e. **Distress Vessel Location.** Determining the precise location of the vessel in distress is assisted by a Search and Rescue Transponder (SART), and/or the 121.5-MHz homing frequency of an EPIRB.

19.6   GMDSS False Alerts. GMDSS is new, and currently the false alert rate is around 95%. False alerts are not desirable simply because of the load placed on SAR services. False alerts are generally caused by operator errors, usually because of incorrect equipment operation. If you look at the extensive GMDSS systems on larger commercial vessels, the reasons are obvious. Another cause of false alerts is the improper acknowledgment of distress alerts leading to excessive DSC calls. Training and understanding of equipment operation is essential and only experience will resolve these problems. At the time of this writing, false alerts had become so frequent that the IMO was considering the imposition of fines for offenders.

19.7   GMDSS and Yachts. The installation of GMDSS is not compulsory for yachts, but due to its universal implementation on commercial vessels, yachts will be forced to install partial GMDSS equipment simply to remain "plugged in" to the system. GMDSS will certainly maximize SAR situations for yachts so in most cases it will enhance offshore safety. GMDSS equipment will accurately identify your boat, current position, and type of emergency, and this information will be broadcast automatically. What you get is automatic activation of alarms at coastal stations and on other vessels simply by pushing one button. Just as GPS, electronic charting, and the EPIRB have opened up the world to cruisers, so will GMDSS significantly improve safety. As a minimum the following equipment will be required for an offshore trip. Few will be able to invest in full INMARSAT terminals. A more advanced training course and operation certificate will also be required.

- NAVTEX receiver (ICS/Alden or NASA Target or Weatherfax software)

- 406 EPIRB (correctly registered)

- VHF DSC (Class D controller)

- VHF (approved handheld type, i.e., Navico Axis range)

- SART (optional but desirable)

- MF/HF DSC (optional but desirable)

19.8   Satellite Communications Systems. Under GMDSS, satellite systems play a major role and prices are getting more affordable for yachts. INMARSAT was established by the IMO to improve distress and safety of life at sea communications and general maritime communications. INMARSAT is based on satellites placed in geostationary orbit. Under GMDSS all commercial vessels operating in areas outside designated areas of International NAVTEX coverage require a receiver for reception of INMARSAT SafetyNET Maritime Safety Information (MSI).

    a.   Standard-A SES. This was the first system implemented and unlike later systems uses analog rather than digital techniques. New standard A systems have dramatically decreased the size of equipment.

b.   **Standard-C SES.** This is a GMDSS-compliant system that offers compact and lightweight terminals. These systems are designed to support data-only services, not voice. Services are telex, e-mail, Internet access, and computer database access. Providers such as British Telecom with their BT SatMail system use the data-only capabilities very efficiently. This system was used on all vessels competing in the recent BT Global Challenge race.

c.   **INMARSAT-B.** This service provides high quality communications that include telephony, telex, fax, and data. This system is the primary one for most commercial vessel operations and complies with all GMDSS requirements.

d.   **INMARSAT-M.** This system is a low cost digital system utilizing relatively small antenna domes. Services include low speed fax and data services as well as voice services. A number of Mini-M systems are on the market, all offering gyro-stabilized antennas that are able to operate up to roll angles of 25°. Unlike standard M services, which provide global coverage, Mini-M systems utilize what is called "spot beam" technology. This means that a signal is beamed to specific areas only, which include main land masses and adjacent coastlines, typically giving coverage up to 100 nm offshore.

e.   **INMARSAT-P.** This system is currently under development and will be a global handheld receiver system with voice, paging, fax, and data services.

f.   **Iridium.** This program consists of 66 satellites inserted into Low Earth Orbit (LEO). Most of the satellites for this system are already in orbit. Headed by Motorola, the system utilizes handheld receivers and will offer global voice, data, fax, and paging services along with geolocation. Switch on date is September 1998. I will be an early customer!

g.   **ORBCOMM.** This data-only service utilizes 26 LEO satellites. The service is digital data only and will offer paging, e-mail, etc. Magellan has already launched the GSC-100 handheld communicator for this system.

h.   **Globalstar.** This constellation comprises 48 LOE satellites and the consortium includes the cellular provider Vodafone. Service will provide mobile handheld digital services worldwide from 1999 and will be integrated with GSM terrestrial services.

19.9   COSPAS/SARSAT System. GMDSS incorporates the COSPAS/SARSAT system as an integral part of the distress communications system. The acronym is based on the former Soviet "Space System for Search of Distress Vessels" and the American "Search and Rescue Satellite Aided Tracking." Under GMDSS if a vessel does not carry a satellite L-band EPIRB in sea areas A1, A2, and A3 (described earlier), then a 406M-Hz EPIRB is required operating in the COSPAS-SARSAT system. This unit must have hydrostatic release and float-free capability. The system is a worldwide satellite-assisted SAR system for location of distress transmissions emitted by EPIRBs on the 121.5/243-MHz and 406-MHz frequencies, where 121.5 is an aircraft homing frequency and 243 MHz is a military distress frequency that enables military aircraft to assist in SAR operations. The Emergency Position Indicating Radio Beacon (EPIRB) is an essential item of safety equipment for any offshore cruising vessel. Earlier EPIRB units relied solely on over-flying aircraft for detection of signals and relay of the position to appropriate SAR authorities; the new systems utilize satellites. The satellite-compatible system relies on four satellites inserted in near polar orbits with orbit times of approximately 100 minutes. Accuracy of the system improved from approximately 10 nm for 121.5/243-MHz units to 3 nm for a 406-MHz unit. Note that the 406-MHz units are far more effective at lower latitudes than the 121.5/243-MHz units. In many coastal areas the use of 243/121.5-MHz units is the best choice for the most cost-effective EPIRB.

19.10   Satellite (L-Band) EPIRBs. This system, developed by the European Space Agency, will alert rescue services to vessels in distress within 2 minutes, rather than in hours as with current systems. The new system combines position determination along with a distress signal using the INMARSAT geostationary satellites. The system uses special EPIRBs that incorporate GPS receivers and ensure a position fix within 200 meters. The distress signal transmits via one of four Land Earth Stations and landline links with appropriate rescue coordination centers. Recent testing shows an average 5-minute delay from activation to reception by rescue services.

19.11   406 EPIRBs. The 406-MHz units also have a unique identification code, and information is usually programmed at time of sale. Some units also have integral strobes and some incorporate 121.5 MHz for homing signal purposes. Units on the market include Kannad 406S, LOKATA 406 2M, ACR Satellite 406, McMurdo 406, and TRON 40S. Float-free units are called Category 1, manual bracket units are Category 2.

19.12   406-MHz EPIRB Registration. If you acquire a vessel with a 406-MHz EPIRB, you must register the unit properly and provide all of the appropriate data, including its Unique Identification Number. Registration should be done immediately upon purchase. Failure to do this can cause absolute havoc if you use it, because a vessel may be incorrectly identified or, worse still, not identified at all, which could seriously jeopardize your rescue. Bad information means real bad rescue problems for everyone. If you have not registered, contact the organizations listed:

- United States of America. SARSAT Operations Division, NOAA-USMCC. Tel +1-301-457 5678. Additional information on registration Tel +1-302-763 4680.

- United Kingdom. EPIRB Registration, Marine Safety Agency, Tel +44-703-329 1449.

- Canada. Canadian EPIRB Registry Director, Search and Rescue, Canadian Coastguard, Tel +1-613-998 1559.

- Australia. Maritime Rescue Co-ordination Center, Australian Maritime Safety Authority. Tel +61-6-247 5244.

19.13   EPIRB Activation Sequence. On activation of an EPIRB the following sequence of events occurs:

- A satellite detects the distress transmission. With 243/121.5-MHz units a satellite and the EPIRB must be simultaneously within view of the Local User Terminal (LUT).

- The detected signal is then downloaded to a LUT. (In 406-MHz units the satellite stores the message and downloads to the next LUT in view.)

- The LUT automatically computes the position of the distress transmission. The distress information is then passed to a Mission Control Center (MCC) before going to a Rescue Control Center (RCC) and then to SAR aircraft and vessels.

19.14   EPIRB Operation. Do not operate an EPIRB except in a real emergency, because you could initiate a rescue operation. Do not even operate it for just a short period of time and then switch it off, because authorities may assume your vessel went down quickly before circumstances stopped transmission. With current attitudes changing toward false alarms, it may reflect very badly on yachtsmen as a whole in terms of wasting taxpayers' money. If you had to activate your EPIRB during a genuine emergency, once rescued, do not leave the EPIRB in the boat or floating off into the deep blue. The beacon may continue to transmit for some time, causing others not aware of your plight and salvation to report a distress signal or to divert course to investigate, which wastes valuable resources and puts others at risk.

19.15   Rescue Reaction Times. There is a mistaken belief that rescues are instantaneous after activation of an EPIRB. The reality, however, is a time lag that can average up to 6 hours or more from detection of a signal and physical location, although position is usually confirmed in less than 2 hours. This is dependent on suitable aircraft, weather conditions, and SAR coordinator response times. Every LUT has a "footprint" coverage area, and the closer you are to the edge of that footprint, the longer the delay. Time lags depend on intervals between satellite passes over a given location. There are six polar orbiting satellites and, although random in orbit, their tracks are predictable. If you have to activate, be patient and wait. Remember, you are not a survivor until you're on the deck of a rescue vessel or in the helicopter. Priority one is a survival training course. Have you evaluated and planned a helicopter evacuation procedure?

19.16   Battery Life and Transmit Times. Much concern has been raised over battery transmit life after activation. Always ensure that the battery pack is replaced well within the listed expiration date. Nominally a lithium battery has a life of 4 to 5 years depending on the manufacturer. Typical transmit times are 80-100 hours at 5W output. Standards require a minimum of 48 hours.

19.17   EPIRB Maintenance. The only maintenance required is to test the EPIRB using the self-test function every six months in accordance with the manufacturer's instructions. Do not self-test by activating the EPIRB distress function. Do not drop unit unless it is in the water.

19.18   Personal Locator Beacons (PLBs). The PLB is essentially a miniature EPIRB. They operate on 121.5 MHz, which is the frequency used for homing in by SAR vessels and aircraft. Due to their small size they can be attached into wet weather gear, or carried in a pocket or panic pack. It is not as accurate as other units and will localize your position to around 12 nm, because the transmitters are line of sight only. Some units are configured to activate in water, and most operate for at least a 24-hour period and some work up to 48 hours. Units available include the LOCAT LDT126 (also 243 MHz), TRON 1E.MK2, ACR Mini B300, Sea-Marshall PLB7, GME MT310, and the McMurdo SOS Rescue PLB. The PLB is not a substitute for a 243/121.5-MHz or 406-MHz EPIRB.

19.19   Radar Target Enhancers (RTEs). These units are relatively new and affordable for the average cruiser. They are an ideal complement to passive radar reflectors. The operation of these devices works by the reception of an incoming radar signal, the amplification of that pulse, and the retransmission of the pulse back to the radar signal source. This has to occur virtually simultaneously and at the same frequency. The returned signal is displayed in enhanced form, with the relatively small return of the yacht appearing significantly larger than it actually is. The recently introduced McMurdo Ocean Sentry RTE claims a target enhancement factor of eight times greater than actual reflected image. This obviously has the advantage of displaying strong and consistent echoes on radar screens. Its effectiveness depends on the incoming radar signal strength, the height at which the RTE is installed, and the height of the other vessel's radar above sea level. The Ocean Sentry unit operates either in standby or transpond modes. In standby mode, the unit is activated only when a radar signal is present. These units operate in response to 3-cm X-band radars only, not S-band. The effective range is typically around 12 nm, but not less than around 3 nm.

19.20 **Search and Rescue Transponders (SARTs).** Under GMDSS these units are required on all vessels over 300 GRT. These devices are designed for use in search and rescue, and are different from RTEs. An EPIRB will put potential rescue vessels in the area, but the transponder will accurately localize your position to search radars. The transponder is not unlike an RTE in operation. Units typically have the following characteristics:

    a.   **Signal Transmission.** The transponder emits a radar signal in the range of 9200-9500 MHz, which is in the same range as most radars (X-band).

    b.   **Signal Reception.** On reception of the radar signal, the position is indicated on radar screens as a line of 12 blips.

    c.   **Transponder Receiver.** The transponder gives an audible alarm when the radar emission of a search and rescue vessel is detected.

19.21 **NAVTEX.** NAVTEX is an integral part of the GMDSS as well as the Worldwide Navigational Warning Service (WWNWS). It is an automated information system providing meteorological, navigation, and urgent safety information. Messages are broadcast on a dedicated frequency of 518 kHz. Message reception requires a dedicated receiver, such as the integrated printer units of the ICS Nav 4 and Alden units, or NASA Marine LCD NAVTEX displays.

    a.   **Message Priorities.** Prioritization of messages is used to define message broadcasts. Those classified as Vital will be broadcast immediately, usually at the end of any transmission in progress. Those classified as Important will be broadcast at the first available period when the frequency is not in use. Those classified as Routine will be broadcast at the next scheduled transmission time. Those messages classified as Vital and Important will be repeated if still valid at the following scheduled transmission times. Messages incorporate a Subject Indicator code (B2 character), which allows acceptance and rejection of specific information. Navigational and meteorological warnings and SAR information are nonselective so that all stations receive important safety information.

    b.   **Station Identification.** Navigation information is broadcast from a number of stations located within each NAVAREA, and broadcast times as well as transmitter power outputs are carefully designed to avoid interference between stations. Each station is assigned an identification code (B1 character). This is essential so that specific geographical region stations can tune in.

19.22   Single Sideband (SSB) Radio. Long-range radio communications depend on radio frequencies in the high-frequency (HF) spectrum of 2 to 24 mHz. Radio waves are transmitted out, but the waves are bent by the ionosphere back down to earth. The ionosphere is constantly changing, and the changes alter the propagation characteristics of the radio waves. This is typified by the differences in night and day transmission characteristics. The higher frequencies offer the greatest ranges, and I have on one occasion had perfect communications with Portishead (U.K.) from Singapore. Good HF communications depend on using the optimum frequencies for the changing conditions. Amateur or ham radio is no substitute for SSB and should not be used as such.

a.   **Signal Propagation.** Skywaves travel up until they reach the ionosphere and reflect back over a wide area. Higher frequencies offer the greatest ranges. Greater ranges are possible at night. The following components affect radio transmissions:

(1)   **F Layer.** The main reflecting layer is called the F layer. Approximately 320 kilometers high, this layer is permanently ionized. During the day, however, energy from the sun causes the intervening layers E and D to form.

(2)   **E and D Layers.** The signals reflected from these layers have lower ranges. Frequencies of 3 mHz or less are absorbed by the D layer, eliminating skywave propagation. Therefore, 2 mHz is not favored.

(3)   **Ground Wave.** Ground wave signals travel along the earth's surface but are absorbed or masked by other radio emissions.

(4)   **Skip Zone.** The skip zone is the area between the transmission zone and the zone where the signal returns to earth. The signal is generally negligible in these zones.

b.   **Propagation Changes.** The ionosphere affects each frequency differently, allowing you flexibility in choosing the most suitable frequency for communication. Remember that your best local transmission times may differ from the area you are calling, and you must consider the lagging effect of ionization.

(1)   **Sunset.** At sunset, lower-layer ionization decreases, and the D layer disappears.

(2)   **Dusk.** At dusk, the range on 2 mHz increases almost instantaneously over thousands of miles as interference levels are dramatically reduced.

(3)   **Night.** The reflecting layer of the ionosphere rises at night, increasing the ranges for 4-6 mHz.

c.   **Optimum Transmitting Frequency Guide (U.K.).** This guide is compiled and published every month and is available from Portishead radio.

(1)   **Prediction Intervals.** It makes predictions based on two-hour intervals for the best frequency for communicating with Portishead from 25 locations around the world. You should use the listed frequency or the one below it.

(2)   **IF2 Index.** This is a measure of the ionosphere's ability to reflect radio waves. The range varies from -30 in poor conditions to +180 on excellent conditions. Changes in the index are cyclical over an 11-year period, with rapid increases over 3 years, and gradual decline over 8 years.

d.   **AXM Facsimile Predictions—Asia/Western Pacific.** These HF prediction charts are the recommended frequencies for Australian weatherfax reception, but they apply to all HF communications. The forecasts are transmitted every day, along with weatherfax transmission schedules. The following information was provided by IPS Radio and Space Services:

(1)   **Charts.** The transmissions consist of 27 contour charts on three pages. Each page has contoured frequency prediction charts superimposed over land and sea masses and covers 9 hours, with the last chart repeating on the following page. The geographic coverage zone is indicated by latitude and longitude on the chart edges and times are in UT (GMT).

(2)   **Frequency Recommendations.** The charts show numbers at various locations, which correspond to recommended frequencies listed at the top of each page. The frequencies are those recommended for weatherfax reception in areas bounded by the contour lines. A comment at the top of the chart gives the expected propagation conditions for the prediction period. For the following charts, frequency recommendation codes are **1**/2628, **2**/5100, **3**/11030, **4**/13920 and **5**/20469. Zero indicates the lack of a suitable channel.

e.   **Frequency Preferences.** The best ocean frequencies are 4 mHz with ranges of up to 300 miles during the day and thousands of miles at night without static at 2 mHz. Characteristics are as follows:

(1)   Low frequencies are weak during daytime and best at night.

(2)   High frequencies are used in the daytime, but are no good at night.

Table 19-1 SSB Optimum Transmission Times

Frequency (mHz)	Sunrise 0600	Noon 1200	Sunset 1800	Midnight 2400
22000	Average 100-2000 nm	Good 2000 nm plus	Good 2000 nm plus	Average 100-2000 nm
12000	Good 2000 nm plus	Good 2000 nm plus	Good 2000 nm plus	Good 2000 nm plus
8000	Good 2000 nm plus	Average 100-2000 nm	Average 100-2000 nm	Good 2000 nm plus
6000	Good 2000 nm plus	Average 100-2000 nm	Average 100-2000 nm	Good 2000 nm plus
4000	Average 100-2000 nm	Bad 50 nm	Bad 50 nm	Good 2000 nm plus
2000	Good 2000 nm plus	Bad 50 nm	Bad 50 nm	Good 2000 nm plus

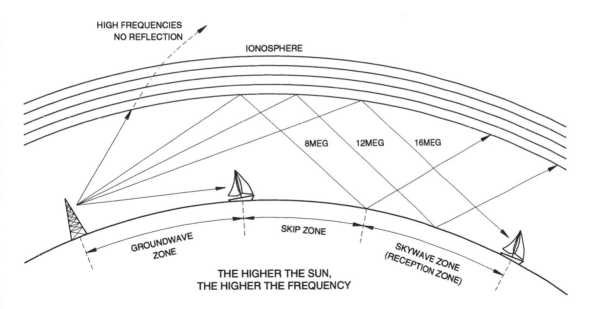

Figure 19-1 HF Radio Wave Behavior

19.23   Operation Requirements. There are certain legal requirements and operational procedures to observe.

   a.   **Ship Station Licensing.** Every vessel must have a license issued by the relevant communication authority. Transmitters must also be of a type approved by the appropriate authority.

   b.   **Operator Licensing.** A restricted radiotelephone operator's certificate is required. The test covers knowledge of distress and safety procedures and related matters of marine communications.

   c.   **Accounts.** You need to have account-keeping features or reverse charges every time a call is placed. Calls can be placed through AT&T, British Telecom, or appropriate national shore stations.

   d.   **Call Signs.** The issued call sign and vessel name must be used with all transmissions.

19.24   HF Radio Frequencies and Bands. Always consult a current list of radio signals to confirm frequencies, times of traffic lists, and navigational and weather forecasts.

   a.   **Listen to Station.** If you can hear traffic clearly on the band, you will probably have relatively good communications on that band.

   b.   **Monitor Bands.** Monitor the various bands and channels and determine the best time for communications. If the signal strength is good but the channel is busy, use a second channel, if available, or wait. Do not tune on a frequency while a call is in progress.

   c.   **Station Identification.** Have name, call sign, position, and accounting code ready for the operator.

19.25   Distress and Safety Service Frequencies. The following are the Global Marine Distress and Safety System (GMDSS) service frequencies.

   •   2182 kHz

   •   4125 kHz (Channel 421)

   •   6215 kHz (Channel 606)

   •   8291 kHz (Channel 833)

   •   12290 kHz (Channel 1221)

   •   16420 kHz (Channel 1621)

19.26   United States SSB Frequencies. AT&T operates three coast stations, aptly named the High Seas Service. The service offers 7-day, 24-hour coverage, and operates assigned duplex channels in the 2-23 mHz bands.

Table 19-2 AT&T Coast Station KMI - California

ITU Channel Number	Receive Frequency	Transmit Frequency
242	2450.0	2406.0
248	2506.0	2003.0
401	4357.0	2065.0
416	**4402.0**	**4110.0**
417	4405.0	4113.0
804	8728.0	8204.0
809	8743.0	8219.0
822	8782.0	8258.0
1201	13077.0	12230.0
202	13080.0	12233.0
1203	**13083.0**	**12236.0**
1229	13161.0	12314.0
1602	17245.0	16363.0
1603	17248.0	16366.0
1624	17311.0	16429.0
2214	22735.0	22039.0
2223	22762.0	22066.0
2228	22777.0	22081.0
2236	22801.0	22105.0

- **Traffic List of Stations with Call Waiting.**

  Channel 416 & 1203

  Times: 0000, 0400, 0800, 1200, 1600, 2000 UTC

- **Weather Forecasts.**

  Channel 416 & 1203

  Times: 0000 & 1200

Table 19-3 AT&T Coast Station WOM - Florida

ITU Channel Number	Receive Frequency	Transmit Frequency
209	2490.0	2031.5
221	2514.0	2118.0
245	2566.0	2390.0
247	2442.0	2406.0
403	4363.0	4071.0
412	4390.0	4098.0
416	**4405.0**	**4113.0**
423	4423.0	4131.0
802	**8722.0**	**8198.0**
805	8731.0	8207.0
810	8746.0	8222.0
814	8758.0	8234.0
825	8791.0	8267.0
831	8809.0	8285.0
1206	13092.0	12245.0
1208	13098.0	12251.0
1209	13101.0	12254.0
1215	13119.0	12272.0
1223	13143.0	12296.0
1230	13164.0	12317.0
1601	**17242.0**	**16360.0**
1609	17226.0	16384.0
1610	17269.0	16387.0
1611	17272.0	16390.0
1616	17287.0	16405.0
2215	**22738.0**	**22042.0**
2216	22741.0	22045.0
2222	22759.0	22063.0

- **Traffic List of Stations with Call Waiting.**

  Channels 413, 802, 1601 & 2215

  Times: 0100, 0300, 0500, 0700, 0900, 1100, 1300, 1500, 1700, 1900, 2100, 2300 UTC

- **Weather Forecasts.**

  Channel 416, 802, 1601 & 2215

  Times: 1300 & 2300

Table 19-4 AT&T Coast Station WOO - New Jersey

ITU Channel Number	Receive Frequency	Transmit Frequency
242	2558.0	2166.5
221	2450.0	2366.0
410	4384.0	4092.0
411	**4397.0**	**4095.0**
416	4402.0	4110.0
422	4420.0	4128.0
808	8740.0	8216.0
811	**8749.0**	**8225.0**
815	8761.0	8237.0
826	8794.0	8270.0
1203	13083.0	12236.0
1210	13104.0	12257.0
1211	13107.0	12260.0
1228	13158.0	12311.0
1605	17254.0	16372.0
1620	17299.0	16417.0
1626	17317.0	16435.0
1631	17332.0	16450.0
2201	22696.0	22000.0
2205	22708.0	22012.0
2210	22723.0	22027.0
2236	22801.0	22105.0

- **Traffic List of Stations with Calls Waiting.**

  Channel 411, 811

  Times: 0000, 0200, 0400, 0600, 0800, 1000, 1200, 1400, 1600, 1800, 2000, 2200 UTC

- **Weather Forecasts.**

  Channel 411 & 811

  Times: 1200 & 2200

19.27   United States SSB Weather Frequencies. While AT&T provides weather broadcasts, two U.S. Coast Guard high seas stations (NAM in Portsmouth, and NMC in San Francisco) also give good weather transmissions. The same channels are also used out of Honolulu and Guam.

Table 19-5 U.S. Coast Guard Channels

ITU Channel Number	Receive Frequency	Transmit Frequency
	2182.0	
	2670.0	
424	4426.0	4134.0
601	6501.0	6200.0
816	8764.0	8240.0
1205	13089.0	12242.0
1625	17314.0	16432.0

19.28   SSB Intership Frequencies. Some of these frequencies have intervessel conversation schedules. They are ideal for making regular contact with other vessels.

Table 19-6 SSB Intership and Limited Coast Channels

ITU Channel Number		Receive Frequency	Transmit Frequency
4A	451	4146.0	4146.0
4B	452	4149.0	4149.0
4C	453	4147.0	4147.0
6A	651	6224.0	6224.0
6B	652	6227.0	6227.0
6C	653	6230.0	6230.0
8A	851	8294.0	8294.0
8B	852	8297.0	8297.0
12A	1251	12353.0	12353.0
12B	1252	12356.0	12356.0
12C	1253	12359.0	12359.0
16A	1651	16528.0	16528.0
16B	1652	16531.0	16531.0
16C	1653	16534.0	16534.0
22A	2251	22159.0	22159.0
22B	2252	22162.0	22162.0
22C	2253	22165.0	22165.0
22D	2254	22168.0	22168.0
22E	2255	22171.0	22171.0

19.29   Caribbean Radio Frequencies and Weather Forecasts. The following are MF/HF/VHF frequencies, weather forecast information, and NAVTEX for the Caribbean. Primary frequencies are indicated in bold.

- **Bermuda (Bermuda Harbor) MMSI: 003100001**

Frequencies	2182, **2582**
VHF channels	10, 12, 16, 27
Weather	Taped continuous broadcast Coastal Waters Bermuda forecast on VHF Channel 38.

- **Bahamas (Nassau)**

Frequencies	2182, **2522**/2126,
VHF channels	16, 27
Weather	Weather messages at every odd hour on 2522 and VHF 27, storm and hurricane warnings are issued on receipt. Radio Bahamas 1540/1240/810, and 107.9-MHz broadcast detailed shipping weather reports M-F at 1205 hrs. Daily weather messages/synopsis 0815, 1315, and 1845 hrs

- **Jamaica (Kingston)**

Frequencies	2182, 2587, 2590, 3535
ITU channels	405, 416, 605, 812, 1224
VHF channels	16, 26
Weather	Weather messages Coast Guard on 2738 kHz at 1330 and 1830 hrs and on VHF 13 at 0130, 1430, and 1900 for SW, NW, and Eastern Caribbean, and Jamaica coastal waters forecast. Radio Jamaica on Montego Bay 550/104.5. Weather messages M-F 0015, 0340, 1104, 1235, 1709, and 2004 hrs. Jamaica Broadcasting Corporation on 560/700/93.3 MHz, fishing and weather forecast M-F 2248 hrs.

- **US Virgin Islands (St Thomas)**

Frequencies	2182, **2506**/2009
ITU channels	401, 604, 605, 804, 809, 1201, 1202, 1602, 1603, 2223
VHF channels	16, 24, 25, 28 (Traffic Lists), **84**, 85, 87, 88
Weather	Weather messages forecast and synopsis West North Atlantic, Caribbean and Gulf of Mexico on 2506

and VHF 28 0000 and 1200. Also 1400, 1600, 1800, and 2000 hr forecasts for Virgin Islands Eastern Caribbean. Virgin Islands Radio on VHF 28 0600, 1400, 2000 detailed Caribbean Weather reports.

- **Puerto Rico (San Juan) USCG**

NAVTEX (518 kHz)	0200, 0600, 1000, 1400, 1800, 2200
Weather	NOAA forecasts broadcast continuously on VHF WX2. Storm warnings on 2670 and VHF 22. Forecast, synopsis East Caribbean, Puerto Rico, Virgin Islands 2670 at 0030 and 1430, VHF 22 at 1210 and 2210.

- **Windward Islands (Martinique)**

Frequencies	2182, **2545**
VHF channels	16, 26, 27 (call Coast Station 26 and 27)
Weather	Storm warnings on receipt 2545 every odd H+33 and VHF 26 and 27 every odd H+30. Weather messages 2545 at 1333 and VHF 26 and 27 at 0330 and 1430.

- **Windward Islands (Barbados)**

Frequencies	2182, **2582**, 2723, 2805
ITU channels	407, 816 (Traffic Lists), 825, **1213**, 1640
VHF channels	16, 26
Weather	Warnings in English, on receipt and every 4 hrs for Caribbean, Antilles, and adjacent Atlantic waters.

- **Windward Islands (Grenada)**

VHF channels	16, 06, 11, 12, 13, 22A
Weather	GBC Radio on 535 and 15105. Storm warnings on receipt and every H+30 and after news 0200, 1030, 1130, 1630, 2030, 2230.

- **Windward Islands (Dominica)**

Weather	Radio Dominica on 595. Storm warnings every H+30 and after new service 0200, 1000, 1100, 1200, 1300, 1400, 1500, 1630, 1715, 2000, 2100, 2200.

- **Windward Islands (Saint-Lucia)**

Weather	Radio Saint-Lucia on 625/660 and 107.3 MHz.

Storm warnings on receipt and after news 1110, 1315, 1715, 2228.

- **Windward Islands (Saint-Vincent)**

  Weather   NBC Radio on 705. Storm warnings on receipt, repeated H+30, and 0200, 1640, 1715, 2030, 2230, 2345 after news.

- **Leeward Islands (St Kitts and Nevis)**

  Weather   Radio ZIZ on 550. Storm warnings on receipt broadcast M-S 1000-0300. Radio Paradise on 1265 storm warnings broadcast at 1030 and 2230.

- **Leeward Islands (Guadeloupe)**

  VHF channels   16, 25

  Weather   Storm warnings on 2250 every H+03 and every H+33. Weather messages on 640/1420 at 1028 and 2258.

- **Netherlands Antilles (Curacao)**

  Frequencies   2182, 2250/2158

  ITU channels   408, 604, 803, 1207, 1607

  VHF channels   16, 26, 27

- **Trinidad and Tobago**

  Frequencies   2182, 2735, 3165, 2049

  VHF channels   16, 24, 25, 26, 27

  Weather   Radio Trinidad on 730. Weather messages M-S 1030, 1200, 1500, 1630, 2000, 2350. NBS on 610 and 98.9/100/91.9 MHz. Weather every H+30, 0800, 1200, 1900 after news.

- **Caribbean SSB Weather Nets.** Synoptic forecasts and analysis including hurricane information and tracks for all of Caribbean. Times are all UTC.

  Frequencies   4003 kHz at 1215 to 1230, 8104 kHz at 1230 to 1300, and in the hurricane season also 8107 kHz at 2215 to 2245.

- **Caribbean Ham Weather Net (8P60M).** Broadcasts out of Barbados on 21.400 MHz daily at 1300 hrs. Receives positions 1300-1330. Translates RFI WFs 1330-1400.

329

19.30 **Pacific Islands Radio Frequencies and Weather Forecasts.** The following are MF/HF/VHF frequencies and weather forecast information for the Pacific Islands. Primary frequencies are indicated in bold. Times are UTC.

- **American Samoa (Pago Pago)**

Frequencies	2182, 2638, 2845, 4143.6, 6215.5, 6218.6
ITU channels	408, 806, 1232, 1638
Weather	Weather messages on 8585 and 6361 at 0400 and 2000 for Samoa and Tokelau Islands.

- **Western Samoa (Apia)**

Frequencies	2182, **2206,** 4125, **4143.6,** 6215.5
ITU channels	401, 603, 820, 1213, 1624, 2219
VHF channels	16, 12, 26

- **Fiji (Suva)**

Frequencies	**2111**/2162, 2182, 6215
ITU channels	406, 602, 810, 1202
VHF channels	16, 26
Weather	Weather messages on Ch 406 and 810 at 0003, 0403, 0803, and 2003. Strong breeze warnings and Fiji coastal waters Radio Fiji 3, on 989/1089/90.6/94.6 and 105 MHz, M-S 0030 0130, 0500, 1800, 1900, and 2000 after news broadcast.

- **Iles de la Societe (Society Islands) (Mahina)**

Frequencies	1755, 2182, 2620, 2845
ITU channels	416, 829, 1605
VHF channels	Tahiti 16, 27, 10 (Distress/Safety only), Bora-Bora 26
Weather	Storm warnings on receipt on 2620 and VHF 26 and 27. After announcements on 2182 and VHF 16 at 0403, 1803, and 1830. Weather messages on Ch 829, VHF 26 and 27 at 2100 and 0640, and on 2620 and VHF 26 and 27, at 2200 and 0700.

- **Cook Islands (Rarotonga)**

Frequencies	2182, **2207,** 4125, **4143.6**
ITU channels	821, **825,** 1222
VHF channels	16, 26

Weather	Weather messages on 2207 at 0015, 0615, and 1815. Arnolds Weather Net, standby on 8815USB for Q & A and forecast on 14.318USB at 0400UTC. Broadcasts translations of French reports for Marquesas, Tuamotus, and Society Islands. Relay reports Fiji, and Wellington, New Zealand.

- **Cook Islands (Penrhyn and Aitutaki)**

Frequencies	**2012**, 2182

- **Niue Island**

Frequencies	2182, **2207**, 4125, 4146, 6215, 6224
VHF channels	16, 68

- **Caroline Islands (Ponape, Truk, Koror, Yap)**

Frequencies	2182, **2616, 2724, 5205**

- **Kiribati (Tarawa)**

Frequencies	2182, **2217**/2210, 6215.5
ITU channels	411, 814
Weather	Weather messages on 4388.4 every even H+00.

- **Tuvalu (Funafuti Island)**

Frequencies	2182, 6215.5
ITU channels	411, 814, 1207, 1607
Weather	Weather messages on 6215.5 at 0500 and 2100. Gale warnings and local forecast on request.

- **Marshall Islands (Majuro)**

Frequencies	2182, **2616, 2724,** 5205

- **Nouvelle-Caledonie (Noumea)**

Frequencies	2182, **2197.5**, 4125, 6215.5
ITU channels	404, **601**, 805
VHF channels	16, 09, 26, 27
Weather	Gale, storm, and cyclone warnings for SW Pacific on receipt on Ch 404, synopsis and 18-hr forecast on 8698 at 0000, and 0930. Coastal forecast Ch 404 at 2000.

- **Tonga (Nuku'alofa)**

Frequencies	**2080**, 2182, 4125, 6215

VHF channel   16

Weather   Weather messages on 2080 and VHF 12 at 0133, 0833, 2033 for Tonga and Niue coastal waters. Vava'u Radio broadcasts weather at 1030 and 1330 LT.

- **Vanuatu (Port Vila)**

Frequencies   **2182**, 2168, 4125, 4143.6, 6215.5, **6218.6**, 5680

ITU channels   **410**, 818

Weather   Warnings on receipt 4385.3 after advice on 4125 and 6215.5. Gale warnings on 4385.3 at 0530 and 2130.

- **Solomon Islands (Honiara)**

Frequencies   **2167**, 2182, 6215.5, **6221.6**, 8294.2

VHF channels   16, 26

- **Pitcairn Island**

Frequencies   **2162**, 2182

Weather   Weather messages on request 522.5 and 12110.9

- **Nauru**

Frequencies   2182, **2201, 6215.5,** 6221.6

ITU channel   817

VHF channels   16, 06, 12, 26, 68

- **Papua New Guinea (Port Moresby)**

Frequencies   4125, **4143.6**, 6215.5

ITU channels   **417, 604**, 409, 805, 1225

VHF channels   16, 26

19.31   Ocean Passage Radio Frequencies and Weather Forecasts. In response to many requests I have incorporated the following MF/HF/VHF frequencies and weather forecast information for ocean voyages. I strongly advise that voyagers purchase an Admiralty List of Radio Signals (ALRS) prior to voyage; the following information is extracted from same.

ATLANTIC CROSSINGS

- **Ascension Island**

Frequencies   2182, 2755/2009

ITU channels   807

VHF channels   16, 26

- **Saint Helena**

  Frequencies   2182, 3162

  ITU channels   414, 807, 1217

  VHF channels 16, 10, 12, 14, 22, 26

- **Cape Verde Islands (Sao Vincente)**

  Frequencies   2182, 2160, 2049

  ITU channels   413, 426, 802, 813, 1203, 1207, 1615, 1635, 2207, 2222

  VHF channels 16, 18, 19, 20, 21, 22, 79

- **Islas Canarias (Las Palmas) DSC:MMSI 002240995**

  Frequencies   2182, 1689/2045-2048-2114, 2191

  ITU channels   406, 604

  VHF channels 16, 04, 05, 26, 28

  Weather   Gale warnings and forecast on 1689, 2820, 4372, 6510 at 0903 and 1803.

  NAVTEX   Gale warnings and synopsis 0920 and 2120.
  (518 kHz)

- **Madeira**

  Frequencies   2182, 2843

  ITU channels   426

  VHF channels 16, 25, 26, 27, 28

  Weather   Gale warnings and forecast on 2657 at 0905 and 2105. VHF 11 1030 and 1630 for Madeira.

- **Azores (Faial)**

  Frequencies   2182, 1663.5, 2742, 2748, 4434.9/4140.5

  VHF channels 16, 23, 26, 27, 28

  Weather   Horta Radio gale warnings and forecast 0935 and 2135 on 2657, and VHF 11 0900 and 2100.

  NAVTEX   0050, 0450, 0850, 1250, 1650, 2050
  (518 kHz)

INDIAN OCEAN

- ### Sri Lanka (Galle)

Frequencies	2182
ITU channels	403, 406, 410, 421, 601, 606, 802, 808, 821, 1221, 1224, 1621
VHF channels	16, 24, 25, 26, 27, 28
Weather	8473 kHz at 0600 and 1300

- ### Mauritius (Port Louis)

Frequencies	2182, 4396.6, 4403
VHF channels	16
Weather	Cyclone warnings 4396.6 and 4403 each H+03. Storm warnings and forecast at 0435 and 1635.

- ### Reunion (Saint-Denis)

Frequencies	2182, 2583, 2600
VHF channels	16, 26
Weather	Weather synopsis on 2583 and 2600 at 0503. Storm warnings incl. Mozambique channel every H+03.

- ### Ile Amsterdam

Frequencies	8690
Weather	Storm warnings and synopsis 50°E-80°E, 50°S-80°S at 1018 and 1148 hrs. Marine weather 24-hr forecast at 1018.

- ### Seychelles

Frequencies	2182, 2595
ITU channels	410, 818, 1215, 1601
VHF channels	16, 26, 27
Weather	Nav warnings at 0518 and 1548 on Ch 818.

- ### South Africa (Capetown) DSC: MMSI 006010001

Frequencies	2182, 2191, DSC2 (4125)
ITU channels	405, **421, 427**, 801, 805, **821**, 1209, **1221**, 1608, **1621**, 1633 2204, 2206, **2221**

VHF channels	16, 01, 03, 04, 23, 24, 26, 27, 28, 84, 85, 87
Weather	Forecasts on 4435 (427), 8719 (801), and VHF 01, 04, 23, 25, 26, 27, 84, 85, 87. Coastal forecasts at 1220 and 1620.
NAVTEX (518 kHz)	0020, 0420, 0820, 1220, 1620 and 2020 UTC.

SOUTH PACIFIC

- ### Hawaiian Islands (Honolulu) USCG

Frequencies	2182, 2670, 8416.5
ITU channels	424, 601, **816, 1205**, 1625
VHF channels	16, 26, 27
NAVTEX (518 kHz)	0040, 0440, 0840, 1240, 1640, 2040
Weather	816 and 1205 at 0000 and 1800; 601 and 816 at 0600 and 1200; 2670 kHz at 0545, 1145, 1745, 2345; 8416.5 kHz at 0130, 0430, 2030, 0730, and 1330.

- ### Mariana Islands (Guam) USCG

ITU channels	601, 1205
VHF channels	16, 22A
NAVTEX (518 kHz)	0100, 0500, 0900, 1300, 1700, 2100

- ### Taupo Maritime Radio (New Zealand)

Frequencies	2182, 4125, 4146, 6215, 6224, 8291, 8297, 12290, 12356, 16420
VHF channels	Contact Auckland Maritime Radio on VHF 16 (working channels are 67, 68, 71)

- ### Isla de Pascua (Easter Island)

Frequencies	2182, **2738**, 4146,
ITU channel	421
VHF channels	16, 09, 10, 14, 26
NAVTEX (518 kHz)	0450, 1250, 2050

- **Callao (Peru)**

Frequencies	2182, 2738
VHF channels	16, 14, 26
NAVTEX (518 kHz)	Weather at 0320, 0720, 1120, 1920, 2320

- **Valparaiso (Chile)**

Frequencies	2182, 1997.5, 2738, 4146
ITU channels	421, 606, 821, 1221, 1621, 2221
VHF channels	16, 25, 26, 27
NAVTEX (518 kHz)	0410, 1210, 2010

- **Magellanes (Magellan Straits) (Punta Arenas)**

Frequencies	2182, 2738, 4146
ITU channels	421, 606, 821, 1221
VHF channels	16, 09, 10, 14, 26
NAVTEX (518 kHz)	Weather at 0440, 1240, 2040
Weather	4322 and 8684 kHz at 0200 and 1400

19.32   Australian Radio Frequencies and Weather Forecasts. This frequency information courtesy of Telstra Australia and Penta Comstat. Distress and emergency calls 2182, 4125, 6215, 8291 and on 12290 and 16420 kHz at 0700-1900 hrs. Times are Local Standard and main broadcast frequencies are in bold:

- **Sydney DSC: MMSI 005030330**

Frequencies	2182, **2201, 8176, 12365**
ITU channels	405, **424, 603,** 607, 802, 1203, 1602, 2203
Weather	0503 and 1703 NSW/Qld coastal waters and navigation warnings. 0503 and 1703 High Seas (South Eastern) and Navarea X warnings.

- **Brisbane**

Frequencies	2182, 8291, 1229, 16420

- **Townsville**

Frequencies	2182, **2201, 8176**, 12365, 12290, 16420
ITU channels	419, **424, 603**, 817, 1231, 1612
Weather	0603 and 1603 Qld/NSW coastal waters and navigation warnings. 1003 and 2203 High Seas (North Eastern) and Navarea X warnings.

- **Darwin**

Frequencies	2182, **2201, 8176**, 12365
ITU channels	415, **424, 603**, 811, 1227, 1622
Weather	0803 and 1803 NT/WA coastal waters and navigation warnings. 1203 and 2203 High Seas (Northern) and Navarea X warnings.

- **Perth MMSI:005030331**

Frequencies	2182, **2201, 8176**, 12365, 12290, 16420
ITU channels	427, **424, 603**, 806, 1226, 1604, 2212
Weather	0718 and 1918 WA/SA coastal waters and navigation warnings. 0918 and 2318 High Seas (Western) and Navarea X warnings.

- **Melbourne**

Frequencies	2182, **2201, 8176**, 12365, 12290, 16420
ITU channels	404, **424, 603**, 607, 811, 1227, 1622
Weather	0748 and 1948 Vic/Tas/SA coastal waters and navigation warnings. 1148 and 2348 High Seas (South Eastern) and Navarea X warnings.

- **Penta Comstat (Gosford) (Private Station).** It is highly recommended that if you cruise the Western and Central Pacific, you subscribe to this service.

Frequencies	2182, 2032, 2524, 4125, 4483, 6215, 12290, 16420
ITU channels	429, 608, 833, 836, 1234, 1642, 2243
VHF channels	16, 67, 73, 78, 81
Storm warnings	0325 and 2325 on 2524, 4483, Ch 836, and VHF 78 0925 on 2524, Ch 429, 4483 and VHF 78.

Weather messages	Forecast/gale warnings Gabo Is. to NSW/Qld border on 2524, 4483, Ch 836 and VHF 78 at 0125, 0625, 2125. NSW/Qld to Bowen, on 4483, Ch 836 and Ch 1234 at 0335, 0635, 2135. High Seas forecast, synopsis, and warnings Equator to 50°S and 142°E and 170°E. On 2524, 4483, Ch 608 and Ch 1234 at 0935, and on 4483, Ch 836, and Ch 1642 at 2335. Bowen to Torres Strait Gale warnings Ch 836 and Ch 1234 at 0700 and 2200. Long-range navigation warnings Equator to 50°S and 142°E and 170°E on 2524, 4483, Ch 608 and Ch 1234 at 0935 and 4483, Ch 836 and Ch 1642 at 2335.

19.33   United Kingdom Radio Frequencies and Weather Forecasts. The following are MF/HF/VHF frequencies and U.K. weather forecast information courtesy of British Telecom (BT).

•   **Portishead Radio**

•   Frequencies   2182

ITU channels	Primary channels 410, 816, 1224, 1602, 1801, 2206
NAVTEX (Niton)	0118, 0418, 0818, 1218, 1618, 2018
Weather	Atlantic weather bulletin, storm warnings and synopsis on 4274, 8559.4, 12835.4, 17113 and Ch 217 at 0930 and 2130. Storm warnings at 0130, 0530, 0730, 1130, 1330, 1730. For U.K. forecasts use the MetCall Direct Service for normal RT call costs Tel No 0374 555 888 (credit card payment). Also contact MetWEB on http://www.met-office.gov.uk
Medical help	Free service connecting directly to Royal Naval Hospital, call Portishead and request "Medico" call.

19.34   Mediterranean Radio Frequencies and Weather Forecasts. The following are MF/HF/VHF frequencies and weather forecast information for principal cruising areas in the Mediterranean.

•   **Izmir (Turkey) (Aegean Sea)**

Frequencies	1850, 2182, 2760
VHF channels	16, 04, 24
NAVTEX	0120, 0520, 0920, 1320, 1720, 2120

- **Antalya (Turkey) (Mediterranean Sea) (DSC MMSI: 002713000)**

  Frequencies   2182, 2693

  VHF channels   16, 25, 27

  NAVTEX   0050, 0450, 0850, 1250, 1650, 2050

- **Iraklion – Kritis (Greece)**

  Frequencies   1742, 2182, **2799**, 3640

  VHF channels   Call Hellas Radio

  NAVTEX   0110, 0510, 0910, 1310, 1710, 2110

  Weather   2799 kHz at 0703, 0903, 1533, 2133

- **Malta**

  Frequencies   2182, 2625

  ITU channels   410, 603, 832, 1233

  VHF channels   01, 02, 03, 04, 16, 28

  NAVTEX   0220, 0620, 1020, 1420, 1820, 2220

  Weather   2625 kHz and VHF 04 at 0003, 1003, 1603, 2103

- **Cyprus**

  Frequencies   2182, 2670, **2700**, 3690

  ITU channels   406, 414, 426, 603, 807, 818, 820, 829, 1201, 1208, 1230, 1603

  VHF channels   16, 26, 24, 25, 27

  NAVTEX   0200, 0600, 1000, 1400, 1800, 2200

  Weather   2700 kHz at 0733 and 1533

19.35   **HF Radio Tuner Units.** The tuner unit's function is to match the antenna length to the frequency being used:

a.   **Manual.** There are many manual tuner units around, although they are rapidly being phased out by fully synthesized systems with automatic units. These entail matching the antennas by adjusting tune and load controls using a built-in tune meter.

b.   **Fully Synthesized Units.** The automatic tuner unit is now almost standard on new synthesized radio sets. It allows inexperienced, non-technical people to communicate easily without worrying about technical factors.

(1)   **Frequency Control.** The synthesized unit consists of EPROM-controlled frequencies. This is normally a full set of ITU frequencies, in accordance with relevant national authorities.

(2)   **Automatic Tuner Unit (ATU).** The tuner unit essentially consists of inductors and capacitors that are automatically switched in series or parallel with the antenna to achieve the correct tuned length.

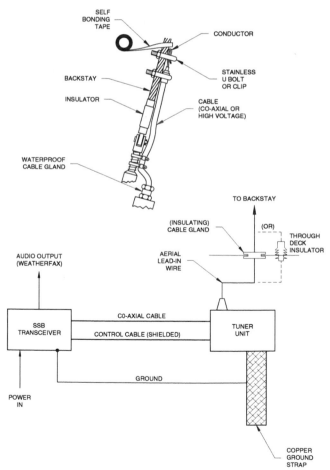

Figure 19-2 Tuner Unit and Aerial Connections

19.36   **HF Radio Aerials.** Aerials are crucial to proper performance of the HF radio.

  a.   **Whip**. The whip is reasonably popular and is often seen on larger vessels. It generally operates over a wider frequency range. There are two types of whip as follows:

  (1)   **Loaded Whip.** These aerials have loading coils and are generally very long.

  (2)   **Unloaded Whip.** These whips have a similar performance to long wire backstay aerials. The ATU provides the required aerial length. As the voltage and currents can be significant at the base, it is essential to use high-quality insulators and insulated feedline cables to minimize losses. A very low resistance ground system is also required.

  b.   **Backstay**. The insulated backstay is the most common aerial system on cruising yachts. It is the most efficient in the 2-8 mHz range. Losses can occur here as the signal radiates into the mast and rigging. It should be at least 11 meters long to be effective. The backstay insulators should be free of chips and have long leakage paths. The illustration below shows various aerial arrangements.

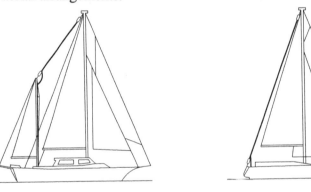

TRIATIC ANTENNA   BACKSTAY ANTENNA

BACKSTAY ANTENNA ON A KETCH

Figure 19-3 SSB Aerial Arrangements

c.   **Aerial Feedline.** The feedline to the aerial is very important as resistance degrades the transmission signals.

(1)   **Conductor Size.** Thin conductors and bad joints result in conductor heating and losses.

(2)   **Insulation Quality.** Insulation losses also occur through conductors and deck-feed insulators. Use cables with good insulation values. Many vessels use RG8 coaxial cable, while others use high-voltage ignition cable. A silicone insulated high-voltage cable should be used.

(3)   **Deck Transits.** Poorly insulated leads close to metal decks and hull can cause arcing or induction losses. External cables can also leak when the insulation cracks due to UV rays. The best system in steel vessels is to use through-deck insulators. These offer long leakage paths and therefore less signal loss. They must be kept clean.

(4)   **Backstay Connections.** The connection between the feedline and the aerial *must* be made properly. Figure 19.2 shows the ideal method.

(5)   **Feedline Cables.** The cable should not run close to metal decks or hull. On some vessels, the cable is mounted clear of the backstay by spacers until it reaches the connection point above the insulator.

19.37   HF Radio Grounds. HF radio transmission and reception problems are more often than not attributable to poor grounding systems. Remember that the ground is an integral part of the aerial system. If it is poor, you may not be able to tune properly to desired frequencies. Ground systems comprise the following options.

a.   **Keel.** The keel offers an excellent ground plate for tuner units. However, because the grounding strap has to be run from the stern-mounted tuner unit forward to the keel, it is rarely used.

b.   **Ground Shoes.** Ground shoes are the most effective method of providing an RF ground on fiberglass and wooden vessels. They provide half of the required aerial length and are an integral part of the radiating system.

c.   **Internal Copper Plates.** Glass or timber vessels may avoid installing ground plates by glassing in a large sheet of copper. Alternatively, a copper screen (Newmar) can be used to achieve the same result.

d.   **Copper Straps.** A copper strap connecting the tuner unit to the ground plate is essential. It must be a strap, not cable; surface area is the critical factor. The ground strap should be 2 inches wide at least and should run clear of bilge areas.

19.38   HF Radio Maintenance. You can perform a number of tasks that will ensure good radio performance.

    a.   **Aerial Connections**. Check regularly the lead wire connections to the aerial for deterioration. If exposed, the wire may anneal and introduce resistance into the circuit. Always tape the connection with self-amalgamating tape.

    b.   **Insulators.** Clean the insulators to remove encrusted salt deposits that result in surface leakages. This includes the upper insulator. It is amazing how many times the upper insulator leaks and causes a serious loss of signal. Grab a volunteer and hoist him up in the bosun's chair. A damp rag is the best tool.

    c.   **Ground Connection.** Check the RF ground connections. Clean and tighten the bolts and connection surfaces. After this, apply a light smear of petroleum jelly to prevent deterioration in the bilge area. Always check and keep this area clean and dry if it is in a bilge; a reaction between the copper strap and adjacent metalwork can cause corrosion problems. I have encountered this problem myself in racers with aluminum keel frames.

19.39   HF Radio Troubleshooting. There are a number of basic troubleshooting procedures to follow. Where the fault is not listed, call in a service agent.

Table 19-7 HF Radio Troubleshooting

Symptom	Probable Fault
No Reception	Wrong channel selected
	Propagation problems
	Aerial lead wire broken
	Aerial connection corroded
	Tuner unit fault
Poor Reception	Propagation problems
	Aerial connection corroded
	Insulators encrusted with signal leakage
	Aerial grounding out
No Transmission	Tuner unit fault
	Aerial connection corroded
	Insulators encrusted with signal leakage
	Aerial grounding out
	Aerial lead wire broken
	Ground connection corroded
	Low battery voltage
	Transceiver fault
Poor Transmission	Propagation problems
	Aerial connection corroded
	Insulators encrusted with signal leakage
	Aerial grounding out
	Tuner unit fault
	Ground connection corroded

19.40   Amateur (Ham) Radio. Ham radio is the realm of a worldwide group of radio enthusiasts. Ham operators have been involved in many lifesaving efforts, but regrettably ham operators and the system have been badly abused by some yachtsmen. Ham radios are a major communication source among cruisers. About 70% of American sailors use ham radio, while in the U.K. and Australia it is probably around 10%. Essential reading for enthusiasts is *Sailing With Ham Radio*, by Ian Keith & Derek Van Loan. Both are sailors and ham operators. Contact Paradise Cay Publications, 1001 Bridgeway #405, Sausalito, CA 94965. There are a number of factors to consider regarding ham operation.

a.   **Operator Licensing.** It is the operator, not the station, that is licensed. There are a number of levels that give either partial or full access to frequencies. Levels require examination in Morse code, radio theory, and the rules and regulations with respect to ham operations. All these requirements scare off many would-be amateurs. A general class license will be required for access to Maritime Mobile Nets in the 15-, 20-, and 40-meter bands.

b.   **Penalties.** You must be licensed for the country of operation. In some third-world countries where communications are controlled, jail and vessel seizure can occur if you use ham in port without authorization. In many cases, you will not be acknowledged on ham bands unless you are licensed and have a call sign.

c.   **SSB vs Ham.** This argument is never ending. Both systems have their use. In an ideal world, you should carry both.

(1)   **SSB.** Radio sets are generally easier to operate, and with automatic tuning it is simple to punch in a channel number and talk. Additionally, radios have automatic emergency channel selection. Radios are also type-approved for marine communications. Only a Restricted Radio Telephone Operators Permit is required. You can operate a SSB radio on amateur frequencies if you have a ham license, though one of the disadvantages of SSB on ham frequencies is that synthesizers are programmed in 0.10 kHz steps. Ham communications may be at frequencies outside of that so an SSB set may be marginally off frequency. Most SSB sets operate on upper sideband (USB) while most ham frequencies below 40 meters are lower sideband (LSB).

(2)   **Ham.** The ham operator must have a license appropriate to the frequency band being worked. Access to Global Marine Distress and Safety System (GMDSS) emergency frequencies is illegal except in emergencies. It is illegal to operate non-type-approved radios such as ham radios on marine frequencies. Ham allows casual conversation and chit chat; marine SSB does not. Ham allows full access to information-packed nets and a worldwide communications network. Ham does not readily allow access to telephone networks, although some stations offer phone patches.

19.41   Standard Time Frequencies. Another useful function of ham (and SSB) is the ability to accurately fix time; it is available from the following stations:

    a.   **WWV (Fort Collins).** Times are announced at the eighth and ninth minute past the hour on 2.5, 5, 10, 15, and 20 mHz. Information is also given on weather, location and movement of storm centers, wind speeds, and propagation data.

    b.   **WWNH (Kekaha, Hawaii).** Times are announced at the forty-eighth, forty-ninth, and fiftieth minute past the hour respectively on 2.5, 5, and 10 mHz. Information is also given on weather, location and movement of storm centers, wind speeds, and propagation data.

    c.   **VNG (Llandilo, Australia).** Times are announced continuously on 5.000, 8.638, 12.984 mHz and 2200-1000 UTC on 16 mHz. Voice broadcasts on 5 and 16 mHz occur at the fifteenth, thirtieth, forty-fifth and sixtieth minute.

19.42   Ham Nets. It is worth investing in a good receiver just to listen to radio broadcasts on ham nets. The information picked up can prove invaluable. Many SSB units can also access these frequencies. The main maritime mobile nets are as follows, but I cannot guarantee the frequencies and times. Note that times could vary an hour either way depending on the summer time changes in respective countries. Frequency 14.314 is monitored virtually 24 hours a day, and is the de facto maritime mobile international calling frequency.

Table 19-8 Atlantic/Caribbean/Mediterranean Nets

UTC	Frequency	Call Sign	Net Name and Area
0100	3.935		Gulf Coast Hurricane Net
0230	14.313	K6QTR	Seafarers Net
0700	14.313		German MM Net
0700	14.303		International Net
0900	14.313		Mediterranean Net
0900	7.080		Canary Island Net (Atlantic)
1030	3.815		Caribbean WX Net
1030	14.265		Barbados Cruising Net
1130	3.815	HP3XWB	Antilles Emergency Weather Net
1130	14.320	G3TJY	South Africa MM Net (South Atlantic)
1230	7.237		Caribbean Net
1300	7.268		Waterway Net (US East Coast/Caribbean)
1300	21.400		Transatlantic Net (operates in crossing season)
1400	7.292		Florida Coast Net
1600	14.313		US Coast Guard Net
1700	7.240		Bejuka Net. (Central America)
1800	14.320/303		UK MM Net
2300	7.190		Admirals' Net (US West Coast)

Table 19-9 Pacific/Asia/Indian Ocean Nets

UTC	Frequency	Call Sign	Net Name and Area
0100	21.407	W6BYS	MM Net (Pacific/Indian Ocean)
0200	7.290	KH6B	Hawaii Interisland Net (MF)
0220	14.315	VK9JA	John's Weather Net (Norfolk Is & Pacific)
0230	14.313	K6QTR	Seafarers Net (Also operates Atlantic)
0300	14.106		Travelers Net
0300	14.313	VE7CEM	DDD (Doers, Dunners & Dreamers) Net
0400	14.318		Arnold's Net (Weather Pacific)
0500	21.200	VK3PA	Aus/NZ/Africa Net (Indian & Pacific Ocean)
0530	14.314	WH6ANH	Pacific MM Net (Covers all Pacific via relay stations)
0530	14.303		Swedish Maritime Net
0630	14.330	255MU	Durban Net (Indian Ocean)
0630	14.180	VR6TC	Pitcairn Net
0700	14.220		Pacific Net
0715	3.820	ZL1BKD	Bay of Islands Net (South Pacific/Aust)
0800	14.315	P29JM	Pacific Interisland Net
1000	14.320	HG3BA	Dixies Net MM (Phillipines, Weather NW Pacific)
1000	14.330		Pacific Gunkholers' Net
1200	14.320	WB8JDR	SE Asian Net
1400	14.330		Durban Net
1430	3.963	WA6VZH	Sonrisa Net (Baja California)
1545	14.340		Marquesas Net
1600	7238.5	W6IM	California Baja Net
1630	21.350	VR6TC	Pitcairn Net
1700	14.329	KH6FWV	MM Hawaii Net
1700	14.115	VR6TC	Pitcairn Net
1700	14.329	KH6OE	Skippers' Net
1700	14.340	K6VDV	California Hawaii Net
1730	14.115	VE7CEM	Jerry's Net
1800	14.282	KH6S	South Pacific Net
1800	7.197	WA2CPX	South Pacific Sailing Net
1900	21.390		MM's Pacific Net
1900	2.738		Children's Hour Society Islands
1900	7.285	KH6BF	Shamaru Net (Hawaii)
1900	14.329	ZL1BKD	Bay of Islands Net
1900	14.340	KA7HYA	Manana Net (Mexico)
1900	7.288		Friendly Net (Hawaii)
1900	3.990		NorthWest MM Net (NW Pacific)
2000	14.305	N6GYR	Confusion Net (Pacific)
2030	7.085		Sydney/New Caledonia Net
2100	14.315	ZL1ATE	Tony's Net (South Pacific MM's Only)
2100	7.060	VK4LZ	Coral Coast Net (Airlie Beach, Aust)
2130	14.318		Daytime Pacific Net
2200	21404	KH6CO	Pacific Maritime Net (2300 in winter)
2300	28.300	VK4ACZ	10-Meter Net (Cairns, Aust)
2300	21.325		Cal-South Pacific Net
2400	14.320	VS6BE	SEA MM Net (Rowdy's Net, SW Pacific/SE Asia)

19.43   Short-Wave Radio Frequencies. The following frequencies are for the main English language services. It is easy to lose touch with what is happening while cruising, and regular monitoring of the news services can often inform you of sudden political changes or other factors that may affect your plans, especially in Third World countries. It is better to know about that war, coup, or revolution *before* you arrive. The frequency schedules are generally valid for up to 6 months or more, and may alter marginally. Contact the broadcasters for free schedules and frequency information.

a. **Voice of America (VOA).** VOA broadcasts worldwide and in some 52 languages. All times are given in GMT (UTC). In many cases you may be able to tune into broadcasts to other areas for limited periods. Frequencies are subject to variation.

  •   **Caribbean Service.** News is broadcast at 0000 on 6130, 9455, and 11695; 0100 on 5995, 6130, 7405, 9455, 9775, and 13740 kHz; and 1000 on 6165, 7405, and 9590 kHz.

  •   **Pacific Service.** News is broadcast at 1900 on 9525, 11870, and 15180 kHz; 2100 on 11870, 15185, and 17735 kHz; 1000 on 5985, 11720, and 15425 kHz.

b. **British Broadcasting Corp. (BBC) World Service, Pacific Service.** The BBC World Service is considered the essential information provider. World Service is rebroadcast in many countries. In the Pacific this includes Papua New Guinea, Radio Fiji, Radio Tonga, Solomon Islands, Western Samoa, Radio Tuvalu, Radio Kiribati, Radio Vanuatu and Radio Niue. Broadcast times are GMT and may vary slightly.

  •   World News is broadcast at 0100, 0130, 0300, 0600, 0700, 0800, 0900, 1200, 1400, 1500, 1600, 1700, 1900, and 2100.

  •   Newsdesk is broadcast at 0000, 0400, 1000, 1800, and 2200.

  •   Newshour is broadcast at 1300 and 2200.

  •   Mornings tune to 5975, 9740, 11955, and 12080 kHz.

  •   Daytime tune to 7145 and 15360 kHz.

  •   Evenings tune to 9740 kHz.

c. **Radio Australia, Pacific Service.** Radio Australia broadcasts to Asia and the Pacific areas. Like other broadcasters, frequencies are subject to variation, and times are UTC.

  •   News is broadcast every hour on the hour.

  •   Mornings tune to 9415, 5890, and 5995 kHz.

  •   Daytime tune to 1180, 7240, 12080, 15510, 17795, 13755, and 12080 kHz.

  •   Evenings tune to 15240, 11880, and 9580 kHz.

19.44   **VHF Radio.** VHF is probably the most useful radio system available as it allows easy ship-to-ship or ship-to-shore communications. Its disadvantage is that its range is line of sight, typically around 35 miles. For local port or coastal communications, it is incomparable.

19.45   **Licensing Requirements.** All countries have licensing regulations that must be adhered to. Failure to comply may result in prosecution and fines.

    a.   **Ship Station License.** All VHF installations must possess a station license issued by the appropriate national communications authority. On issue of the first license, a call sign is issued.

    b.   **Operator License.** At least one operator, normally the person registering the installation, should possess a Restricted Radiotelephone Operator's Certificate. This is obtained on completion of a short course.

19.46   **Theory.** The frequency spectrum consists of 55 channels in the band 156-163 mHz.

    a.   **Range.** As VHF operation is effectively line of sight, the higher the two antennas are mounted, the greater the distance. There are theoretical ways to work beyond this range, but for simplicity I have left them out. Atmospheric conditions and the installation itself also affect the actual range. The typical range for a coast station is approximately 35-40 nm.

    b.   **Power Consumption.** Typical units consume 5-6 amps when transmitting. Reception-only consumption, typically 0.1 to 0.7 amps, can add up if the set is on for 24 hours. That can add up to 12-17 amp-hours, depending on the set. Even so, your VHF should be left on, regardless of power consumption. Merchant ships can sight you and try to communicate well before you are aware of them.

19.47   **VHF Operation.** As VHF is widely used by official and commercial operators, it is essential to use your set properly for optimum performance.

    a.   **Power Setting.** Always use the 1-watt low-power setting for local communications and the 25-watt high-power for distance contacts.

    b.   **Squelch Setting.** Squelch reduces the inherent noise in the radio. Don't reduce the squelch too far.

    c.   **Simplex and Duplex.** Simplex means that talk is carried out on one frequency. With Duplex, transmit and receive are on two separate frequencies.

    d.   **Dual Watch.** This feature enables continuous monitoring on Channel 16 and the selected channel.

    e.   **Talk Technique.** Hold the microphone approximately 2 inches from the mouth and speak only slightly louder than normal. Be clear and concise.

19.48 **Radio Procedure.** After selecting the required channel, use the following procedures:

    a. **Operating Procedure.** Wait until any current call in progress is terminated. Even if you do not hear speech, listen for dial tones or other signals. Do not attempt to cut in or talk over conversations. Sometimes traffic may be busy and patience is required. Observe the following basic rules:

        (1) Always identify your vessel and call sign both at the beginning and end of transmission.

        (2) Keep conversations to a minimum, ideally less than 3 minutes.

        (3) After contact with other vessels, allow at least 10 minutes before contacting them again.

        (4) Always observe the 3-minute silence period on the hour and half hour.

    b. **Coast Station Calls.** Operate your transmitter for at least 7-8 seconds when calling and use the following format:

        (1) Call the coast station 3 times.

        (2) "This is [vessel name & call sign], repeat [vessel name & call sign]."

        (3) Response will be: "Vessel calling [station name] this is [station name] Radio on Channel [No.]".

        (4) "[station] Radio, this is [call sign]. My vessel name is [name]. Transfer Charge/account call please."

        (5) State account details if required.

        (6) "I have [x number of calls] for you. The number I require is [number]".

19.49 **Distress, Safety and Urgency Calls.** Channel 16 should only be used for the following.

a. **Mayday**. Use this distress call only under the direst circumstances. The Mayday call imposes a general radio silence on Channel 16 until the emergency is over. Use the following procedure, and allow time before repeating:

(1)   "MAYDAY, MAYDAY, MAYDAY."

(2)   "This is the vessel [name]."

(3)   "MAYDAY, vessel [name]"

(4)   "My position is [latitude and longitude, true bearing and distance from known point]".

(5)   State nature of distress.

(6)   State type of assistance required.

(7)   Provide additional relevant information, including number of people on board.

b. **Pan-Pan.** (Pronounced pahn-pahn) Use this call to transmit an urgent message regarding the immediate safety of the vessel or a crewmember. It takes priority over all traffic except Mayday calls. The call is used primarily in cases of injury or serious illness or man overboard:

(1)   "All Ships."

(2)   "PAN PAN, PAN PAN, PAN PAN."

(3)   "This is the vessel [name]."

(4)   Await response and transfer to working channel.

c. **Security.** (Pronounced say-cure-ee-tay). This is usually used by shore stations regarding navigational hazards, gale warnings, etc.

(1)   "SECURITY, SECURITY, SECURITY."

(2)   "This is the vessel/station [name]."

(3)   Give safety message.

d. **Medical Services.** Use this call to advise of an urgent medical emergency. It takes priority over all traffic except Mayday calls. The call is used primarily in cases of serious injury or illness:

(1) "PAN PAN, PAN PAN, PAN PAN."

(2) "MEDICO."

(3) "This is the vessel [name, call sign, nationality]."

(4) "My position is [latitude and longitude]. Diverting to [location]."

(5) Give patient details, name, age, sex, medical history.

(6) Report present symptoms and advice required.

(7) List medication carried on board.

e. **Phonetic Alphabet**

A.	ALFA	N.	NOVEMBER
B.	BRAVO	O.	OSCAR
C.	CHARLIE	P.	PAPA
D.	DELTA	Q.	QUEBEC
E.	ECHO	R.	ROMEO
F.	FOXTROT	S.	SIERRA
G.	GOLF	T.	TANGO
H.	HOTEL	U.	UNIFORM
I.	INDIA	V.	VICTOR
J.	JULIETT	W.	WHISKEY
K.	KILO	X.	X-RAY
L.	LIMA	Y.	YANKEE
M.	MIKE	Z.	ZULU

f. **Phonetic Numbers.**

1.	WUN	6.	SIX
2.	TOO	7.	SEVEN
3.	THUH-REE	8.	AIT
4.	FO-WER	9.	NINER
5.	FI-YIV	0.	ZERO

19.50   United States VHF Radio Channels. The following table gives VHF coastal frequency allocations in the U.S. for recreational and some commercial vessels

Table 19-10 United States VHF Channels

Channel Number	Channel Designation
16	DISTRESS, SAFETY and CALLING
06	Intership Safety Communications & SAR Coms only
22A	Primary Liaison USCG Vessels to USCG Shore Station USCG Marine Information Broadcasts
83A	USCG Auxiliary
7A	Commercial intership & ship to çoast
08	Intership commercial
09	Commercial intership and ship to coast
10	Commercial intership and ship to coast
12	Port operations, traffic advisory, USCG Coast Stations
13	Port operations: bridge and lock tenders non-commercial intership and ship to coast (1 watt only)
14	Port operations: bridge and lock tenders
18A	Commercial intership & ship to coast
19A	Commercial intership & ship to coast
20	Port operations
24	Public telephone
25	Public telephone
26	Public telephone (First priority)
27	Public telephone (First priority)
28	Public telephone (First priority)
65A	Port operations
66A	Port operations
68	Non-commercial intership and ship to coast
69	Non-commercial intership and ship to coast
70	Digital Selective Calling (DSC)
71	Non-commercial intership and ship to coast
72	Interyacht (non-commercial intership) communications
73	Port operations
74	Port operations
78	Non-commercial intership and ship to coast
78A	Non-commercial intership and ship to coast
79A	Commercial intership & ship to coast
80A	Commercial intership & ship to coast
84	Public telephone
85	Public telephone
86	Public telephone
87	Public telephone
88	Public telephone
WX-1 to WX-7	NOAA weather broadcasts

Notes: Channel 68 is the most common channel for local cruiser nets in Mexican Pacific coast ports (i.e., Cabo San Lucas and La Paz), and in the Caribbean. Intracoastal Waterway (ICW) bridgetenders monitor Channel 13 as well as all commercial vessels. Keep a dual watch on 16 and 13. When using this channel, do not use call signs. Use abbreviated operating procedures only.

19.51 **United Kingdom VHF Radio Channels.** The following table gives U.K. coastal stations, and broadcast and working channels. Parent stations are indicated in brackets.

Table 19-11 United Kingdom VHF Coast Stations

Shore Station	Safety & Calling	Working Channel
Collafirth	24	
Shetland	27 (MF1770 kHz)	
Orkney	26	
Cromarty	28	84
Buchan	25	87
Stonehaven	26 (MF2691 kHz)	
Forth	24	62
Cullercoats	26 (MF2719 kHz)	
Whitby	25	28
Grimsby (Humber)	27	04
Humber	26 (MF1869 kHz)	24, 85
Bacton (Humber)	7	3, 63, 64
Orfordness (Niton)	62	82
Thames (North Foreland)	2	83
North Foreland	26 (MF 1707 kHz)	5, 65, 66
Hastings (Niton)	7	63
Niton	28 (MF 1641 kHz)	4, 64, 81, 85, 87
Weymouth Bay (Niton)	5	
Start Point	26	60, 65
Pendennis (Land's End)	62	66
Land's End	27 (MF 2670 kHz)	64, 85, 88
Ilfracombe (Niton)	5	7
Burnham (Niton)		25
Celtic (Niton)	24	
Cardigan Bay	3	
Anglesey	26	28, 61
Morecambe Bay	4	82
Portpatrick	27 (MF1883 kHz)	
Clyde	26	
Islay	25	60
Oban	7	
Skye	24	
Hebrides	26 (MF1866 kHz)	
Lewis	5	

Navigation Warnings South Region: 0133, 0233, 0533, 0633, 0933, 1033, 1333, 1433, 1733, 1833, 2133, 2233

Gale Warnings: 0303, 0903, 1503, 2103. **Weather Bulletins:** 0733, 1933

Navigation Warnings Northern Region: 0203, 0233, 0603, 0633, 1003, 1033, 1403, 1433, 1803, 1833, 2203, 2233

Gale Warnings: 0303, 0903, 1503, 2103. **Weather Bulletins:** 0703, 1903

19.52   **Australian VHF Radio Channels.** The following table gives the main Australian VHF coastal stations and supplementary safety channels. Primary channels are given first. (The asterisk denotes Autocall channel only.)

Table 19-12 Australian VHF Coast Stations

Shore Station	Safety & Calling	Working Channel
Brisbane Radio (VIB)	16, 67	
Port Clinton/Keppel Island		01, 04*
Gladstone/Bundaberg		27, 24*
Fraser Island		62
Sunshine Coast		28, 25*
Brisbane Central		02
Gold Coast/Tweed Heads		26, 87, 23*,84*
Coffs Harbour		27, 24*
Darwin Radio (VID)		
Broome		28
Darwin	16, 67	26, 23
Melbourne Radio (VIM)		
Lakes Entrance		27, 24*
Wilsons Promontary		60
Western Port/Port Phillip	16, 67	26, 23*
Northern Tasmania		28
Hobart		07
Bruny Island		27, 24*
Adelaide		26, 23*
Port Lincoln		27, 24*
Perth Radio (VIP)		61
Perth	16, 67	26, 23
Rottnest Island		60
Geraldton		28, 25
Sydney Radio (VIS)		
Camden Haven		62
Port Stephens/Newcastle	16, 67	28, 25*
Newcastle/Lake Macquarie		01
Hawkesbury River		02, 60, 05*, 66*
Sydney	16, 67	26, 23*, 63*
Sydney Sth/Wollongong		88, 86*
Nowra	16, 67	27
Townsville Radio (VIT)		
Darnley Island		60
Torres Strait		26, 23*
Thursday Island		66*
Cooktown	16, 67	61
Cairns		27, 24*
Townsville		26, 23*
Ayr/Home Hill		60
Whitsunday Island		28, 86, 25*,83

19.53 **VHF Aerials**. The aerial is the principal component of good VHF communications.

a.   **Masthead**. The aerial length relates directly to the aerial gain. The higher the gain, the narrower the transmission beam. Ideally, yachts have a low-gain, 3-decibel (dB) whip mounted at the mast top. The illustration below shows the RF radiation patterns from high- and low-gain antennas. The high-gain antenna has a greater range, but when a vessel is rolling and pitching, the low-gain antenna is more reliable and has a greater coverage pattern:

(1)   **Half Wave Whip Aerials**. They are typified by a stainless steel rod. The radiation pattern has a large vertical component which suits heeling yachts. These antennas can also come in the form of a whip with lengths between 1-3 meters. The fiberglass whip effectively increases the height and therefore range of the radiating element. Gain is typically 3 dB.

(2)   **Helical**. The biggest advantage of these aerials is that they generally survive a knockdown without being torn away. They have a gain slightly less at 2.5 dB, but do have a characteristically wider signal beamwidth, which is an advantage on a heeling yacht. The helical aerial is my personal choice.

b.   **Emergency Aerial**. Always carry an emergency aerial for easy clipping to the stern pulpit in case of dismasting. I recommend permanently mounting a base unit on a stern arch or stern pulpit (pushpit) so it is ready for easy connection.

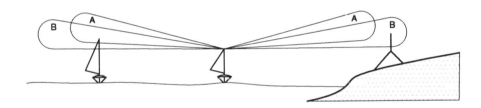

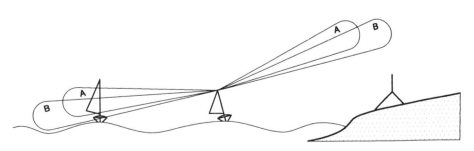

Figure 19-4 VHF Antenna Radiation and Aerials

19.54   VHF Aerials and Testing. Many vessel VHF installations operate poorly, with often undiagnosed problems. Many cruisers install their own cables, connectors, and aerials, but in the majority of cases the installation is never tested. If the maximum range is to be realized, then the installation requires proper testing. With the increasing reliance on new technology, in particular with the incoming GMDSS DSC units, reliability is of crucial importance. In an earlier chapter I highlighted the importance of installing the correct coaxial cable to reduce losses. The attenuation inherent within the cable is only part of the loss equation, and the following should be observed.

   a.   **Voltage Standing Wave Ratio (VSWR).** When a signal is transmitted via the cable and aerial a portion of that signal energy will be reflected back to the transmitter. The effect is that coverage is reduced due to the reduced power output. Measure the VSWR with a meter. Up until recently you had to hire a technician to bring along an expensive meter (I am fortunate to possess a Bird meter), but now Shakespeare offers a small and inexpensive meter (less than $100), the ART-1, which can be left permanently in the circuit to monitor performance. This allows easy fault diagnosis and timely repairs, and installation of an in-circuit meter is highly commended.

   b.   **Failure Causes.** A number of problems can reduce the VSWR. Regular testing of reflected power and detection of excessive values will alert you to potential installation problems. It may even save your life.

   (1)   **Damaged or Cut Ground Shields.** This is common on yachts where the cable has been jointed, or improperly terminated at the connector. Make sure the shield is both properly prepared and installed.

   (2)   **Dielectric Faults.** Another common yacht problem occurs when cables are run tightly around corners, through bulkheads, and through cable glands. Make sure that cables are bent with a relatively large radius; the tighter the bend, the more dielectric narrowing will occur with increased reflected power.

   (3)   **Pinched Cable.** This common problem also occurs where a cable has not been properly passed through a bulkhead with the gland or connector impinging on the cable and reducing its dielectric diameter. Radio waves pass along the outside of the central core and along the inner side of the braiding, so any deformation will alter the inductance and reduce the power output.

   (4)   **Connector Faults.** The most common problem is that of connectors not being installed or assembled correctly. Ensure that connectors are properly tightened, that pins are properly inserted, and that the pin-to-cable solder joint is sound and not a dry joint. Ensure that shield seals are properly made. Many connectors appear good at time of assembly, but deteriorate very quickly when exposed to rain, salt spray, and resultant metallic corrosion.

(5)   **Antenna Faults.** If an antenna is out of spec or suffered storm damage, or if a new antenna has been damaged in transit, then functional efficiency will decrease and losses increase. Inspect the antenna and connectors regularly. I always wrap the masthead aerial connection with self-amalgamating tape to reduce ingress of moisture and salt air.

19.55   Aerial Cables and Connections. This is one of the principal reasons why performance is degraded. A number of yachts have thin RG58U coaxial cable installed up the mast, which results in unacceptable attenuation and a large signal loss. The amount of signal that gets out depends on keeping losses within the cable and its connections low.

a.   **Cabling.** For mast cabling and masthead aerials, always use RG213/U or RG8/U to minimize attenuation. Ensure that the cable has no sharp bends. The typical cable attenuation for both types over a 100-foot run is as follows:

  (1)   **RG58/U.** This is nominally 7.1 dB, a signal loss of approximately 80%.

  (2)   **RG213/U.** This is nominally 2.6 dB, a signal loss of approximately 45%.

b.   **Connections.** Ensure that connections are properly fitted. Check for short circuits between the core and screen with a multimeter. I recently was involved on a job where the owner wanted no breaks in the coaxial cable, but I reminded him that he had to allow for pulling the mast. Install a good VHF terminal box or in-line connector to facilitate disconnection. After installation, always get the Standing Wave Ratio (SWR) checked by a technician if possible .

c.   **Standing Wave Ratio (SWR) Measurements.** SWR measurements are made using a special instrument that measures the level of transmitted RF power and how much is reflected back. These measurements quickly show poor connections and cable faults. Marine installations have a typical reading of 2:1 or (hopefully) lower.

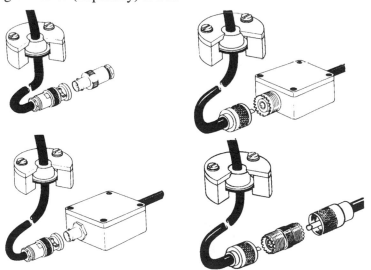

Figure 19-5 VHF Mast Connections

357

19.56   VHF Radio-Frequency Information, Changes, and Developments. GMDSS has caused some frequency allocation changes. In addition, changes have occurred in watchkeeping monitoring. To date, these are identified as follows, along with other useful cruising information. There may be others as well, so checking with your local regulator is necessary. Like many countries, use of cellular phones has lead to significant drops in link call activity. As a result coast stations and repeaters are closing also. In the U.S. a company called Maritel in Gulfport, Mississippi, has bought up and opened new stations. In the near future there will be total VHF US coastal coverage with automated link call capabilities, something which has been a reality for years in the U.K. and Australia, and a development that should assist U.S. cruisers immensely. Some VHF updates are as follows:

- **United States**

  VHF Channel 09 is now allocated for intership communications.

- **Europe**

  VHF Channel 06 is for intership business only.

  VHF Channel 77 is used for intership chat only.

  VHF Channel 13 is used for bridge-to-bridge common channel only.

- **Adriatic Sea (Serbia)**

  VHF Channels 67, 69, and 73 have continuous weather forecasts for Northern and Central Adriatic Sea updated three times per day. Broadcast in English.

- **Aegean Sea (Greece)**

  VHF Channel 86 has continuous shipping forecasts for Southern Aegean Sea.

19.57   Cellular Telephones. The rapid development of the mobile cellular telephone has made personal communications for the cruiser in coastal waters much easier. Many of us are fortunate to be able to utilize GSM technology; I can use my phone in more than 30 countries. This technology has not been without a price. The rapid drop in placement of link calls has meant the closure of many coast stations and repeaters. The media often highlight a rescue that has occurred via cell phone, direct from the life raft. This makes great headlines but this trend is of major concern. It must be emphasized that the cell phone is not a substitute for VHF or HF marine communications systems. GMDSS implementation in Europe has aggravated this problem, because some local SAR authorities have already ceased VHF 16 watch-keeping and to date GMDSS equipment is not available for small vessels.

- A vessel in distress cannot communicate with other potential rescue vessels in the area. This has the effect of delaying rescues considerably, and uses greater resources and increases the risks to all involved.

- If you are in distress, you simply may not get through to an appropriate authority, or may be at the outside of the cell range and drop out repeatedly.

- Vessels in distress who cannot provide exact position information cannot be located using direction-finding (DF) equipment. VHF allows this function.

- Vessels in distress cannot activate priority distress alerting using cell phones. This has the effect of creating delays (on hold!).

- Rescue scene communications can be severely disrupted because normal cell phone communications can only occur between two parties. Most rescue vessels and SAR aircraft do not have cellular phones. These communications problems and resulting message passing have the potential to cause disruptions or delays to the extent that a safe rescue opportunity is lost with catastrophic results.

19.58   **Weatherfax**. Weather facsimiles give skippers access to weather maps from over 90 stations worldwide. The maps are easier to interpret than foreign language voice forecasts and provide a lot of useful information. No more heading southwest then turn right when the wind changes; no more surprise gales In early 1993, it was announced in the U.S. that all HF weatherfax transmissions were to cease to save a paltry amount of money. A concerted campaign by many, including *Cruising World* magazine, managed to reverse that decision. Remember that for weather maps to be useful, you must know how to interpret the pictures.

    a.   **Weatherfax Data.** Transmitted data includes the following:

- Ocean current positions

- Sea temperature charts

- Current weather maps every 6 hours

- Forecasts up to 5 days in advance

- Sea-state and swell forecasts

- Ionospheric forecasts

    b.   **Facsimile Signal Components.** A fascimile transmission consists of a number of distinct components:

    (1)   **Continuous Carrier.** This single tone is emitted before the start of any broadcast. It allows the receiver to be tuned to maximum signal strength before data is received.

    (2)   **Start Tone.** Also called the Index of Cooperation (IOC) select tone, this enables receivers to recognize the start of a transmission and to select the appropriate IOC drum speed.

    (3)   **Phasing Tone.** This tone synchronizes the edge of the transmitted image.

    (4)   **Scale Tone.** Some systems enable the tone variations within the broadcast to be selected or varied.

    (5)   **Body of Transmission.** The characteristic rhythmic "crunching" tone is the fascimile data being decoded into an image.

    (6)   **Stop Tone.** The stop tone is similar to a start tone and indicates the end of the transmission.

    (7)   **Close Carrier.** This tone follows conclusion of the transmission.

c. **Decoders**. To obtain weatherfax data, it is necessary to obtain signals via a SSB or shortwave radio and decode them for display on a laptop computer or printer. The basic function of a decoder is to convert transmitted audio signals into data. The audio signal is taken from the audio jack (if fitted) or a terminal on the rear of the SSB set. Some units such as the Furuno integrate the HF receiver as well, which makes for a power-hungry system as well as unnecessary duplication and added expense.

d. **Printers**. The Kodak Diconix is probably the printer most used for weatherfax printouts. The Diconix 150 is a high-resolution ink-jet printer suited to function also as a laptop computer printer. As a plain paper printer, it is also significantly cheaper to operate than thermal paper roll types. One factor to consider is the ease of printing and the size and quality required. The Diconix (or equivalent units such as Canon) do provide printed images with much better resolution, along with greater size. Make sure you carry enough spare paper and ink cartridges for your voyage. Often these items are hard to procure.

e. **Discrete Systems**. The integrated decoder/printer is the most practical for cruising yachts because you do not have to fiddle with loading paper sheets into printers. I find the ICS Fax-2 to be the best in this regard, as its paper roll lasts a long time. The unit also has a number of useful features: an additional aerial can be added for full Navtex reception, marine page can be utilized, and the reception of RTTY and FEC signals is possible. Like most weatherfax units, you can program it to receive at specific times, which takes the worry out of looking up and catching broadcasts.

f. **Computer Based Systems**. These are covered in the chapter on computer systems (Chapter 23). The laptop is making rapid inroads into vessel information systems, and weatherfax capable laptops offer many advantages over traditional discrete decoders and printers. In most cases, an image can be stored and looked at without requiring a printout and these images can be zoomed down to small areas. Most software packages also allow reception of cloud cover images, amateur radio transmissions, and even photographs.

g. **Power Consumption**. Surprisingly, the rate of power consumption is relatively low, although you should take into account SSB consumption if both units are left on to capture transmissions. If you are energy conscious, you will have to power up before the required broadcast and shut down again after receiving. A decoder and SSB together will consume at least 25-30 amp-hours over 24 hours, which is considerable. Typical drains are as follows:

   (1) **Standby Listening Mode.** The ICS Fax-2 unit has a drain of only 2.5 watts. An SEA SSB 222 unit drains 2 amps, while the 322 model is only 1.0 amp.

(2) **Print Mode.** The drain increases to approximately 4 amps when printing. The SSB drain remains the same unless the audio is turned up, which adds about 0.5 amp.

h. **Troubleshooting.** If you cannot get images at all, it is generally a case of operator error, wrong frequencies, etc. Most problems occur with poor image quality. The following should be checked:

(1) **Electrical Interference.** Check all sources of noise, including fluorescent lights, motors, etc. If necessary, install suitable suppression equipment, which will protect other equipment as well. See Chapter 21 on interference.

(2) **Propagation Conditions.** The frequencies may be affected by the same adverse conditions which affect all HF transmissions. It is advisable to tune to another frequency and try again or wait until conditions improve. If this is a regular problem, obtain propagation forecasts or use the contour charts, if available.

(3) **Tuning Problems.** Be sure that the frequency is tuned accurately. If instability and drifting occur, the signal will not be consistent or clear. Often, weatherfax reception problems indicate that the aerial and ground connections in the SSB system are defective. Check these out first.

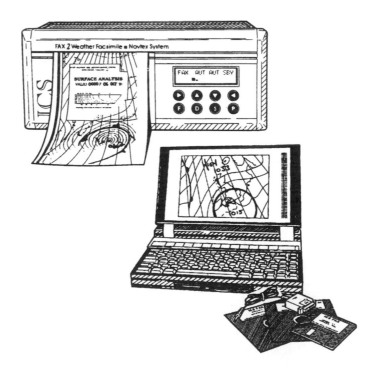

Figure 19-6 ICS Weatherfax

Table 19-13 Weather Facsimile Frequencies

Station	Frequencies
Pacific Ocean	
Vancouver (Canada)	2754, 4268, 6456, 12753
San Francisco (USA)	4346, 8682, 12730, 17151.2, 22527,
Agana (Guam)	5258, 5262, 10253, 10257, 16027.6, 19858, 23008
Honolulu (Hawaii)	9982.5, 11090, 16135, 23331.5
Pearl Harbor (Hawaii)	4855, 9398, 21839
Canberra (Australia)	2628, 5100, 11030, 13920, 20469
Auckland (New Zealand)	5807, 9459, 13550, 16340.1
Valparaiso (Chile)	4228, 8677, 17144.4
Santiago (Chile)	4766, 6418, 8594, 13525, 22071
Atlantic Ocean	
Halifax (Canada)	122.5, 4271, 6496.4, 10536, 13510
Boston (USA)	3242, 7530
Norfolk (USA)	3357, 8080, 10865, 15959, 20015
Hamburg (Germany)	3855, 7880, 13882.5
Bracknell (UK)	2618, 3289.5, 4610, 4782, 8040, 9203, 11086.5, 14436, 14582.5,18261,
Northwood (UK)	2374, 3652, 4307, 6446, 8334, 8342.5, 12844.5, 16115
Rota (Spain)	4623, 5864.5, 9373, 11485
Monsanto (Portugal)	4236.9, 8527.9, 13003.9, 17058
Pretoria (SA)	4014, 7508, 13538, 18238
Buenos Aires (Argentina)	5185, 10720, 18621.5
Indian Ocean	
Darwin (Australia)	5755, 7535, 10555, 15615, 18060
Bangkok (Thailand)	6765, 7394, 17519
New Delhi (India)	4993.5, 7403, 10105, 14842, 18225
Nairobi (Kenya)	9045, 16187, 17367, 17445, 22869
Diego Garcia	582, 12806, 20302
St Denis (Reunion)	8176, 16335
Mediterranean Sea	
Madrid (Spain)	3650, 6918.5, 10250
Cairo (Egypt)	4526, 10123, 11015, 9365, 14738, 15664, 17635
Rome (Italy)	4777.5, 8146.6, 13597
Caribbean Sea	
Martinique	5013, 14515
Red Sea	
Jeddah (Saudi Arabia)	3560, 5452, 10296

NOTE: In upper sideband mode, adjust frequency 1900 Hz lower. If in lower sideband mode, adjust 1900 Hz higher.

19.59   HF Radio E-Mail Services. Marginal HF communications with all the vagaries of ionospheric conditions, language difficulties, and high call costs are all good reasons to consider alternatives. There is always "snail mail"; if you're lucky letters will be waiting at your chosen destination, although they'll be weeks old. For most cruisers an INMARSAT terminal is not a viable economic alternative, although GMDSS-inspired changes make communications improvements essential. If, like myself, you have a quality SSB radio on board, then that valuable piece of equipment is your means to get connected to the world. In the last 18 months I have encountered a number of cruisers who have e-mail services on board via the SSB radio, and the results are impressive.

a.   **E-Mail System Components.** The three required basic components are:

(1)   **SSB Radio.** Not all SSB radios are configured for e-mail and may require modification to operate. New radios coming out such as the ICOM M710 are e-mail ready. I have an SEA 225, which already has a port for an alternative transmitter audio source such as a modem.

(2)   **Modem.** Modems are generally part of the service providers' systems, although those using other non-service company systems such as packet radio enthusiasts use what is called a Terminal Node Controller (TNC); one successful system I have encountered uses the Kantronics modem from Kansas. A modem has a power input, data port, and radio port, along with operating software.

(3)   **Notebook/Laptop Computer.** Many cruisers are incorporating this as an essential part of the equipment inventory, for use in voyage planning, chart plotting, weather fax reception, etc., so the addition of an e-mail function further enhances the investment. Software for the most part is simple to use. You merely prepare messages using the text editor and attach word processing files with point-and-click simplicity.

b.   **Transmission System Modes and Configurations.** Both the principal service providers and alternative systems utilize different methods for handling e-mail traffic. Although similar equipment is used, the systems cannot communicate with each other.

(1)   **Clover.** These modems are used by PinOak and are made by HAL Communications in the U.S. These modems use a four-tone signal and are used in the PinOak PODLink-e service. Currently Globe establishes a link in SITOR (marine telex) and then switches over to Clover mode. PinOak does not use SITOR but establishes links either in Clover or PacTOR 2.

(2)   **PacTOR 2.** These modems are made by SCS in Germany. They use a two-tone signal and are far more effective and reliable with data transfer in noisy environments. Effectively, they are a hybrid

Packet/Amtor modem. They are becoming the favored modem type for use in marine HF e-mail systems. The new PinOak PODLink-f service utilizes PacTOR modems. PacTOR is replacing Amtor communications due to improved capabilities and is supported by many Aplink stations.

c. **Service Providers.** The two main service providers and pioneers of this service are listed below. Both offer comprehensive services that will offer GMDSS-level services that cannot be afforded without installing satellite systems, such as weather and navigational warnings.

(1) **Globe Wireless.** Stations worldwide in San Francisco, New Orleans, Hawaii, Bahrain, Sweden, Newfoundland, Australia, and New Zealand. Service offered is called GlobeEmail, along with GPS position reporting tied with USCG AMVER system. Contact Globe Wireless, One Meyn Road, Half Moon Bay, CA 94019; Tel 415-367-8232; Fax 415-367-9995. Users are charged a subscription fee, which allows a specific amount of data transfer, and then a charge per kilobit transferred. Subscribers will require a Selective Call (Selcall) Number. To operate, a background routine scans all Globe Radio stations for availability, and automatically contacts and sends the message. Message reception is similar with automatic message notification.

(2) **PinOak Digital.** Stations located worldwide include Galapagos, Falkland Islands, Capetown, Cape Verde Islands, Grand Banks, West Greenland, Eastern Mediterranean, Sri Lanka, Hawaii, Tahiti, Wellington, South China Sea, Perth, and others. Coverage varies from 5 hours up to a full 24 hours. PinOak Digital, P.O. Box 360, Gladstone, NJ 07934; Tel 800-746-6251; Fax 908-234-9685. Users are charged a subscription fee, which allows a specific amount of data transfer, and then a charge per kilobit transferred. Over 4000 worldwide weather forecasts are available, along with e-mail services and Internet access.

(3) **AMTOR (Amateur Teletype Over Radio).** This is probably the cheapest option that I have seen in wide use. The system uses what is termed Amtor Packet Link (Aplink). These Aplink stations are ham stations configured for automatic reception, storage, and transmission of Amtor messages. Messages are transferred between stations until the designated destination station is reached. Addressing mail requires the recipient MBO (Electronic Mail Box) details. What I found most attractive with on-board systems using this system is the ability to "talk" with other vessels on a chat net. These nets were very effective to see in operation.

d. **Alternative E-Mail Systems.** The main systems offer a seagoing system, but there are other land-based options.

(1) **Acoustic Couplers.** This system still requires a notebook computer with an appropriate modem card installed, as well as an acoustic coupler. Subscribing to an Internet provider such as Compuserve gives you appropriate e-mail access. Download or send your mail from a phone on land and then you're back off to the boat. It is an economical alternative if you don't mind taking your PC ashore to a phone box.

(2) **E-Mail Holding Services.** A number of forwarding and holding services are appearing that allow e-mail to be forwarded for collection. A number of Caribbean sites enable e-mail to be sent and held, including Antigua Yacht Services (antyacht@candw.ag) and The Mariners Office, Crews Inn, Trinidad (mariner@trinidad.net). There are plenty of services, so you will have to scout around to find them if you're based around one port.

19.60 **Internet Services.** Internet web surfing is the hottest topic around. If you are coastal cruising you can access the Internet via your cellular telephone, or if further out utilize the services of Globe Wireless and PinOak Digital (discussed in previous section). This section lists some useful sites.

Books, Magazines, Software, and Charts

- http://www.sheridanhouse.com Sheridan House America's Favorite Sailing Books

- http://www.seafaring.com Latitudes and Attitudes Magazine

- http://www.sailnet.com Sailing Magazine

- http://www.cruisingworld.com. Cruising World Magazine

- http://.ybw.com Yachting Monthly and Practical Boat Owner Magazine

- http://www.hypernet.com/WoodenBoat.html Wooden Boat Magazine

- http://aladdin.co.uk/cpy Yachting World Magazine

- http://www.paw.com/sail/ The Internet Sailing Magazine

- http://www.bookshop.co.uk/ Internet Bookshop

- http://www.rngend.com International Boating Library

- http://www.mdnautical.com Maryland Nautical Sales (charts, publications, etc.)

- http://www.waypoints.com Complete Cruising Solutions (software, charts, etc.)
- http://www.capjack.com Captn. Jack's Software Source (software catalog)

Weather and Navigation Sites

- http://www.navcen.uscg.mil// USCG Navigation Information Center
- http://ourworld.compuserve.com.homepages/caribwx. Caribbean Weather
- http://www.meto.govt.uk/cgi-bin/offshore UK Offshore Weather Forecasts
- http://www.meteo.govt.uk/ UK Met Office
- http://www.cwp.co.uk/ UK Weather Page
- http://www.ecmwf.int/ European Center for Medium Range Weather Forecasts
- http://www.satobsys.co.uk/ Satellite Observing System (Wave Height Analysis)
- http://www.met.fsu.edu/explores/tropical.html Tropical Weather Data
- http://cirrus.sprl.umich.edu/wxnet/radsat.html Weathernet
- http://www.bom.gov.au Bureau of Meteorology Australia
- http://www.ccc.nottingham.ac.uk/pub/sat-images/meteosat.html World Satellite Images
- http://lumahai.soest.hawaii.edu University of Hawaii – Pacific Weather
- http://www.ccc.nottingham.ac.uk/ Nottingham University Satellite Imagery
- http://www.bom.gov.au/climate/glossary/elnino/elnino.shtml Everything about El Niño

Destination Information

- http://pathfinder.com/travel/maps/index.html Maps for virtually any location
- http://www.hydro.navy.gov.au Australian Hydrographic Office
- http://www.lonelyplanet.com.au Lonely Planet Guide Travel Information

Communications

- http://www.globewireless.com Globe Wireless
- http://www.pinoak.com PinOak Digital
- http://www.ozemail.com.au/~pentacom Australian Penta Comstat Sea-Mail services
- http://www.sma.gov.au/ Spectrum Management Agency Australia (radio information)
- http://www.bbc.co.uk/worldservice BBC Radio World Service
- http://www.ips.gov.au/rwc/ IPS (Ionospheric Prediction Service) Australia

Associations and Clubs

- http://www.rya.org.uk/ Royal Yachting Association
- http://www.sailing.org/ IYRU
- http://www.merlin.com.au/offshore Cruising Yacht Club of Australia

General Yachting Information

- http://www.marinedata.co.uk/start.html UK Marinedata
- http://www.alaska.net/~gusto/asst.html Seasickness Solutions and Treatments
- http://www.gosailing.com.ussail.html Sailing Subjects
- http://www.telegraph.uk Electronic Telegraph
- http://www.boatus.com BOAT/U.S.
- http://www.paw.com/sail/thelist/ Sailing Index
- http://www.boatfacts.com Large Marine Information Site
- http://www.iwol.com/ Internet Waterway

Electronics and Equipment Information

- http://www.inmet.com/~pwt/gps_gen.htm Paul Tarr's GPS Reference Links
- http://www.heartinterface.com Inverters, Chargers, Switchboards
- http://www.icomamerica.com Icom Marine (SSB, VHF)
- http://www.magellangps.com Magellan Satellite Navigation (GPS)

- http://www.kvh.com KVH (instruments)
- http://autohelm.com Autohelm (instruments, autopilots)
- http://www.technauticsinc.com Technautics Refrigeration
- http://www.huron.sailnet.com/navico Navico (instruments, autopilots)
- http://www.paw.com.sail.harken/ Harken (deck equipment)
- http://www.balmarvst.com Balmar (marine power equipment)
- http://www.glacierbay.com Glacier Bay Refrigeration
- http://www.kenyonmarine.com Kenyon Marine Refrigeration
- http://www.sailrite.com Sailrite (sail repairs, sewing machines—essential!)
- http://www.westmarine.com West Marine
- http://www.biz.com.au/ebp Electric Boat Parts Australia

Miscellaneous

- http://www.sailomat.com (windvane steering)
- http://www.sailnet.com/profurl (furlers)
- http://www.raytheon.com (electronics)
- http://www.standardcomm.com/marine (radios)
- http://www.celestaire.com (navigation instruments)
- http://www.marlowropes.com (ropes)
- http://www.bluewaterweb.com

Contact the author, John Payne, at jolly-jack@cheerful.com or http:wwwcruising-yacht.net.

Instrument Systems

20.0 **Instrument Systems.** Discrete stand-alone instruments are all but obsolete. Now integrated instrument systems are in the forefront due to the rapid advances in microprocessor computing power, miniaturization, and appropriate software developments. Integration as such is not new. The reliable Datamarine Link 5000 and Brookes and Gatehouse Hydra have been on the market for years. Low cost fluxgate compasses were a key development as they enabled a wider range of sailing parameters to be calculated and displayed. An incredible 75 separate measurements can now be taken with these systems. Discrete instrument systems without the ability to either communicate or calculate anything other than the measured function will be around for some years, but more and more purchasers will opt for the components of an overall system, whether they wish to expand or not. New Autohelm systems are also incorporating a security system called CodeLock.

> **Integration.** One big advantage of integrated systems is that duplicated equipment such as fluxgate sensors, wind vanes, and log transducers is eliminated. The two primary system configurations are as follows:
>
> **(1)** All inputs from transducers and other sources are processed by a single Central Processor Unit (CPU). The information displayed at the instrument heads is distributed via a single "daisy-chain" network to all instrument heads and connected peripherals, such as autopilots and GPS.
>
> **(2)** Total integration is where all electronic equipment, including the instrumentation, position-fixing systems, autopilot, and chart plotters, are physically matched and use a manufacturer-specific interfacing language. In some cases, engine instrumentation and communications are also matched as part of that integration.

20.1 **Systems Architecture.** The basic architecture of integrated instrument systems varies between manufacturers. The three systems in use are as follows:

> **a.** **Discrete Instrument Systems.** These systems have a transducer serving each dedicated instrument head. The head processes and displays the information. Data is exchanged between each instrument on a dedicated network for computing related data. This is the approach of B&G's Network and VDO's Logic systems.
>
> **b.** **Central CPU Systems.** These systems have a CPU to which all all transducers and some external data are connected. Instrument displays are connected on a daisy chain. The daisy-chain cable can convey data in NMEA sentences (or a manufacturer's protocol) and supply power to each instrument head. Stowe/Robertson Dataline and Datamarine Link 5000 use this system. There is a misconception that routing everything through one CPU risks total failure if the CPU fails. Stowe processes data from each source independently to prevent this.

c. **Active Transducer Systems.** This new innovation on Navico's Corus system utilizes active transducers. Each transducer has a microprocessor in it where all raw data is processed. The transducers are all connected by a single cable network and all data is available through user-definable instrument displays. These multifunction displays can be configured with simple key strokes.

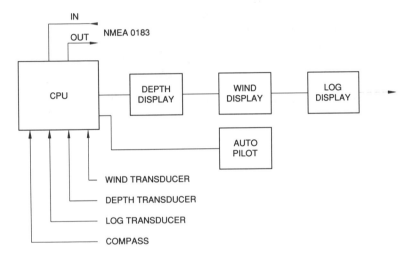

CENTRAL PROCESSING SYSTEM

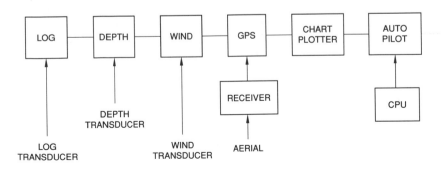

DISTRIBUTED SYSTEM

Figure 20-1 Integrated Instrument Systems

20.2   Interfacing. Interfacing is the process of connecting various electronic equipment so that digitally encoded information can be transferred between its components and used for processing tasks or for display. Manufacturers have to consider, among other things, the connectors and cables, voltages, impedances, current values, and signal timing, as well as the data structure and the transfer rate. Then there is the protocol, which determines the information to communicate and the frequency of error corrections. All the data messages must have compatible structures and content. In short, interfacing is frighteningly complex. The National Marine Electronics Association (NMEA) devised the first general digital standard in 1980 (NMEA 0180) to link position fixing systems with autopilots. This was followed up by NMEA 0182 which interfaced plotters with position fixing systems. The current and most comprehensive standard is NMEA 0183.

a.   **NMEA 0183.** This standard was designed to enable a variety of information to be transferred among position fixing systems, radar, compass, plotters, and autopilots, as well as any other systems either sending or requiring data. NMEA uses what is called single-talker, multiple-listener architecture. The next version will no doubt be multi-talker, multi-listener. Compliance with the standards is voluntary and there are cases where communication is poor or impossible because of flawed standards implementation. The NMEA has standard message sentences that may be divided into input and transmit sentences, whereas many are simply transmitted as inputs to processors with other information transmitted to the appropriate systems or displays. Message sentences have the following formats, e.g., HDM = Compass heading, magnetic; WPL = Waypoint location; XTE = Cross track error. There are as many sentences as there are parameters.

b.   **Private Protocols.** There has been a marked trend towards in-house communications protocols, in part because manufacturers are seeking faster data transfer speeds and because they want to "hook" purchasers into a single system. NMEA 0183 is gradually being relegated to a protocol for external communication between peripherals, though Robertson/Stowe Dataline uses NMEA 0183 for daisy-chain communications. The major in-house protocols in use are:

(1)   **Autohelm SeaTalk.** This protocol ensures compatibility among all SeaTalk equipment. A separate interface for NMEA 0183 equipment is sometimes required.

(2)   **B&G Network.** This protocol permits communication among B&G systems. NMEA interfaces are provided.

(3)   **VDO Logic.** This protocol is used for inter-instrument communications, but all instrument heads have an NMEA 0183 output to allow easy connection to other systems.

(4)   **Bosch Can.** This vehicle electronics standard is used in Navico's Corus system. The system requires an interface for NMEA communications.

c. **Interface Installation and Problems.** Virtually all problems with interfacing occur at installation. The majority of faults are related to the following:

(1) **Connections.** Unless the interface cable and connector are supplied by an equipment manufacturer, make sure the correct pins are used on the output port connector. These vary between equipment and manufacturers. Check with the supplier or get them to make up the cable and connector. All connections should have the correct polarity with respect to ground references. Incorrect connections mean no signals.

(2) **Grounding.** Terminate and connect screens and reference grounds. If not grounded properly, data corruption can occur, or the instrument simply will not work.

(3) **Set-up.** At commissioning, ensure that the appropriate interface output ports are selected along with the correct NMEA output format. In many cases, problems are directly attributable to this oversight and most manuals do not explain the process clearly. Go through the set-up procedures carefully. Also, where there are other protocols, always select NMEA 0183.

(4) **Cables.** All cables should be shielded, twisted pair. Using other cables may lead to data corruption caused by the induced "noise" from adjacent electrical cables and radio transmissions.

d. **Interfacing Cable Designations.** There are a number of variations in designating interface cable connections. The standard NMEA terminology is signal (positive) and return (negative). NMEA output port variations are as follows. They can be confusing and obviously lack any standard notation.

(1) **Data Signal Output:** Data O/P; Tx; Tx hot; A Line; Positive data; Signal O/P; NMEA O/P; NMEA Sig Out; O/P Sig; Data Out; Tx - ve; Tx Data O/P.

(2) **Data Return Output:** Gnd; Tx Cold; Ground; Signal Rtn; Return Out; O/P Return; NMEA Rtn; Data Rtn; I/P Gnd; Ref; Negative.

(3) **Data Signal Input:** Signal I/P; NMEA Sig In; I/P Sig; NMEA I/P; Rx Data I/P.

(4) **Data Return Input:** Signal Return In; Signal Rtn; I/P Rtn; NMEA Rtn; Gnd; Negative; Reference; Ref.

20.3 **Selection Criteria.** When selecting a system, consider the following factors:

a. **Display Types.** Ergonomic design is important, but the major decision is whether you want digital or analog displays. An array of digital displays can be confusing, which is why the aviation and vehicle industries have invested heavily in researching ways to make data easier to assimilate, from a safety viewpoint. Display types are as follows:

(1) **Digital Liquid Crystal Display (LCD).** Most displays use a 7-segment display with chunky numerals. Some displays are difficult to read at wide angles or in bright sunlight, although new technology is making higher contrasts and wider viewing angles possible. All units generally have a 3-level backlit illumination system.

(2) **Analog Display.** The analog display still seen on some instruments can make instrument displays easier to monitor; a changed needle position is easier to see than an altered digit. I personally prefer analog displays, particularly on depthsounders. With the sun behind, analog displays are easier to see. Many manufacturers such as Autohelm, VDO, and Danaplus still make analog repeaters part of their line.

(3) **LCD Analog Display.** Some manufacturers are incorporating an analog display using LCDs.

(4) **LCD Supertwist Displays.** These displays are relatively new, and they do allow viewing at much wider angles. Navico's Corus line has a 14-segment display with increased character sizes and improved visibility.

b. **Information Requirements.** Ask yourself how much data do you need or can use and interpret. If you are a full-blown racer out to squeeze every last bit of performance from the boat, then 75 parameters may be of use. Most cruisers just want the essentials, plus a few added features such as VMG (velocity made good).

c. **System Expandability.** Most systems offer you the chance to start with the basics and add as your budget allows. Remember, once you start with one line, you generally will continue as your requirements change. This is not a problem since most electronics manufacturers make everything from GPS to autopilots. If you want to add equipment from another manufacturer, however, you must ensure it is compatible.

20.4 **Electronic Compasses.** Most electronic compasses are fluxgate, though these are already being surpassed by new electronic units. The two types are as follows:

    a. **Fluxgate Compasses.** A fluxgate sensor detects the earth's magnetic field electronically, sampling hundreds of times per second. The sensing part of the compass consists of coils mounted at right angles in a horizontal plane. Each coil is fed a precisely controlled current which is modified by the earth's magnetic field. The processor compares the signals within each coil, automatically correcting for variation. The resulting analog output is then converted to digital signals for processing.

    b. **Electronic Compasses.** These compasses, like the Ritchie MagTronic, are entirely solid state. Purely electronic sensing overcomes the problems of analog-to-digital conversion by outputting and processing a digital signal.

    c. **Sensor Location.** The sensor must be mounted in the area of least magnetic disturbance, so that no interference is induced into it resulting in errors and degraded accuracy. It must also be positioned close to the center of vessel motion to prevent errors caused by vessel heeling. On steel vessels, the compass must be at least 5 feet above the deck.

    d. **Accuracy.** Accuracy depends on having a proper location clear of interference. Accuracy is typically + or - 1°. Although some self compensate to 0.5°, the display accuracy is still 1°.

    e. **Damping.** Typically, there are 5 to 10 damping levels to reduce the effects of boat motion. The rougher the seastate, the more damping is required. A low damping level can result in erratic or rapidly altering headings.

    f. **Power Consumption.** Current drains are very low, typically 100 milliamps.

    g. **Compensation.** Automatic compensation for deviation involves steering in a circle at commissioning. The deviation may vary if you have electrical devices running, but with electronic compasses, recompensation is simple and quick.

20.5 **Speed Logs**. The log indicates speed through the water and distance travelled, which makes it one of the most important instruments aboard. Not so long ago, in the mid-70s, the merchant vessels I served on towed a Walker's log. As soon as we were clear of port and full away on passage, the turbine was streamed and the mechanical counter was mounted on the poop rail. Occasionally, the turbine was mistaken for bait, but generally it was very reliable and accurate. Of course, drag was not a problem. Things have progressed somewhat and there are now a variety of systems to choose from which can be interfaced to other instruments.

a. **Paddlewheel Logs**. The common paddlewheel simply has magnets imbedded in the blades. Magnetic pulses are picked up by a detector as the water spins the wheel, giving a pulse that can be counted and processed. Earlier units had a glass reed switch that was prone to fail. New units have a Hall effect device. The pulses are normally seen as a voltage change, such as 0 and 5 volts, to give a stepped signal that can be counted. The result is directly proportional to the speed and distance travelled. The transducer may count either the pulses per second or the pulse length.

b. **Sonic Logs.** This log, developed by B&G, measures the transmission time of a sound signal between 2 transducers. The system is very sensitive—I have seen readings of minute tidal currents in boats tied up at marinas—and because it measures clear of the turbulent boundary layer, readings are accurate to 0.001 knot. This greater accuracy and sensitivity come at a greater cost.

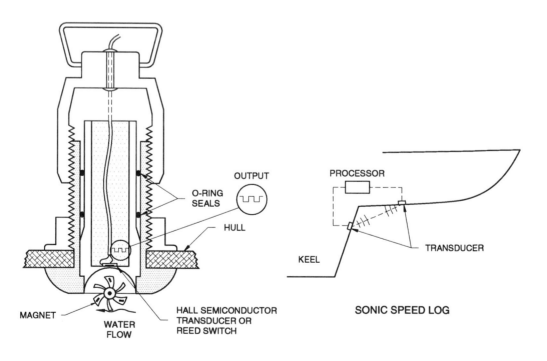

PADDLEWHEEL LOG

Figure 20-2 Log Transducers

c.   **Doppler Logs**. Unlike other logs which give speed through the water, these logs report actual speed over the ground by transmitting acoustic pulses which reflect off the bottom.

d.   **Electromagnetic Logs.** These systems measure changes to the magnetic field in the water, which alters with boat speed. On this system, there is no impeller to foul up.

e.   **Impeller Logs.** These systems measure propeller rotations, which are picked up and transmitted to the instrument head.

f.   **Dual Transducer Systems.** Catamarans often require a transducer in both hulls, and some monohulls use a dual system to compensate for heeling. Gravity switches are commonly used in racing monohulls to turn on the appropriate transducer for port or starboard tacks, but in multihulls where heel angles are less, a switch that activates when the mast rotates may be used.

g.   **Trailing Logs**. These logs are still a great standby, and some skippers use nothing else. It makes good sense to carry one as a spare. Unlike earlier versions such as the reliable unit from Stowe, these trailing logs do not have a rotating line, but have a sensor at the end of a 10-meter cable that sends a signal to the freestanding control box. As these units use a rechargeable or carbon battery, they do not have the risks of a spike induced by the power supply, although it is possible to connect them. There are a few basics to remember when using these logs.

   (1)   **Pre-Streaming.** Prior to streaming the log, make sure that the line is hooked onto the log. (This is a common error!)

   (2)   **Streaming.** Pay out the line quickly and at a constant speed *before* launching the turbine. Do not pay out the turbine first and allow the line to follow; its rotation will cause tangling.

   (3)   **Recovery.** The challenge here is to retrieve line and turbine without tangles. Ideally, you should slow the vessel to reduce drag on the line, and initiate a small turn to put some slack into the line. As soon as this is done, disconnect the line from the log and pay it under or over the stern pulpit. This will take out the turns put in the line by the turbine before the turbine is recovered.

   (4)   **Stowage.** Dry out the rope before stowing.

h. **Installation.** Correct installation is essential if the log is to be accurate and reliable. Observe the following notes:

(1) **Location.** The log transducer is normally mounted in the forward third of the hull and must be in an area of minimal turbulence, called the boundary layer.

(2) **Cabling.** Do not run depthsounder and log cables together as interference may result.

i. **Calibration.** Calibrating a log normally requires the use of a measured mile. These are always clearly marked on charts. Many new logs are self-calibrating or have an optional manual calibration. The calibration run should be carried out at slack water in calm, wind-free conditions to minimize inaccuracies. Before making a run, check that the vessel is on the correct magnetic course, and this means making appropriate corrections for variation and compass deviation. Make the runs under power at a constant throttle setting. Ensure that your transits are accurately observed at the start and finish of each run. Speed under sail may be different as heeling errors and leeway come into play. The formula for determining log error is as follows:

(1) $$\frac{\text{Runs } 1 + 2 \text{ (ground measurement)}}{\text{Runs } 2 + 2 \text{ through water}} = \text{Correction K}$$

(2) The resulting figure will show either under or over reading, which is used either to calibrate log or correct readings.

j. **Transducer Maintenance.** Logs in general need little maintenance, though paddlewheels require more than most. Perform the following checks:

(1) Regularly remove the paddlewheel to see that it is rotating smoothly and freely. Apply some light oil to the spindle.

(2) Check to see if the O-ring seals are in good condition to prevent leakage into the bilge.

k. **Transducer Troubleshooting.** To test whether the transducer or instrument head is at fault:

(1) Disconnect the log input cables to the instrument head or processor.

(2) Using a small piece of wire, rapidly short out the terminals and observe whether a reading is indicated. If there is, the transducer is faulty. If there is no reading, the instrument head is probably at fault.

20.6   **Wind Instruments.** The typical wind system comprises an integral windspeed and direction masthead unit, an instrument head, and usually a combination analog and digital display unit.

a.   **Wind Speed.** The anemometer is essentially a rotating pulse counter similar to the log. The pulses are counted and processed to give speed.

b.   **Wind Direction.** This part of the masthead unit consists of a simple wind-vane. A number of methods can be used to measure the angle and transmit the signals to the instrument head or processor. Some units use an electro-magnetic sensing system. Others use an optical sensing system to identify coded markings that relate to the windvane direction.

(1)   **Apparent Wind Direction.** The measured wind direction is apparent wind. The display indicates the close hauled angles and gybe points.

(2)   **True Wind Direction.** True wind data is a result of the instrument processing vessel course and speed and apparent wind direction and speed.

c.   **Combination Units.** Autohelm's new Rotavecta transducers incorporate the wind direction sensor in the anemometer. The wind direction is sensed from the anemometer's rotation.

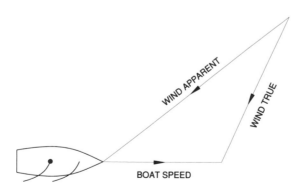

Figure 20-3 Wind Vectors

d. **Masthead Unit Installation.** The masthead unit is always mounted on the end of a boom in front of the mast to reduce turbulence. The position is not perfect—the masthead unit is subject to updrafts and turbulence from the sail—but it is still the best alternative.

   (1) **Fastening.** It is important that the unit be properly fastened down, especially as masthead units are often installed in a simple bracket assembly and are removable. Check fore-and-aft alignment to reduce inaccuracies in angle readings. Besides birds and lightning, the main cause of masthead damage is vibration.

   (2) **Electrical Connections.** Make sure the cable connector is securely fastened. It is good practice to put a few wraps of self-amalgamating tape around it to prevent water entry. If you must put on petroleum jelly or silicone grease, do not smother the socket as many do. It simply gets pushed into the masthead unit and contributes to poor electrical contact. It is better to keep electrical connections dry with tape, as suggested. You can put grease on the screw threads to minimize seizing.

e. **Mast Base Installation.** Make cable connections in a water-resistant instrument connection box and be sure all connections are tight.

f. **Masthead Unit Maintenance.** Every 6 months:

   (1) Check securing bolts and frame, and tighten as required.

   (2) Check cable connector for moisture and water, as well as for signs of corrosion on the pins. Smear a small amount of petroleum jelly or silicone grease around the threads when replacing it, and rewrap with self-amalgamating tape. Examine cable insulation for signs of chafing at any mast access point.

   (3) Check that the anemometer rotates freely without binding or making any noises, which may indicate bearing seizure or failure. Check the cups for splitting or damage, which frequently is caused by birds.

   (4) Apply a few drops of the manufacturer's light oil into the lubrication hole and rotate to ensure that it penetrates the bearing.

   (5) Check the connections in the connection box at the mast base. They should be tight and show no corrosion.

g. **Velocity Made Good (VMG).** A sailboat's VMG to a mark or waypoint is an important piece of data with respect to steering and sail trim. VMG is derived from calculation of true wind, course, and speed and is usually combined with one of the wind instruments. Monitoring VMG enables the helmsman to sail the optimum course so that maximum speed is made toward the destination. The following are used to achieve optimum VMG, which is indicated with a higher reading:

(1) **Sail Trim.** Adjusting sail trim will increase or decrease speed and VMG.

(2) **Course Adjustment.** Changing course off the wind or into it will also change the VMG reading.

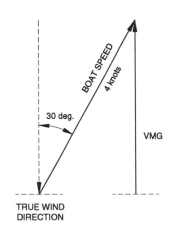

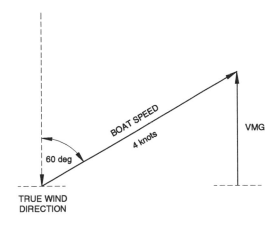

Figure 20-4 VMG Vectors

20.7   Depthsounders. The depthsounder is an important and indispensable piece of electronic equipment, unless you still prefer a lead line. It converts an electrical signal to an acoustic signal via a piezoelectric element and transmits it toward the sea bottom. The time between transmission and return is measured to give depth. The lower the frequency, the deeper the capability. Most depthsounders operate at 200 kHz. The sounder normally projects the acoustic signal directly down in a cone of coverage.

a.   **Digital**. The most common depth instrument is a digital unit incorporating an anchor watch alarm.

b.   **Forward Looking Echosounders.** Incastec in the U.K. has finally developed the answer to reef cruising yachtsmen. A powerful processing unit enables the transducer to angle sonar beams down and up to 80 meters ahead of a vessel. The instrument head's liquid crystal display shows a profile of the sea bed up to a maximum range of 200 meters.

c.   **Keel Offset.** This adjustment is important so that the depth of the water under the keel is measured. In many installations, this is set inaccurately. Read the manual and adjust accordingly.

d.   **Accuracy.** A number of factors influence sounder accuracy, and these should be taken into account at all times. Intermittent or spurious data can often be attributed to water temperature, salinity, density, aeration, bottom layers, or even fish schools.

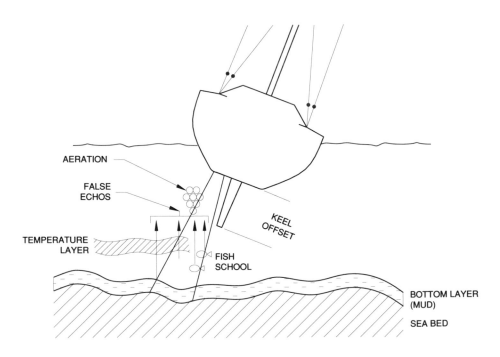

Figure 20-5 Depth Sonic Cone

e.   **Installation.** The transducer consists of a ceramic element encapsulated in epoxy. Be careful not to bump the transducer and damage the ceramic element.

(1)   **Through-Hull Mounting.** Most installations are mounted on a fairing block to ensure that beam faces directly down when the boat is on an even keel and to reduce turbulence. The transducer should be located somewhere from amidships to just forward of the mast in an area of minimal turbulence away from the keel. This prevents signal reflections when heeling. Water bubbles from turbulence is a common cause of problems.

(2)   **In-Hull Mounting.** Transducers on fiberglass boats can be mounted inside the hull in an oil bath. This technique can reduce a depth-sounder's range by 60-70% and therefore should be avoided if possible.

(3)   **Cabling.** Always install cables clear of heavy current-carrying cables or radio aerial cables. Never install next to log cables as the interference problem can be significant.

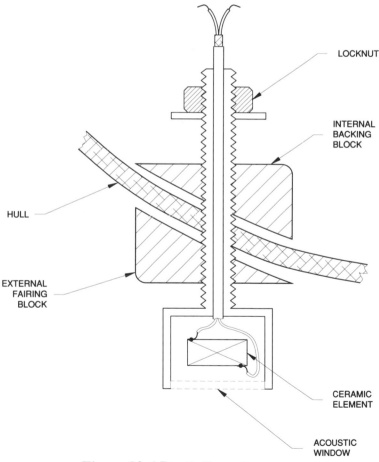

Figure 20-6 Depth Transducer

383

f.   Maintenance. The transducer is the only item that can be maintained. If neglected, performance will be dramatically reduced.

  (1)   Cleaning. Regular cleaning is essential to remove growth. Do not bash it or apply any impact to the surface.

  (2)   Antifouling. Avoid putting antifouling on the transducer surface, as it reduces sensitivity. If you must, smear on a very thin layer with your finger.

20.8   Instrument Installation. The following should be observed when installing an instrument system:

  a.   CPU Location. Always install the CPU or data box in a clean, dry area that permits easy access to transducer cables. Mount the CPU unit well away from fluxgate compasses, SatNav, Loran, Decca, and GPS receivers, and VHF, SSB, and AM/FM radios. The CPU must be one meter minimum from a magnetic compass.

  b.   Transducer Cables. Transducer cables should not be lengthened or shortened. Coil up the extra length at the transducer end.

  c.   Instrument Covers. Do not cover or mount your instruments behind perspex or plastic sheeting. This magnifies the heat from the sun and burns them out. When the instruments are not in use, always use the covers provided to prevent sun damage and weathering.

  d.   Cables. Do not stress or bend the cables sharply. All cables must be run through proper deck transits to connection boxes. Always run cables well away from radio antennas and heavy current carrying cables.

20.9   Instrument Maintenance. The following precautions should ensure maximum reliability:

  a.   Check Connections. Bad electrical connections are the source of many failures, as is moisture in the connection boxes and plugs. When a short occurs, the spike that is generated often causes a failure in the electronics. See that all boxes are dry, well waterproofed, and have tight connections.

  b.   Remove Transducers. If possible when at a mooring or in port, remove the log and depth transducers and replace them with dummies. Clear them of any growth. If the vessel will not be used for some time, also remove the masthead wind transducer to prevent excess wear or damage from birds or lightning.

Table 20-1 Instrument Troubleshooting

Symptom	Probable Fault
No Display	Loss of power
	Cable connection fault
	Instrument fault
Partial Display	Processor fault
	LCD fault
	Transducer fault
Erratic Readings	Connection degradation
	Interference from radios, electrical, etc.
	Low battery voltage
	Transducer fault
No or Low Boat Speed	Transducer not installed
	Transducer not connected
	Fouled transducer
	Transducer misaligned
	Paddlewheel seizing
High Boat Speed	Electrical interference
No Wind Speed	Mast base connection fault
	Masthead unit plug fault
	Anemometer seized
	Masthead unit fault
	Processor fault
	Low battery voltage
Erratic Wind Angle	Loose connections
	Corroded masthead unit plug
	Water in masthead unit plug
	Masthead unit fault
No Depth Indication	Transducer damaged
	Transducer fouled
	Low battery voltage
Intermittent Shallow Indication	Weed or fish
	Water aeration
Shallow Readings in Deep Water	Check your charts!
	Outside depth range
Inconsistent Depth Readings	Muddy or silted bottom
	Low battery voltage
	Poor transducer interface (in hull only)

Interference

21.0   Interference. Interference is the major enemy of electronic systems. It corrupts position fixes, reduces performance, and often is the cause of electronics damage. Interference and noise superimpose a disturbance or voltage transient onto power or signal lines and this corrupts or degrades the processed data. The following describes problems and some solutions:

    a.   **Voltage Transients.** The voltage transient is the most damaging and comes from many sources. The best known is the corruption of GPS and Loran data where the power is taken off an engine-starting battery. If a significant load is applied, there can be a momentary voltage drop, followed by an increase. This disturbance can exceed 100 volts in some cases, damaging power supplies, wiping out memories, or corrupting data. The same applies to battery systems where the house bank supplies items such as electric toilets and equipment with large current demands. Variation or interruption of current in the equipment power conductor also causes noise.

    b.   **Induced Interference.** Electrical fields radiate from cables and equipment. This is induced into other nearby cables or equipment. The most common causes of induced interference are cables running parallel to or within the same cable bundle. Always run power-supply cables and data cables separately and make sure the cables cross at 90°. Also, power cables to sensitive equipment should be separate from the main power cables.

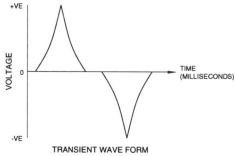

TRANSIENT WAVE FORM

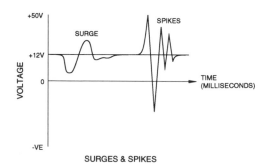

SURGES & SPIKES

Figure 21-1 Transient Waveforms

21.1 **Noise Sources.** There are a number of noise sources on yachts. Noises can be classified as Radio Frequency Interference (RFI) or Electromagnetic Interference (EMI). Noise also occurs in differing frequency ranges, and equipment may only be prone to problems within a particular frequency range.

a. **Electric Motor Noise.** These are repetitive spikes caused by commutators and sparking brushes. Wind generators are a common source.

b. **Alternator Noise.** The brushes on any alternator, particularly dirty brushes, can cause sparking and noise. Another source of noise is the diode bridge that converts AC to DC. This is usually a high-pitched whine.

c. **Static Charges.** These have a number of sources:

(1) **External Charges.** This type of interference can arise due to static build-up in rigging. On reaching a certain voltage level, the static will discharge to the ground, causing interference. Also, when dry winds occur, a static charge can build up on fiberglass decks. The problem is prevalent on larger fiberglass vessels and multihulls with large decks. A good lightning protection ground will effectively ground out these charges.

(2) **Engine Charges.** This type of interference arises due to static build-up both induced and due to moving parts in the engine. When the static charge discharges to ground, it causes interference.

(3) **Shaft Charges.** This type of interference comes from static build-up on propeller shafts. The static charge reaches a certain voltage level, and then discharges to the ground, causing interference. Grounding the shaft with a brush system is a typical cure.

d. **Electromagnetic Pulse.** In areas of lightning activity, pulses can be induced into electrical wiring and aerials.

e. **Induced Interference.** Where data cables run parallel to those carrying larger currents, the electromagnetic field (which may vary in intensity) can be induced into the data cables.

f. **Fluorescent Lights.** This is a common source of interference in cheaper fixtures with low grade electronics. Always install fittings with suppressed electronics.

g. **Turn-on Spikes.** These result from the initial charging of input filters on power supplies.

h. **Turn-off Spikes.** These arise when magnetic fields collapse on inductive loads such as transformers and relay or contactor coils.

i. **Electrical Arcing.** This is often caused by charging systems. The most common cause is loose connections or poor engine return paths for alternators. The negative path arcs across points of poor electrical contact.

21.2   **Suppression Methods**. A number of methods can be used to reduce or eliminate interference.

    a.   **Filters.** A filter or capacitor installed close to the "noisy" equipment effectively short circuits noise in the protected frequency range. Filters may take a number of forms:

        (1)   The filter is either a capacitor, or a combination of capacitor and inductor, connected across the power supply lines. These are simple, discrete components.

        (2)   Another option is to supply sensitive equipment through a Navpac from NewMar. This conditioning module filters out spikes and noise, regulates supply voltage, and has an internal power pack to ensure supply continuity.

    b.   **Power System Stabilization.** In cases of high voltage induction, it is necessary to clamp voltages to a safe level, typically around 40 volts. One of the major causes of lightning strike damage is the failure of equipment power supplies to cope with high voltage transients. The easiest way to achieve this to connect a metal oxide varistor (MOV) across the power supply. As the voltage rises, the resistance changes, shunting excess voltage. A second method uses an avalanche diode across the supply.

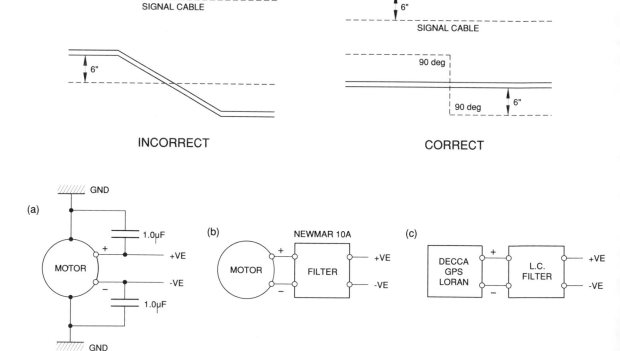

Figure 21-2 Noise Filtering and Stabilization

c.   **Screening.** Screening masks sensitive equipment from radiated interference. The most common source of this is HF- and VHF- induced interference on autopilots. The equipment or cables are covered and grounded by a metal cover or screen called a Faraday cage. This may be a simple aluminum cover grounded to the RF ground point.

   (1)   **Equipment Covering.** One of the best new products on the market is the Sonarshield conductive plastic sheet. Simply cover the Loran, GPS, radar, or radio casing (Southwall Technologies, 1029 Corporation Way, Palo Alto, CA 94303).

   (2)   **Cable Covering.** Noisy power cables can be wrapped in noise tape such as that made by NewMar. This tape is a flexible copper foil with an adhesive backing.

   (3)   **Cable Shields.** Most manufacturers specify that shields should be terminated. Never ground at both ends, always ground one end only, typically the equipment end.

d.   **Grounding.** When grounding static causing equipment such as shafts and engine blocks, pay close attention to the negative connections to the engine block. Ensure that the starter motor negative is attached close to the starter. Add an additional negative to the alternator. Engines that are part of the negative return conductor often have internal arcing and sparking that can cause interference. Modifying the negative system eliminates this problem.

e.   **Cancellation.** Twisting together the wires to a piece of equipment effectively causes cancellation as the electrical fields are reversed.

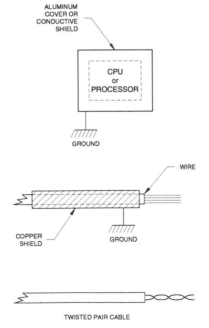

Figure 21-3 Grounding and Screening

389

Safety Systems

22.0 **Gas Detectors.** Propane gas is potentially lethal on a boat. If leaking gas accumulates in the bilges, once ignited it takes only a small amount of gas to destroy a vessel. If gas is installed, a quality gas detector is essential.

a. **Theory**. All gases have a lower explosion limit (LEL). As long as the gas/air ratio remains within this range, no explosion can occur. Once this level is exceeded, a significant explosion risk exists. A detector must indicate the presence of gas concentrations before the limit is exceeded, typically 50% of LEL. Better units have a sensitivity of 25% LEL.

b. **Detector Types.** Two types of gas detectors are in use in detection systems.

   (1) The main commercial sensor is the catalytic type. On offshore installations, we recalibrated these units weekly to ensure precise operation.

   (2) The most common type of sensor on small vessels is the semi-conductor type, which consists of a sintered tin oxide element. When gas is detected, the resistance alters and activates the alarm circuit. It takes several days of operation before the sensor stabilizes and final calibration can be made. Detectors may be subject to temperature drift in the sensing circuit. Good gas detectors incorporate a temperature sensor to correct this and ensure accuracy.

   (3) Other detection devices use what is called the pellister principle. These devices consist of two heated platinum wire elements. One is coated with gas-detecting material, the other is used for temperature and humidity compensation.

c. **Installation**. Sensor elements must be mounted in areas where gas may accumulate. The problem is that bilgewater or moist salt air can contaminate the element, causing degradation or failure.

d. **Testing**. Ideally, a precise gas/air mix of the appropriate LEL ratio would be used to calibrate the alarm level. In practice, however, this is never done. The simplest method to test whether the system functions is by activating a butane or disposable cigarette lighter at the sensor. Activation should be almost immediate.

e. **Alarm Outputs.** All detectors should have a gas bottle solenoid interlock that closes when gas is detected. This function should be fail safe in operation. An external alarm or exhaust fan can also be connected to the detector, as illustrated below.

f. **Troubleshooting.** Note the following important factors:

(1) **Alarms.** If an alarm goes off, assume it is real. If the alarm proves to be false, you can normally readjust the alarm threshold. Do so only enough to compensate for the sensor drift causing the nuisance activation.

(2) **Sensor Element.** The principal cause of problems is a degraded sensor element. Carry a spare sensor for replacement. If after replacing the sensor the alarm still causes problems, have the electronic unit tested.

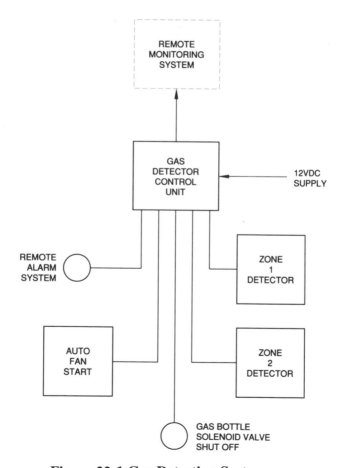

Figure 22-1 Gas Detection Systems

22.1   Security Systems. Trying to keep villains off your boat is always a major undertaking. You can never keep out a determined thief, but my approach has always been to make the exercise as difficult as possible. A variety of detectors can be coupled with control units and alarms, including:

a.   **Ultrasonic Sensors.** These sensors are unsuited to vessel installation. They are easily set off by spurious signals and have a relatively high power consumption.

b.   **Infrared.** These sensors direct a pattern of infrared beams over a set area. When a heat source crosses a beam, the alarm is activated. Contrary to the theory that cats and other animals set them off, they can be calibrated to only react to human-sized heat sources. One unit, properly located, can cover a typical saloon, but the installation site must be carefully selected so that it is not easily visible. They consume relatively little power.

c.   **Magnetic Switches.** The most reliable and power-efficient security systems use magnetic switches on hatches and other access points. These are connected directly to the control unit. This system detects the thief before he enters the boat; so the alarm catches him on deck or in view. It is also fail safe, so that the alarm still activates if a sensor cable is cut.

d.   **Pressure Pads.** Pressure activated pads can be installed under carpets and mats. They are not suitable in smaller boats, but I have installed them on larger vessels.

22.2   Security Alarm Indication Systems. Once an intruder is detected, an alarm has to be activated to indicate his presence. The following alarm systems are recommended:

a.   **Strobe Light.** A high-intensity xenon strobe light mounted on the stern arch or mast is the most common indication method. Many install a blue light, but you simply cannot see it easily. That is why police vehicles worldwide now use a red/blue light combination. I always fit an orange xenon strobe light, which is far more visible, but cannot not be relied upon on its own.

b.   **Audible Alarm.** Install the highest output, two-tone siren you can find. Put one outside and one below. A high output unit wailing in a cabin is very painful and will cut short any intruder's stay, A number of audible alarms may also panic or disorientate a thief.

c.   **Interlocking Systems.** Connecting various systems to the alarm is another popular method.

(1)   Spreader and foredeck spotlights, as well as any spotlight on stern post and arches can be interlocked to come on with alarm activation.

(2)   One yachtsman I know was robbed so many times he attached a high-voltage, electric fence energizer to the stern pulpit of his fiberglass boat to give thieves a "rude shock." Such a system, however, may get you in legal trouble if it causes injury or death.

d.   **Time Delays.** Entry and exit delays give you time to leave after you activate the alarm, or to disable the alarm when you return. I prefer to fit a remote isolator in a sail locker and have minimal delay. Generally, laws restrict alarm operation to 10 minutes. After that, the alarms must cease. Really ambitious thieves will set off the alarm and come back when the silence returns, so make sure that yours resets automatically.

e.   **Back-to-Base Alarms.** This alarm method transmits a radio signal to a 24-hour monitoring station that can take corrective action. These systems can monitor all vessel alarms, including bilge levels, smoke and fire, gas, as well as security.

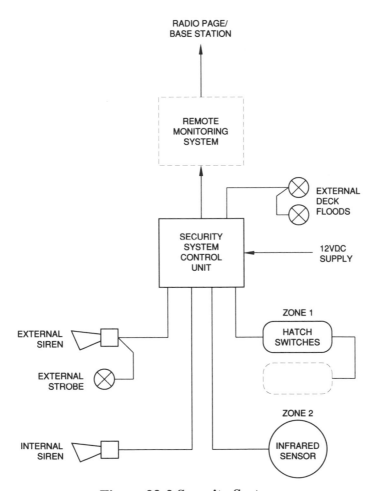

Figure 22-2 Security Systems

393

Computers

23.0   Computers. The notebook computer is making a rapid transition onto the cruising yacht. A large amount of software has been specifically designed for yachts, including a vast range of programs such as databases and word processors and, of course, we musn't forget the favorite game packages. The massive increases in laptop and notebook processing power in conjunction with powerful user-friendly programs allows anyone to learn how to use notebooks effectively. The minimum specifications will depend on your budget and software requirements. Many cruisers are happy to use off-the-shelf units, although a number of manufacturers have launched waterproof units.

23.1   Weather Software. A number of weather programs are available.

   a.   **ICS Fax-III (U.K.) and PC Weatherfax Fax V7 (U.S.).** These two leading packages include software, an interface cable, and a demodulator to link the PC to your radio and decode radio signals. I have both systems on board and am pleased with the results. Both systems have an on-screen tuning indicator. Auto-tuning and signal tracking are also possible. Once an image is received, you can zoom in, scroll or save, or print it. The programs can also receive RTTY, FEC, and CW, as well as NAVTEX transmissions. Both systems can be adapted for automatic frequency control of Lowe and ICOM receivers.

   b.   **PC WeatherFax for Windows 95.** This 32-bit Windows package incorporates on-line help systems, worldwide weatherfax schedules, etc.

   c.   **ICS Synop.** This package is able to decode IMO Synop coded information, which is the raw data used by forecasters. It plots observational data as it is transmitted in real time. Data can include wind speed and direction, temperature, barometric pressure, and cloud cover. Isobars and isotherms are automatically generated on screen.

   d.   **MetMap.** MetMap enables reception of NOAA satellite photos direct from polar orbiting and geostationary satellites. In addition to software, it requires 1-meter Quadrifilar Helix aerial, receiver, and interface cables.

   e.   **WinSat Pro.** WinSat receives, processes, displays, and stores images from both geostationary and polar orbiting satellites at close to photographic standards. Allows animation of weather patterns and cloud formations. Comes with parabolic dish, downconverter, receivers, etc.

   f.   **Starpath® Weather Trainer™.** This is an interactive weather training package that ranges from basic to advanced meteorology. It covers barometric changes, clouds and sea state analyses, and useful weatherfax, NAVTEX, and HF voice broadcast information, and a lot more information.

23.2 **Navigation Programs.** This area of software offers a significant range of information processing that can replace stand-alone equipment such as chart plotters.

    a.   **Chart Plotting and Route Planning.** A number of useful systems are on the market.

        (1)   **PC Wayplanner (U.K.).** I have found this package to be very useful. It is a chart plotting and route planning program, using the Livechart format. It is upgradable to Navmaster, and incorporates tidal heights, correctable charts, etc.

        (2)   **Navmaster (U.K.) (approved for ARCS) for Windows.** Easy-to-use software, using the latest ARCS raster chart format. It allows navigation monitoring, plotting and interfacing, full navigation information display of all parameters, chart management, route and chartpoint databases, passage planning using any criteria you require, tidal calculations, logbook function, and various utilities.

        (3)   **The Cap'n (U.S.).** One of the leading packages, it incorporates a lot of things, including electronic charting, tide and current predictions, celestial computations for easier sight reductions, a log book, a float plan, and a record-keeping function. Optional features are also worth having such as its GPS waypoint save function, graphical representation of tides and currents, light listings, World Port Reporter, which is invaluable, instrumentation interface, undersea feature reference list, and worldwide tide finders.

    b.   **PolyPlot.** Polyplot is a very versatile package. Polyplot consists of a number of programs as follows; I use mine frequently:

        (1)   **Celestial Navigation.** This includes dead reckoning, great circle navigation, compass deviation control, star, sun, moon and planet sight reductions, sight clustering, two-plot and running fixes, twilight forecast, star, moon and planet finders, night sky planispheres, and the perpetual calendar of the nautical ephemeris.

        (2)   **Quick Calculator.** This is used for wind and tide corrections, tack assistance, traverse summation, Beaufort scale data, vertical and horizontal sextant positions, compass error checks, temperature, distance and time-arc conversions, and sunrise and sunset times.

        (3)   **Great Circle Plots and Logs.** This calculates and plots great circle courses, stores and plots fixes, and generates plotting sheets.

        (4)   **Star Finding Tutorial.** This is a training program with on-screen star charts for those beginning to learn celestial navigation.

        (5)   **Celestial Navigation Training Course.** This program instructs users in the art of celestial navigation using a nautical almanac and sight reduction tables, calculation of DR positions, reduction of sun, moon and planet sights to lines of position, and plotting LOPs to fixes.

23.3   Training and Simulators. The software written for laptops provides a whole world of training. Some of the packages are as follows:

a.   **PC Navigator.** One of my favorite training aids, this package is really challenging and instructive. Navigator simulates tides, weather, and vessel performance. The display incorporates instruments, landfalls, depth contours, buoyage, and lights. The exercise involves choosing the appropriate sailing conditions, and commencing a passage through the Channel Islands or US-based areas. The program also includes full night navigation, with buoys and lighthouses flashing.

b.   **E-Nav Trainer.** This interactive program uses graphics very effectively to instruct users in the basics of radio-wave behavior, Loran C, and Decca. It has an easy question-and-answer type format, and provides a clear understanding of electronic navigational aids and position fixing systems.

c.   **Sail Simulator.** A real sail and boat handling simulator, which includes sail setting controls, mast settings, crew positions, maneuvering, gybes and tacks, capsizes, grounding, realistic simulation of vessel motion, waves heights, depth, wind strengths, and turbulence.

d.   **LiSim.** A complete light simulation program with own boat control and various scenarios that include land, lighthouses, buoyage, and moving target vessels, both pleasure and commercial. It tests and instructs in an interactive format on the correct knowledge, identification, and interpretation of lights.

e.   **The Yacht Racing Rules (CD-ROM).** IYRU rules tutorial, with video, audio, animation, graphics, illustrations, etc., from Mary Pera. If you race, it's invaluable.

f.   **Laser Match Racing (CD-ROM).** Having raced a Laser for a few years, I find this package very entertaining, and challenging. You get to experience capsizes without the cold water and swimming.

g.   **Radar Training Software.** There are a number of useful training packages:

•   RaTech: structured tutorial with animated graphics, incorporates principles of aerials, transmitters, etc.

•   RaPlot: radar plotting tutorial, interactive.

•   RaSim: simulated display of operating system.

•   Starpath Radar Trainer: incorporates radar training and similator.

23.4   **Computer Maintenance.** The following basics will ensure reliability.

    a.   **Disk Drive.** All disk drives are sealed and maintenance free. Ensure that dust is blown out regularly. Disk head cleaning kits are also available.

    b.   **Printer.** Whether it is a dot matrix or ink jet printer, a few basic maintenance tasks are required to maintain optimum performance:

        (1)   Clean out the interior using a soft brush or mini vacuum cleaner.

        (2)   Outside casings should be wiped using a damp cloth. Do not use solvents or abrasive cleaners. Never apply lubricants or electrical cleaners on mechanisms.

    c.   **Keyboard.** Brush out dust and particles regularly, and wipe the board with a slightly damp cloth. Keep wet fingers, coffee mugs, etc., well away. A battery-powered vacuum cleaner is ideal to extract dust and particles.

    d.   **Battery Packs.** Many laptops and notebooks have rechargeable nickel-cadmium and lithium battery packs. The major problem is that battery packs are not properly cycled and develop what is called memory effect. Discharge them properly on a regular basis and then recharge completely.

    e.   **Power Supply.** The majority of problems on computers in vessels can be attributed to poor quality power supplies, both AC and DC carrying voltage transients. Most externally powered laptops have a 15-volt maximum. If using an alternator fast charge device, disconnect the computer from the vessel DC system.

    f.   **Printers.** The most common problem is caused by moisture being absorbed into the paper. Use only as much paper as required in sheet feeders; keep the rest packaged and dry.

    g.   **Virus Checks.** Do not try out software from external sources before you scan it for viruses.

Entertainment Systems

24.0   **Music Systems.** Without music, your boat is not ready for sea. On new vessels, there is a definite psychological lift when the stereo goes on for the first time. When selecting or installing a music system, there are a number of important factors to consider:

a.   **Power Output.** Power output is rated in watts, and is either specified in "watts per channel" (RMS), or "total power output" (PMPO). Watts per channel is the power through each speaker, total power output is combined power. There is no need for high rated units with 60 watts per channel simply because the area involved is relatively small, and the ear cannot distinguish between a 30-watt and a 60-watt system. Quality, not volume, is what counts.

b.   **Cassette Players.** The cassette player is still the backbone of any onboard music system. Choosing the equipment is the problem because of manufacturers' claims about marine, waterproof models. If you want reasonable quality, buy from manufacturers such as Pioneer, Alpine, or similar. I always recommend a unit designed for RV or four-wheel drive vehicles. These units can stand severe vibration and are moisture resistant, making them ideal for yachts. Beware of the term "marine stereo". Many are relatively cheap compared to a car stereo system, and their advertised superiority in the marine environment is rather suspect. If you buy a recognized brand, chances are you can get it repaired fairly easily at any automotive sound specialist. Virtually all players now incorporate Dolby noise reduction to reduce background hiss. There is a wide selection of audio cassette tapes available. The C90 offers the best overall performance in terms of reliability and reproduction. Tapes are easily damaged at sea, where they are left in the sun, fall in the bilge, etc. Take plenty with you. Tape types are:

(1)   **Normal Bias (Ferric Oxide).** These are made in a variety of quality levels. Choose according to your budget.

(2)   **Chromium Dioxide (CrO2).** Tape decks incorporate a separate switch to use these tapes. They have a lower background hiss, and better reproduction.

(3)   **Metal Tapes.** These are the most expensive, but they offer the highest quality reproduction. Tape players should have a separate switch for use with these tapes or sound quality will suffer slightly.

c.   **CD Players.** The units designed for vehicles are obviously the choice for boats. Choose those designed for RVs. If like me you hate continually changing CDs, use the 5 or 10 CD cartridge pack from Kenwood or Pioneer; it gives a lot of music without reloading.

d. **Speakers.** For internal speakers, reasonable quality vehicle types are sufficient. For the deck speakers, use only waterproof types, such as those made by Pioneer. Virtually all stereo systems can accommodate 4 and 6 speaker setups, with appropriate balance control. I prefer a set of speakers in the saloon, a set in the main cabin for nighttime, and a set up in the cockpit, ideally on the stern arch. Many of the new all-weather speakers are made entirely of plastics and do not degrade.

(1) **Two-Way Speakers.** These consist of a large woofer for bass sounds, and a smaller tweeter for high-frequency sound reproduction.

(2) **Three-Way Speakers.** These consist of a woofer and tweeter with an additional mid-range speaker. They are much more expensive but offer far better reproduction. I suggest installing three-way speakers in the saloon, and waterproof, two-way speakers in the cockpit.

(3) **Speaker Cables.** It is very important to install the best quality speaker cable you can. Long runs are normal in boats, and quality suffers accordingly. For speakers mounted in the cockpit or on the stern arch, use tinned cables.

e. **Graphic Equalizers.** The equalizer makes the difference between good music and great music. Its function is to divide the music into different frequency ranges, which you can adjust to suit your own tastes. A boat's shape and materials do not facilitate ideal acoustic reproduction; the equalizer overcomes this to a considerable extent.

24.1 **Television.** Television aerials and how they perform on vessels is a subject fraught with misconceptions and misleading claims. Apart from that, they can be outrageously expensive. One certainty is that performance comparable to home aerials should not be expected. Attempting to get a reasonable picture under sail is generally out of the question; the offwatch should stick to videos. At anchorages, the principal problem is getting a good picture without the continual ghosting that occurs as the boat swings around the anchorage. Ghosting is caused largely by the transmitted signal's path and its frequency characteristics.

a. **Signal Distortion.** Television signals are essentially straight-line transmissions and do not bend significantly when meeting obstructions. As a result, shadows and areas of low signal are created behind the obstruction. Reflection causes signals to arrive at the aerial from a direction other than the straight line path from the transmitter. The receiver then picks up the same signal at different times, i.e., a distorted signal pattern. The distortion of a signal can occur from a number of sources, including hills, other boats, rigging, and the water surface.

b. **Signal Polarization.** Signal transmissions are generally horizontally polarized. When signal is reflected, the polarization is altered, causing distortion.

24.2 **TV Aerials.** There are a number of aerial types:

a. **Directional Aerials.** These aerials can be aligned with the transmitted signal. Intended for domestic use, such aerials may be of use if you live on board and rarely venture out from the marina, but at an anchorage they are fairly useless and require constant adjustment.

b. **Omnidirectional Aerials.** These aerials can receive transmission signals consistently and are not affected by the vessel's swinging at anchor. Commonly a ring or loop, the aerial is hoisted when required. This type cannot discriminate between directly transmitted and reflected signals and so perform poorly in marinas where other vessels are tied up.

c. **Active Aerials.** These units typically have a fiberglass or plastic dome with an integral omnidirectional loop inside. The signal is amplified to compensate for the smaller aerial and performance depends on a good gain value within the amplifier. Active aerials are also designed to receive UHF signals as well as AM/FM radio transmissions, which eliminates the need for additional aerials. The best active aerials are the new Omnimax Gazelle and the UFO by Triax.

d. **Installation Factors.** The following factors should be considered when mounting and installing aerials:

(1) **Aerial Height.** Install the aerial as high as possible, at the masthead preferably. The low-profile Omnimax Gazelle units are compact enough for masthead mounting.

(2) **Aerial Cables.** Cables should always be low loss coaxial (RG59) which normally has 75-ohm impedance.

e. **Video Players.** Most yachts are fitting simple 12-volt players. Purists may scoff at the installation of such luxuries, but a foul night in some unpleasant anchorage can be made infinitely more bearable by a good videotape. With new acquaintances, it is also an invaluable ice breaker, especially when the rain sends you all below. Be sure the video is in a dry location, and is well protected behind a cupboard door, when not in use. A bag of silica gel and perhaps a corrosion inhibitor will help ward off the damp. Current demands are relatively small, typically around 1 amp. Combined with an average TV consumption of 3 amps, the average movie will consume around 8 amp-hours.

Troubleshooting

25.0 **Troubleshooting.** There is a definite philosophy behind troubleshooting that should be understood and followed if it is to be effective. Troubleshooting is a logical process of evaluating a system and how it operates. It involves collecting evidence, such as burn marks or heat, unusual sounds, acrid smells, temperature variations, etc. All the senses can be used to compile a problem profile. This can be supported by using instruments correctly and by analyzing the data displayed on them. This information forms the basis for testing theories and assumptions, so that the precise fault can be identified and rectified. The following factors must be considered in any troubleshooting exercise.

a. **Systems Knowledge.** Understand the basic operations of the equipment. It is common to find that "faults" are in fact only improperly operated equipment. If there is a basic understanding of the system, it is considerably easier to break it down into functional blocks, which makes troubleshooting much easier.

b. **Systems Configuration.** Understand where all the system components are installed, where connections and cables are, and where supply voltages originate from.

c. **Systems Operation Parameters.** Understand what is "normal" during operation, and what are the parameters or operating ranges of the system. All too often, expectations are different from the realities.

d. **Test Equipment.** Understand how to use a basic multimeter. Be able to make the simple tests of voltage and continuity of conductors.

25.1 **Troubleshooting Procedure.** The following approach should be used:

a. **System Inputs.** Check that the system has the correct power input. Don't assume anything. For example, there may be a voltage input, but it may be too low. Check it with a multimeter.

b. **System Outputs.** Does the system have an output? Is the required voltage or signal being put out? If there is input and no output, then you have already isolated the main problem.

c. **Fault Isolation.** In any troubleshooting exercise, split the system in two. This method is ideal when troubleshooting lighting circuits. It instantly isolates the problem into a smaller, more specific area.

d. **Fault Complexity.** Most problems usually turn out to be rather simple. Start with the basics, and don't try to apply complex theoretical ideas you do not fully understand. Stand back and think first.

e. **Failure Causes.** When a fault has been isolated and repaired, try to ascertain why the failure has occurred.

25.2   Instrument Use. Effective troubleshooting of electrical devices requires the proper use of the multimeter.

a.   **Continuity Tests.** The continuity test, which requires the use of the ohms setting, simply tests whether a circuit is open or closed. Power must be switched off before testing. Set the scale to one of the megOhm ranges. Place the probes on each wire of the circuit being tested. What you are looking for is a simple over-range reading if the circuit is open, and low or no resistance if closed. Many multimeters also incorporate a beeper to indicate a short circuit.

b.   **Resistance Tests.** Set the range switch to the circuit being tested. Typically, a 20-ohm range is used. Turn off circuit power and discharge any capacitors. When testing, do not touch probes with your fingers as this may alter readings. Before testing, touch the probes together to see that the meter reads 0.

c.   **Voltage Tests.** The most practical of all measurements is voltage, either to detect that it is present or to precisely measure its exact level, as is done when testing charging systems and batteries. I did 99% of all troubleshooting on complex oil rigs and commercial vessels with this function alone. The voltmeter is connected across a load with negative probe to negative and positive to positive (it is measuring the voltage potential between the two). Reversing the probes will show a negative reading. Set the scale to the one that exceeds the expected or operating voltage of the circuit under test.

d.   **Current Tests.** The ammeter function on a multimeter is rarely used or required, although some use it for locating leakages. The ammeter on the switchboard can normally be used for all measurements. An ammeter is always connected in series with a circuit as it is measuring the current passing through the wire. The circuit should be switched off before inserting the ammeter in circuit.

e.   **Meter Maintenance.** Look after your meter. Do not drop it or let it get wet. A few basics will ensure reliability and safety:

(1)   **Probes.** Keep the probes in good condition. On many probes, the tips sometimes rotate out and short circuit the terminals being tested. Another problem is that the solder connections of test leads can break away due to twisting and movement.

(2)   **Cables.** Keep the cables clean and the insulation undamaged. Cables do age and crack. Do not attempt to test higher voltages, in particular AC voltages, with damaged cables. If a cable is damaged, replace it.

(3)   **Batteries.** Replace the internal battery every 12 months, or carry a spare. Many meters will have a low battery warning function.

On Board Spares

26.0   Spare Parts and Tools. To maintain a reasonable level of self sufficiency, the following tools and equipment should be carried onboard every vessel. This list can be used as an itemized checklist.

Table 26-1 Tools and Spares List

Recommended Tools	Consumables & Spares
Electrical pliers	Self-bonding tape, 2 rolls
Long nose pliers	Insulation tape, 2 rolls
Side cutters	Nylon cable ties (black), 3 sizes
Cable crimpers (ratchet type)	Electrical cleaner, 2 cans (CRC)
Electrical screwdriver set	Water dispersant, 2 cans (WD40)
Phillips-head screwdriver set	Silicone grease, 1 tube
Soldering iron (gas)	Silicone compound, 1 tube
Soldering iron (12-volt)	Petroleum jelly, 1 can
Solder	Distilled water, 1 gallon
Adjustable wrench	Heatshrink tubing
File, small half round	Oil (for wind instrument)
File, small round	Fan belts, 2 of each type
Socket wrench set	Spiral wrapping
Bearing puller set	2.5mm twin tinned cable, 50m
Wire brush	2.5mm single tinned cable, 100m
Junior hacksaw	Circuit breaker (15A)
Battery-powered drill	Lamp-bicolor, 2
Adjustable wrenches	Lamp-stern/masthead, 2
Allen keys set	Lamp-tricolor/anchor, 2
Digital multimeter	Switchboard indicator lamps, 2
Meter battery	Butt crimp connectors
Jumper wires and clips (Tandy)	Spade connectors
	Alternator regulator
	Alternator diode plate
	Alternator bearings
	Alternator warning light
	Start relay (if fitted)
	Alternator fuses (if fitted)
	Fuses for electronics equipment
	Anchor windlass fuses, 2
	Brushes-windlass
	Brushes-starter motor
	Brushes-refrigerator motor
	Brushes-alternator
	Coaxial connectors
	Battery terminals, 2

Table 26-2 Basic Three Language Electrical Glossary

English	French	Spanish
Audible Alarm	Avertisseur sonore	Bocina electrónica
Alternator	Alternateur	Alternador
Alternator Rating	Puissance de l'alternateur	Potencia del alternador
Alarm Panel	Tableau des alarmes	Tarjeta de instrumentos
Battery	Batterie	Bateria (Acumulador)
Bolt	Boulon	Perno, tornillo
Brushes	Balais	Escobilla
Circuit Breaker	Disjoncteur, interrupteur	Fusible
Connection	Cablage	Conexión
Circuit Diagram	Schéma de cablage électrique	Esquema de conexiones electricas
Current (electrical)	Courant	Corriente
Drive Belt	Courroie de transmission	Correa de ventilador
Disconnect	Déconnecter, isoler	Desconector
Electrician	Electricien	Electricista
Element	Elément	Elemento
Fault	Faute	Falta
Ignition Switch	Contact (moteur)	Llave de contacto
Insulation	Isolement	Aislamiento
Current level	Intensité (amps)	Intensidad
Fuse	Fusible	Fusible
Ground (earth)	Mettre à la masse	Conectar con masa
Lights	Feux	Luz
Light Bulb	Ampoule électrique	Bombilla, foco
Lightning	Eclair	Relampago, rayo
Navigation lights	Feux de position	Luz de navigación
Overheat	Surchauffe	Recalentarse
Oil Pressure Sensor	Sonde de pression d'huile	Sensor presión aceite
Oil Pressure Gauge	Manomètre d'huile	Manómetro de aceite
Preheating Glowplugs	Bougies de préchauffage	Bujia de precalentamiento
Relay	Relais	Rele
Recharge	Recharge de batterie	Recargar
Short Circuit	Court-circuit	Corto circuito
Starter Motor	Démarreur	Motor de arranque
Sensor	Capteur/sonde	Sensor
Switch	Starter/interrupteur	Pulsador
Tachometer	Compte-tours, tachymètre	Tacometro
Temperature Sensor	Sonde de température	Sensor temperatura
Transmitter	Emetteur	Trasmisor
Voltmeter	Voltmètre	Voltimetro
Voltage	Tension de système	Tensión del sistema
Voltage drop	Chute de tension	Caida de voltaje
Water Pump	Pompe à eau	Bomba
Wire	Cable ou fil (électrique)	Alambre
Engine Not Starting!	Le moteur ne démarre pas	El motor no arranca

Service Directory

27.0   Installation and Service List. Following are lists of marine electricians, marine electronics technicians and companies, and other qualified electrical experts who come highly recommended. Marine electricians have a merchant marine or naval background, and will probably have many years of sea service behind them. They have an understanding of the environmental factors affecting marine electrical installations and are qualified to work on both AC and DC systems, as well as on many electronics. Beware of automotive electricians claiming to be marine electricians—they are not. Most good ones doing marine work do not hide that fact. There are some very good automotive electrical tradesmen doing marine work. Many are included in the lists. Go on recommendations, if at all possible. (Ask them if they own a boat!) Beware also of the domestic electrician who makes similar claims. Again, there are a few good tradesmen around who have an industrial background and can do a good job. If you are getting AC work done, ask to see a license or some qualification. Get references or check their backgrounds if at all possible. It's your life in the balance.

27.1   How to Assist Service Technicians. I remember a recent episode when a yacht arrived from a Pacific cruise and the skipper told me that his radar had been out for some months. He could get the display partially working, but there was no picture. I went to the stern-mounted scanner, and flipped on the local power switch. Imagine his reaction; he simply had forgotten to check it. (Grown men do cry.) Consider the following points before calling for service:

    a.   Did you operate the equipment properly? Read the manual again and go back to basics. It is only when you are sure that you have operated the equipment properly and it doesn't work that you should call the service technician.

    b.   Are all the plugs in and the power on? It is amazing how many people forget to plug in an aerial or to put the power on. If the power is on at the breaker and not at the equipment, double check that the circuit connection on the back of the switchboard is not disconnected. Check that the equipment fuse has not ruptured. In short, check the obvious.

    c.   What you were doing immediately before the fault? Many faults occur immediately after working on unrelated systems. Check to see if you inadvertently disturbed a connection.

    d.   Write down clearly the fault and the situation when the unit failed. If a profile can be built up, it may point to some other problem. Not only will it assist the service person, it may assist you to resolve the problem yourself.

    e.   Don't keep asking your service technician whether he has fixed or located the fault. Not only does this ruin his concentration (and slow his work), it can lead to sharp verbal exchanges, especially when he is jammed in some tight space.

f.   Keep a good technical file on board. If possible, obtain copies of all the technical manuals. No service technician can carry or get every manual. Giving him this information will save him time and save you money.

g.   Clean up the area to be worked on. It is unfair to expect service people to work on filthy engines and in dirty bilges. If you don't mind grime tracked through the boat, then ignore this advice, and if the fellow is good, he'll simply decline to come back again.

h.   Have a good tool kit ready. It is impossible to carry a complete tool set onto every boat. Assistance like this is greatly appreciated. Make sure your flashlights work, and empty or clear any locker through which equipment is accessed.

i.   Don't offer beer or coffee until the job is finished. They are appreciated but they don't get the job done.

j.   Make sure your crew is dressed for early morning service calls. It is no fun to be greeted by hangover-afflicted or scantily-clad crewmembers when troubleshooting or tracing cable runs, and the crew doesn't like it either.

k.   If collecting a service person from shore, make sure you both know where to meet. I have been left standing many times due to confusion about the pick-up point. Please bale the dinghy out first and have a dry towel to sit on. In most cases, the tools and spares will need someplace dry as well.

l.   Don't blame the service technician for all the other electrical problems that exist on your boat. Some of the more undesirable types floating around do this to avoid paying accounts. Write down clearly the job you want done and pay for it. If you do not, I can assure you word travels fast and you may end up without help when you need it.

m.   Do not sail off without settling your account. You may be arrested at the next port, have a writ nailed to your mast, lose your yacht to pay accounts, and end up in jail. I know these things can happen because I have had to do them. Technicians and electricians do not just get mad, they get even.

n.   There are quite a number of yachtsmen who do not mind paying a $60 fee for a service call plus $60/hour for a washing machine mechanic to fix a $1000 machine. But when it comes to paying a highly qualified marine electrical/electronics service technician to fix essential and very expensive equipment on $200,000 vessels, they think that $40 an hour is exorbitant, even though only hourly rates (no travel time or service fee) are charged.

Table 27-1 Service Directory—United States/Canada

Port	Person/Company	Contact Numbers
Oakland, CA	Collins Marine Corp	(415) 957 1300
San Francisco, CA	Cal Marine Electronics	(415) 391 7550
Marina Del Rey, CA	Baytronics South	(213) 822 8200
Newport Beach, CA	Alcom Marine Electronics	(714) 673 1727
San Diego, CA	Power & Wind Marine Electrical	(619) 226 8600
Santa Barbara, CA	Ocean Aire Electronics	(805) 962 9385
Fort Lauderdale, FL	Avalon Marine Electronics	(305) 527 4047
Miami, FL	Electro Marine	(305) 856 1924
Houston, TX	Able Communication	(713) 485 8800
Portland, ME	Ross Marine Electronics	(207) 272 7737
Stamford, CT	Maritech Communications Corp	(203) 323 2900
Chesapeake, VA	Seaport Electronics	(804) 543 5600
Annapolis, MD	Coast Navigation	(301) 268 3120
Portsmouth, NH	Cay Electronics	(401) 683 3520
Seattle, WA	Seamar Electronics	(206)622 6130
Tacoma, WA	J & G Marine Supply	(206) 572 4217
Hawaii (Honolulu)	Navtech	(808) 834 7672
Hawaii (Kailua-Kona)	West Hawaii Electronics	(808) 329 1252
Vancouver, BC	Maritime Service	(604) 294 4444
Victoria, BC	Victoria Marine Electronics	(604) 383 9731
Halifax, NS	Gabriel Aero Marine	(902) 634 4004
Quebec, QUE	GAD Electronics	(418) 986 3677

Table 27-2 Service Directory—UK/European Channel Coast

Port	Person/Company	Contact Numbers
Electrical		
Plymouth (England)	Ocean Marine Services	(0752) 500121
Plymouth (England)	Western Marine Power	(0752) 225679
Southampton (England)	Marinapower Electrical	(0703) 332 123
West Sussex (England)	Keith Howlett	(0798) 813 831
Winchester (England)	Power & Air Systems	(0962) 841828
Brighton (England)	K McCallum	(0243) 775 606
Medway (England)	David Holden	(0795) 580 930
Jersey (Channel Islands)	Jersey Marine Electrics	(0534) 21603
Calais (France)	Bernus Shipyard	(21) 34 3040
Gothenburg (Sweden)	Wahlborgs Marina	(42) 29 3245
Stockholm (Sweden)	Linds Boatyard	(715) 624 211
Haringvliet (Holland)	Stellendam Marina	1879 2600
Ostend (Belgium)	Nordzee Yachtwerf	(59) 78100
Electronics		
Jersey (Channel Islands)	Jersey Marine Electronics	(534) 21603
Guernsey (Channel Islands)	Radio & Electronic Services	(481) 728837
Plymouth (England)	Tolley Marine	(752) 222530
Hamble (England)	Hudson Marine Electronics	(703) 4551 29
Southampton (England)	Regis Electronics	(983) 293 996
Lymington (England)	Regis Electronics	(590) 679 251
Brighton (England)	DMS Seatronics	(273) 605 166
Falmouth (England)	Western Electronics	(326) 73438
Poole (England)	Fleet Marine	(202) 6326 66
Ipswich (England)	R & I Marine Electronics	(473) 659737
Boulogne (France)	Ocel	(21) 317592
Honfleur (France)	La Barriere	(31) 890517
Dunkerque (France)	Marine Diffusion	(28) 591 819
St Valery-sur-Somme	Lattitude 50	(22) 26 82 06
Le Havre (France)	Electronique Equip.	(35) 546070
Carentan (France)	Gam Marine	(33) 711 702
St Vaast La Hougue	Marelec	(33) 546 382
Granville (France)	Nautilec	(33) 500496
Cherbourg (France)	Ergelin	(33) 532 026
La Rochelle (France)	Pochon	(45) 413 053
Port Camargue (France)	Y.E.S.	(66) 530 238
Nieuwpoort (Belgium)	Sea Trade & Service	(058) 237230
Sneek (Holland)	Jachtwerf Rimare	(05150) 12396
Hamburg/Wedel (Germany)	Yachtelektrik Wedel	(04103) 87273
Cork (Ireland)	Rider Services	0002 841176

Table 27-3 Service Directory—Mediterranean

Port	Person/Company	Contact Numbers
Valetta (Malta)	S & D Yachting	54 Gzira Rd, Gzira
Bodrum (Turkey)	Motif Yachting	(6141)2309 VHF 71
Marmaris (Turkey)	ATC Yacht Service	(612) 13835
Kusadasi (Turkey)	Dragon Yachting	(636)12257 VHF71
Fethiye (Turkey)	Alesta Yachting	(615)11861 VHF 16
Venice (Italy)	Cantiere Zennaro	71 7438
Larnaca (Cyprus)	IMF Marine Elect.	(04) 655 377
Larnaca (Cyprus)	KJ Electronics	(41) 636 360
Rhodes (Greece)	Y Paleologos	(0241) 25460
Syros (Greece)	E Bogiatzopoulos	(0281) 22254
Corfu (Greece)	P Mavronas	(0661) 26247
Piraeus (Greece)	General Electronic Repairs	461 4246
Mallorca (Spain)	Euro Marine Services	(71) 676141
Torrevieja (Spain)	Torrevieja Int'l Marina	571 3650
Benalmadena (Spain)	M Blenkinsopp	(52) 560906
Gibraltar	H Shephard & Co.	75148
Monaco	Electronic Services	(93) 26 76 67
Antibes (France)	GMT Maritime (electronics)	(93) 34 23 87
	Georges Electricite (electrical)	(93) 33 73 72
Nice	Electronique Marine	(93) 56 58 73
St Laurent du Var	International Marine Tecnic	(93) 07 74 55
Cannes La Bocca	Radio-Ocean	(93) 47 72 15
Port de Ste Maxime	Express Electronique	(94) 96 53 48
	Paulo Services (electrical)	(94) 96 67 15
Port Grimaud	Electronic Services	(94) 56 44 60
Les Marines de Cogolin	Electronique Marine	(94) 56 05 69
Mandelieu	Elec Marine Napouloise	(93) 49 06 02
	Mandelieu Electricite Marine	(93) 49 57 07
Menton	Mar-Elec	(93) 41 62 62
Beaulieu	CRM	(93) 01 09 09
Cap Ferat	Electro Mechanique	(93) 01 67 57
Hyeres	Monmartre Boulanger(electronics)	(94) 38 88 84
	SIARI (electrical)	(94) 38 73 71
Toulon	Pro Electronique	(94) 03 00 50
Marseille	Marseille Marine (electronics)	(91) 91 31 42
	Electric Auto Yachting (electrical)	(91) 73 30 14

Table 27-4 Service Directory—Caribbean

Port	Person/Company	Contact Numbers
Electrical Services		
Castries (St Lucia)	Rodney Bay Marina	(809) 452 9922
	Columban Ellis	(809) 452 7749
St Maarten (Neth Antilles)	Bobbys Marina	Call on VHF 16
St Georges (Grenada)	Moorings Marina (Gill Findlay)	4402119 Ch66/71
Jolly Harbor (Antigua)	Electro Tek	(809) 462 7690
Electronics Services		
St Maarten (Neth. Antilles)	Radio Holland	(599) 525414
English Harbour (Antigua)	Signal Locker	(809) 463 1528
	Cay Electronics	(809) 460 1040
Falmouth Harbour (Antigua)	Marionics Caribbean	(809) 460 1780
Hamilton (Bermuda)	Electronic Communications	(809) 295 2446
	Marine Comms	(809) 295 0558
San Juan (Puerto Rico)	Master Marine Electronics	(809) 788 6888
	Caribbean Radio & Telephone	(809) 724 2035
St. Thomas (U.S.V.I.)	Geary Electronics	(809) 776 1444
Tortola (B.V.I.)	Cay Electronics	(809) 494 2400
Castries (St Lucia)	Cay Electronics	(809) 452 9922
	Morne Doudon	(809) 452 2652
St Barth (French West Indies)	GME Int. (Port de Gustavia)	(590) 27 89 64
Guadeloupe	Marina	(590) 908919
Martinique	Samafon	(596) 660564
Bridgetown (Barbados)	Williams Electrical	(809) 425 2000
Point Cumana (Trinidad)	Goodwood Marina	(809) 632 4612
La Guaira (Venezuela)	Rich Electronics (SEA)	(31)941 789
	Caraballeda YC	
Refrigeration		
Castries (St Lucia)	Mars Refrigeration Services	(809) 452 2994

Table 27-5 Service Directory—Australia

Port	Person/Company	Contact Numbers
Electrical Services		
Sydney	Malbar Marine Electrics	(02) 476 4306
Pittwater	Barrenjoey Marine Electrics	(02) 997 6822
NSW South Coast	Ken King (Seaboard Electrics)	(044) 465 012
Lake Macquarie	Hunter Marine Electrics	(049) 532 353
Southport	Southport Industrial & Marine	321 167
Runaway Bay	Runaway Bay Marine Electrics	572 188
Mooloolaba	Lawries Marina	(071) 441 122
Townsville	Manlin Electrical & Marine	(077) 796 231
Cairns	All Marine Electrics	517 219
Hobart	M & K Madden	295 195
Melbourne	Goaty's Marine Electrical	(018) 327 403
Darwin	Percy Mitchell Electrical	(89)814 288
Adelaide	John Yandell	(08)47 5660
Fremantle	Cully's Electrical Service	430 5181
Electronics Services		
Sydney (NSW)	Peter Morath (Radar Specialist)	(02) 883959
	Ted McNally	(02) 522 8235
	Olympic Instruments (VDO Agent)	(02) 449 9888
Port Macquarie (NSW)	Peter Long (Computel)	(018) 653 128
Whitsundays (QLD)	Phillip Pleydell	(079) 467 813
Runaway Bay (QLD)	Micro Logic	(075) 37 1455
Mooloolaba (QLD)	Mooloolaba Radio	(074) 44 4707
Bundaberg (QLD)	Rampant Marine Elec.	(071) 534 994
Gladstone (QLD)	Rigneys Electronics	(079) 727 839
Cairns (QLD)	Pickers Marine	(070) 511 944
Townsville (QLD)	Breakwater Chandlery	(077) 713 063
Melbourne (VIC)	John Powell	(018) 591 780
Port Adelaide (SA)	International Comms.	(08) 473 688
Fremantle (WA)	Maritime Elect. Services	(09) 335 2716
Darwin (NT)	NavCom	(089) 811 311
Refrigeration		
Sydney	Dave Bruce Moorebank Marine	(02) 602 9571

Table 27-6 Service Directory—Pacific

Port	Person/Company	Contact Numbers
Electrical Services		
Noumea (New Caledonia)	Gerard Destaillets	(687) 25 43 00
Suva (Fiji)	Yacht Help (VHF 71)	(679) 311982
Port Moresby (PNG)	Marine & Industrial Electrical Eng.	(675) 25200
Lae (PNG)	Lae Battery Services	(675) 421125
Auckland (NZ)	MJJ Electrics Afloat	(09)473 871
Whangarei (NZ)	Orams Marine	(89)489 567
Opua (NZ)	Elliots Boat Yard	4027705
Honiara (Solomons)	Pacific Electrics	22454
Apia (Western Samoa)	Samoa Marine	(685) 22721
Nuku'alofa (Tonga)	Flemming Electric	(676) 21095
Nuku Hiva (Marquesas)	Alain Bigot	920 334
Kowloon (Hong Kong)	Islander Yacht Basin	3719 1336
Electronics Services		
Fukuoka-Shi (Japan)	Nakamura Sengu	(092) 531 4995
Majuro (Marshall Islands)	Mariscom	(692) 9 3271
Noumea (New Caledonia)	Marine Corail	(687) 275 848
Guam (Marianas)	Pacific Isle Communications	(671) 649 9797
Nuku'alofa (Tonga)	Tait Electronics	Tungi Arcade
Nuku Hiva (Marquesas)	Alain Barbe	920 086
Bay of Islands (New Zealand)	Rust Electronics	(09) 403 7247
Whangarei (New Zealand)	Ray Roberts Marine	(09) 438 3296
Auckland (New Zealand)	Seaquip Marine	(09) 424 1260
Bay of Plenty (New Zealand)	Bay Marine Electronics	(07) 577 0250
Papeete (Tahiti)	Marine Corail	(689) 428 222
Vina del Mar (Chile)	Nauticos Mauricia Opazo	(32) 66 31 50
Santiago (Chile)	Parker y Cia	(41) 740 730
Callao (Peru)	Marco Peruana	(14) 659 497
Panama	Marco Panama	(27) 3533

Table 27-7 Service Directory—Atlantic & Indian Oceans

Port	Person/Company	Contact Numbers
Las Palmas (Canary Islands)	Internatica Gran Canaria	(28) 246 590
Las Palmas (Canary Islands)	Servicios Electronicos	(28) 243 935
Tenerife (Canary Islands)	Heinemann Hennanos	(22) 680 859
Funchal (Madeira)	Maria-Faria	(91) 368 858
Horta (Azores)	JBN Electronica	(96) 23781
Ponta Delgada (Azores)	Mid Atlantic Yachts Serv.	(92) 31616
Montevideo (Uruguay)	Electromaritima Uruguaya	(02) 203 857
Buenos Aires (Argentina)	Sistemas Electronicos	(01) 343 0069
Galle (Sri Lanka)	Windsor Yacht Services	(09) 22927
Mombasa (Kenya)	Comarco Communications	(11) 318 778
Antanarive (Madagascar)	Landis Madagaskar	(02) 25151 55
Cape Town (South Africa)	Sea Gear	(21) 448 3777
Cape Town (South Africa)	Wilbur Ellis Co.	(21) 448 4517
Durban (South Africa)	Durban Yacht Services.	(31) 0 1953/4

MARINE ELECTRICAL SUPPLIERS

28.0   Marine Electrical Suppliers. The following are suppliers for a range of marine electrical and electronics equipment.

UNITED STATES

Ample Technology 2442 NW Market St. #43, Seattle, WA 98107

Tel (206) 784-4255 Fax (206) 781-9631

Cruising Equipment Co Ltd 6315 Seaview Ave NW, Seattle, WA 98107

Tel (206)782 8100 Fax (206)782 4336 (Alternator regulators, trace inverters)

Hamilton Ferris. PO Box 126-C, Ashland, MA 01721

Tel (508)881 4602 Fax (508)881 3846 (Large catalog marine electrical range)

Marinco One Digital Drive, Novato, CA 94949

Tel (415)883 3347 Fax (415)883 7930 (Shore power electrical equipment)

NewMar PO Box 1306, Newport Beach, CA 92663.

Tel (714)751 0488 Fax (714)957 1621 (Battery chargers, inverters)

UNITED KINGDOM

Adverc BM 245 Trysull Rd, Merry Hill, Wolverhampton WV3 7LG

Tel (0902)380494 Fax (0902)380435 (Charging system specialists)

Aquaman Unit 7, Bessemer Park, 250 Milkwood Rd, London SE24 OHG

Tel (071) 738 4466 Fax (071) 738 6801 (NewMar Euro Warehouse)

Index Marine Clump Farm Industrial Estate, Blandford Forum, Dorset DT11 7TE

Tel (0258) 452398 Fax (0258) 459660 (Complete wiring accessory range)

AUSTRALIA

Electric Boat Parts 11 Babbage Road, Roseville, NSW, 2069

Tel (61)2 9417 8455

Quins 77 St Vincent Street, Port Adelaide, Sth Australia, 5015

Tel (61)8 847 1277 Fax (61)8 8341 0567

Quirks Unit1/590 Old South Head Road, Rose Bay, NSW, 2029

Tel (61)2 9371 6600 Fax (61)2 9371 6623 E-mail: sneill@ibm.net

28.1 **Worldwide Parts Supply.** The following companies supply parts worldwide and offer fast service.

UNITED STATES

NYS Worldwide,

Wellington Square, 580 Thames St, PO Box 149, Newport RI 02840

Tel (401) 846 7720 (800)782 6660 Fax (401) 846 6850

Wayfarer Marine Corporation

Sea St, PO Box 677, Camden, ME 04843

Tel (207) 236 4378 Fax (207) 236 2371

PACIFIC

Thirty Seven South Ltd

PO Box 1874, Auckland, New Zealand

Tel (64) 9302 0178 Fax (64) 93078 170

MEDITERRANEAN

Versilia Supply Service

Via Coppino 433, Viareggio, Italy

Tel (39) 584 387 461 Fax (39) 584 387 652

UNITED KINGDOM

Alex Spares

14a High Street, Battle, East Sussex, England

Tel (44) 4246 4888 Fax (44) 4246 4766

CARIBBEAN

Outfitters International

English Harbour, Antigua, West Indies

Tel (809) 460 1966 Fax (809) 460 3490

Sources and Literature

American Boat and Yacht Council Inc. *Standards and Recommended Practices for Small Craft*, ABYC, Amityville, NY.

AT&T Frequency Finger Tip Guides and Brochures

Battery Service Manual, Battery Council International. 1982

Chloride Batteries Technical Brochures

Cruising World (February 1993, June 1993, September 1993, and February 1994 issues)

Donat, Hans. *Engine Monitoring on Yachts*, VDO Marine.1985

Graves, Frederick. *Big Book of Marine Electronics*, SevenSeas Press, Camden, ME. 1985

Guide to Facsimile Stations, Klingenfuss Publications

International Regulations for Preventing Collisions at Sea, 1972

Lloyd's Rules for Yachts and Small Craft

Maloney, Elbert S. *Chapman Piloting : Seamanship & Small Boat Handling*, Hearst Marine Books, New York, NY.1983

Marine Electrical Systems, Lucas Marine. 1982

Mariners Guide to Single Sideband, Frederick Graves, SEA. 1992

Maritime Radio Services Guide, British Telecom

National Geographic (July 1993)

Mychael. *Electric Circuits and Machines*, McGraw Hill, NY.1972

SEA 222 Instruction & Maintenance Manual 1993

The Straightshooters Guide to Marine Electronics, West & Pittman. 1987

Warren, Nigel. *Metal Corrosion in Boats*, 2E, Sheridan House, Dobbs Ferry, NY. 1998

Ocean Navigator (Issues 52, 55, and 60)

Acknowledgments

I would like to thank the following friends, colleagues and companies for their advice and assistance during the preparation of this handbook. I am also grateful for the various drawings and circuits that were redrawn and modified from technical information and service manuals.

Paul Checkley, for the illustrations on Autocad 12 and his enormous patience; Don McIntyre; Mick Paget (VK2ARG) for editorial assistance; David Avdall (for his computer wizardry); Bill Dainton and Gary Pierce, (Eagle Batteries); Bill Ritchie, Olympic Instruments (VDO Agent); Dr Steve Bell; Kenneth Parker; The U.K. Cruising Association and its members; David and Susan Dreux (Index Marine); Eddie Rooms (VK4AER, Asia/Pacific Agent Van De Stadt Design); D. Guignet; T. Dalton; Australian Maritime Safety Authority; Autohelm (Oceantalk Australia); Autohelm UK; Ingram Corporation (Alternator and starter manufacturers); Bosch Australia; Derek Barnard, (Penta Comstat); Telstra Maritime (Telecom Australia); Wayworld Yachts; IPS Radio & Space Service; Peter Collins, (Collins Marine); Andrew Brodie (Datamarine International); Ken King; IEI (Sonnenschein Batteries); Quinns (Koden Agents); DVK Monitors; Solarex; ES Rubin (ETA circuit breakers); Hayden Rough, Coastal Cruising Club; Ian Baird (Quality Marine); D. Maclean, (Hella Australia); Steve Bik(Mastervolt); Peter Snare, (SeaFresh Watermakers); Marconi-Firdell; Trevor Scarratt (Adverc BM); PC Maritime (Marine Software Developers); ICS Electronics (Weatherfax manufacturers); British Telecom; Brookes and Gatehouse; M.G.Duff & Co.; Marlec Engineering (Rutland & Leisurelights); Lewmar; Whitlock (Steering systems); Perkins Diesels; Ampair; Megalans AB (TWC Manufacturers); Maths Hedlund, LEAB; Volvo AT &T; NewMar; US Coast Guard; American Boat and Yacht Council; Magnavox; Lestek; Balmar; Motorola; Lighthouse Manufacturing Co (Windlasses); The Cruising Equipment Company; Ample Power Company; Marinco; Glacier Bay.

And special thanks to the following for their unwavering commitment in lobbying to retain threatened services, and for supporting yachting and cruising in every area from politics to equipment standards: Australian Sailing, Cruising Helmsman; Peter Rendle (Rendle Media); Multihull World; Amateur Boat Builder; Cruising World; Ocean Navigator; Practical Boat Owner; Yachting Monthly.

INDEX